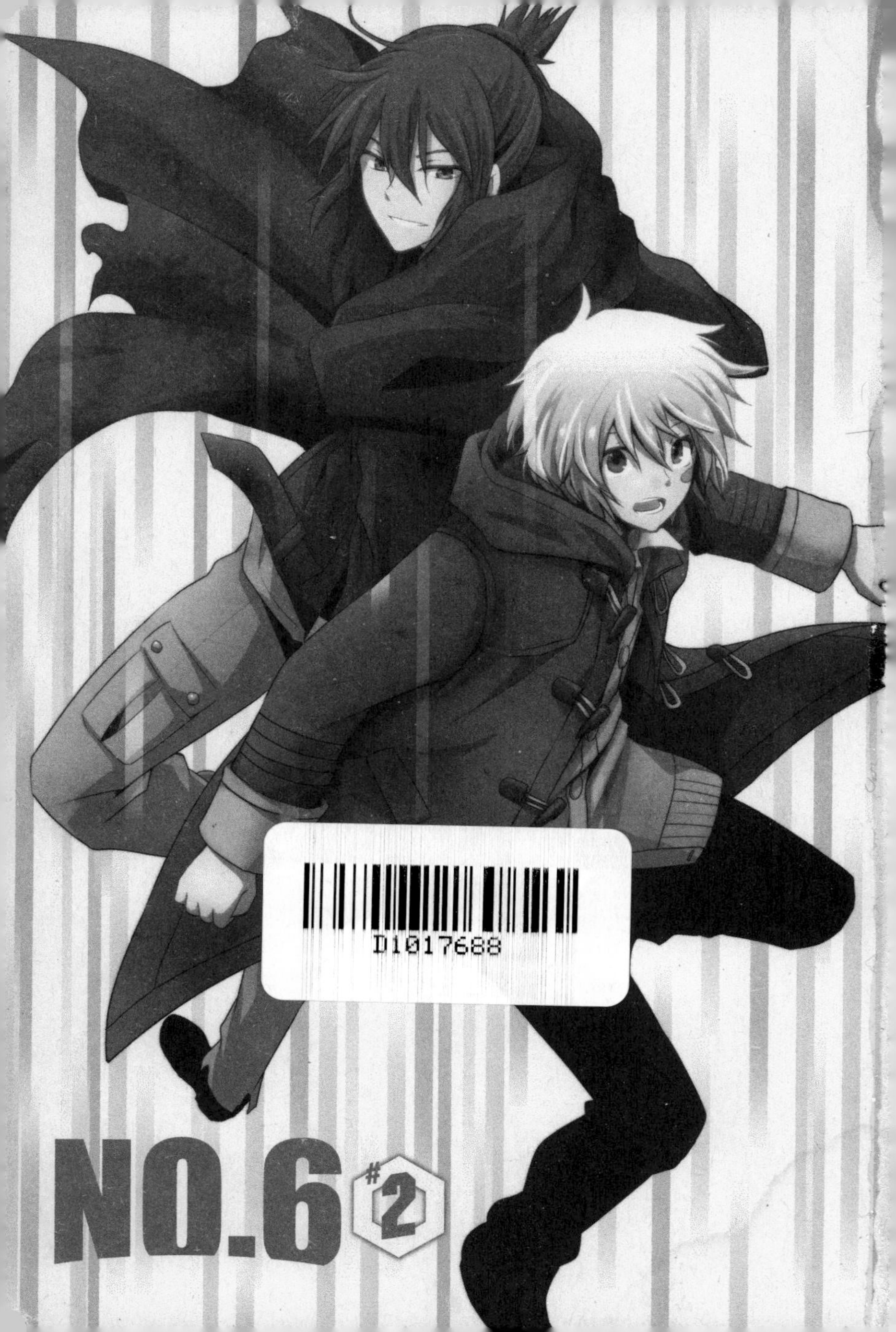
NO.6
#2

NO.6

#2

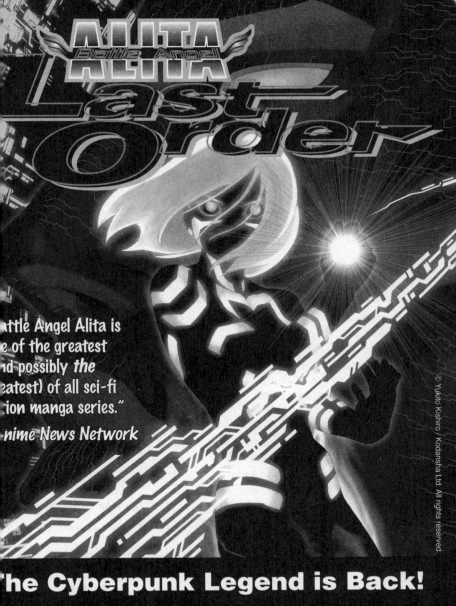

ALITA
Battle Angel
Last Order

"...ttle Angel Alita is
...e of the greatest
...nd possibly *the*
...eatest) of all sci-fi
...ion manga series."

...nime News Network

The Cyberpunk Legend is Back!

...deluxe omnibus editions of 600+ pages,
...cluding ALL-NEW original stories by
...ita creator Yukito Kishiro!
...ol. 1 Coming March 2013

KC
KODANSHA
COMICS

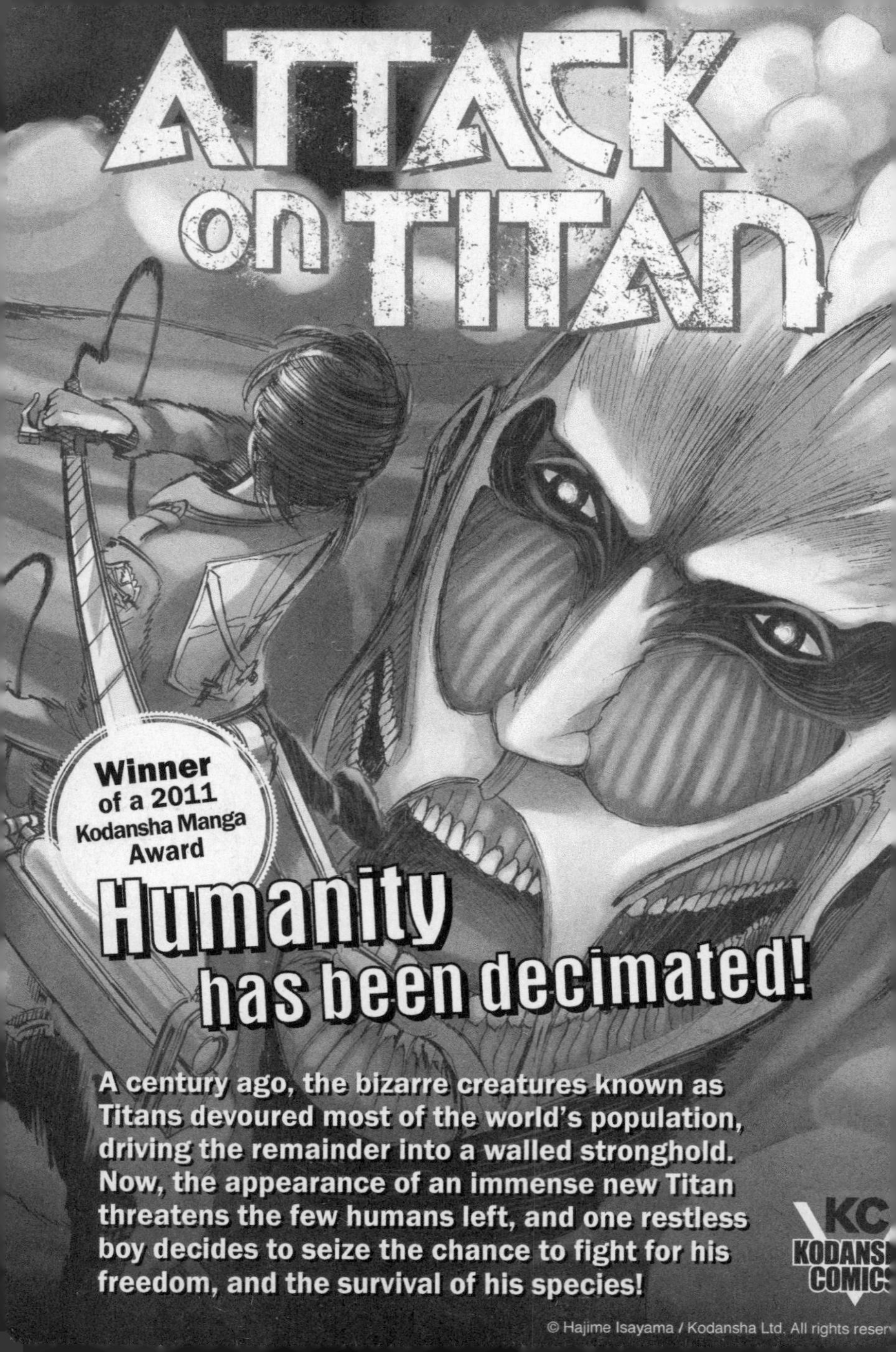
ATTACK on TITAN
Winner of a 2011 Kodansha Manga Award
Humanity has been decimated!
A century ago, the bizarre creatures known as Titans devoured most of the world's population, driving the remainder into a walled stronghold. Now, the appearance of an immense new Titan threatens the few humans left, and one restless boy decides to seize the chance to fight for his freedom, and the survival of his species!
KC KODANSHA COMICS
© Hajime Isayama / Kodansha Ltd. All rights reser

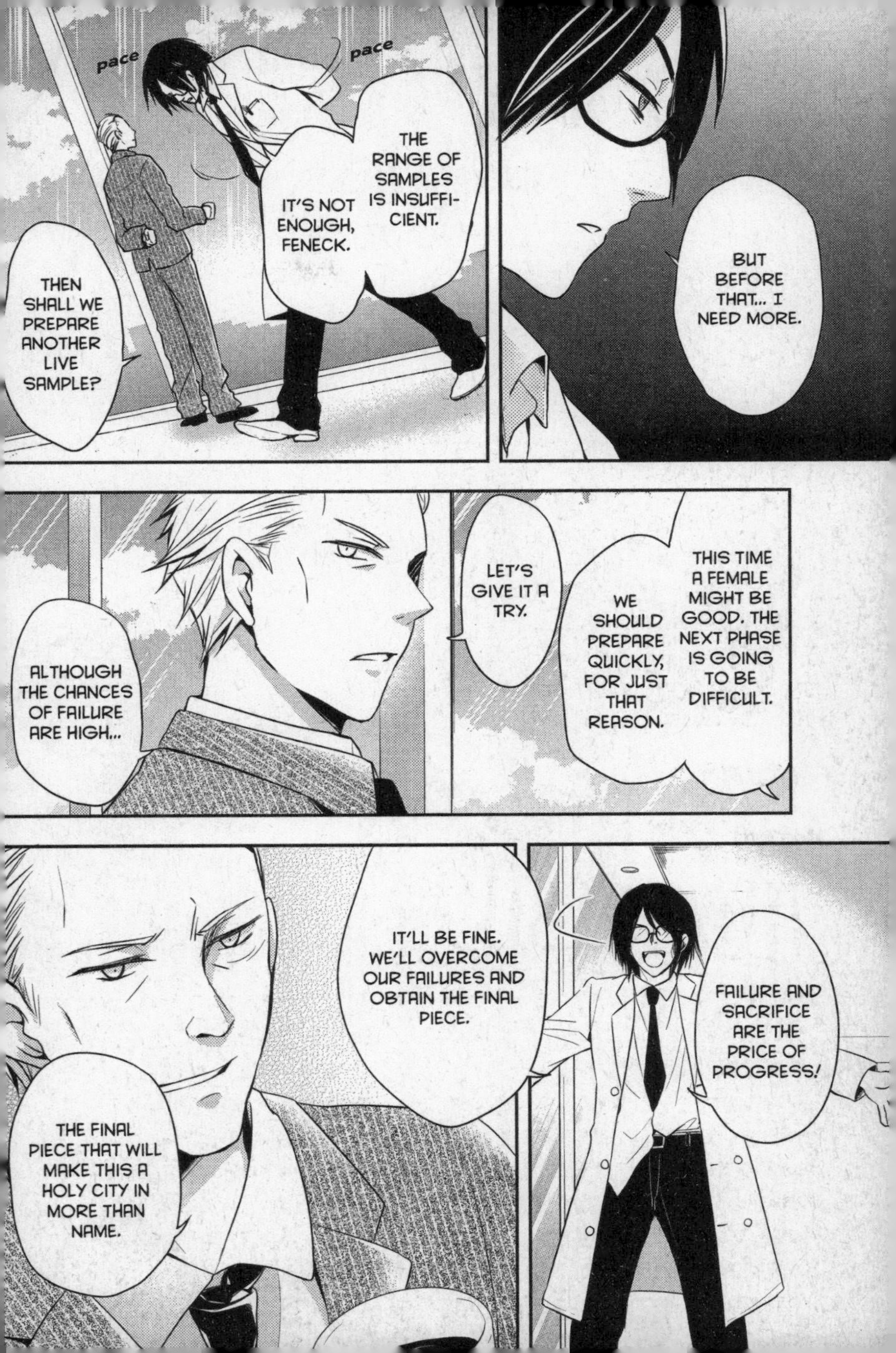
BUT BEFORE THAT... I NEED MORE.
pace
pace
THE RANGE OF SAMPLES IS INSUFFICIENT.
IT'S NOT ENOUGH, FENECK.
THEN SHALL WE PREPARE ANOTHER LIVE SAMPLE?
THIS TIME A FEMALE MIGHT BE GOOD. THE NEXT PHASE IS GOING TO BE DIFFICULT.
WE SHOULD PREPARE QUICKLY, FOR JUST THAT REASON.
LET'S GIVE IT A TRY.
ALTHOUGH THE CHANCES OF FAILURE ARE HIGH...
FAILURE AND SACRIFICE ARE THE PRICE OF PROGRESS!
IT'LL BE FINE. WE'LL OVERCOME OUR FAILURES AND OBTAIN THE FINAL PIECE.
THE FINAL PIECE THAT WILL MAKE THIS A HOLY CITY IN MORE THAN NAME.

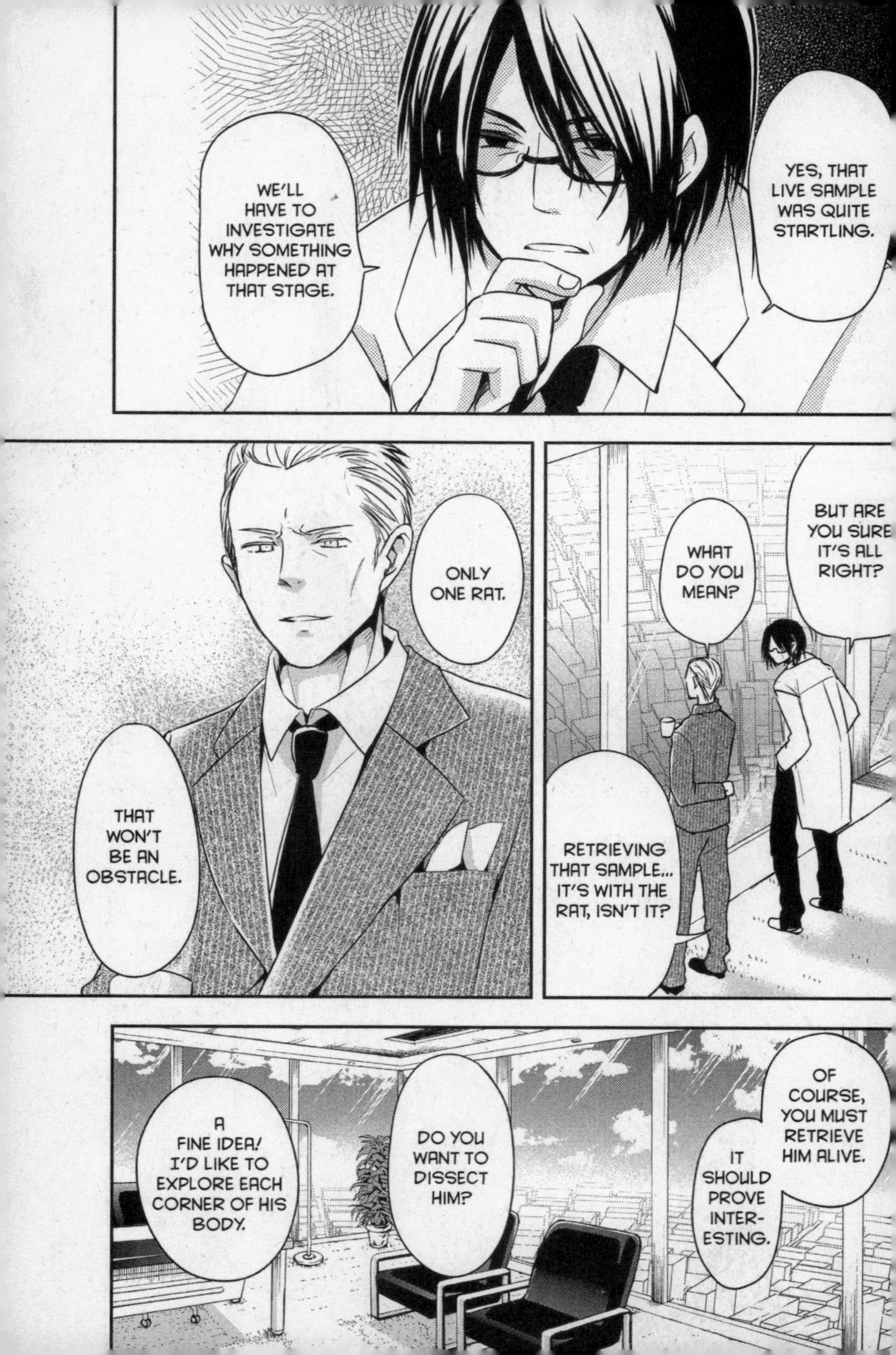
YES, THAT LIVE SAMPLE WAS QUITE STARTLING.
WE'LL HAVE TO INVESTIGATE WHY SOMETHING HAPPENED AT THAT STAGE.
BUT ARE YOU SURE IT'S ALL RIGHT?
WHAT DO YOU MEAN?
RETRIEVING THAT SAMPLE... IT'S WITH THE RAT, ISN'T IT?
ONLY ONE RAT.
THAT WON'T BE AN OBSTACLE.
OF COURSE, YOU MUST RETRIEVE HIM ALIVE.
IT SHOULD PROVE INTER-ESTING.
DO YOU WANT TO DISSECT HIM?
A FINE IDEA! I'D LIKE TO EXPLORE EACH CORNER OF HIS BODY.

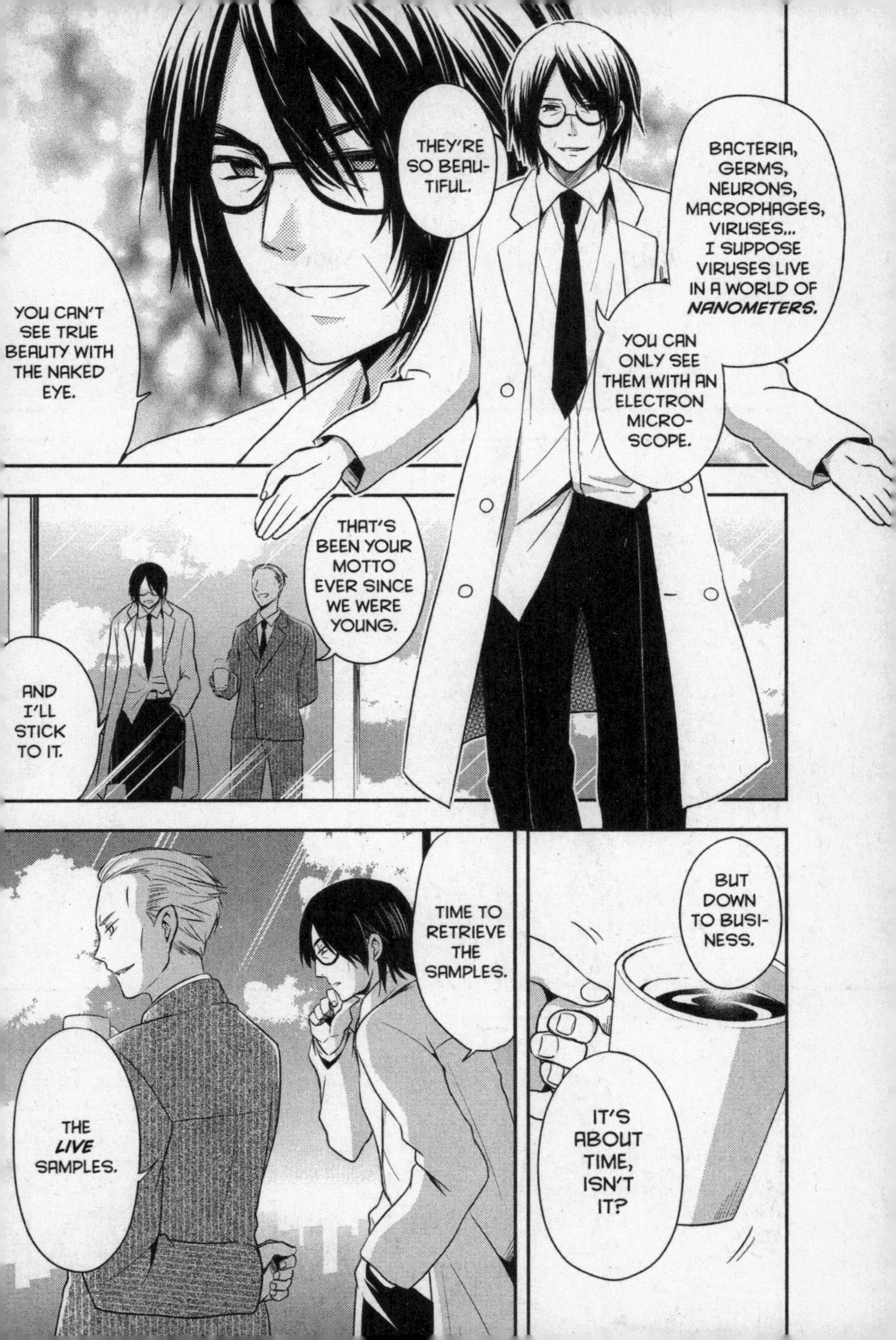

BACTERIA, GERMS, NEURONS, MACROPHAGES, VIRUSES... I SUPPOSE VIRUSES LIVE IN A WORLD OF ***NANOMETERS.***
YOU CAN ONLY SEE THEM WITH AN ELECTRON MICRO-SCOPE.
THEY'RE SO BEAU-TIFUL.
YOU CAN'T SEE TRUE BEAUTY WITH THE NAKED EYE.
THAT'S BEEN YOUR MOTTO EVER SINCE WE WERE YOUNG.
AND I'LL STICK TO IT.
BUT DOWN TO BUSI-NESS.
IT'S ABOUT TIME, ISN'T IT?
TIME TO RETRIEVE THE SAMPLES.
THE ***LIVE*** SAMPLES.

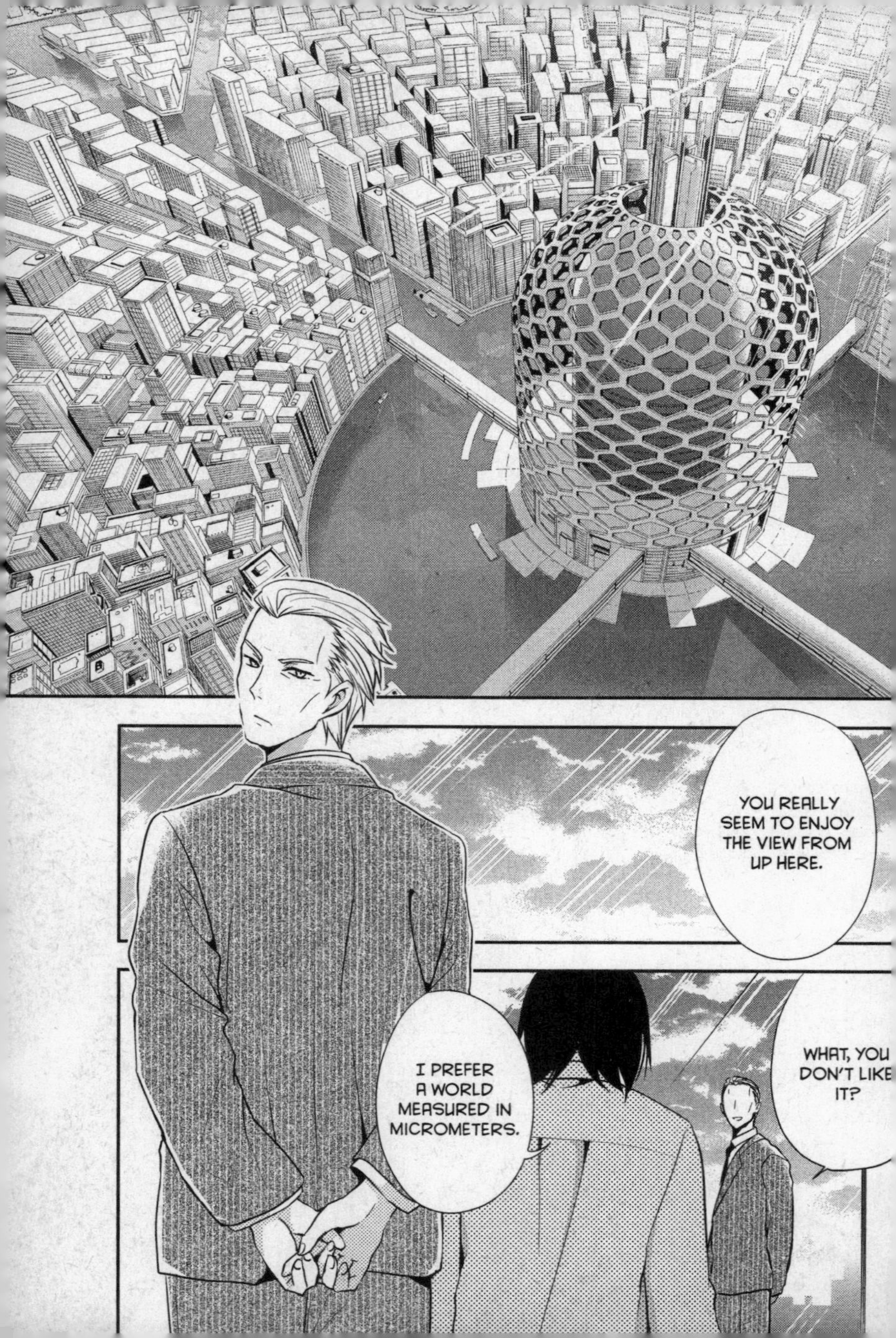
YOU REALLY SEEM TO ENJOY THE VIEW FROM UP HERE.
WHAT, YOU DON'T LIKE IT?
I PREFER A WORLD MEASURED IN MICROMETERS.

Chapter 8: Angel of Death

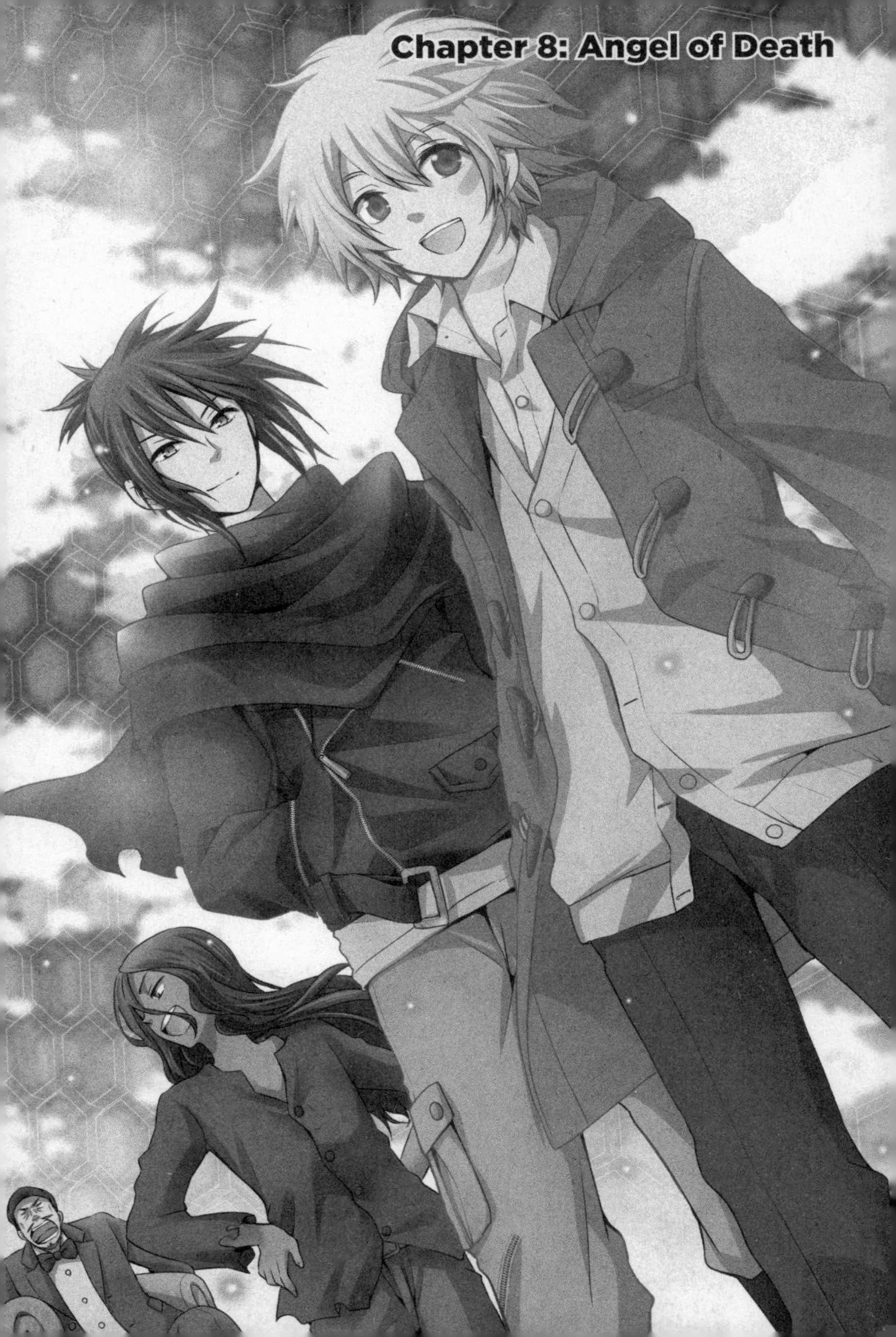

Preview of Vol. 3

Coming Oct. 2013 from
Kodansha Comics

kodanshacomics.com

NO.6 VOLUME THREE

Story by ATSUKO ASANO Art by HINOKI KINO

NO.6

SPECIAL THANKS!

Ms. Atsuko Asano

Everyone in the Kodansha Aria Editorial Department

Everyone on the No. 6 Team
Editor K
toi8
Everyone on the anime staff
Everyone at NARTI;S
Ginkyo

* Production Cooperation
Honma
Megi
Netanon
Sayuri Noguchi

* Finishing
Tsunocchi
Pareko

* 3D
Kei Rinkan

* Color Backgrounds
Mr. dominori (Big Brother)
Family
And everyone else who helped out

Also, all you readers!

Thank you all so very much!

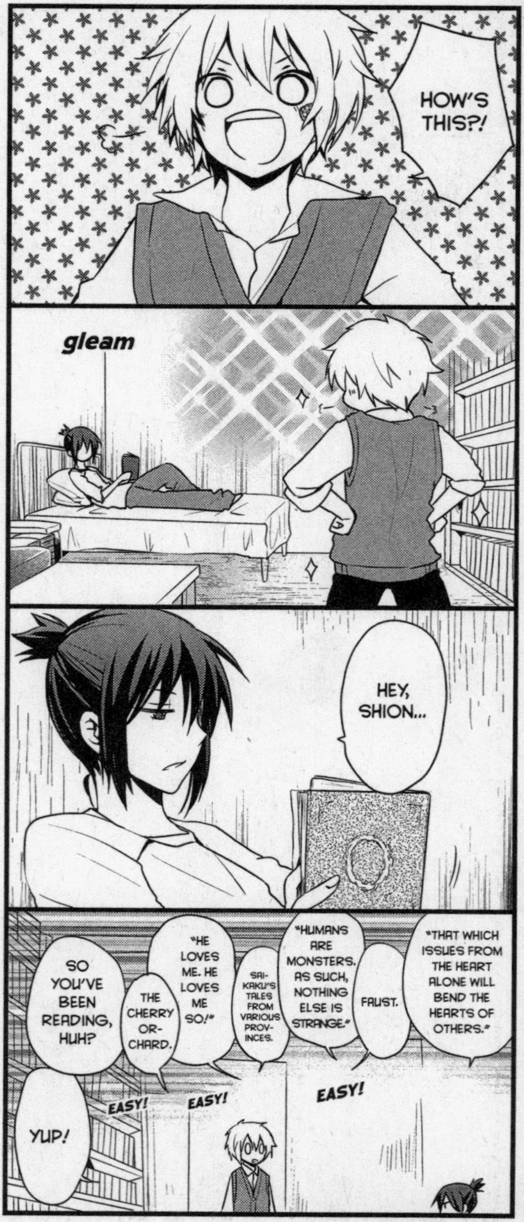
HOW'S THIS?!
gleam
HEY, SHION...
"THAT WHICH ISSUES FROM THE HEART ALONE WILL BEND THE HEARTS OF OTHERS."
FAUST.
"HUMANS ARE MONSTERS. AS SUCH, NOTHING ELSE IS STRANGE."
SAIKAKU'S TALES FROM VARIOUS PROVINCES.
"HE LOVES ME. HE LOVES ME SO!"
THE CHERRY ORCHARD.
SO YOU'VE BEEN READING, HUH?
EASY!
EASY!
EASY!
YUP!

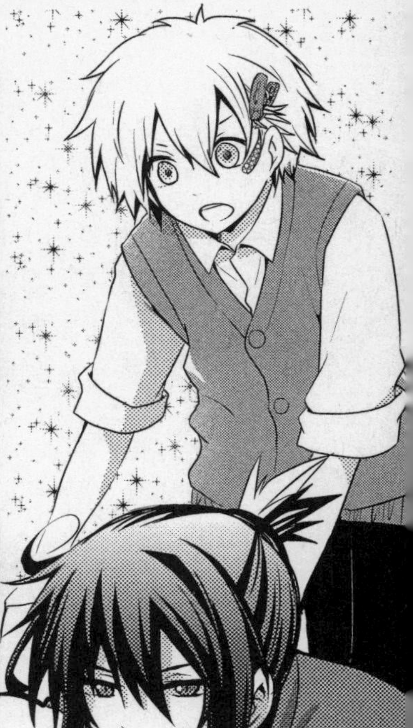

Hello. I'm Hinoki Kino. How did you like No. 6 Vol. 2? I hope I've made a little progress since Vol. 1. If you enjoyed it, then I'm happy. There was an idea for a scene where Shion cleans up Rat's room, which I couldn't add to the story, so I'm drawing it here (I've got some really crazy ideas). I really enjoyed drawing it all, so if you haven't read it, please do (Vol. 2, I mean). And now, I look forward to seeing you all in Vol. 3!

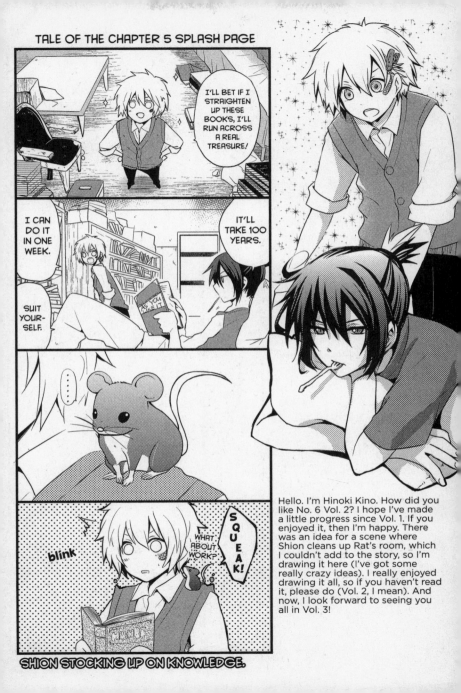

TALE OF THE CHAPTER 5 SPLASH PAGE

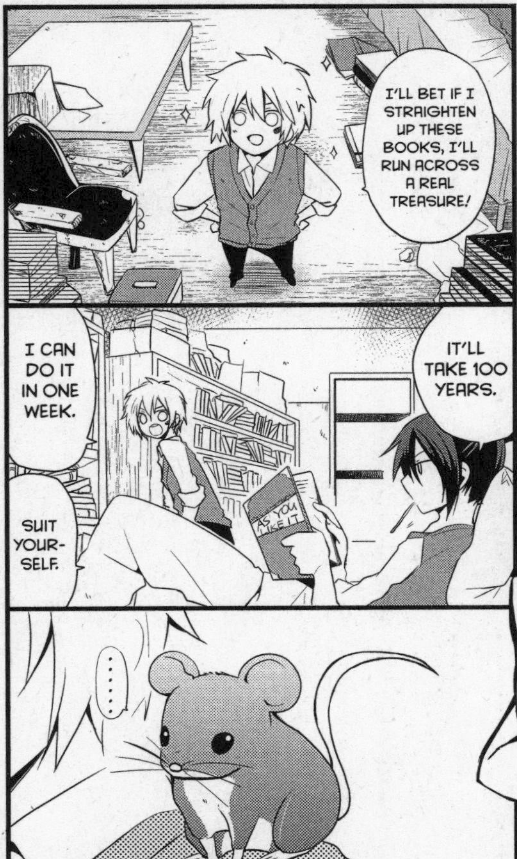
I'LL BET IF I STRAIGHTEN UP THESE BOOKS, I'LL RUN ACROSS A REAL TREASURE!
IT'LL TAKE 100 YEARS.
AS YOU LIKE IT
I CAN DO IT IN ONE WEEK.
SUIT YOURSELF.
......
SQUEAK!
WHAT ABOUT WORK?
blink

SHION STOCKING UP ON KNOWLEDGE.

ANIME'S ON! GATHER 'ROUND!

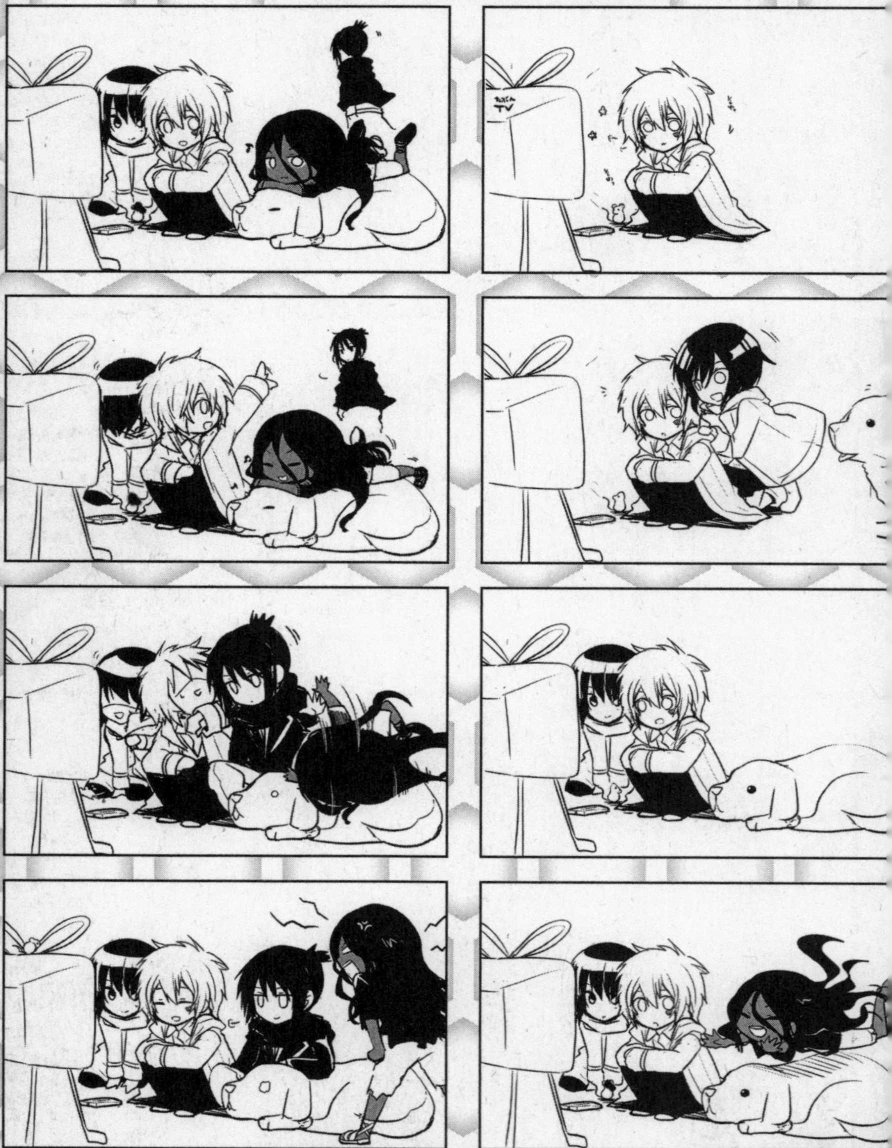

TV

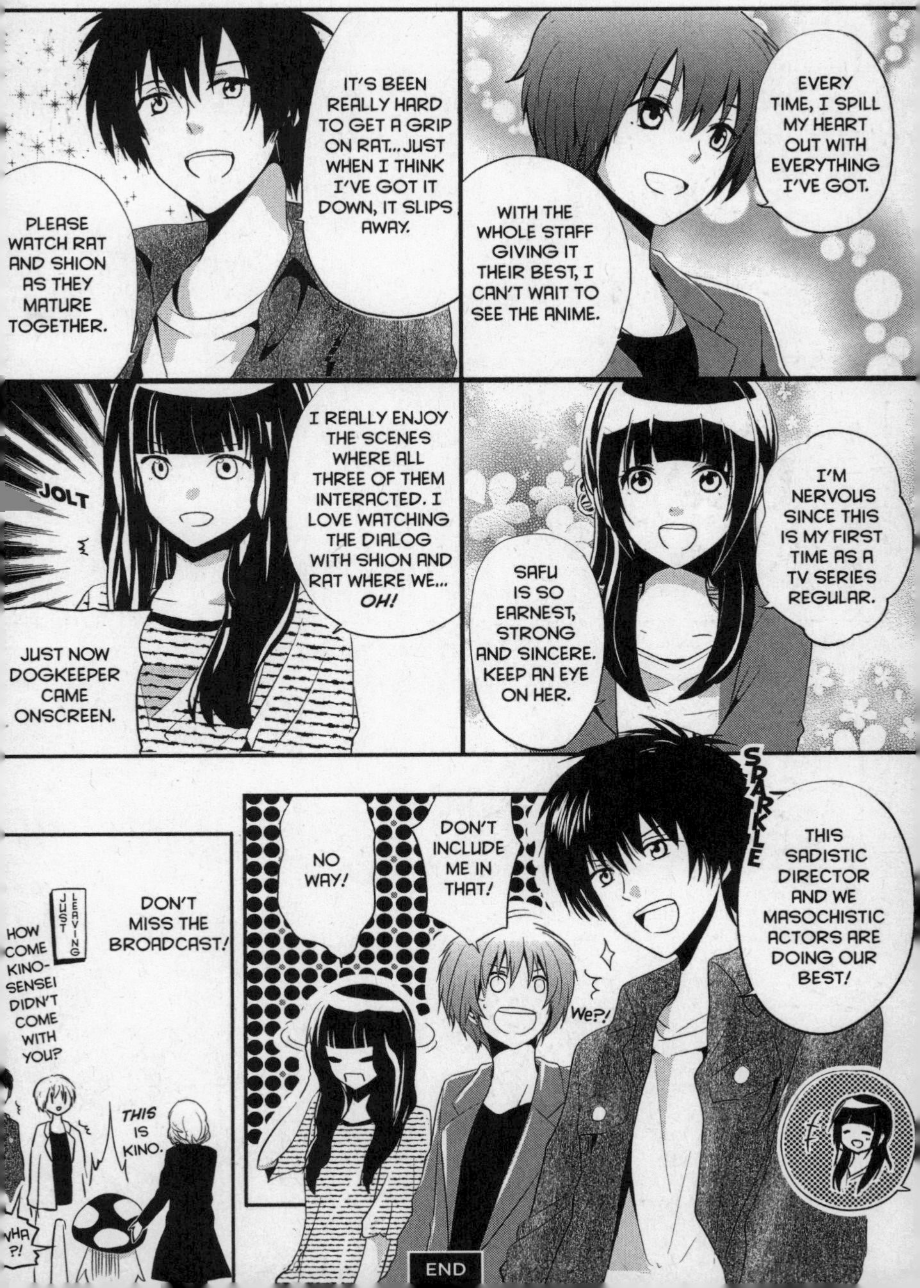
EVERY TIME, I SPILL MY HEART OUT WITH EVERYTHING I'VE GOT.
WITH THE WHOLE STAFF GIVING IT THEIR BEST, I CAN'T WAIT TO SEE THE ANIME.
IT'S BEEN REALLY HARD TO GET A GRIP ON RAT... JUST WHEN I THINK I'VE GOT IT DOWN, IT SLIPS AWAY.
PLEASE WATCH RAT AND SHION AS THEY MATURE TOGETHER.
I'M NERVOUS SINCE THIS IS MY FIRST TIME AS A TV SERIES REGULAR.
SAFU IS SO EARNEST, STRONG AND SINCERE. KEEP AN EYE ON HER.
I REALLY ENJOY THE SCENES WHERE ALL THREE OF THEM INTERACTED. I LOVE WATCHING THE DIALOG WITH SHION AND RAT WHERE WE... *OH!*
JOLT
JUST NOW DOGKEEPER CAME ONSCREEN.
SPARKLE
THIS SADISTIC DIRECTOR AND WE MASOCHISTIC ACTORS ARE DOING OUR BEST!
We?!
DON'T INCLUDE ME IN THAT!
NO WAY!
DON'T MISS THE BROADCAST!
JUST LEAVING
HOW COME KINO-SENSEI DIDN'T COME WITH YOU?
THIS IS KINO.
WHA?!
END

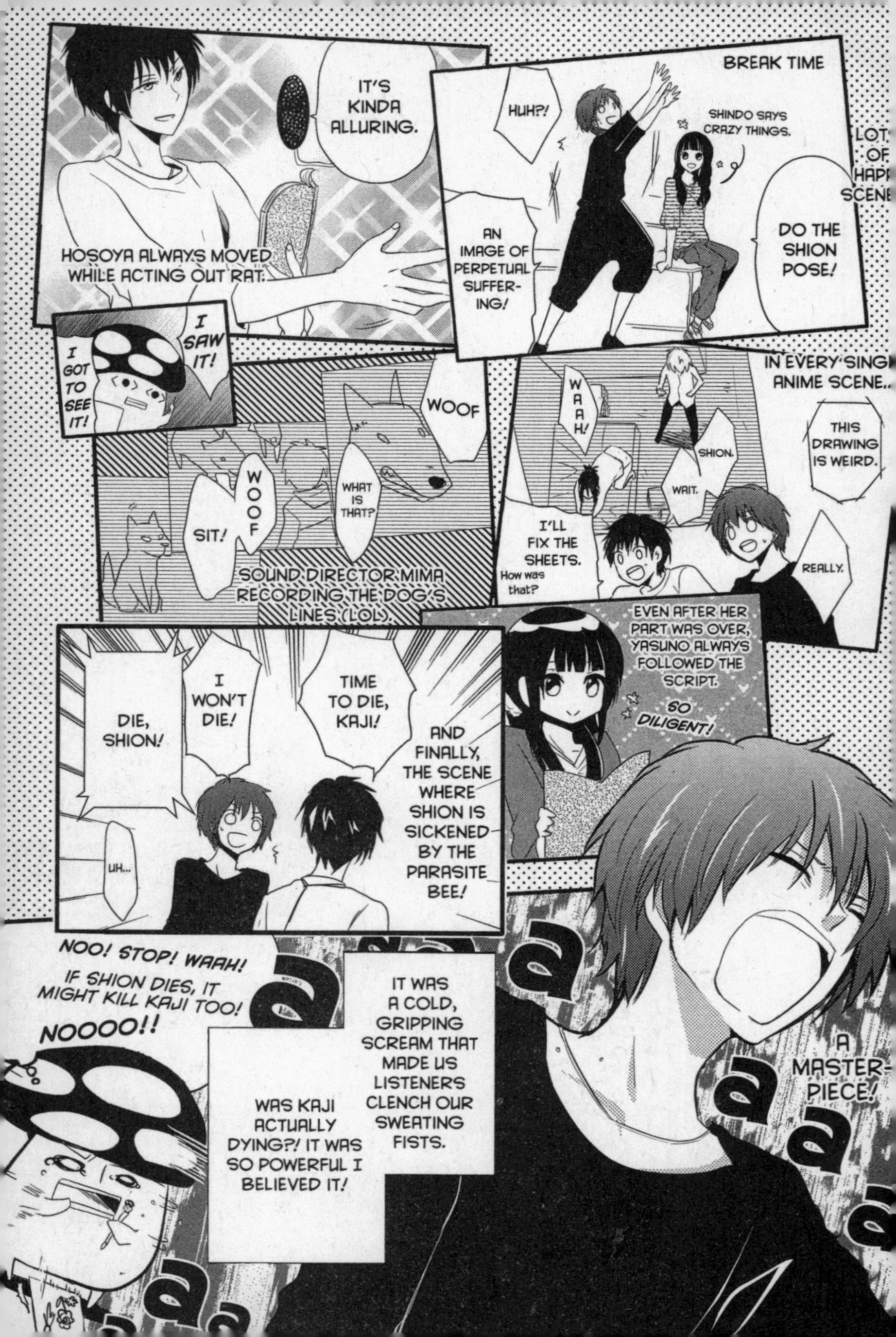
BREAK TIME
LOT OF HAPP SCENE
DO THE SHION POSE!
SHINDO SAYS CRAZY THINGS.
HUH?!
AN IMAGE OF PERPETUAL SUFFERING!
IT'S KINDA ALLURING.
HOSOYA ALWAYS MOVED WHILE ACTING OUT RAT.
IN EVERY SING ANIME SCENE..
THIS DRAWING IS WEIRD.
WAAH!
SHION.
WAIT.
REALLY.
I'LL FIX THE SHEETS.
How was that?
I SAW IT!
I GOT TO SEE IT!
WOOF
WHAT IS THAT?
WOOF
SIT!
SOUND DIRECTOR MIMA RECORDING THE DOG'S LINES (LOL).
EVEN AFTER HER PART WAS OVER, YASUNO ALWAYS FOLLOWED THE SCRIPT.
SO DILIGENT!
TIME TO DIE, KAJI!
I WON'T DIE!
DIE, SHION!
AND FINALLY, THE SCENE WHERE SHION IS SICKENED BY THE PARASITE BEE!
UH...
A MASTERPIECE!
IT WAS A COLD, GRIPPING SCREAM THAT MADE US LISTENERS CLENCH OUR SWEATING FISTS.
WAS KAJI ACTUALLY DYING?! IT WAS SO POWERFUL I BELIEVED IT!
NOO! STOP! WAAH!
IF SHION DIES, IT MIGHT KILL KAJI TOO!
NOOOO!!

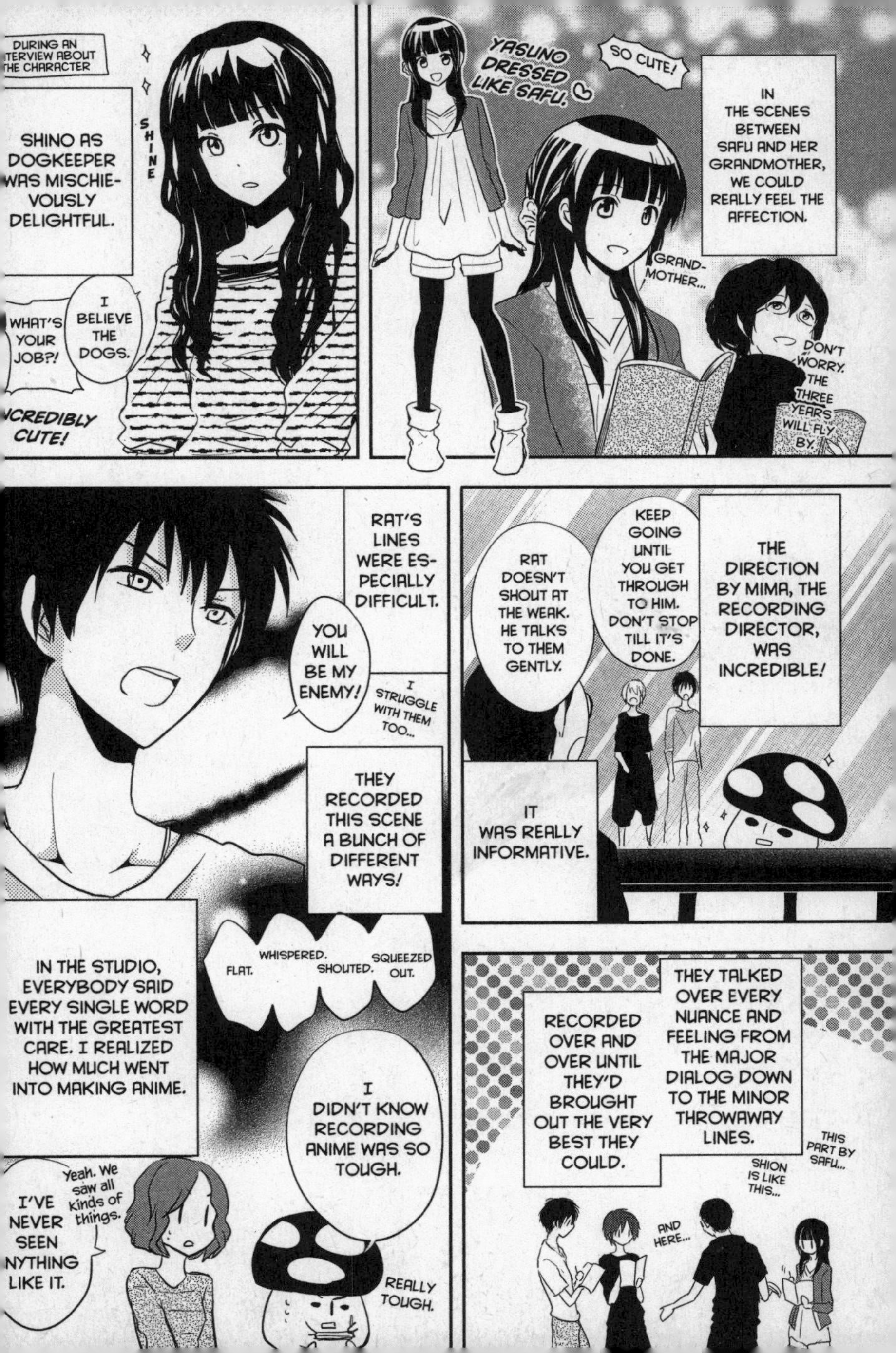
IN THE SCENES BETWEEN SAFU AND HER GRANDMOTHER, WE COULD REALLY FEEL THE AFFECTION.
SO CUTE!
YASUNO DRESSED LIKE SAFU.
GRAND-MOTHER...
DON'T WORRY. THE THREE YEARS WILL FLY BY.
DURING AN TERVIEW ABOUT THE CHARACTER
SHINO AS DOGKEEPER WAS MISCHIE-VOUSLY DELIGHTFUL.
SHINE
I BELIEVE THE DOGS.
WHAT'S YOUR JOB?!
NCREDIBLY CUTE!
THE DIRECTION BY MIMA, THE RECORDING DIRECTOR, WAS INCREDIBLE!
KEEP GOING UNTIL YOU GET THROUGH TO HIM. DON'T STOP TILL IT'S DONE.
RAT DOESN'T SHOUT AT THE WEAK. HE TALKS TO THEM GENTLY.
IT WAS REALLY INFORMATIVE.
THEY TALKED OVER EVERY NUANCE AND FEELING FROM THE MAJOR DIALOG DOWN TO THE MINOR THROWAWAY LINES.
RECORDED OVER AND OVER UNTIL THEY'D BROUGHT OUT THE VERY BEST THEY COULD.
THIS PART BY SAFU...
SHION IS LIKE THIS...
AND HERE...
RAT'S LINES WERE ES-PECIALLY DIFFICULT.
YOU WILL BE MY ENEMY!
I STRUGGLE WITH THEM TOO...
THEY RECORDED THIS SCENE A BUNCH OF DIFFERENT WAYS!
SQUEEZED OUT.
SHOUTED.
WHISPERED.
FLAT.
IN THE STUDIO, EVERYBODY SAID EVERY SINGLE WORD WITH THE GREATEST CARE. I REALIZED HOW MUCH WENT INTO MAKING ANIME.
I DIDN'T KNOW RECORDING ANIME WAS SO TOUGH.
REALLY TOUGH.
Yeah. We saw all kinds of things.
I'VE NEVER SEEN NYTHING LIKE IT.

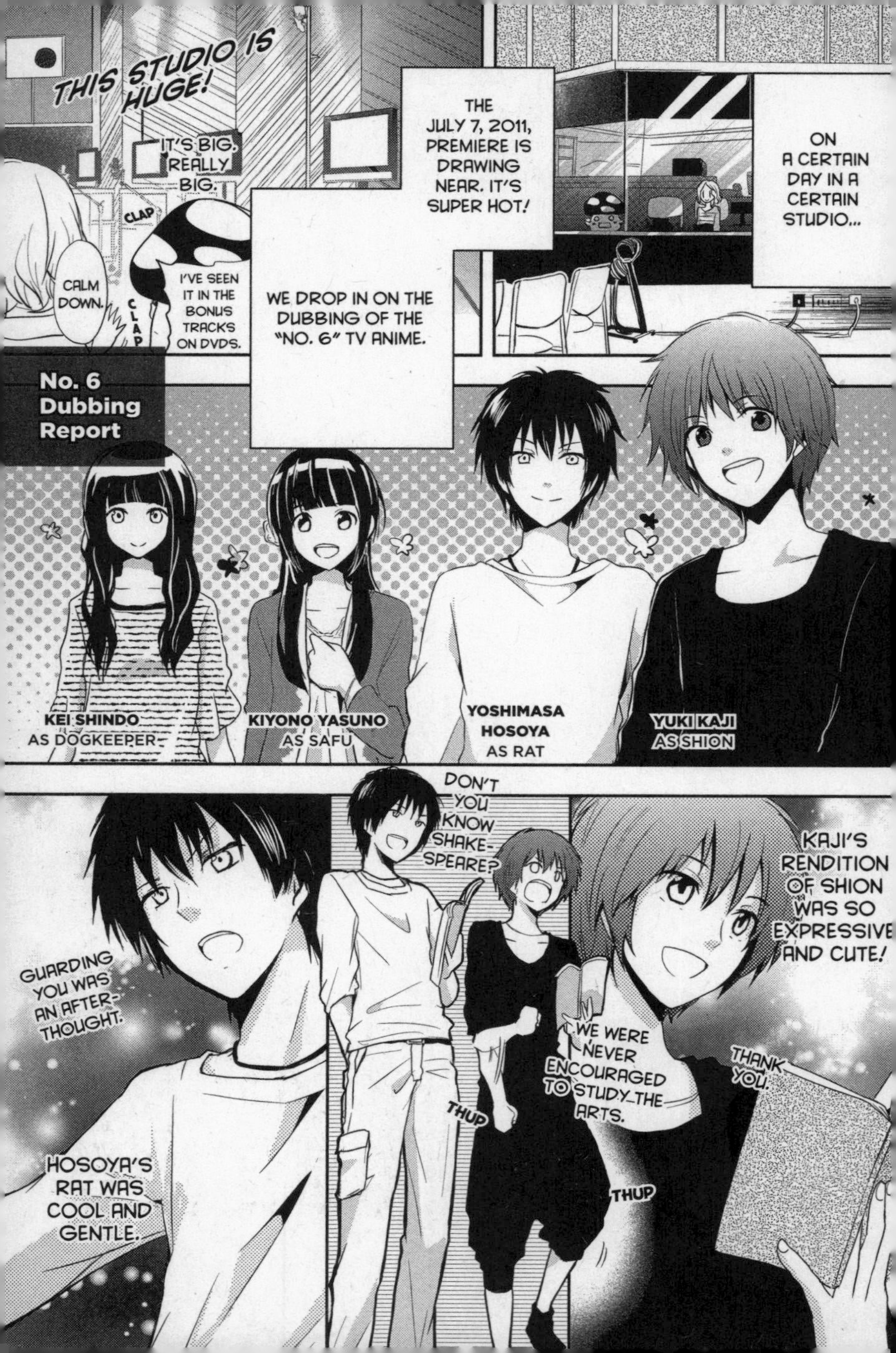
ON A CERTAIN DAY IN A CERTAIN STUDIO...
THE JULY 7, 2011, PREMIERE IS DRAWING NEAR. IT'S SUPER HOT!
WE DROP IN ON THE DUBBING OF THE "NO. 6" TV ANIME.
THIS STUDIO IS HUGE!
IT'S BIG. REALLY BIG.
CLAP
I'VE SEEN IT IN THE BONUS TRACKS ON DVDS.
CALM DOWN.
CLAP
No. 6 Dubbing Report
YUKI KAJI AS SHION
YOSHIMASA HOSOYA AS RAT
KIYONO YASUNO AS SAFU
KEI SHINDO AS DOGKEEPER
KAJI'S RENDITION OF SHION WAS SO EXPRESSIVE AND CUTE!
THANK YOU.
DON'T YOU KNOW SHAKE-SPEARE?
WE WERE NEVER ENCOURAGED TO STUDY THE ARTS.
THUP
THUP
GUARDING YOU WAS AN AFTER-THOUGHT.
HOSOYA'S RAT WAS COOL AND GENTLE.

NO.6

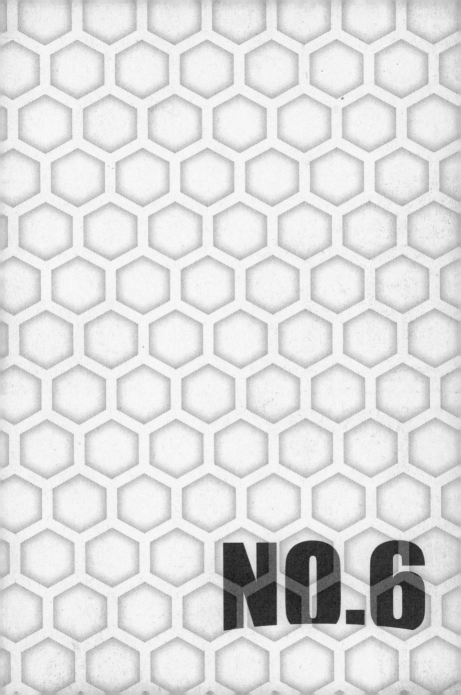

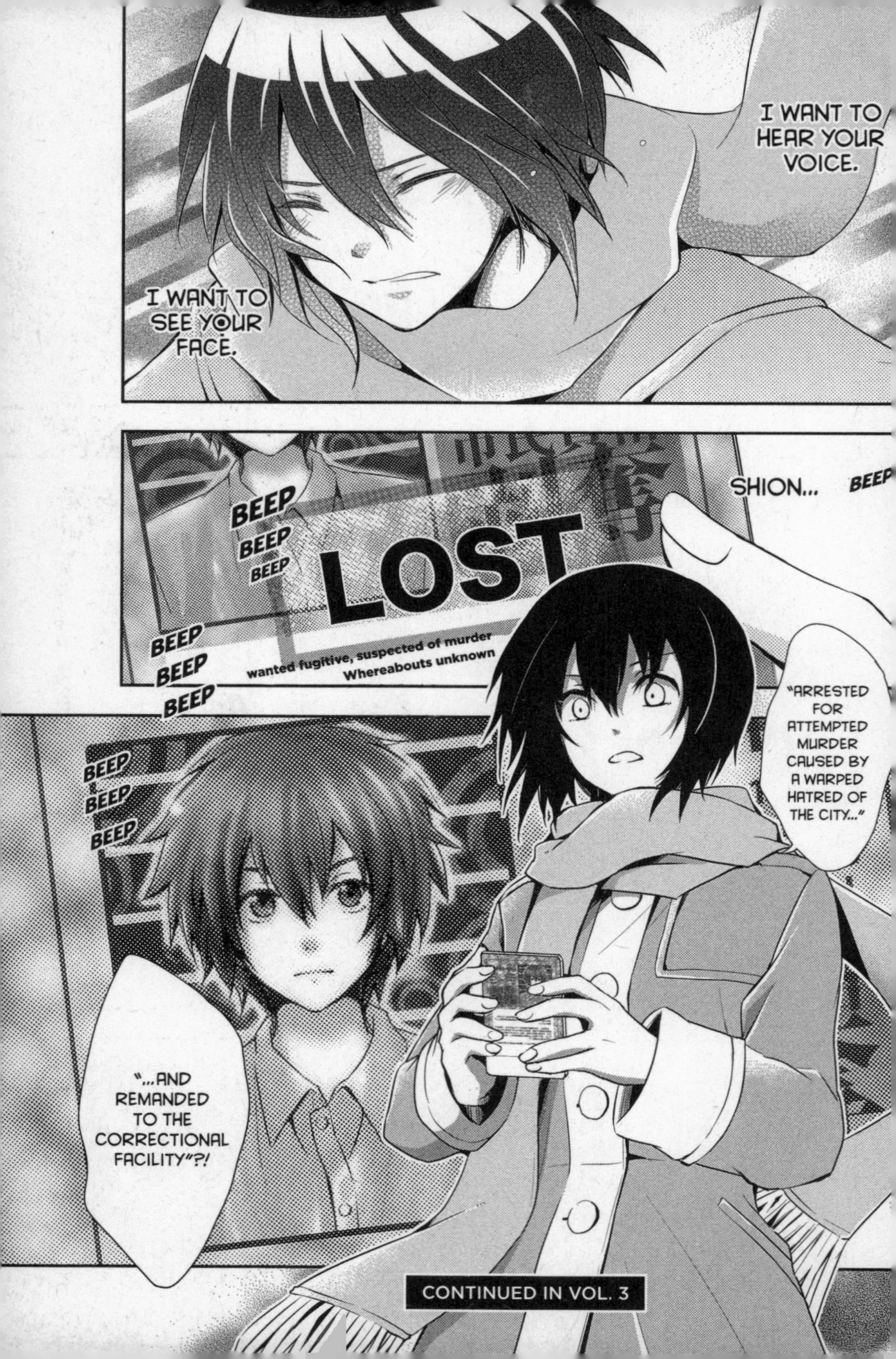

I WANT TO HEAR YOUR VOICE.
I WANT TO SEE YOUR FACE.
SHION...
BEEP
BEEP
BEEP
BEEP
LOST
wanted fugitive, suspected of murder
Whereabouts unknown
BEEP
BEEP
BEEP
"ARRESTED FOR ATTEMPTED MURDER CAUSED BY A WARPED HATRED OF THE CITY..."
BEEP
BEEP
BEEP
"...AND REMANDED TO THE CORRECTIONAL FACILITY"?!
CONTINUED IN VOL. 3

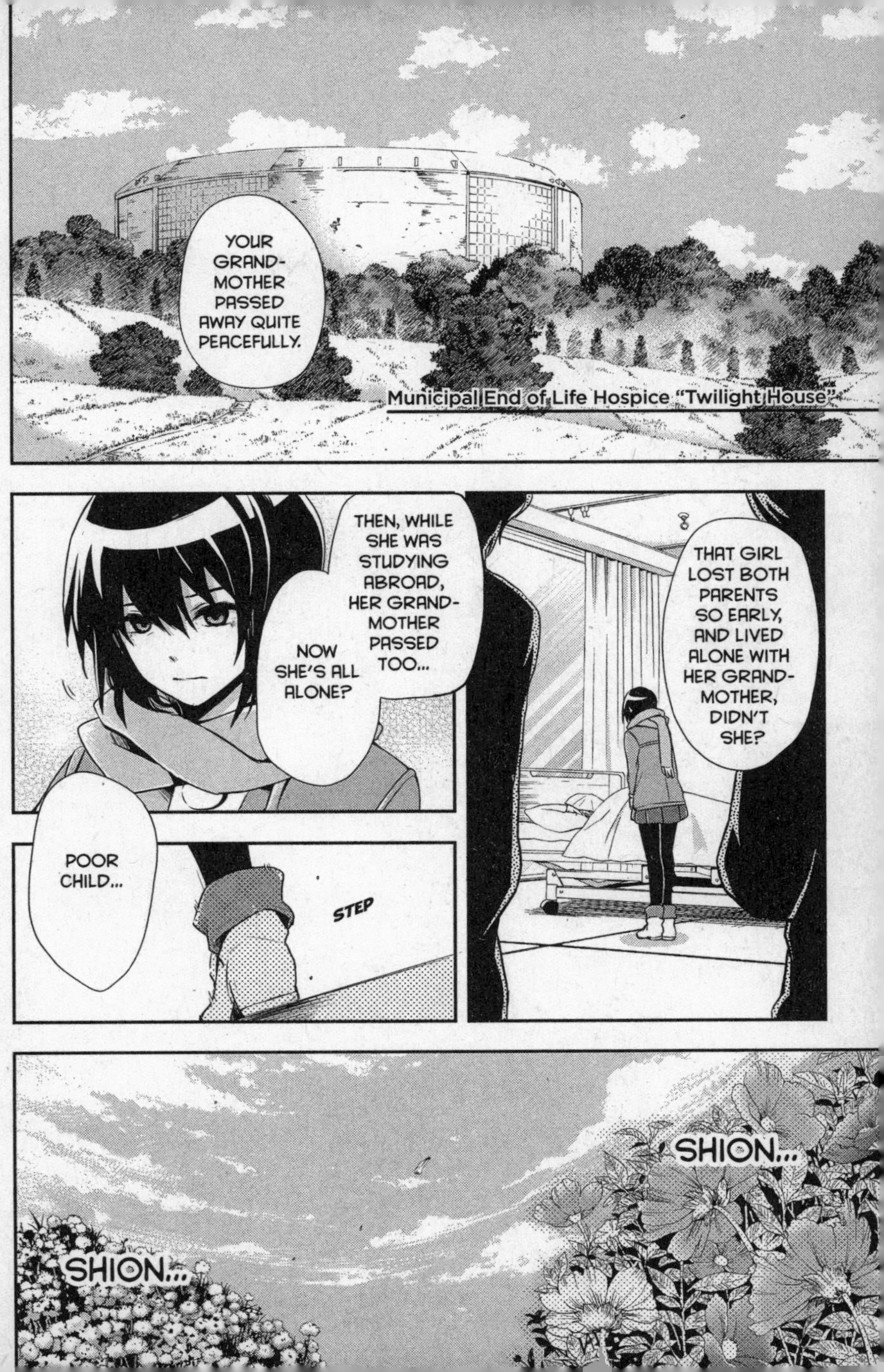
Municipal End of Life Hospice "Twilight House"
YOUR GRANDMOTHER PASSED AWAY QUITE PEACEFULLY.
THAT GIRL LOST BOTH PARENTS SO EARLY, AND LIVED ALONE WITH HER GRANDMOTHER, DIDN'T SHE?
THEN, WHILE SHE WAS STUDYING ABROAD, HER GRANDMOTHER PASSED TOO...
NOW SHE'S ALL ALONE?
POOR CHILD...
STEP
SHION...
SHION...

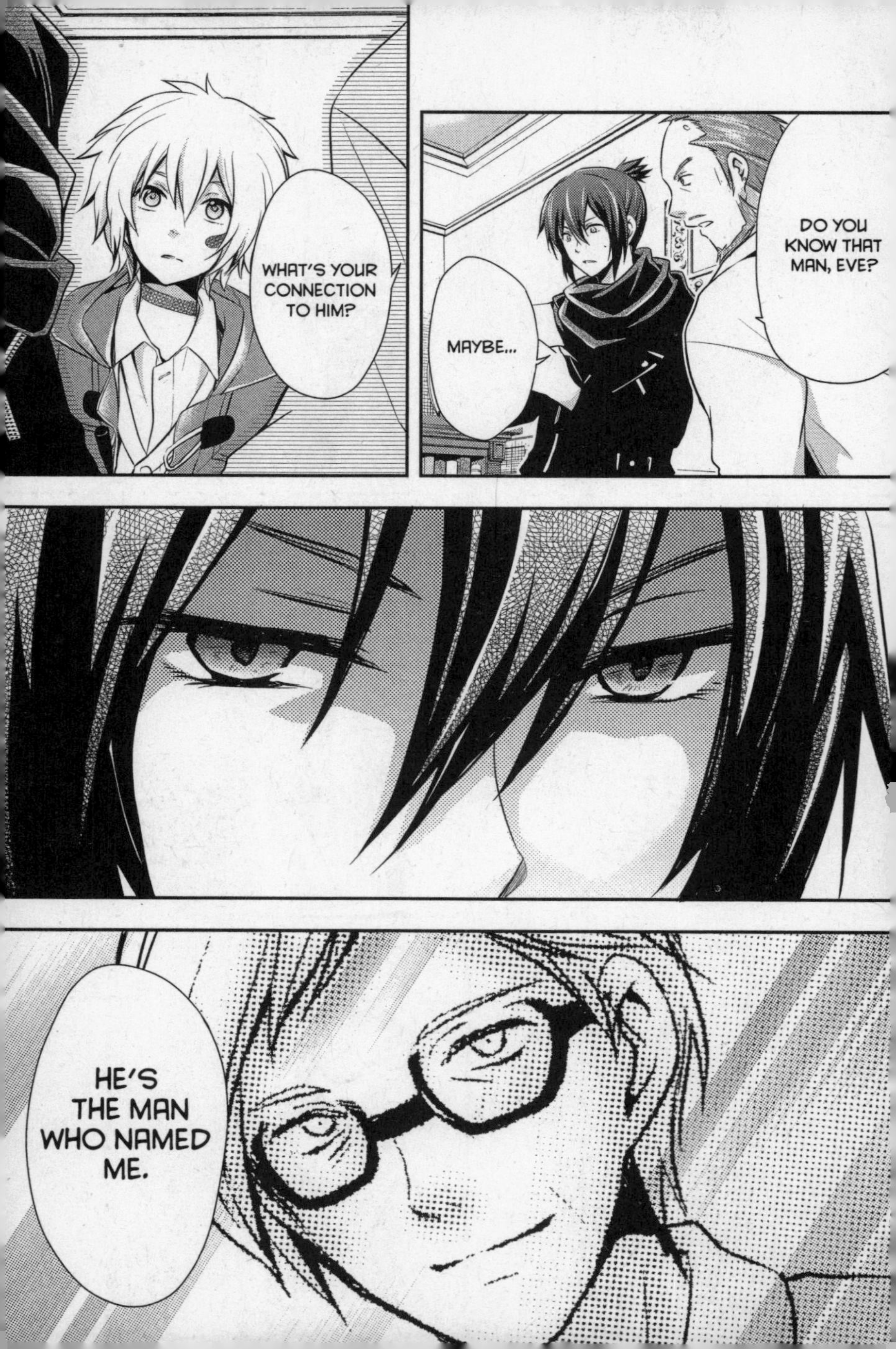
DO YOU KNOW THAT MAN, EVE?
MAYBE...
WHAT'S YOUR CONNECTION TO HIM?
HE'S THE MAN WHO NAMED ME.

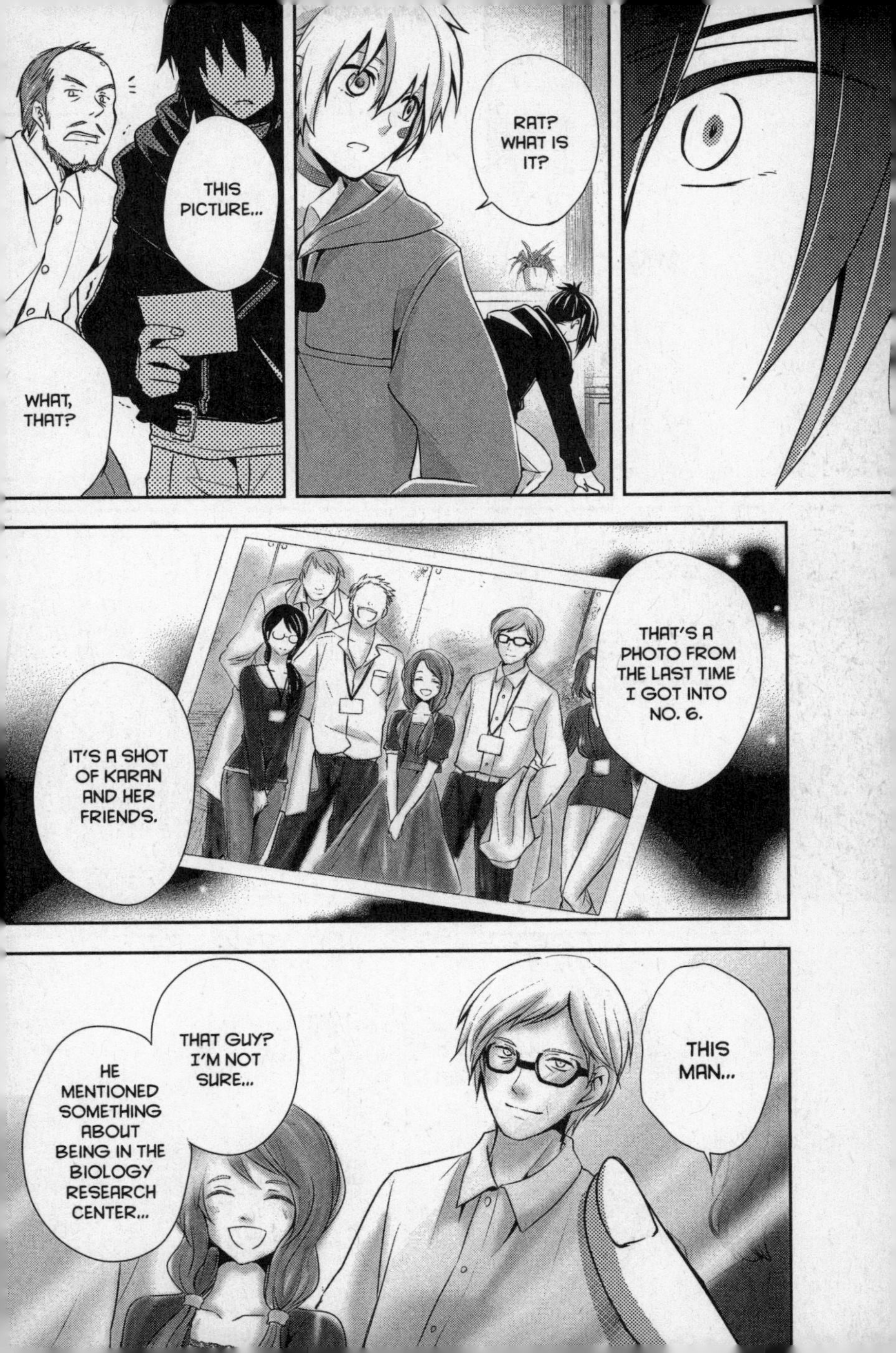
RAT? WHAT IS IT?
THIS PICTURE...
WHAT, THAT?
THAT'S A PHOTO FROM THE LAST TIME I GOT INTO NO. 6.
IT'S A SHOT OF KARAN AND HER FRIENDS.
THIS MAN...
THAT GUY? I'M NOT SURE...
HE MENTIONED SOMETHING ABOUT BEING IN THE BIOLOGY RESEARCH CENTER...

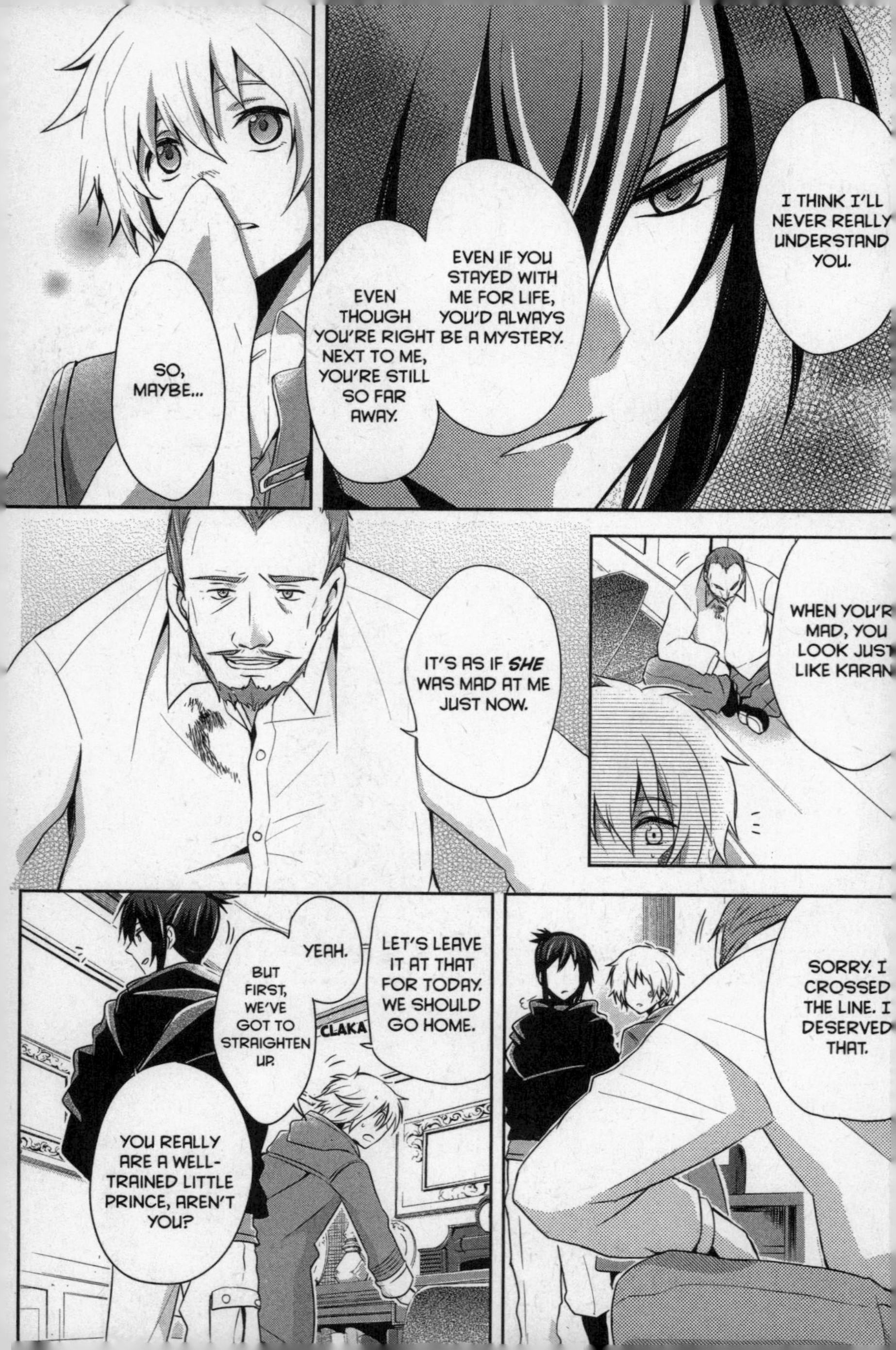
I THINK I'LL NEVER REALLY UNDERSTAND YOU.
EVEN IF YOU STAYED WITH ME FOR LIFE, YOU'D ALWAYS BE A MYSTERY.
EVEN THOUGH YOU'RE RIGHT NEXT TO ME, YOU'RE STILL SO FAR AWAY.
SO, MAYBE...
WHEN YOU'R MAD, YOU LOOK JUST LIKE KARAN
IT'S AS IF *SHE* WAS MAD AT ME JUST NOW.
SORRY. I CROSSED THE LINE. I DESERVED THAT.
LET'S LEAVE IT AT THAT FOR TODAY. WE SHOULD GO HOME.
YEAH.
BUT FIRST, WE'VE GOT TO STRAIGHTEN UP.
CLAKA
YOU REALLY ARE A WELL-TRAINED LITTLE PRINCE, AREN'T YOU?

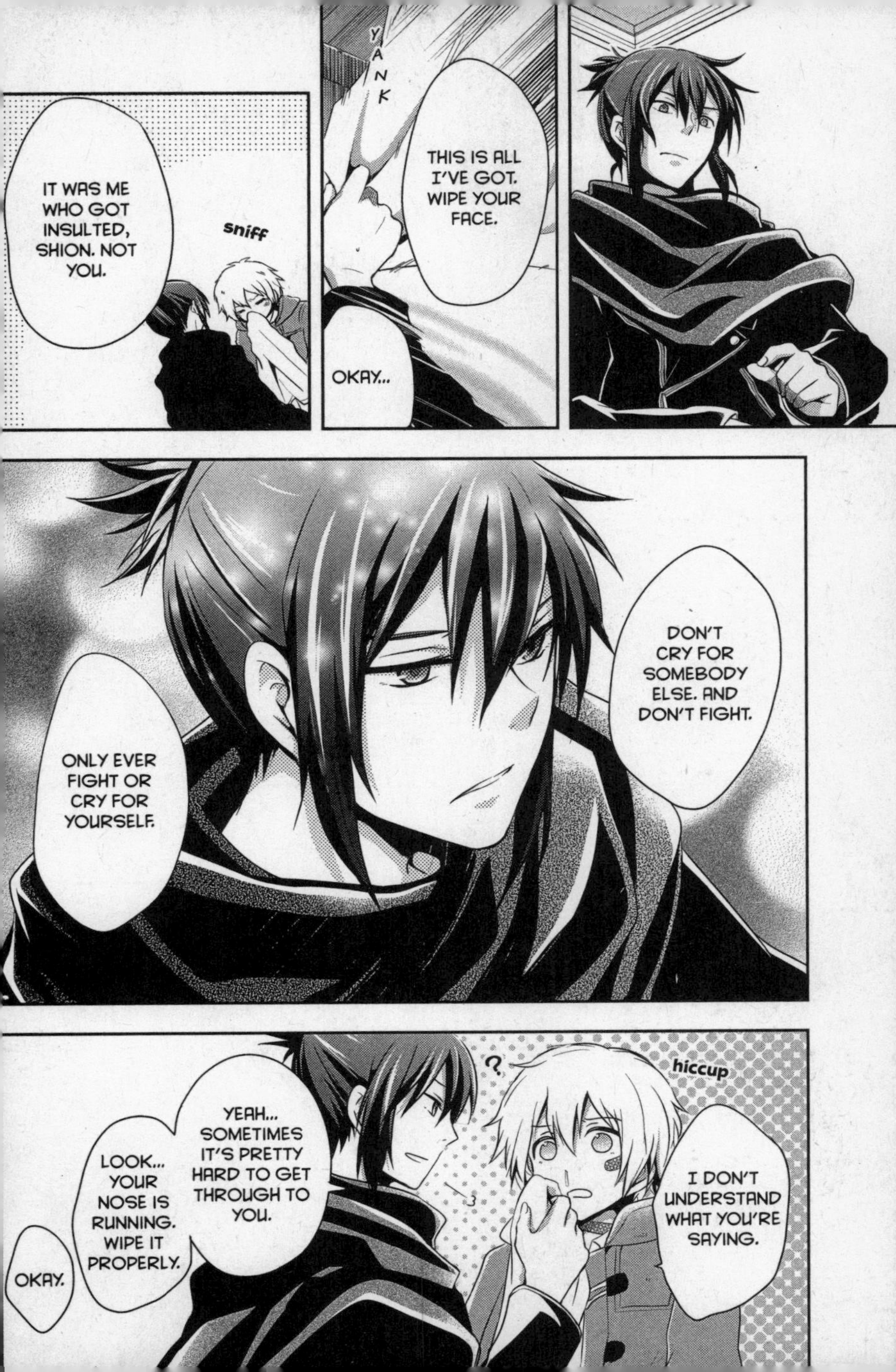
YANK
THIS IS ALL I'VE GOT. WIPE YOUR FACE.
OKAY...
sniff
IT WAS ME WHO GOT INSULTED, SHION. NOT YOU.
DON'T CRY FOR SOMEBODY ELSE. AND DON'T FIGHT.
ONLY EVER FIGHT OR CRY FOR YOURSELF.
hiccup
?
I DON'T UNDERSTAND WHAT YOU'RE SAYING.
YEAH... SOMETIMES IT'S PRETTY HARD TO GET THROUGH TO YOU.
LOOK... YOUR NOSE IS RUNNING. WIPE IT PROPERLY.
OKAY.

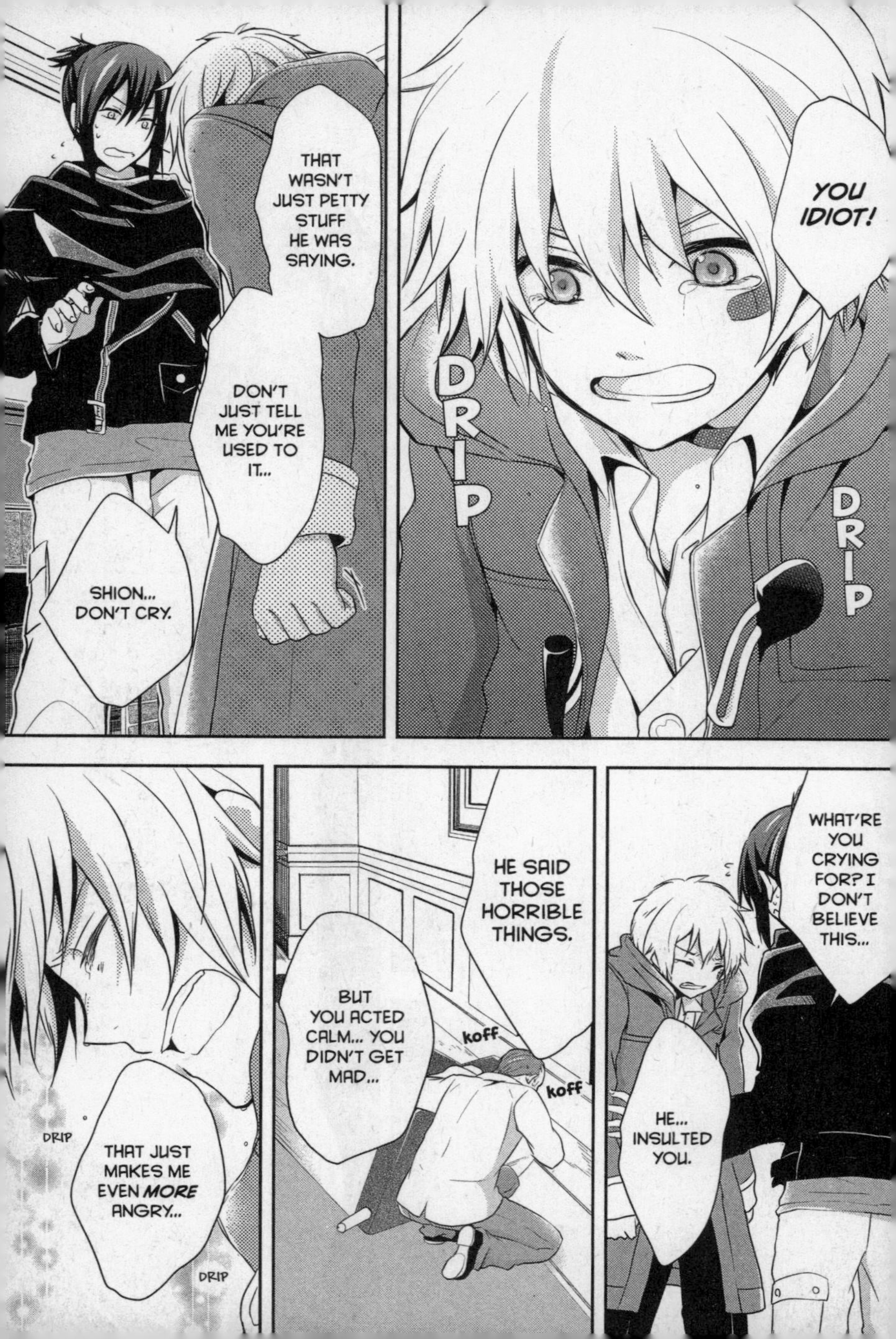
YOU IDIOT!
DRIP
DRIP
THAT WASN'T JUST PETTY STUFF HE WAS SAYING.
DON'T JUST TELL ME YOU'RE USED TO IT...
SHION... DON'T CRY.
WHAT'RE YOU CRYING FOR? I DON'T BELIEVE THIS...
HE... INSULTED YOU.
HE SAID THOSE HORRIBLE THINGS.
koff
koff
BUT YOU ACTED CALM... YOU DIDN'T GET MAD...
DRIP
THAT JUST MAKES ME EVEN *MORE* ANGRY...
DRIP

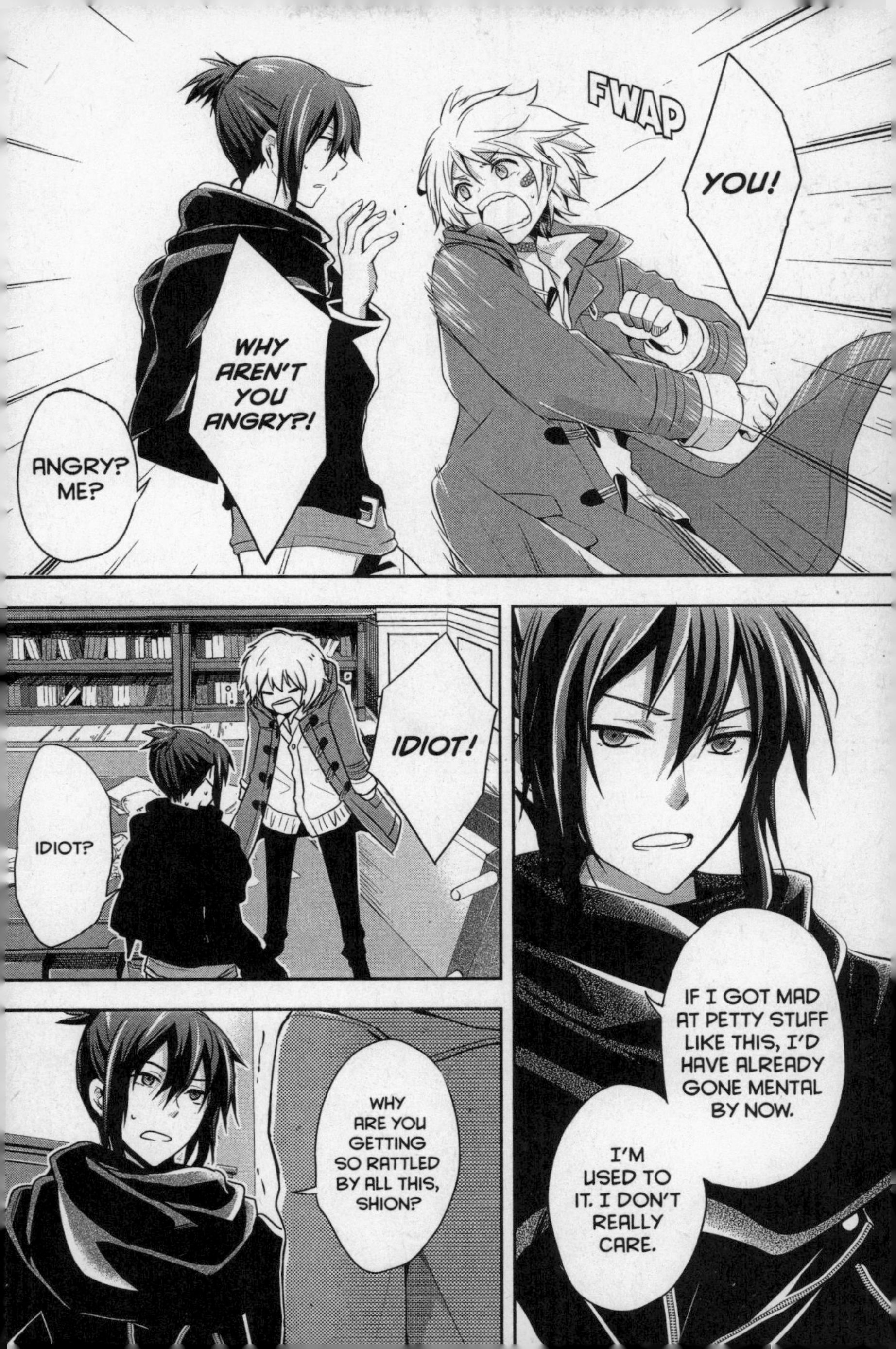
FWAP
YOU!
WHY AREN'T YOU ANGRY?!
ANGRY? ME?
IF I GOT MAD AT PETTY STUFF LIKE THIS, I'D HAVE ALREADY GONE MENTAL BY NOW.
I'M USED TO IT. I DON'T REALLY CARE.
IDIOT!
IDIOT?
WHY ARE YOU GETTING SO RATTLED BY ALL THIS, SHION?

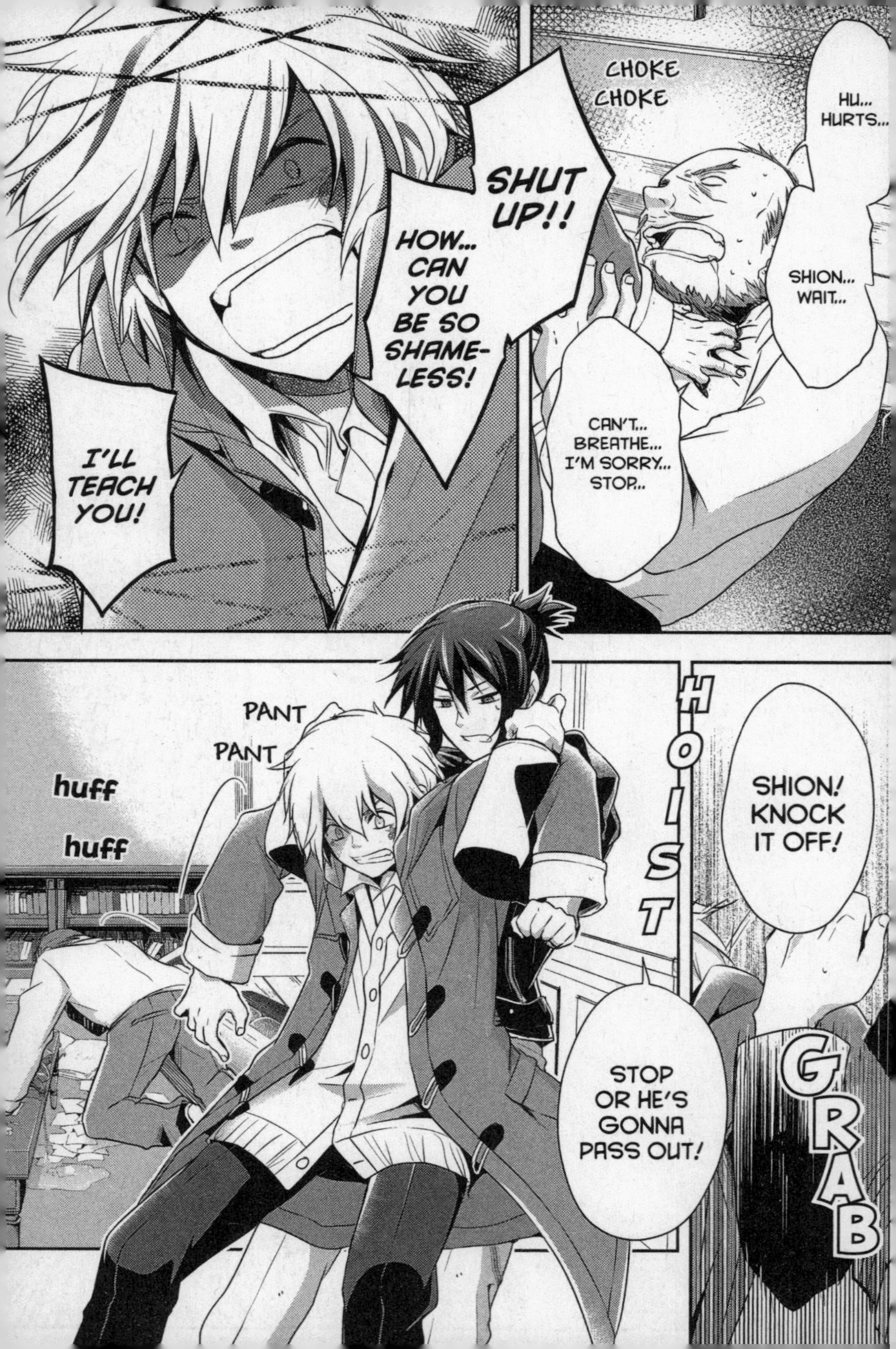
HU... HURTS...
CHOKE CHOKE
SHION... WAIT...
CAN'T... BREATHE... I'M SORRY... STOP...
SHUT UP!!
HOW... CAN YOU BE SO SHAMELESS!
I'LL TEACH YOU!
SHION! KNOCK IT OFF!
HOIST
GRAB
STOP OR HE'S GONNA PASS OUT!
PANT PANT
huff huff

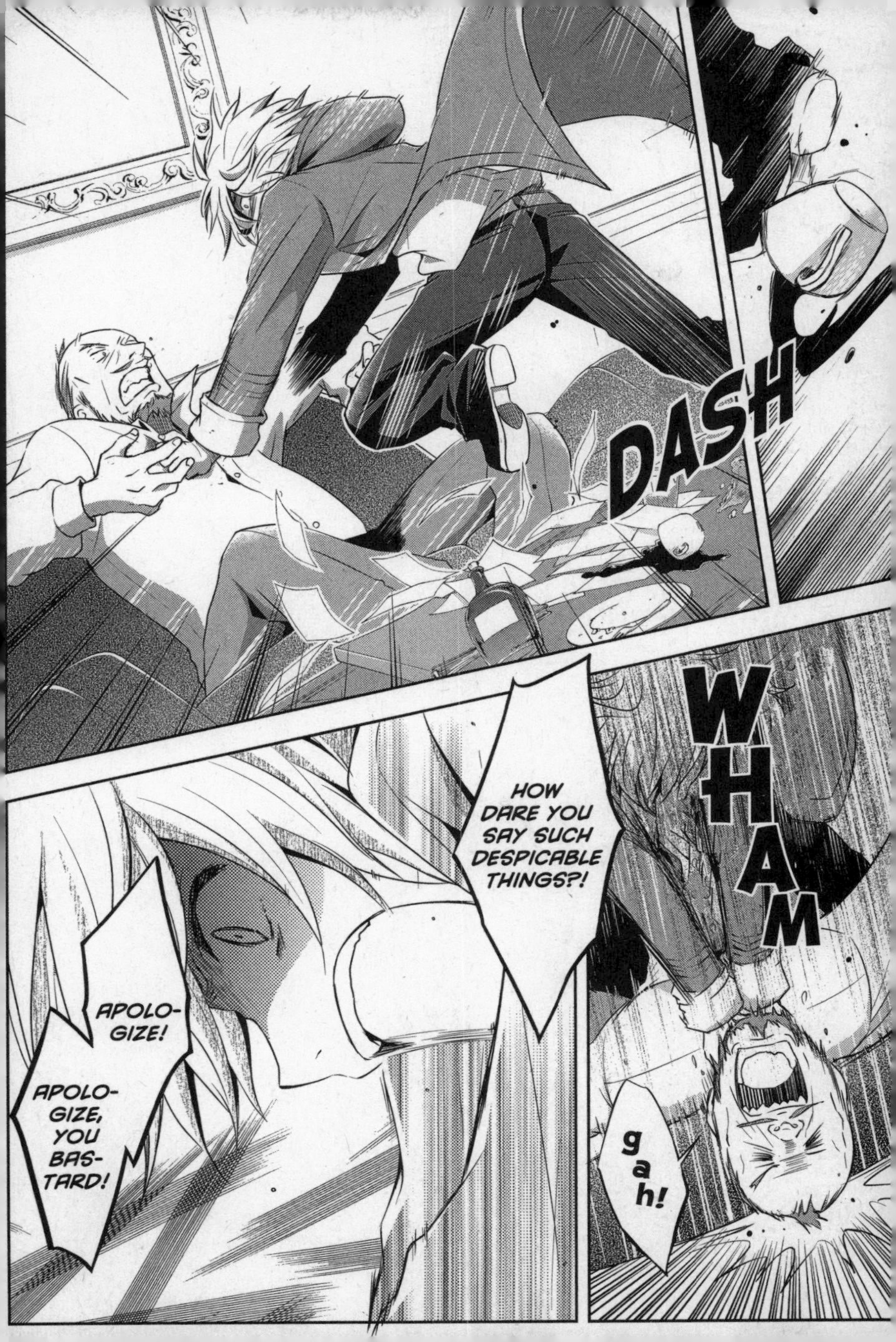
DASH
WHAM
gah!
HOW DARE YOU SAY SUCH DESPICABLE THINGS?!
APOLO-GIZE!
APOLO-GIZE, YOU BAS-TARD!

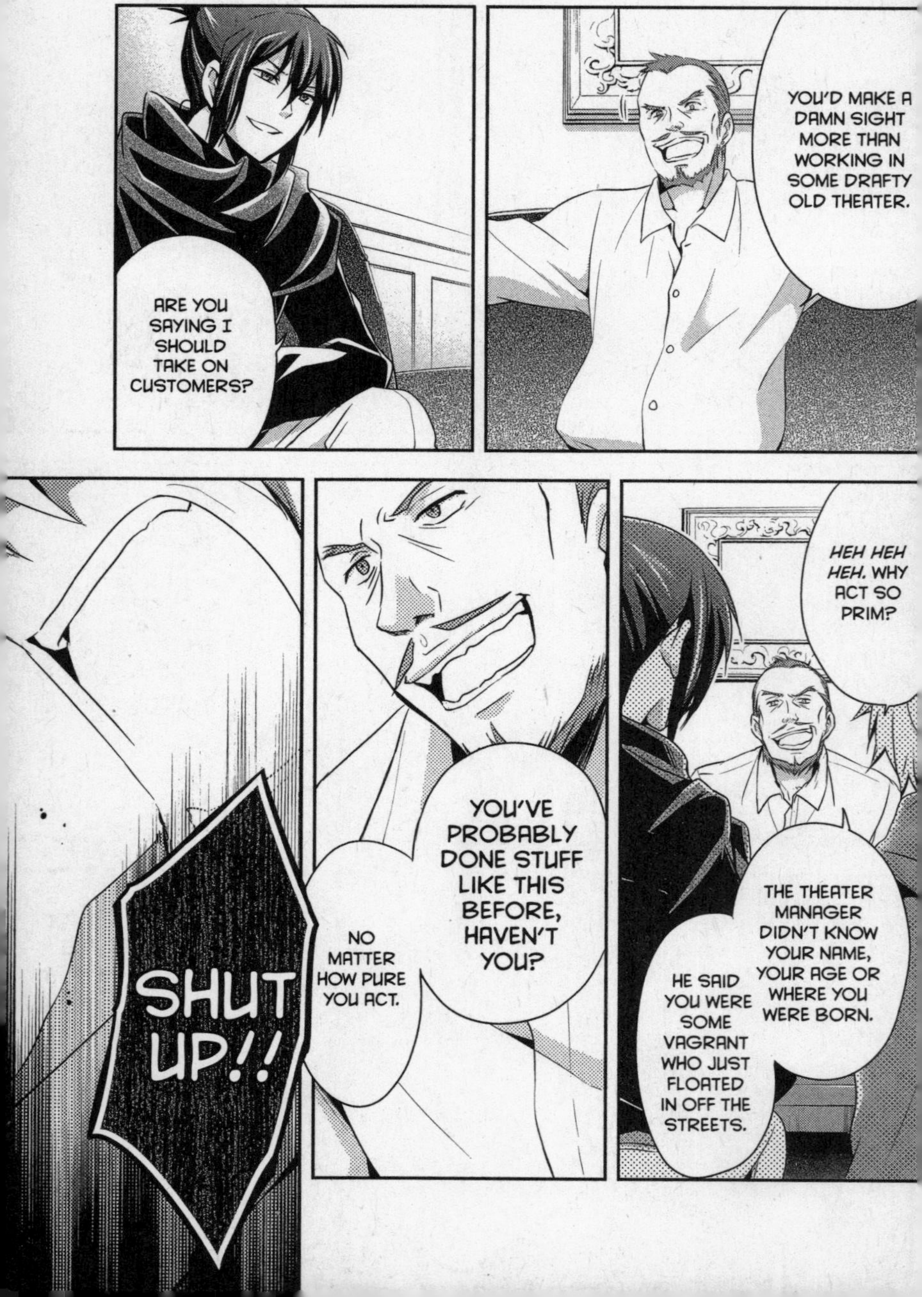
YOU'D MAKE A DAMN SIGHT MORE THAN WORKING IN SOME DRAFTY OLD THEATER.
ARE YOU SAYING I SHOULD TAKE ON CUSTOMERS?
HEH HEH HEH. WHY ACT SO PRIM?
THE THEATER MANAGER DIDN'T KNOW YOUR NAME, YOUR AGE OR WHERE YOU WERE BORN.
HE SAID YOU WERE SOME VAGRANT WHO JUST FLOATED IN OFF THE STREETS.
YOU'VE PROBABLY DONE STUFF LIKE THIS BEFORE, HAVEN'T YOU?
NO MATTER HOW PURE YOU ACT.
SHUT UP!!

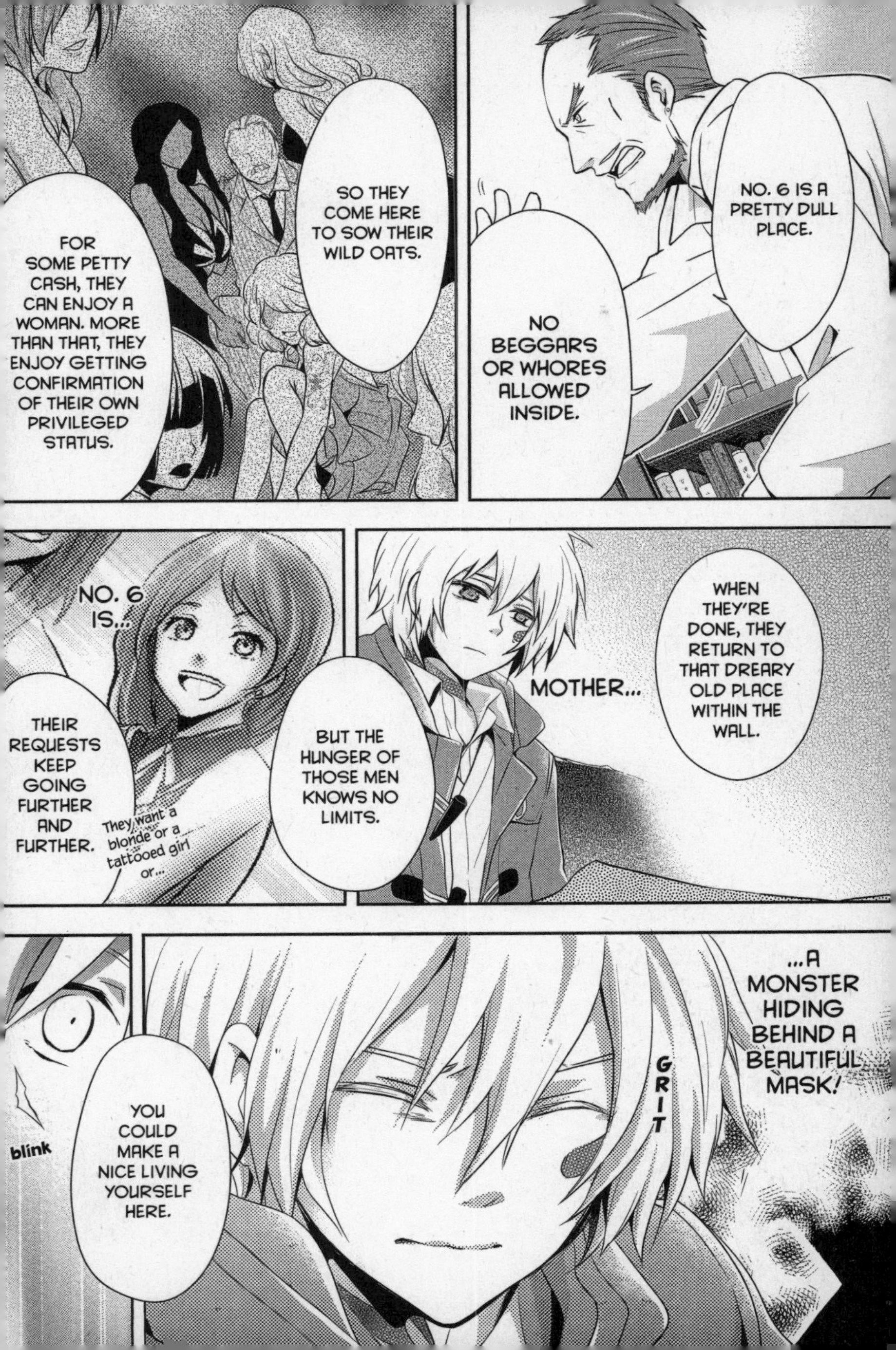
NO. 6 IS A PRETTY DULL PLACE.
NO BEGGARS OR WHORES ALLOWED INSIDE.
SO THEY COME HERE TO SOW THEIR WILD OATS.
FOR SOME PETTY CASH, THEY CAN ENJOY A WOMAN. MORE THAN THAT, THEY ENJOY GETTING CONFIRMATION OF THEIR OWN PRIVILEGED STATUS.
WHEN THEY'RE DONE, THEY RETURN TO THAT DREARY OLD PLACE WITHIN THE WALL.
MOTHER...
BUT THE HUNGER OF THOSE MEN KNOWS NO LIMITS.
NO. 6 IS...
THEIR REQUESTS KEEP GOING FURTHER AND FURTHER.
They want a blonde or a tattooed girl or...
...A MONSTER HIDING BEHIND A BEAUTIFUL MASK!
GRIT
YOU COULD MAKE A NICE LIVING YOURSELF HERE.
blink

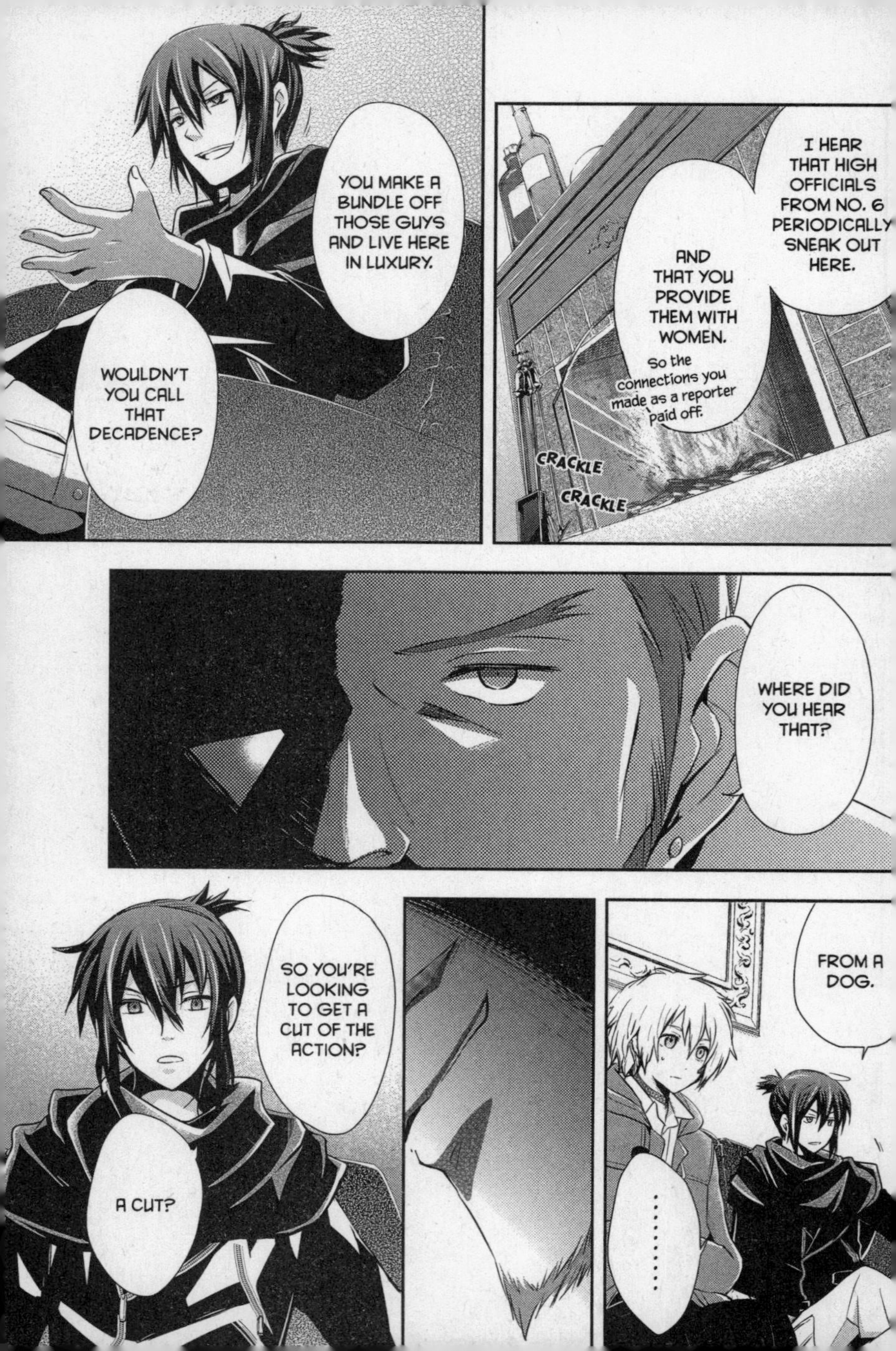
I HEAR THAT HIGH OFFICIALS FROM NO. 6 PERIODICALLY SNEAK OUT HERE.
AND THAT YOU PROVIDE THEM WITH WOMEN.
So the connections you made as a reporter paid off.
CRACKLE
CRACKLE
YOU MAKE A BUNDLE OFF THOSE GUYS AND LIVE HERE IN LUXURY.
WOULDN'T YOU CALL THAT DECADENCE?
WHERE DID YOU HEAR THAT?
FROM A DOG.
....
SO YOU'RE LOOKING TO GET A CUT OF THE ACTION?
A CUT?

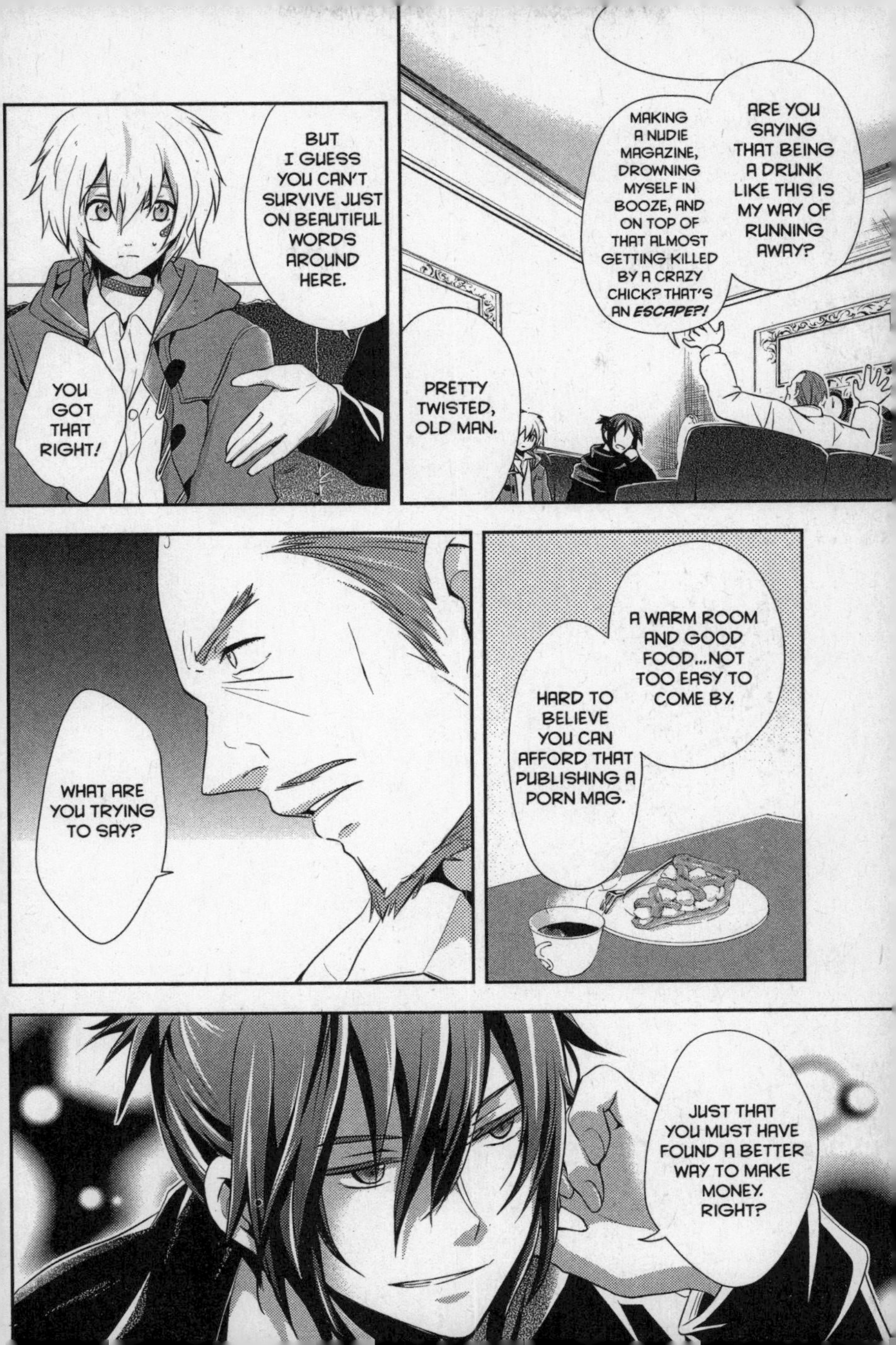
ARE YOU SAYING THAT BEING A DRUNK LIKE THIS IS MY WAY OF RUNNING AWAY?
MAKING A NUDIE MAGAZINE, DROWNING MYSELF IN BOOZE, AND ON TOP OF THAT ALMOST GETTING KILLED BY A CRAZY CHICK? THAT'S AN *ESCAPE?!*
PRETTY TWISTED, OLD MAN.
BUT I GUESS YOU CAN'T SURVIVE JUST ON BEAUTIFUL WORDS AROUND HERE.
YOU GOT THAT RIGHT!
A WARM ROOM AND GOOD FOOD...NOT TOO EASY TO COME BY.
HARD TO BELIEVE YOU CAN AFFORD THAT PUBLISHING A PORN MAG.
WHAT ARE YOU TRYING TO SAY?
JUST THAT YOU MUST HAVE FOUND A BETTER WAY TO MAKE MONEY. RIGHT?

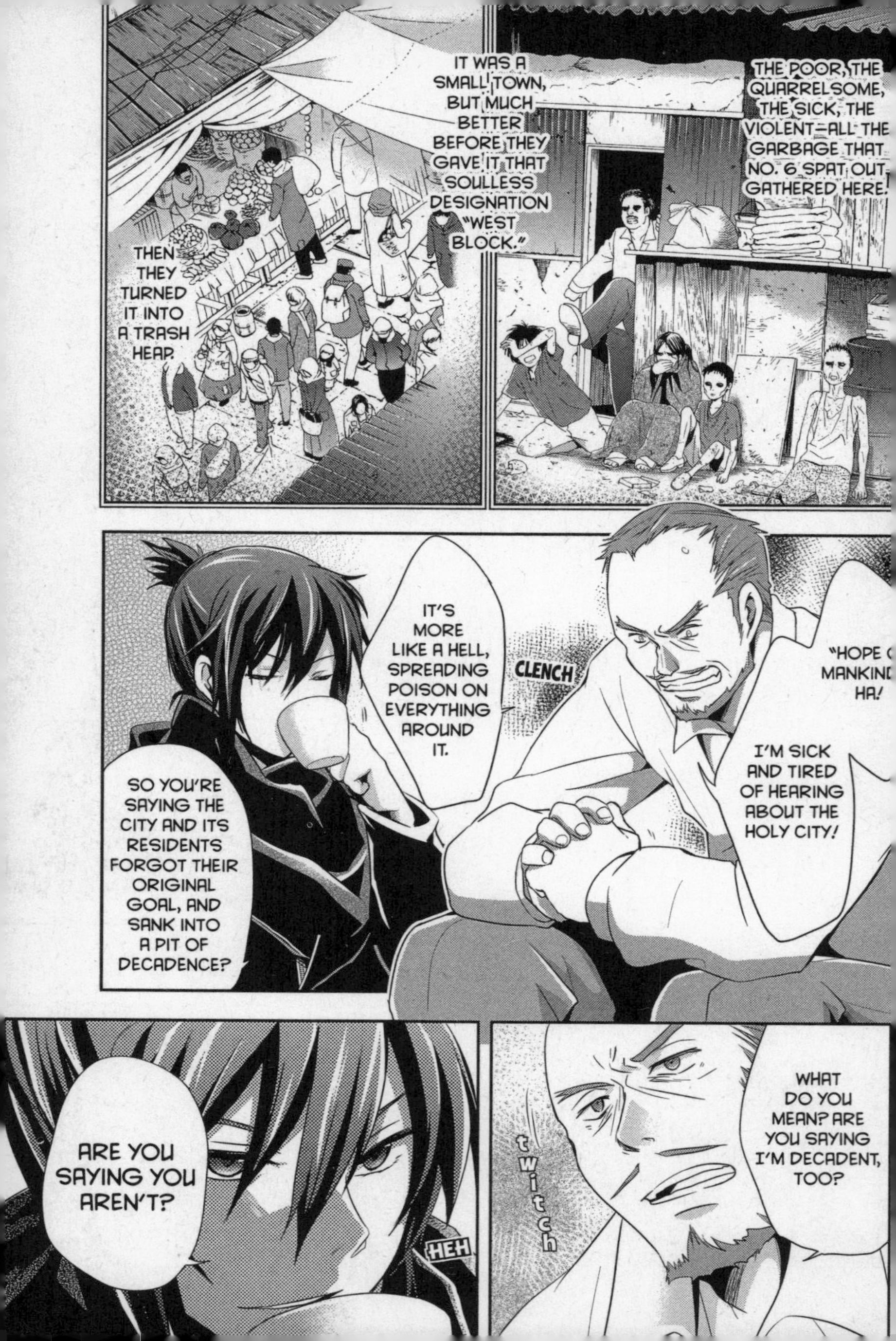
THE POOR, THE QUARRELSOME, THE SICK, THE VIOLENT—ALL THE GARBAGE THAT NO. 6 SPAT OUT GATHERED HERE.
IT WAS A SMALL TOWN, BUT MUCH BETTER BEFORE THEY GAVE IT THAT SOULLESS DESIGNATION "WEST BLOCK."
THEN THEY TURNED IT INTO A TRASH HEAP.
"HOPE MANKIND HA!
I'M SICK AND TIRED OF HEARING ABOUT THE HOLY CITY!
CLENCH
IT'S MORE LIKE A HELL, SPREADING POISON ON EVERYTHING AROUND IT.
SO YOU'RE SAYING THE CITY AND ITS RESIDENTS FORGOT THEIR ORIGINAL GOAL, AND SANK INTO A PIT OF DECADENCE?
WHAT DO YOU MEAN? ARE YOU SAYING I'M DECADENT, TOO?
twitch
HEH
ARE YOU SAYING YOU AREN'T?

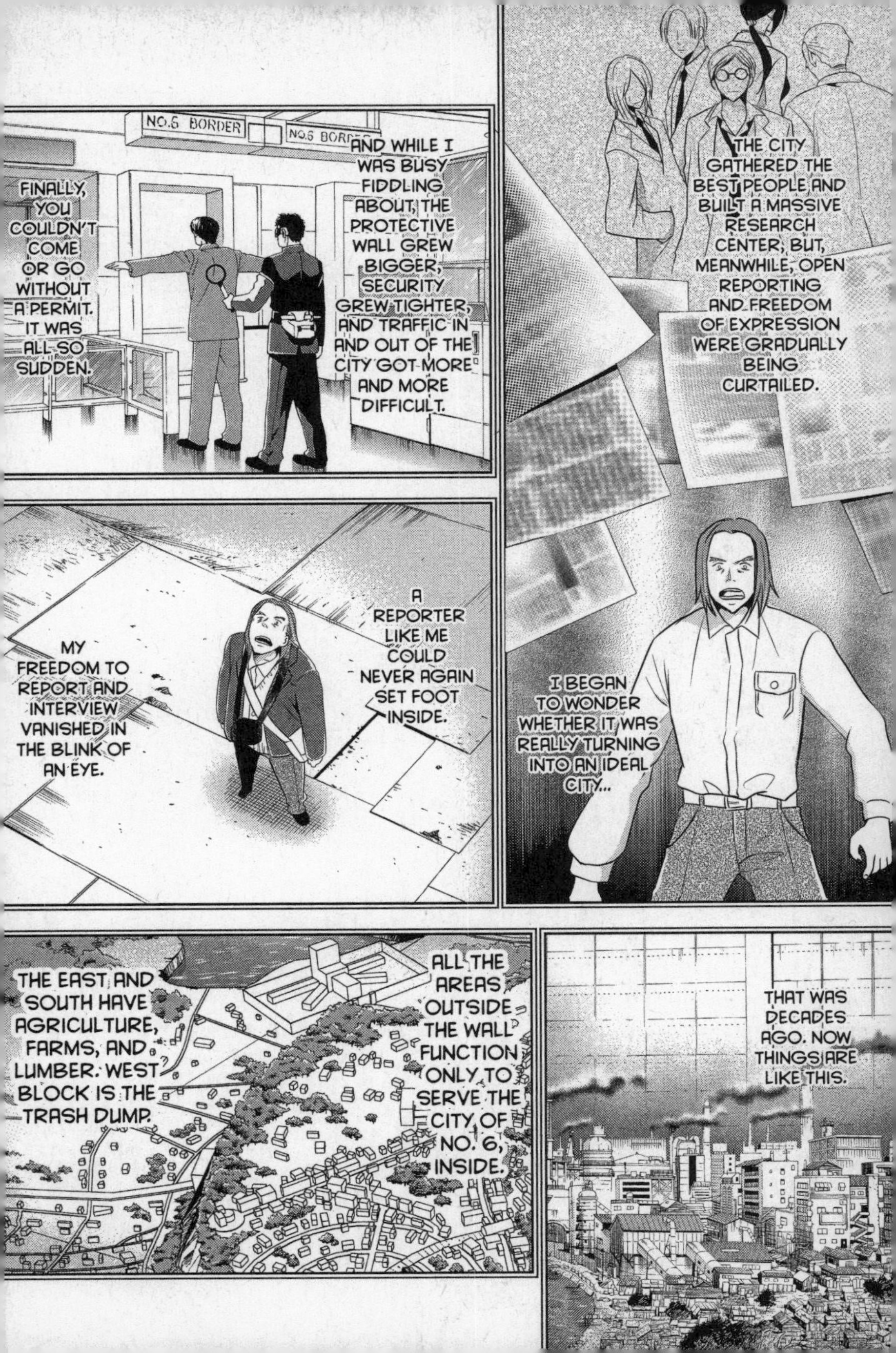
THE CITY GATHERED THE BEST PEOPLE AND BUILT A MASSIVE RESEARCH CENTER, BUT, MEANWHILE, OPEN REPORTING AND FREEDOM OF EXPRESSION WERE GRADUALLY BEING CURTAILED.
I BEGAN TO WONDER WHETHER IT WAS REALLY TURNING INTO AN IDEAL CITY...
NO.6 BORDER
NO.6 BORDER
AND WHILE I WAS BUSY FIDDLING ABOUT, THE PROTECTIVE WALL GREW BIGGER, SECURITY GREW TIGHTER, AND TRAFFIC IN AND OUT OF THE CITY GOT MORE AND MORE DIFFICULT.
FINALLY, YOU COULDN'T COME OR GO WITHOUT A PERMIT. IT WAS ALL SO SUDDEN.
A REPORTER LIKE ME COULD NEVER AGAIN SET FOOT INSIDE.
MY FREEDOM TO REPORT AND INTERVIEW VANISHED IN THE BLINK OF AN EYE.
THAT WAS DECADES AGO. NOW THINGS ARE LIKE THIS.
ALL THE AREAS OUTSIDE THE WALL FUNCTION ONLY TO SERVE THE CITY OF NO. 6, INSIDE.
THE EAST AND SOUTH HAVE AGRICULTURE, FARMS, AND LUMBER. WEST BLOCK IS THE TRASH DUMP.

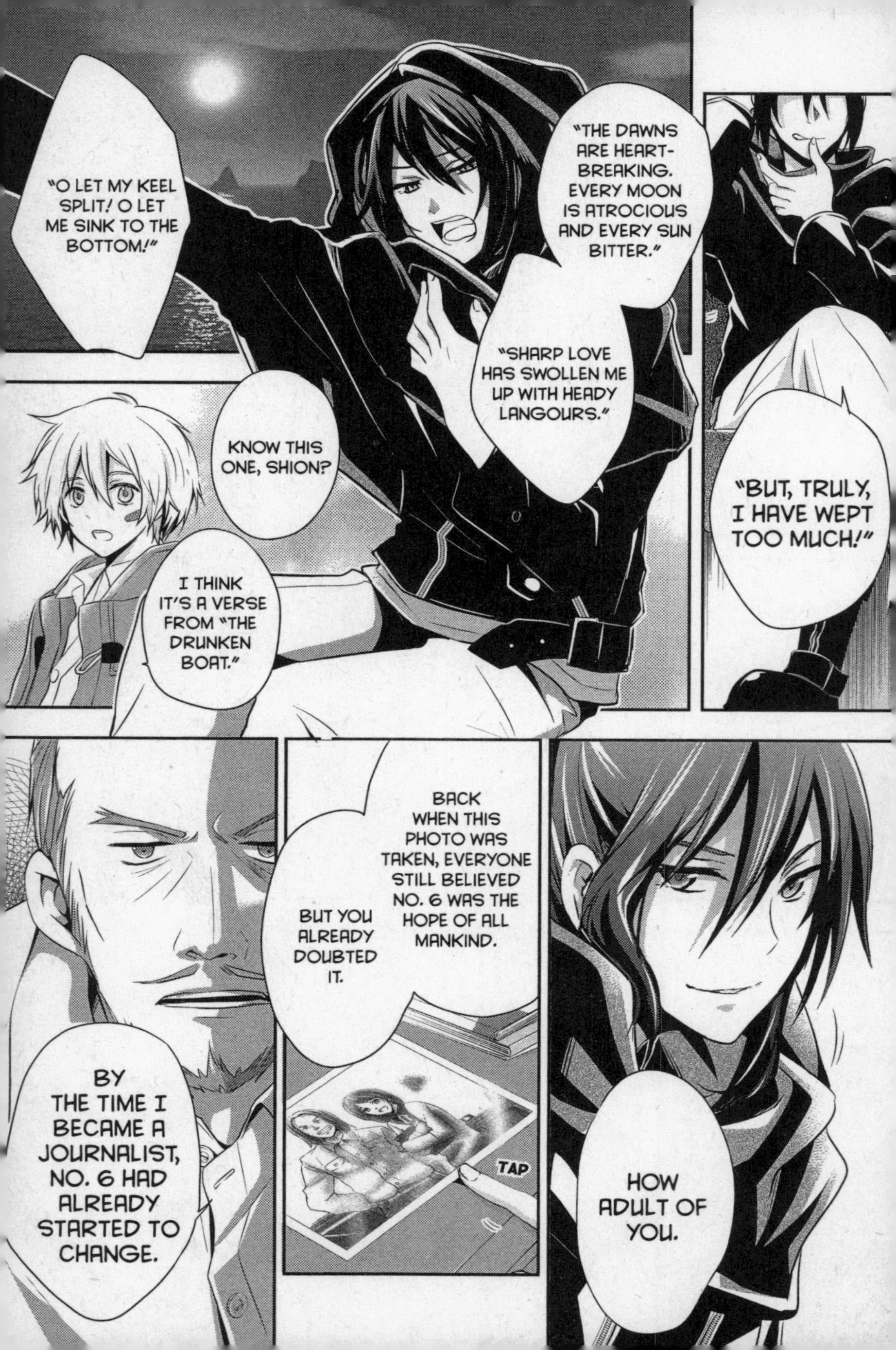
"BUT, TRULY, I HAVE WEPT TOO MUCH!"
"THE DAWNS ARE HEART-BREAKING. EVERY MOON IS ATROCIOUS AND EVERY SUN BITTER."
"SHARP LOVE HAS SWOLLEN ME UP WITH HEADY LANGOURS."
"O LET MY KEEL SPLIT! O LET ME SINK TO THE BOTTOM!"
KNOW THIS ONE, SHION?
I THINK IT'S A VERSE FROM "THE DRUNKEN BOAT."
HOW ADULT OF YOU.
BACK WHEN THIS PHOTO WAS TAKEN, EVERYONE STILL BELIEVED NO. 6 WAS THE HOPE OF ALL MANKIND.
BUT YOU ALREADY DOUBTED IT.
TAP
BY THE TIME I BECAME A JOURNALIST, NO. 6 HAD ALREADY STARTED TO CHANGE.

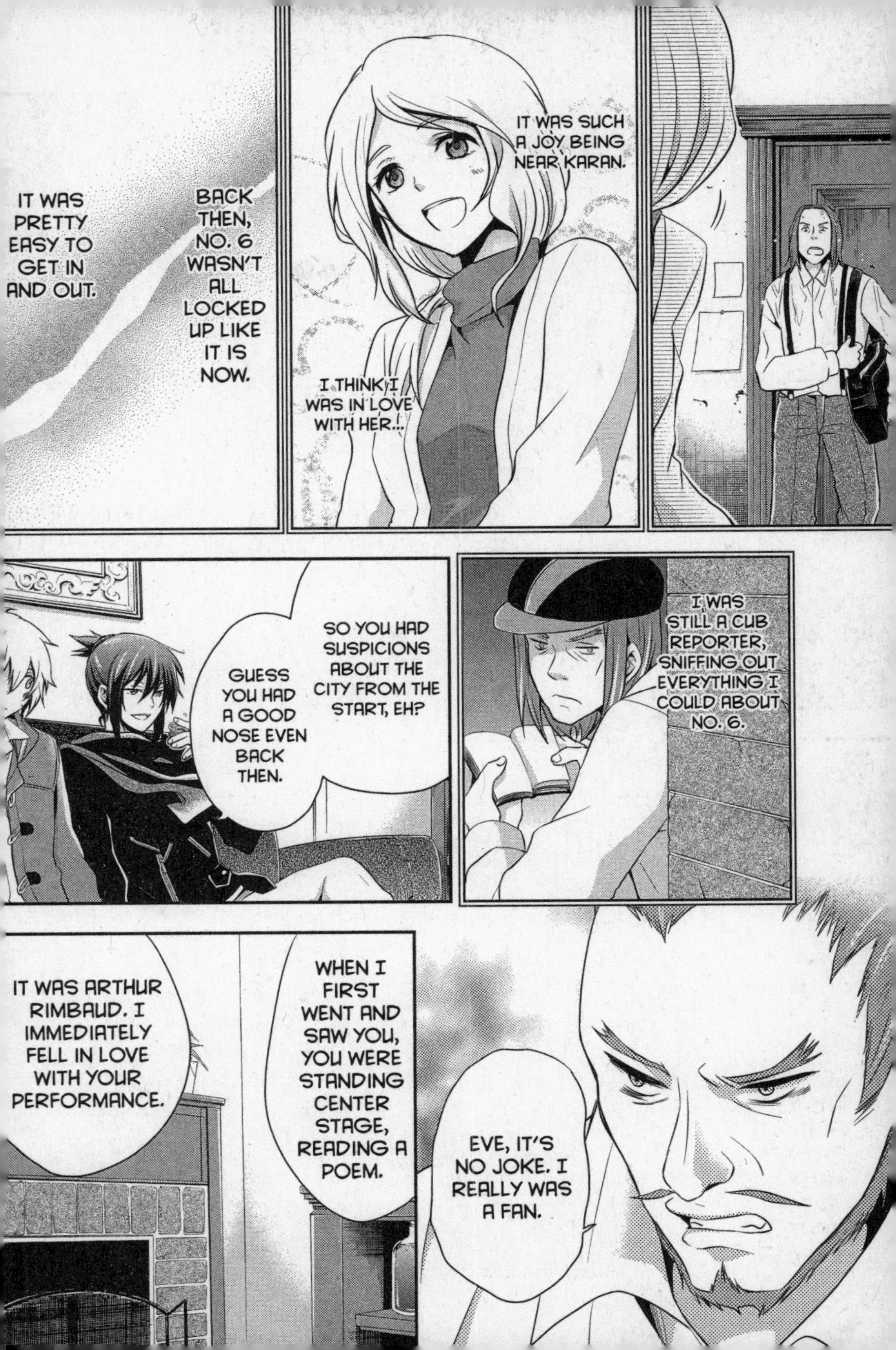
IT WAS SUCH A JOY BEING NEAR KARAN.
I THINK I WAS IN LOVE WITH HER...
BACK THEN, NO. 6 WASN'T ALL LOCKED UP LIKE IT IS NOW.
IT WAS PRETTY EASY TO GET IN AND OUT.
I WAS STILL A CUB REPORTER, SNIFFING OUT EVERYTHING I COULD ABOUT NO. 6.
SO YOU HAD SUSPICIONS ABOUT THE CITY FROM THE START, EH?
GUESS YOU HAD A GOOD NOSE EVEN BACK THEN.
EVE, IT'S NO JOKE. I REALLY WAS A FAN.
WHEN I FIRST WENT AND SAW YOU, YOU WERE STANDING CENTER STAGE, READING A POEM.
IT WAS ARTHUR RIMBAUD. I IMMEDIATELY FELL IN LOVE WITH YOUR PERFORMANCE.

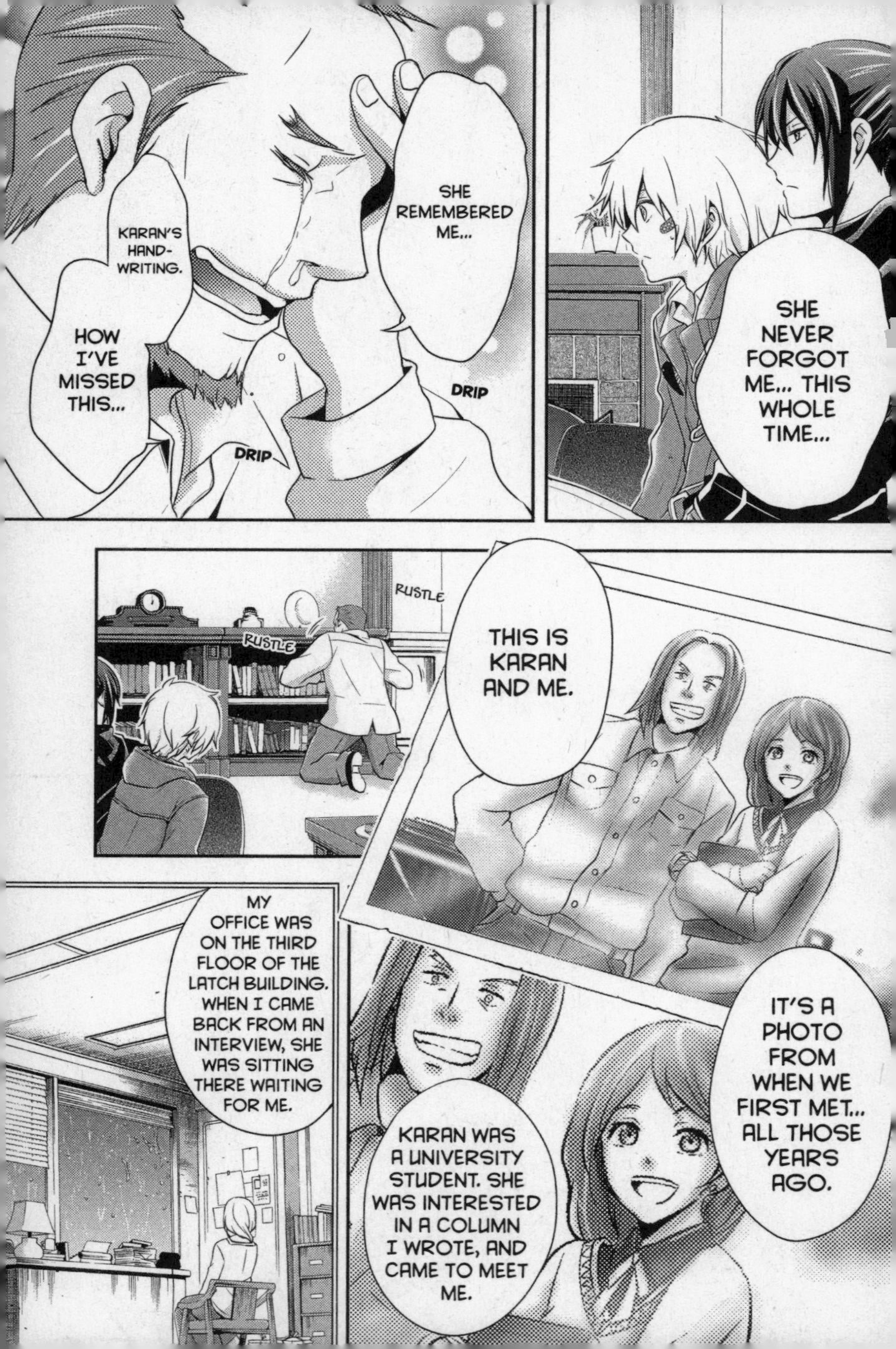
SHE NEVER FORGOT ME... THIS WHOLE TIME...
SHE REMEMBERED ME...
KARAN'S HAND-WRITING.
DRIP
HOW I'VE MISSED THIS...
DRIP
THIS IS KARAN AND ME.
RUSTLE
RUSTLE
IT'S A PHOTO FROM WHEN WE FIRST MET... ALL THOSE YEARS AGO.
KARAN WAS A UNIVERSITY STUDENT. SHE WAS INTERESTED IN A COLUMN I WROTE, AND CAME TO MEET ME.
MY OFFICE WAS ON THE THIRD FLOOR OF THE LATCH BUILDING. WHEN I CAME BACK FROM AN INTERVIEW, SHE WAS SITTING THERE WAITING FOR ME.

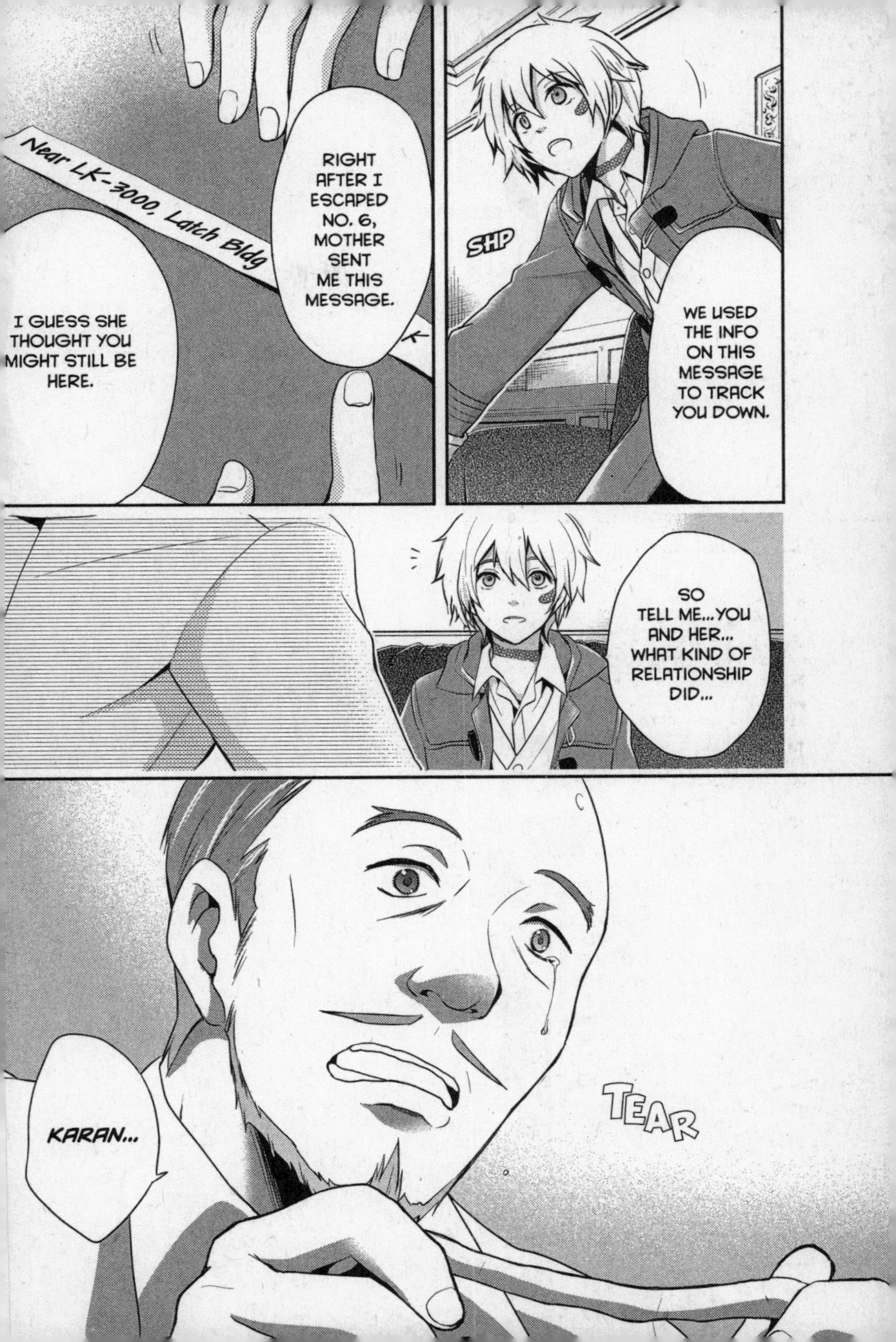
SHP
WE USED THE INFO ON THIS MESSAGE TO TRACK YOU DOWN.
RIGHT AFTER I ESCAPED NO. 6, MOTHER SENT ME THIS MESSAGE.
Near LK-3000, Latch Bldg
I GUESS SHE THOUGHT YOU MIGHT STILL BE HERE.
SO TELL ME...YOU AND HER... WHAT KIND OF RELATIONSHIP DID...
TEAR
KARAN...

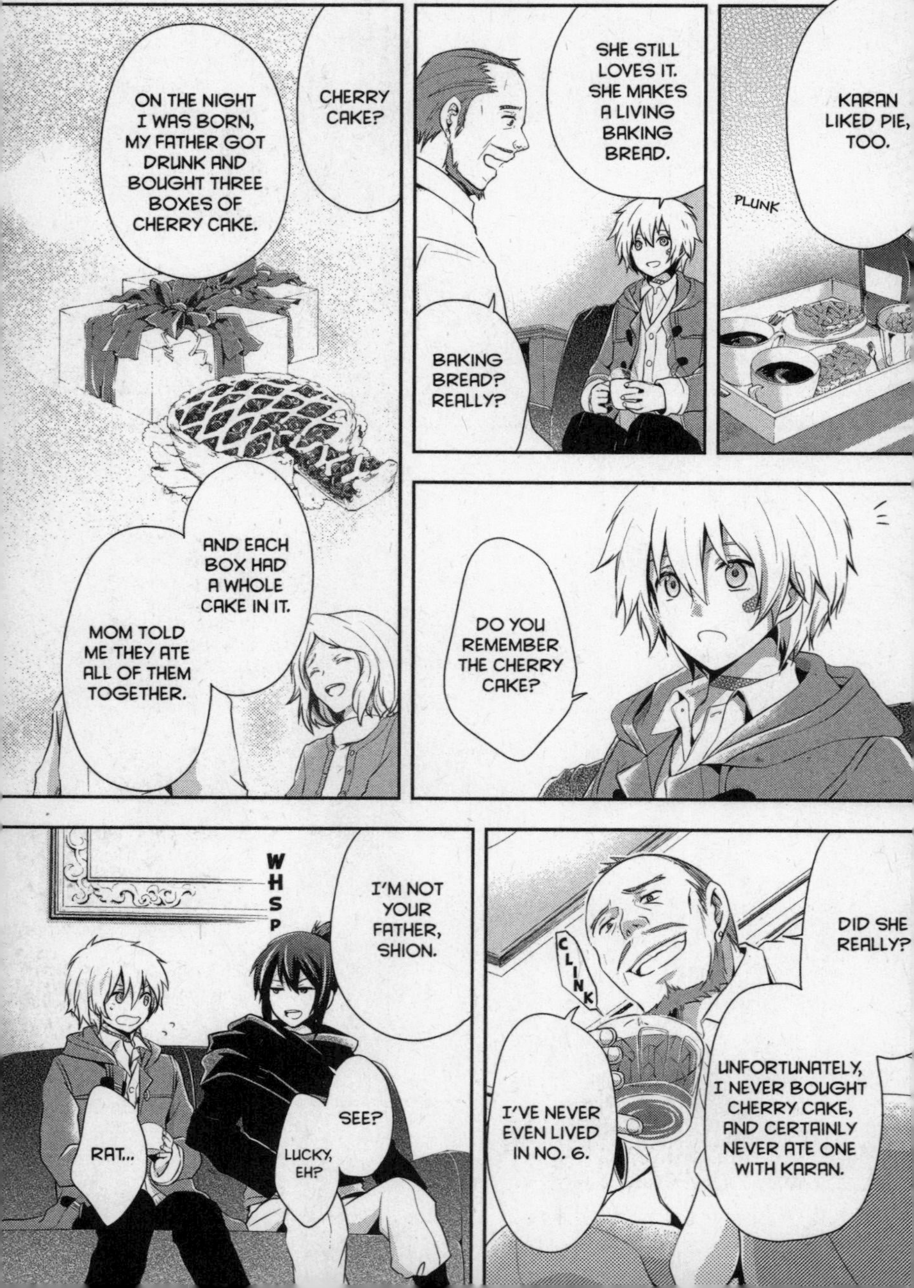
KARAN LIKED PIE, TOO.
PLUNK
SHE STILL LOVES IT. SHE MAKES A LIVING BAKING BREAD.
BAKING BREAD? REALLY?
DO YOU REMEMBER THE CHERRY CAKE?
CHERRY CAKE?
ON THE NIGHT I WAS BORN, MY FATHER GOT DRUNK AND BOUGHT THREE BOXES OF CHERRY CAKE.
AND EACH BOX HAD A WHOLE CAKE IN IT.
MOM TOLD ME THEY ATE ALL OF THEM TOGETHER.
DID SHE REALLY?
CLINK
UNFORTUNATELY, I NEVER BOUGHT CHERRY CAKE, AND CERTAINLY NEVER ATE ONE WITH KARAN.
I'VE NEVER EVEN LIVED IN NO. 6.
I'M NOT YOUR FATHER, SHION.
WHSP
SEE?
LUCKY, EH?
RAT...

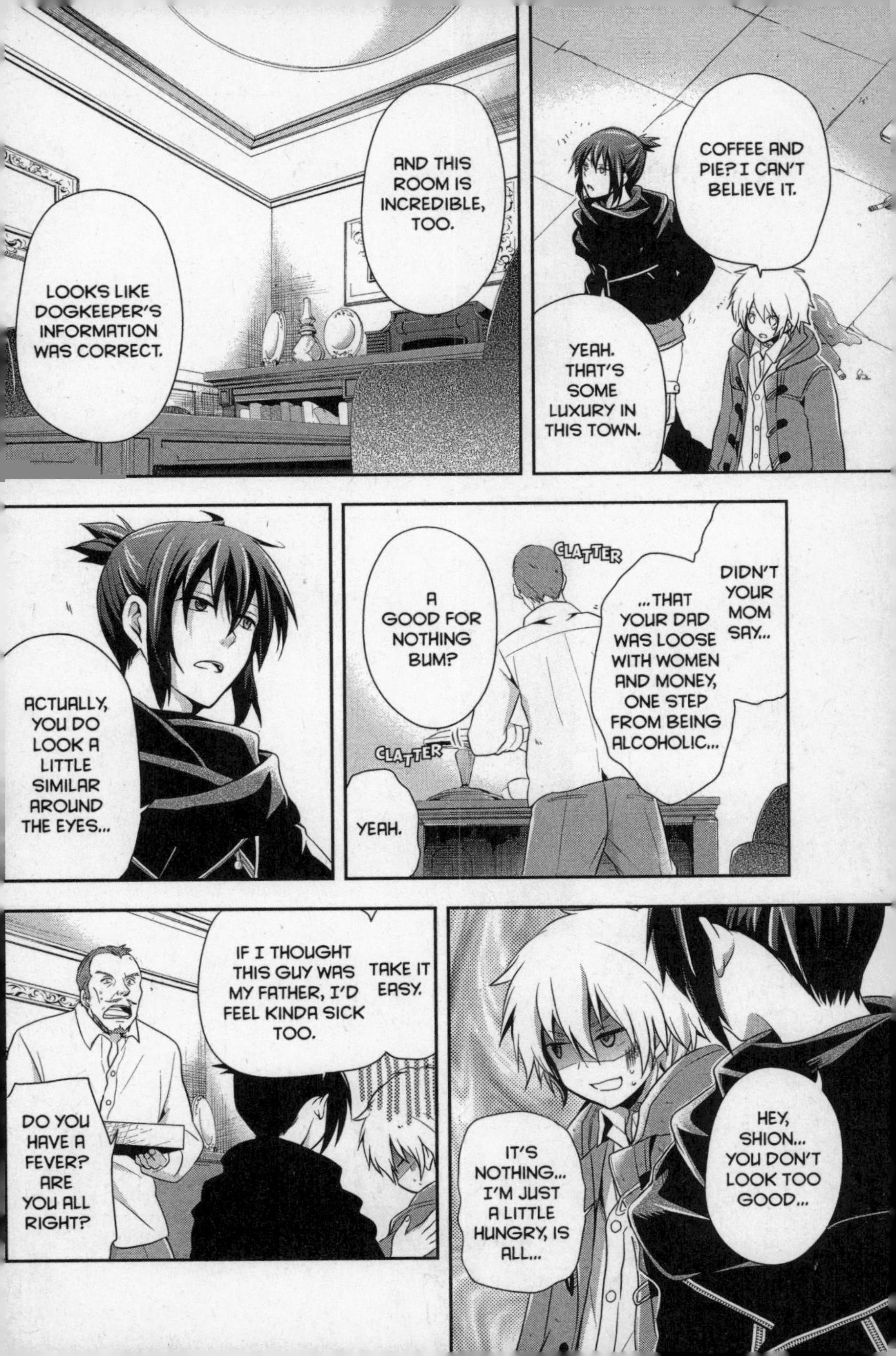
COFFEE AND PIE? I CAN'T BELIEVE IT.
YEAH. THAT'S SOME LUXURY IN THIS TOWN.
AND THIS ROOM IS INCREDIBLE, TOO.
LOOKS LIKE DOGKEEPER'S INFORMATION WAS CORRECT.
CLATTER
DIDN'T YOUR MOM SAY...
...THAT YOUR DAD WAS LOOSE WITH WOMEN AND MONEY, ONE STEP FROM BEING ALCOHOLIC...
A GOOD FOR NOTHING BUM?
CLATTER
YEAH.
ACTUALLY, YOU DO LOOK A LITTLE SIMILAR AROUND THE EYES...
HEY, SHION... YOU DON'T LOOK TOO GOOD...
IT'S NOTHING... I'M JUST A LITTLE HUNGRY, IS ALL...
TAKE IT EASY.
IF I THOUGHT THIS GUY WAS MY FATHER, I'D FEEL KINDA SICK TOO.
DO YOU HAVE A FEVER? ARE YOU ALL RIGHT?

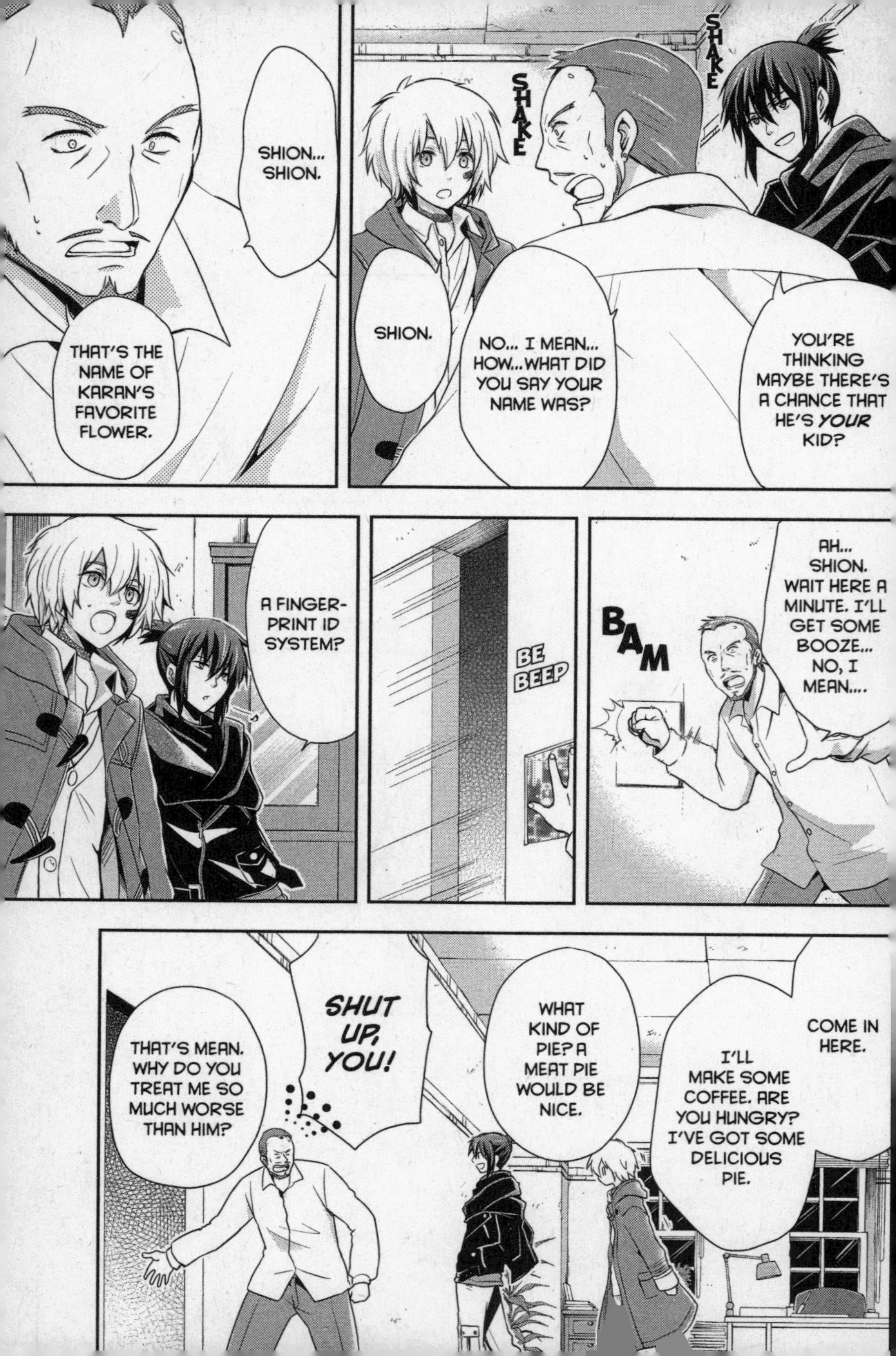
SHAKE
SHAKE
YOU'RE THINKING MAYBE THERE'S A CHANCE THAT HE'S *YOUR* KID?
NO... I MEAN... HOW...WHAT DID YOU SAY YOUR NAME WAS?
SHION.
SHION... SHION.
THAT'S THE NAME OF KARAN'S FAVORITE FLOWER.
AH... SHION. WAIT HERE A MINUTE. I'LL GET SOME BOOZE... NO, I MEAN....
BAM
BE BEEP
A FINGER-PRINT ID SYSTEM?
COME IN HERE.
I'LL MAKE SOME COFFEE. ARE YOU HUNGRY? I'VE GOT SOME DELICIOUS PIE.
WHAT KIND OF PIE? A MEAT PIE WOULD BE NICE.
SHUT UP, YOU!
THAT'S MEAN. WHY DO YOU TREAT ME SO MUCH WORSE THAN HIM?

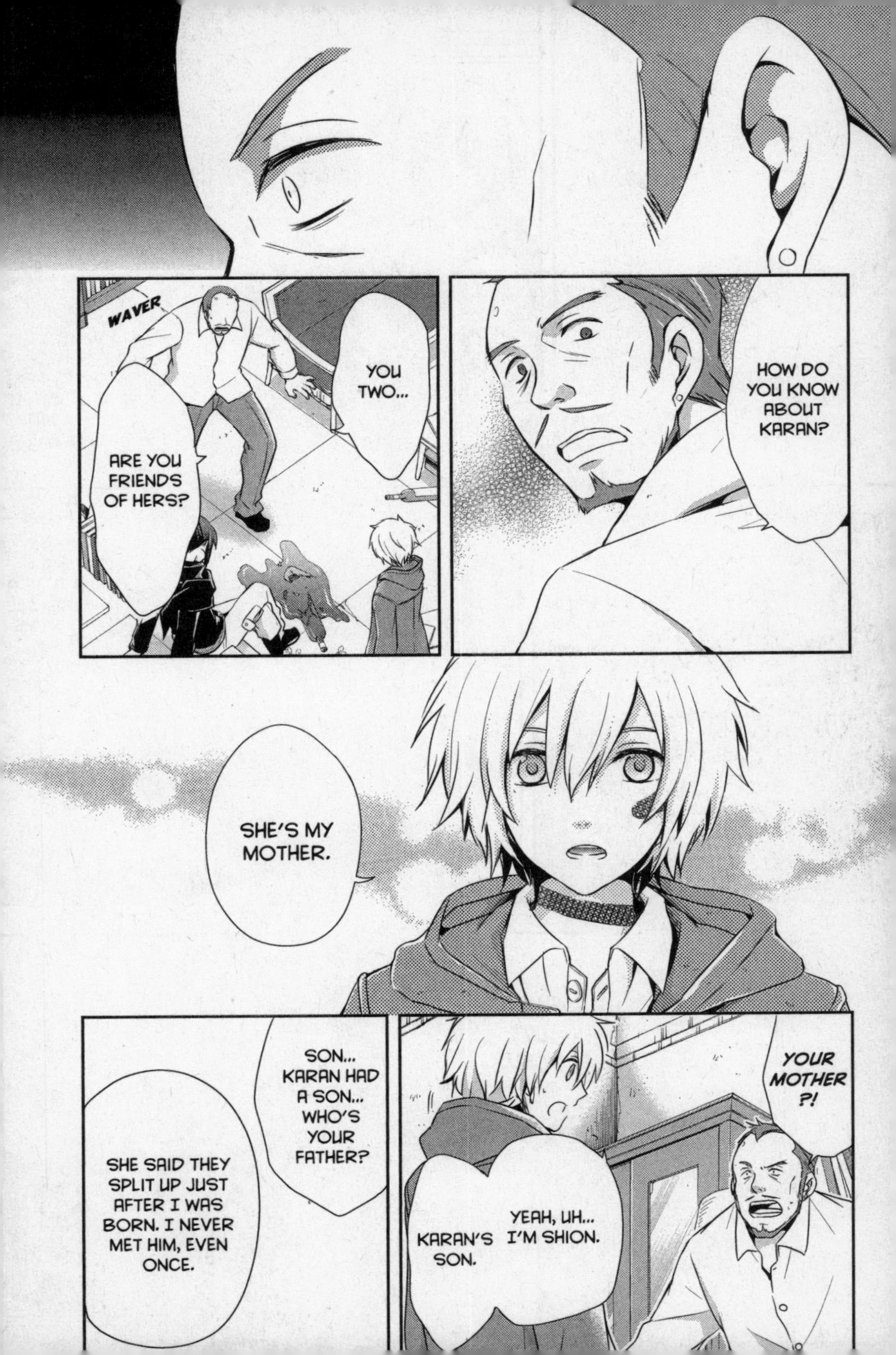
HOW DO YOU KNOW ABOUT KARAN?
WAVER
YOU TWO...
ARE YOU FRIENDS OF HERS?
SHE'S MY MOTHER.
YOUR MOTHER ?!
YEAH, UH... I'M SHION.
KARAN'S SON.
SON... KARAN HAD A SON... WHO'S YOUR FATHER?
SHE SAID THEY SPLIT UP JUST AFTER I WAS BORN. I NEVER MET HIM, EVEN ONCE.

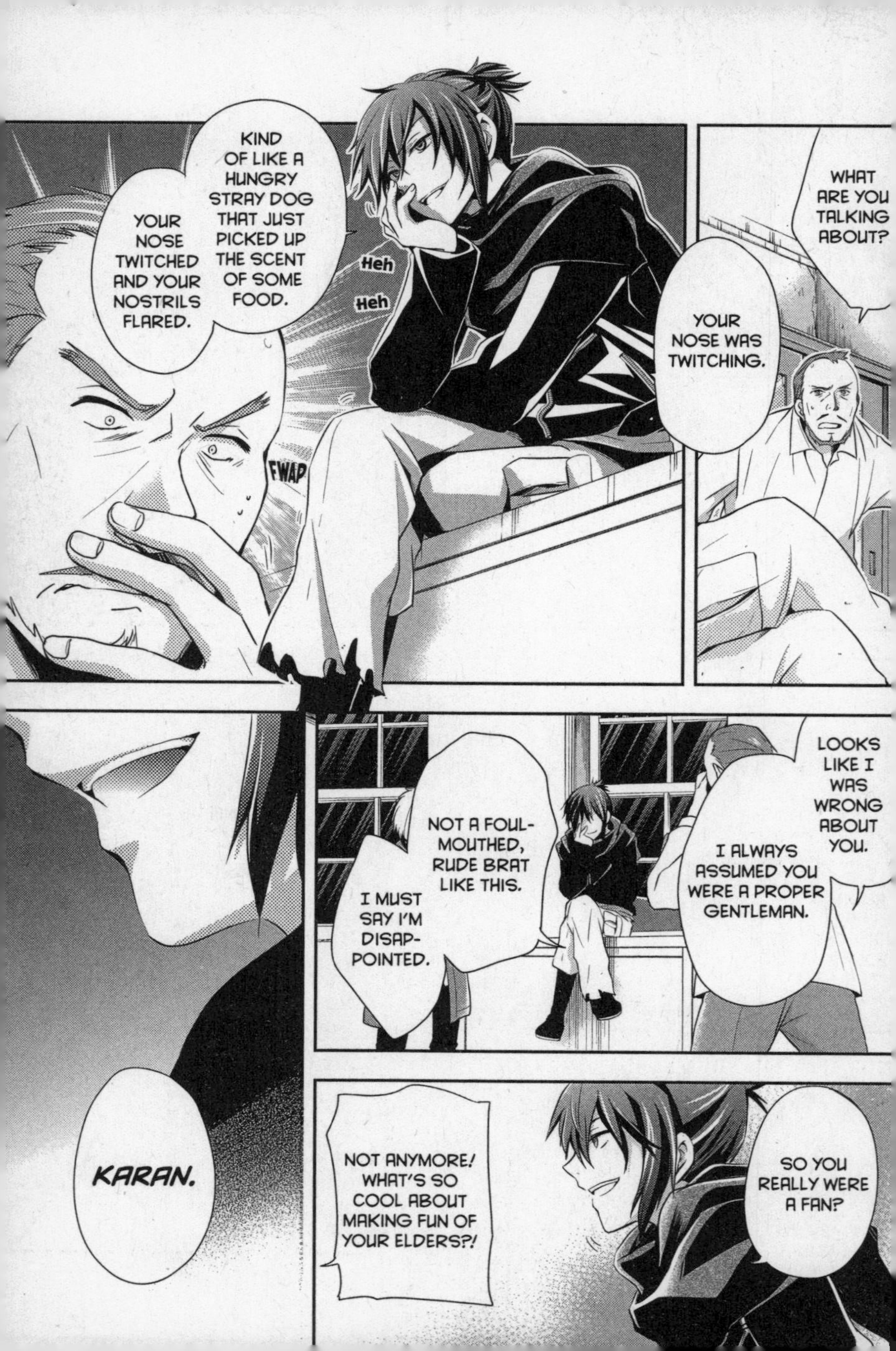
WHAT ARE YOU TALKING ABOUT?
YOUR NOSE WAS TWITCHING.
KIND OF LIKE A HUNGRY STRAY DOG THAT JUST PICKED UP THE SCENT OF SOME FOOD.
YOUR NOSE TWITCHED AND YOUR NOSTRILS FLARED.
Heh
Heh
FWAP
LOOKS LIKE I WAS WRONG ABOUT YOU.
I ALWAYS ASSUMED YOU WERE A PROPER GENTLEMAN.
NOT A FOUL-MOUTHED, RUDE BRAT LIKE THIS.
I MUST SAY I'M DISAP-POINTED.
SO YOU REALLY WERE A FAN?
NOT ANYMORE! WHAT'S SO COOL ABOUT MAKING FUN OF YOUR ELDERS?!
KARAN.

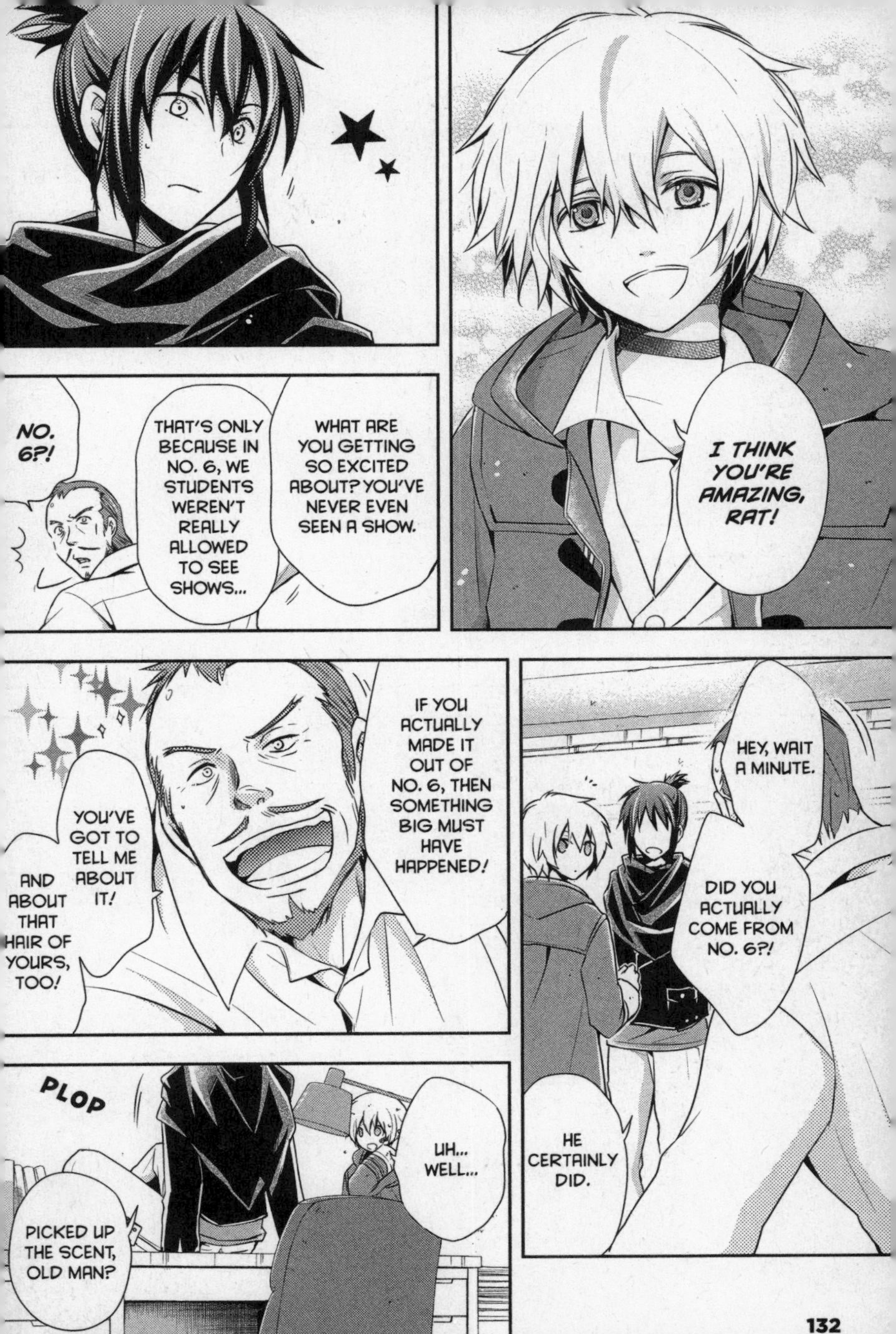
I THINK YOU'RE AMAZING, RAT!
WHAT ARE YOU GETTING SO EXCITED ABOUT? YOU'VE NEVER EVEN SEEN A SHOW.
THAT'S ONLY BECAUSE IN NO. 6, WE STUDENTS WEREN'T REALLY ALLOWED TO SEE SHOWS...
NO. 6?!
HEY, WAIT A MINUTE.
DID YOU ACTUALLY COME FROM NO. 6?!
HE CERTAINLY DID.
IF YOU ACTUALLY MADE IT OUT OF NO. 6, THEN SOMETHING BIG MUST HAVE HAPPENED!
YOU'VE GOT TO TELL ME ABOUT IT!
AND ABOUT THAT HAIR OF YOURS, TOO!
PLOP
UH... WELL...
PICKED UP THE SCENT, OLD MAN?

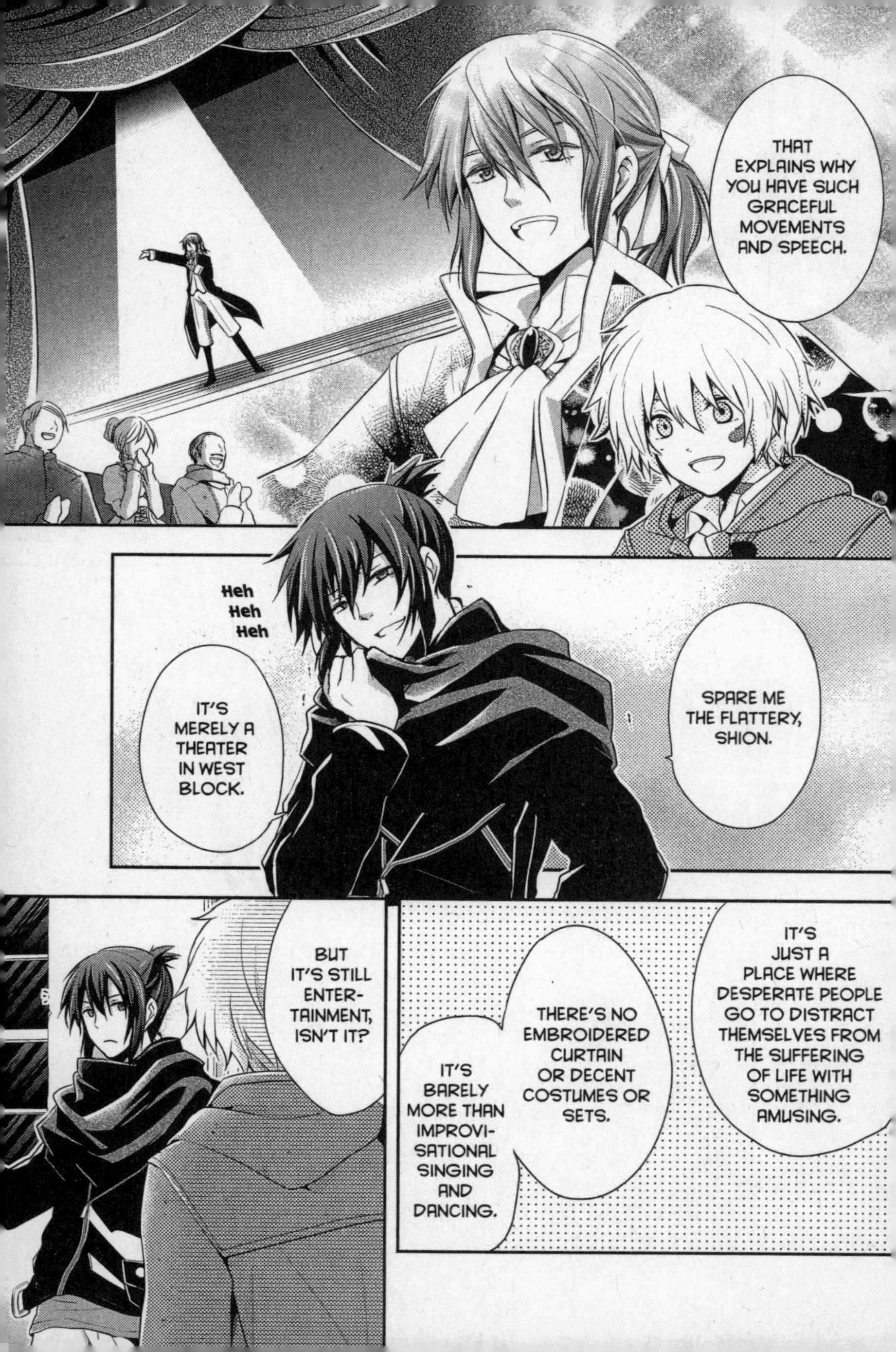
THAT EXPLAINS WHY YOU HAVE SUCH GRACEFUL MOVEMENTS AND SPEECH.
SPARE ME THE FLATTERY, SHION.
Heh Heh Heh
IT'S MERELY A THEATER IN WEST BLOCK.
IT'S JUST A PLACE WHERE DESPERATE PEOPLE GO TO DISTRACT THEMSELVES FROM THE SUFFERING OF LIFE WITH SOMETHING AMUSING.
THERE'S NO EMBROIDERED CURTAIN OR DECENT COSTUMES OR SETS.
IT'S BARELY MORE THAN IMPROVI-SATIONAL SINGING AND DANCING.
BUT IT'S STILL ENTER-TAINMENT, ISN'T IT?

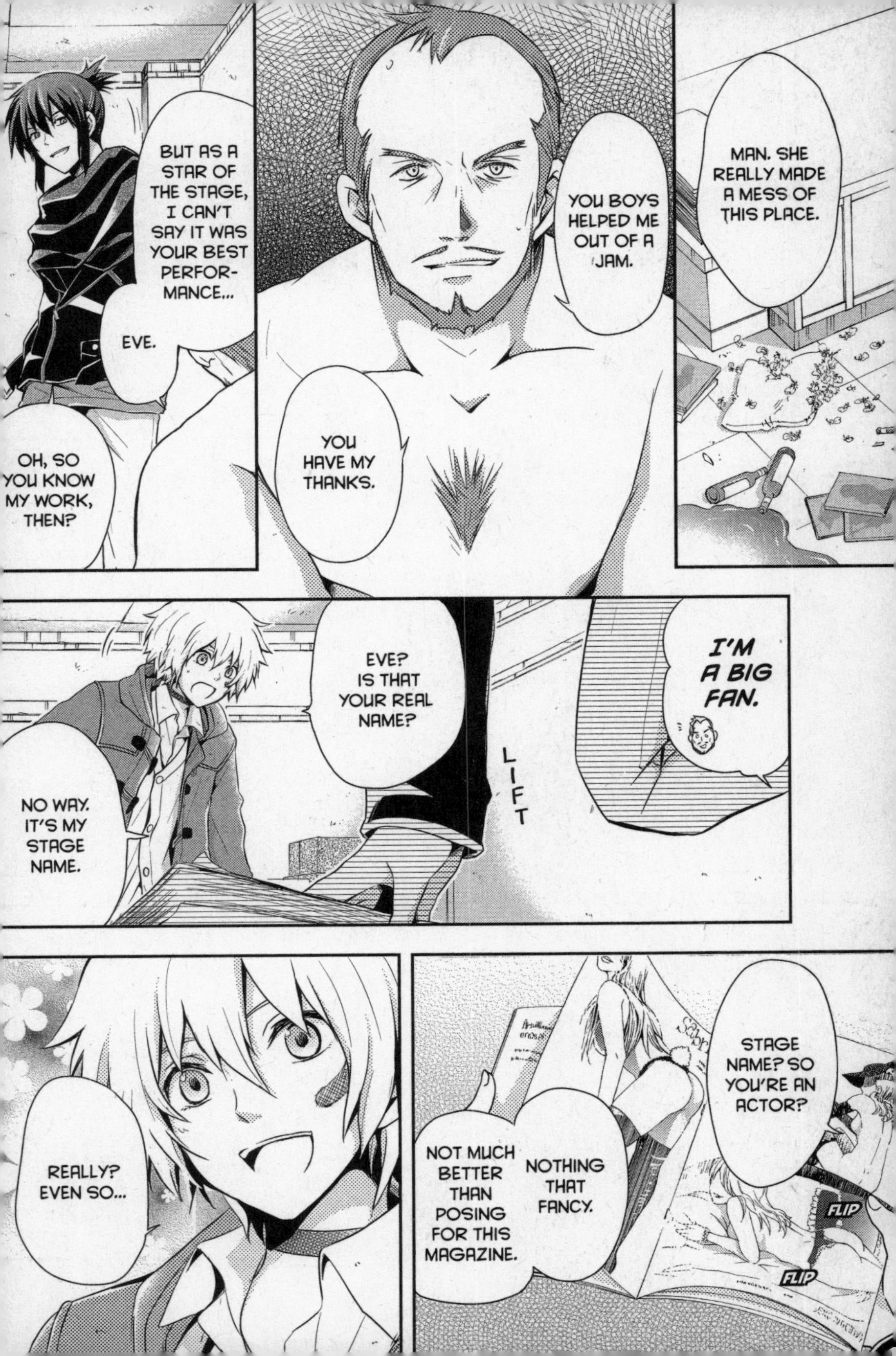
MAN. SHE REALLY MADE A MESS OF THIS PLACE.
YOU BOYS HELPED ME OUT OF A JAM.
YOU HAVE MY THANKS.
BUT AS A STAR OF THE STAGE, I CAN'T SAY IT WAS YOUR BEST PERFORMANCE...
EVE.
OH, SO YOU KNOW MY WORK, THEN?
I'M A BIG FAN.
LIFT
EVE? IS THAT YOUR REAL NAME?
NO WAY. IT'S MY STAGE NAME.
STAGE NAME? SO YOU'RE AN ACTOR?
NOTHING THAT FANCY.
NOT MUCH BETTER THAN POSING FOR THIS MAGAZINE.
FLIP
FLIP
REALLY? EVEN SO...

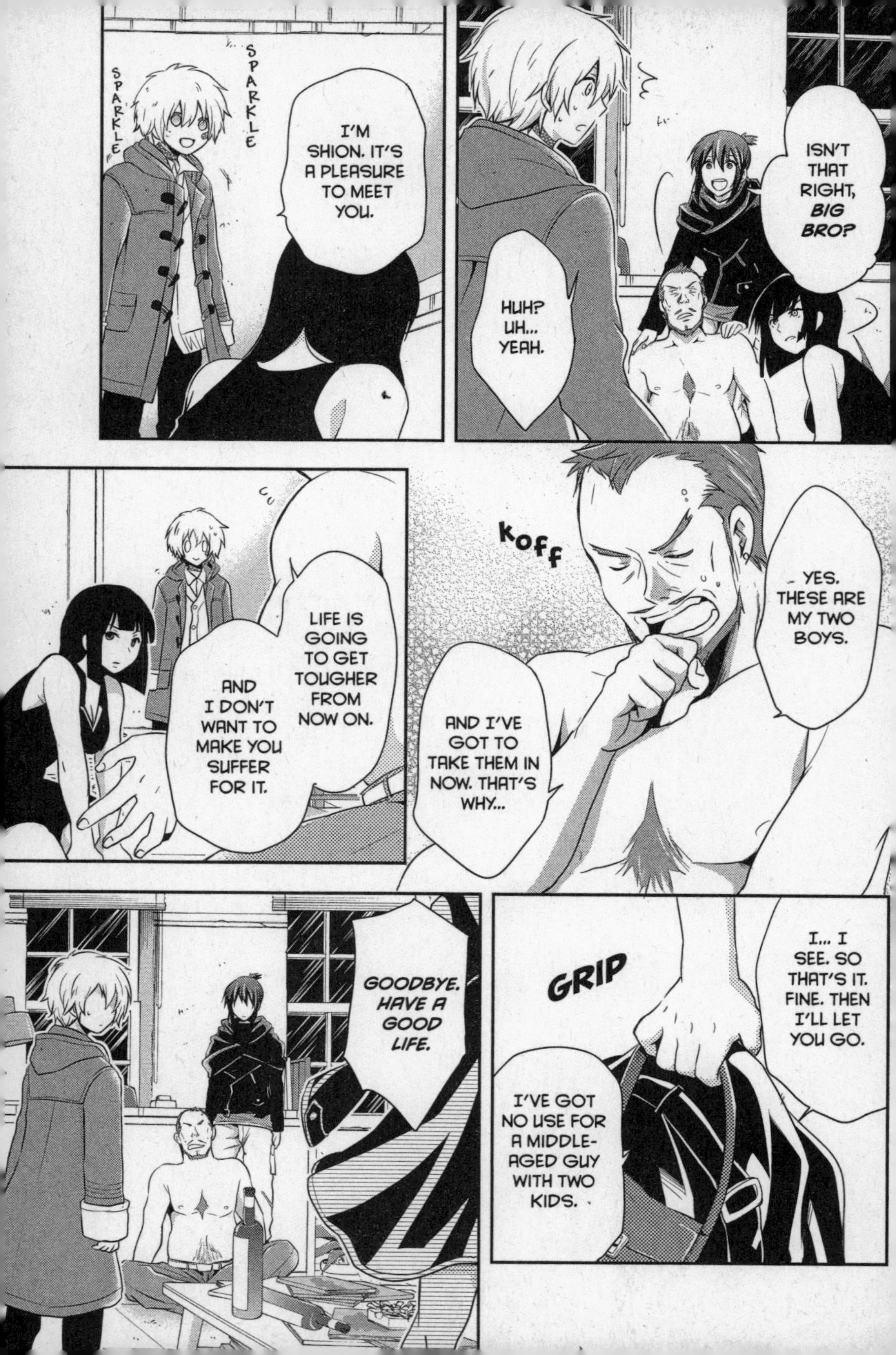
ISN'T THAT RIGHT, BIG BRO?
HUH? UH... YEAH.
I'M SHION. IT'S A PLEASURE TO MEET YOU.
SPARKLE
SPARKLE
YES. THESE ARE MY TWO BOYS.
koff
AND I'VE GOT TO TAKE THEM IN NOW. THAT'S WHY...
LIFE IS GOING TO GET TOUGHER FROM NOW ON.
AND I DON'T WANT TO MAKE YOU SUFFER FOR IT.
I... I SEE. SO THAT'S IT. FINE. THEN I'LL LET YOU GO.
GRIP
I'VE GOT NO USE FOR A MIDDLE-AGED GUY WITH TWO KIDS.
GOODBYE. HAVE A GOOD LIFE.

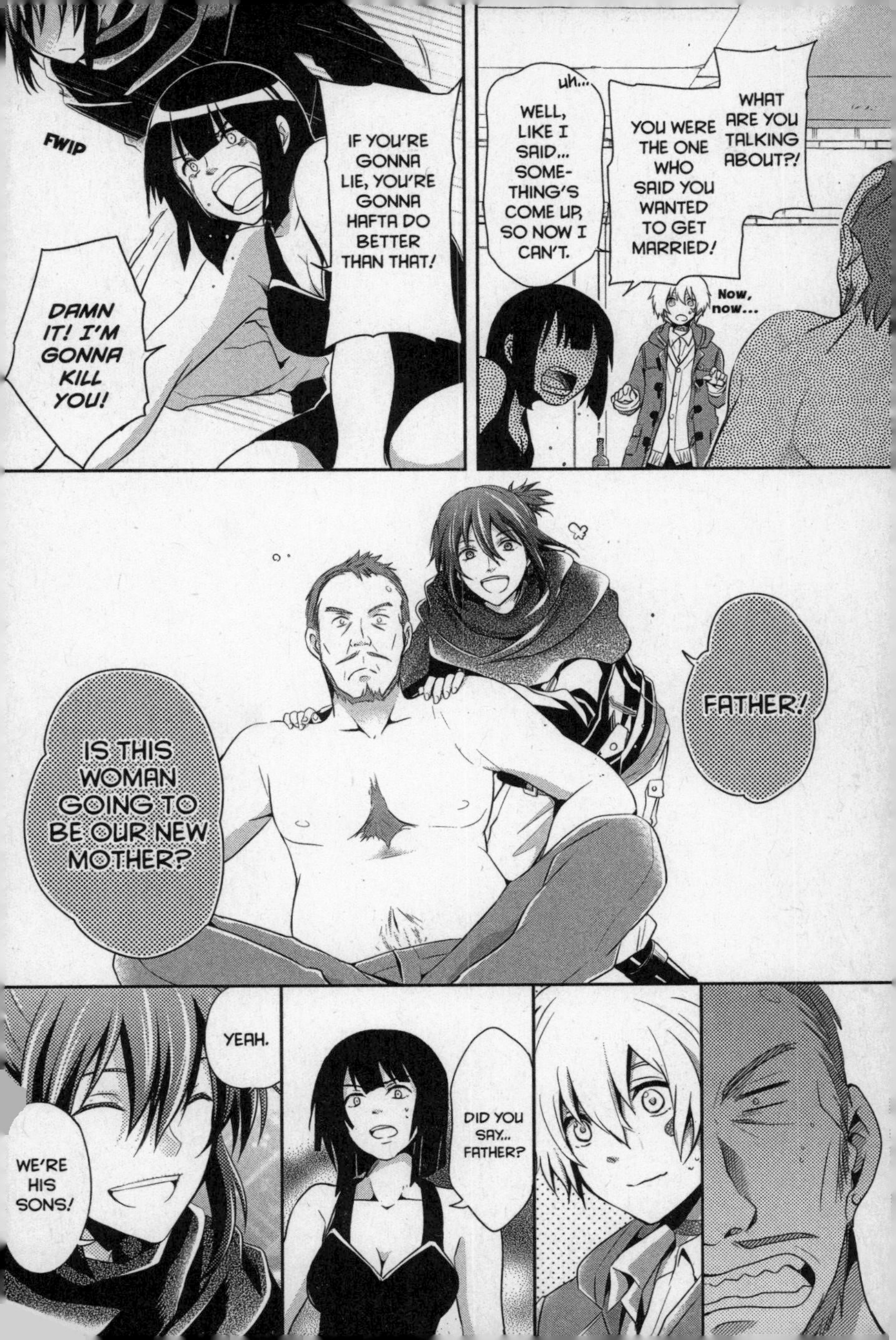
WHAT ARE YOU TALKING ABOUT?!
YOU WERE THE ONE WHO SAID YOU WANTED TO GET MARRIED!
uh...
WELL, LIKE I SAID... SOME-THING'S COME UP, SO NOW I CAN'T.
Now, now...
IF YOU'RE GONNA LIE, YOU'RE GONNA HAFTA DO BETTER THAN THAT!
FWIP
DAMN IT! I'M GONNA KILL YOU!
FATHER!
IS THIS WOMAN GOING TO BE OUR NEW MOTHER?
DID YOU SAY... FATHER?
YEAH.
WE'RE HIS SONS!

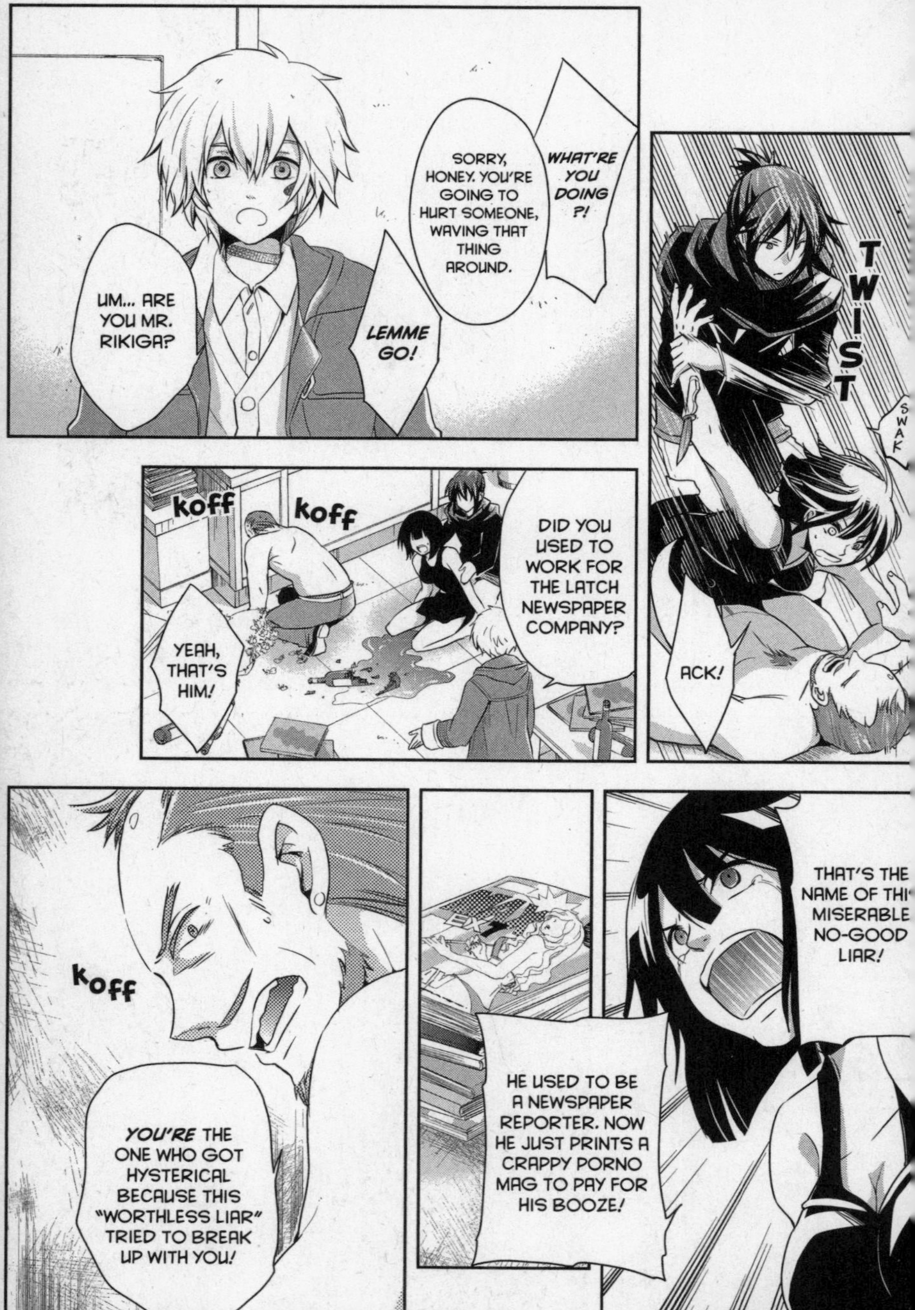
WHAT'RE YOU DOING?!
SORRY, HONEY. YOU'RE GOING TO HURT SOMEONE, WAVING THAT THING AROUND.
LEMME GO!
UM... ARE YOU MR. RIKIGA?
TWIST
SWAK
ACK!
DID YOU USED TO WORK FOR THE LATCH NEWSPAPER COMPANY?
koff koff
YEAH, THAT'S HIM!
THAT'S THE NAME OF THI MISERABLE NO-GOOD LIAR!
HE USED TO BE A NEWSPAPER REPORTER. NOW HE JUST PRINTS A CRAPPY PORNO MAG TO PAY FOR HIS BOOZE!
koff
YOU'RE THE ONE WHO GOT HYSTERICAL BECAUSE THIS "WORTHLESS LIAR" TRIED TO BREAK UP WITH YOU!

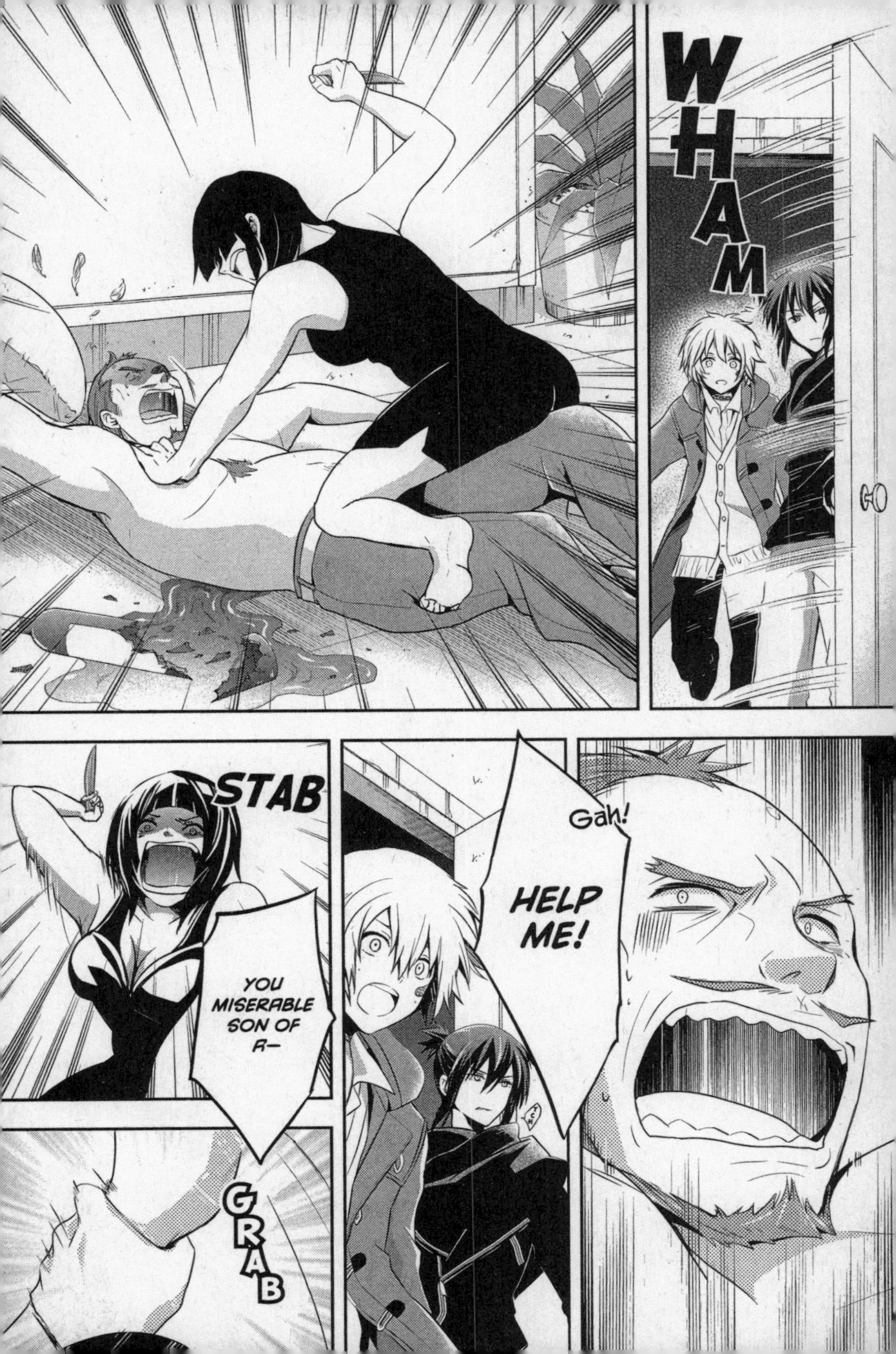
WHAM
Gah!
HELP ME!
STAB
YOU MISERABLE SON OF A—
GRAB

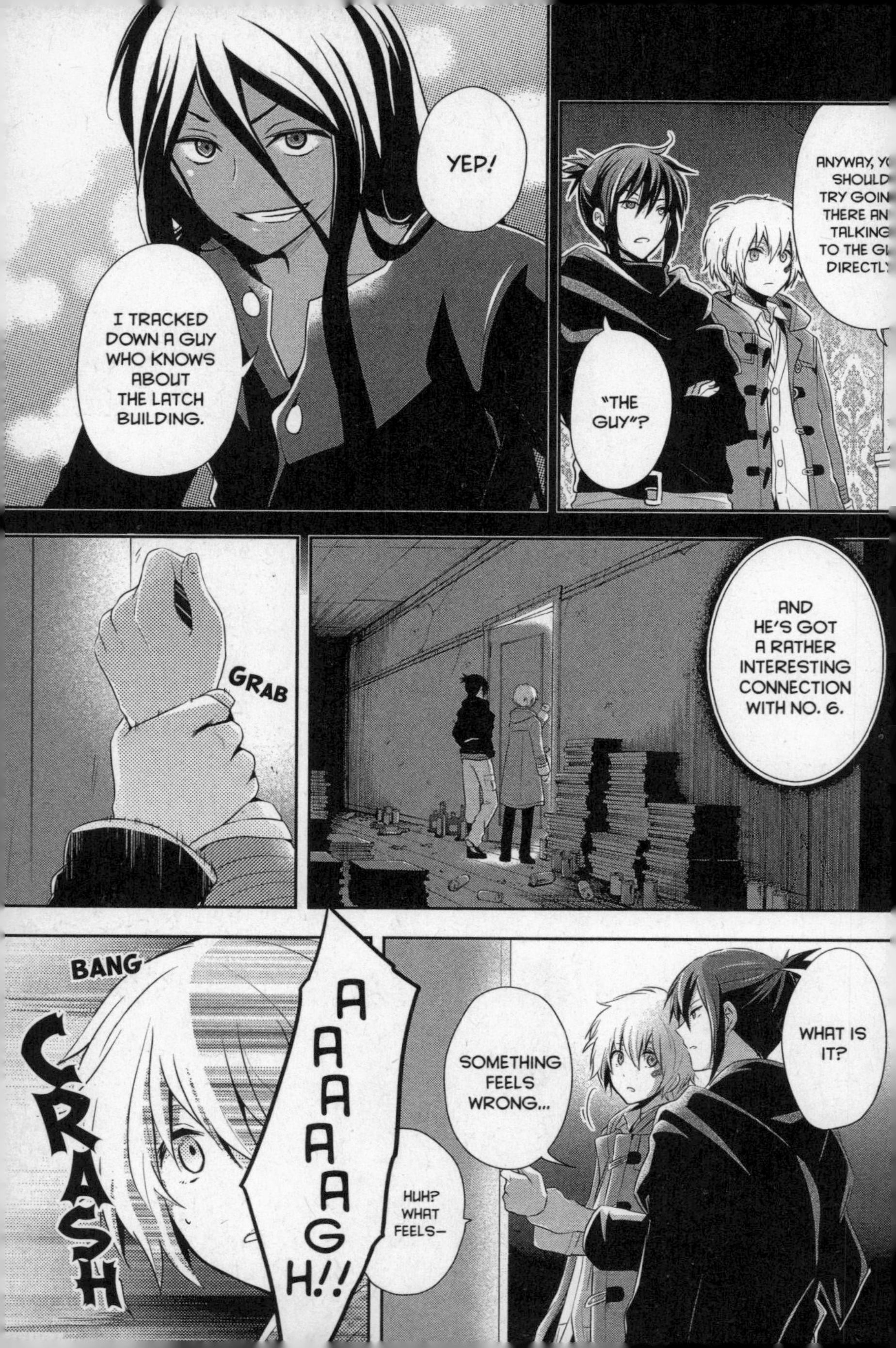
ANYWAY, YO SHOULD TRY GOIN THERE AN TALKING TO THE GI DIRECTLY
"THE GUY"?
YEP!
I TRACKED DOWN A GUY WHO KNOWS ABOUT THE LATCH BUILDING.
AND HE'S GOT A RATHER INTERESTING CONNECTION WITH NO. 6.
GRAB
WHAT IS IT?
SOMETHING FEELS WRONG...
HUH? WHAT FEELS—
AAAAAAGH!!
BANG
CRASH

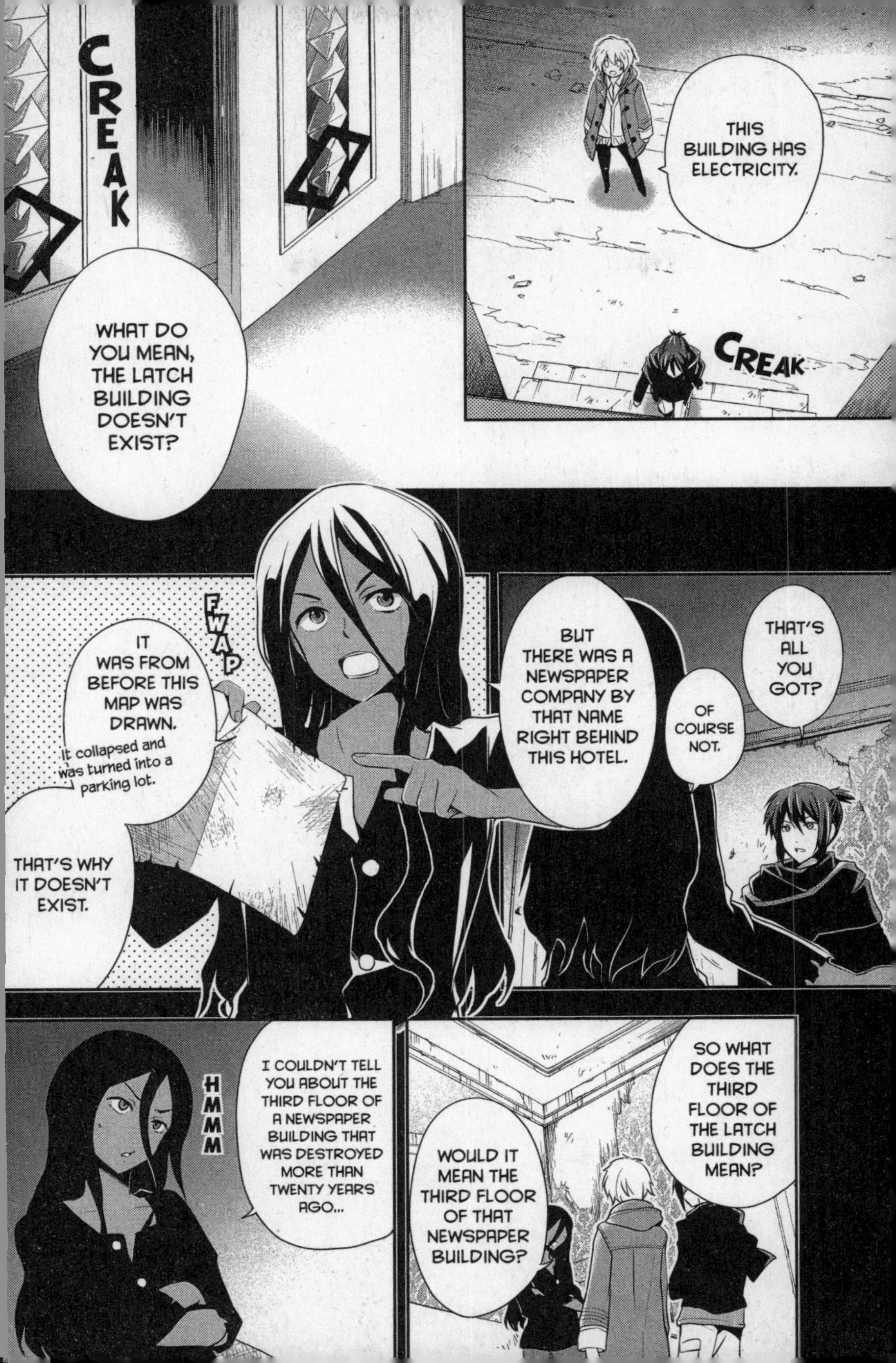
THIS BUILDING HAS ELECTRICITY.
CREAK
CREAK
WHAT DO YOU MEAN, THE LATCH BUILDING DOESN'T EXIST?
THAT'S ALL YOU GOT?
OF COURSE NOT.
BUT THERE WAS A NEWSPAPER COMPANY BY THAT NAME RIGHT BEHIND THIS HOTEL.
FWAP
IT WAS FROM BEFORE THIS MAP WAS DRAWN.
It collapsed and was turned into a parking lot.
THAT'S WHY IT DOESN'T EXIST.
SO WHAT DOES THE THIRD FLOOR OF THE LATCH BUILDING MEAN?
WOULD IT MEAN THE THIRD FLOOR OF THAT NEWSPAPER BUILDING?
I COULDN'T TELL YOU ABOUT THE THIRD FLOOR OF A NEWSPAPER BUILDING THAT WAS DESTROYED MORE THAN TWENTY YEARS AGO...
HMMM

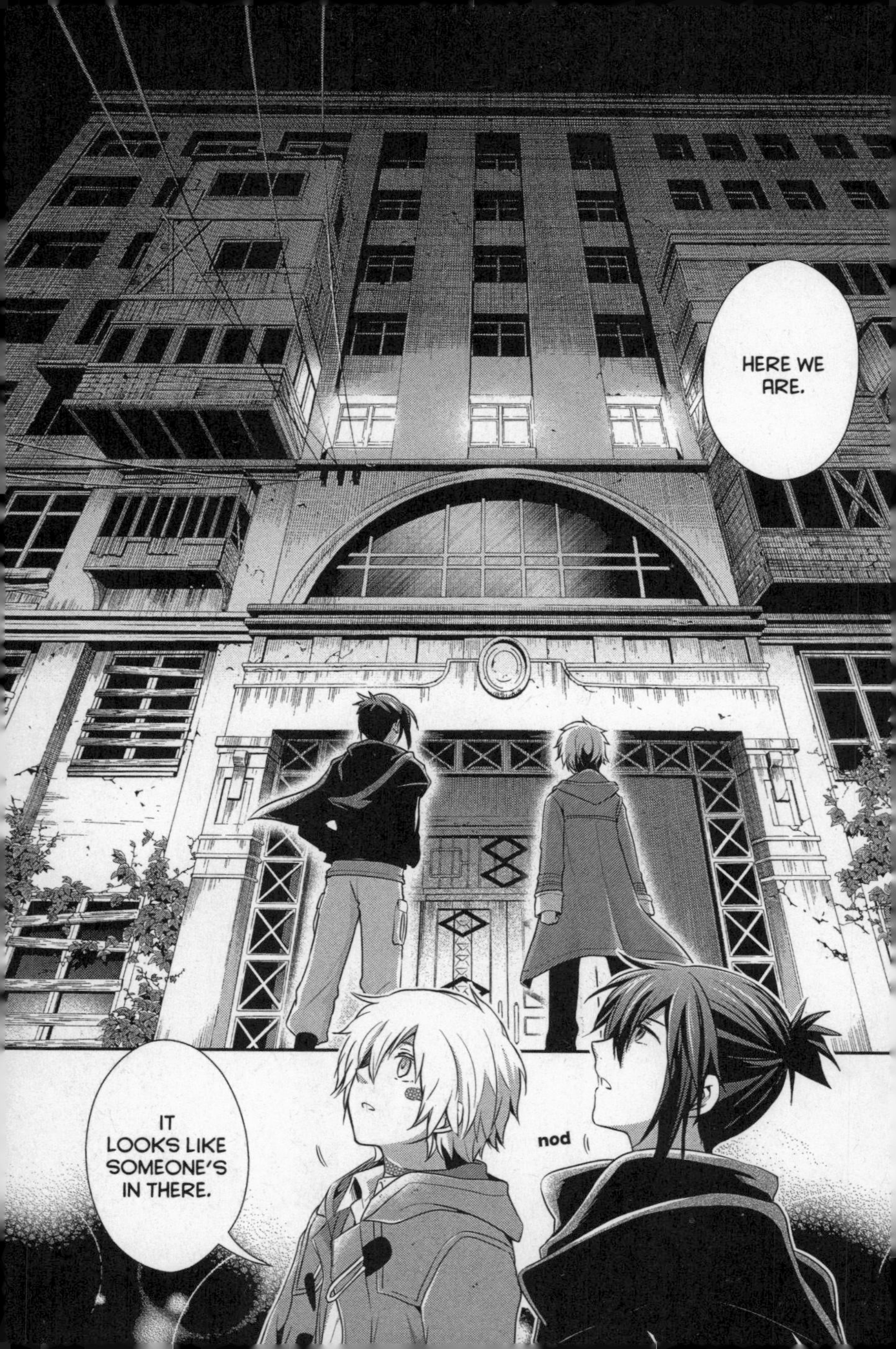
HERE WE ARE.
IT LOOKS LIKE SOMEONE'S IN THERE.
nod

NO.6

Chapter 7: Sacred and Profane, part 2

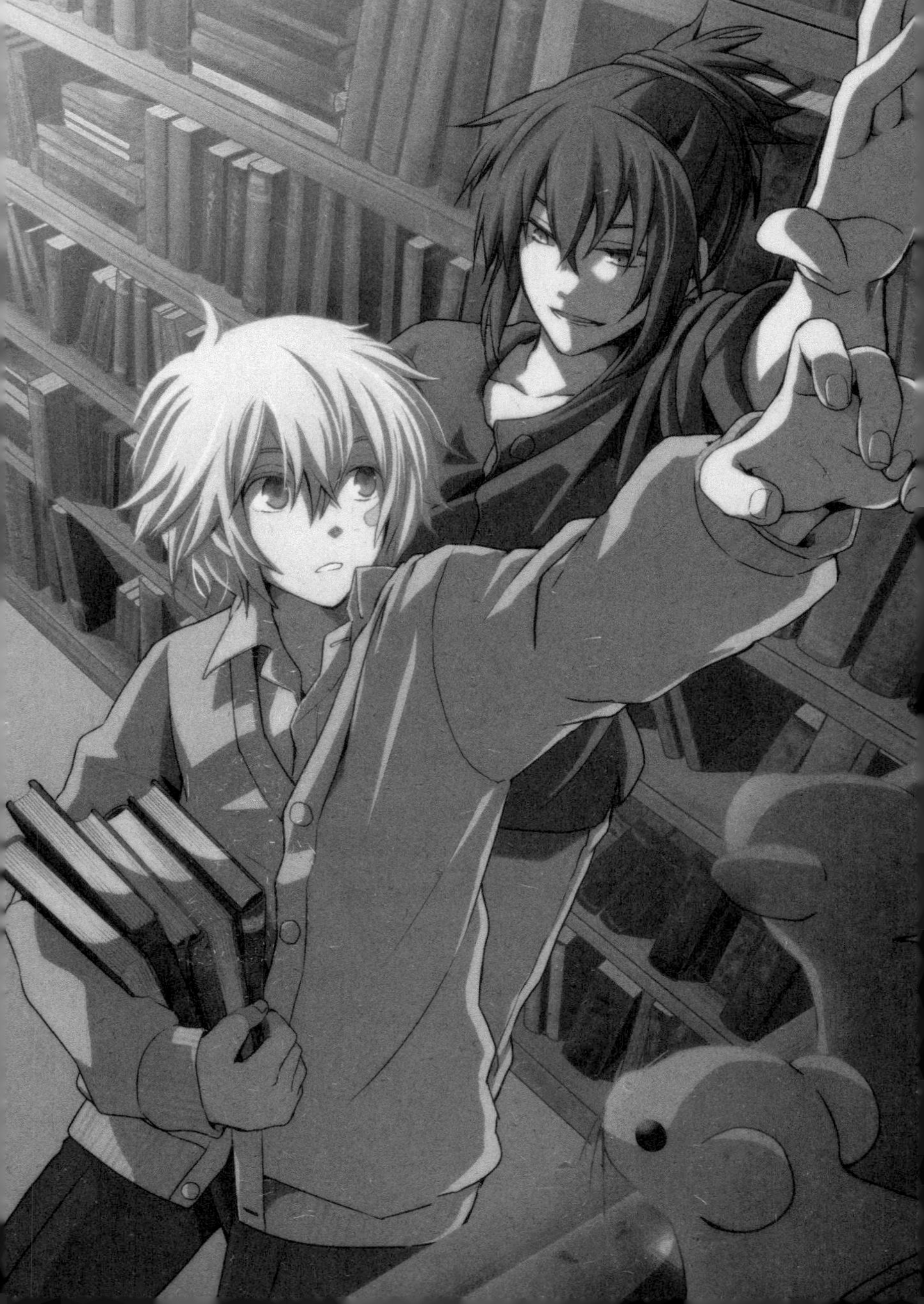

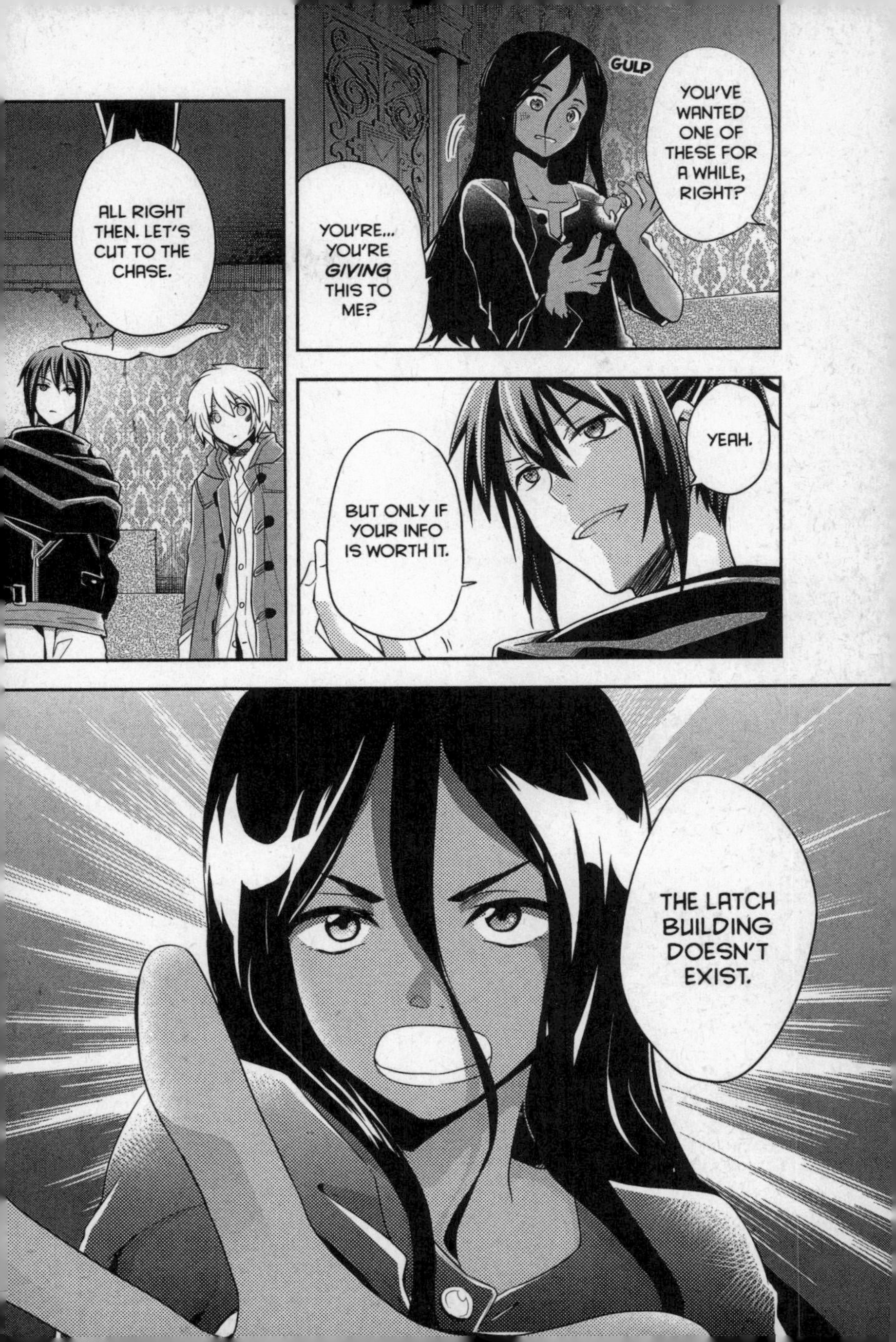
GULP
YOU'VE WANTED ONE OF THESE FOR A WHILE, RIGHT?
YOU'RE... YOU'RE *GIVING* THIS TO ME?
YEAH.
BUT ONLY IF YOUR INFO IS WORTH IT.
ALL RIGHT THEN. LET'S CUT TO THE CHASE.
THE LATCH BUILDING DOESN'T EXIST.

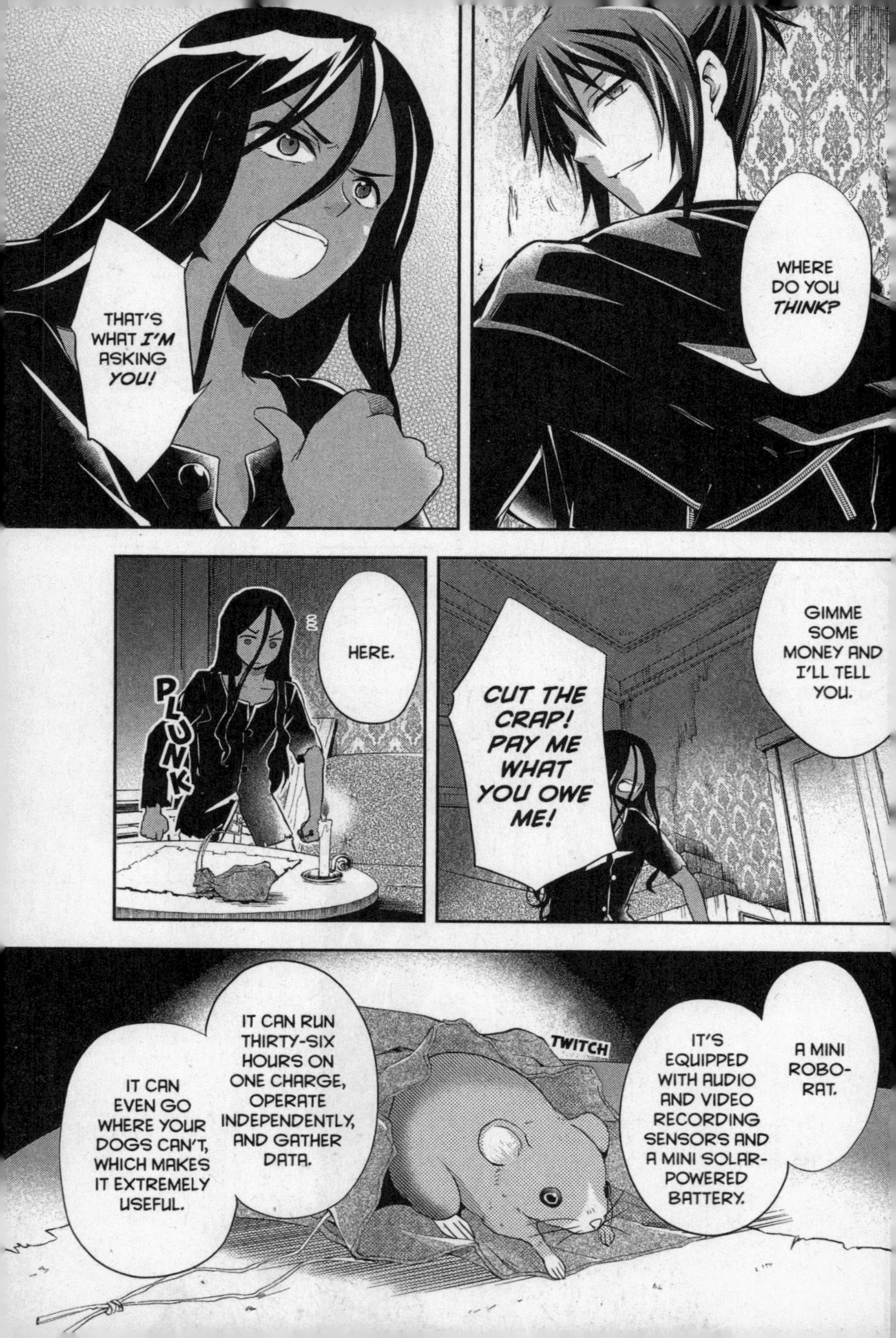
WHERE DO YOU *THINK?*
THAT'S WHAT *I'M* ASKING *YOU!*
GIMME SOME MONEY AND I'LL TELL YOU.
CUT THE CRAP! PAY ME WHAT YOU OWE ME!
HERE.
PLUNK
A MINI ROBO-RAT.
IT'S EQUIPPED WITH AUDIO AND VIDEO RECORDING SENSORS AND A MINI SOLAR-POWERED BATTERY.
TWITCH
IT CAN RUN THIRTY-SIX HOURS ON ONE CHARGE, OPERATE INDEPENDENTLY, AND GATHER DATA.
IT CAN EVEN GO WHERE YOUR DOGS CAN'T, WHICH MAKES IT EXTREMELY USEFUL.

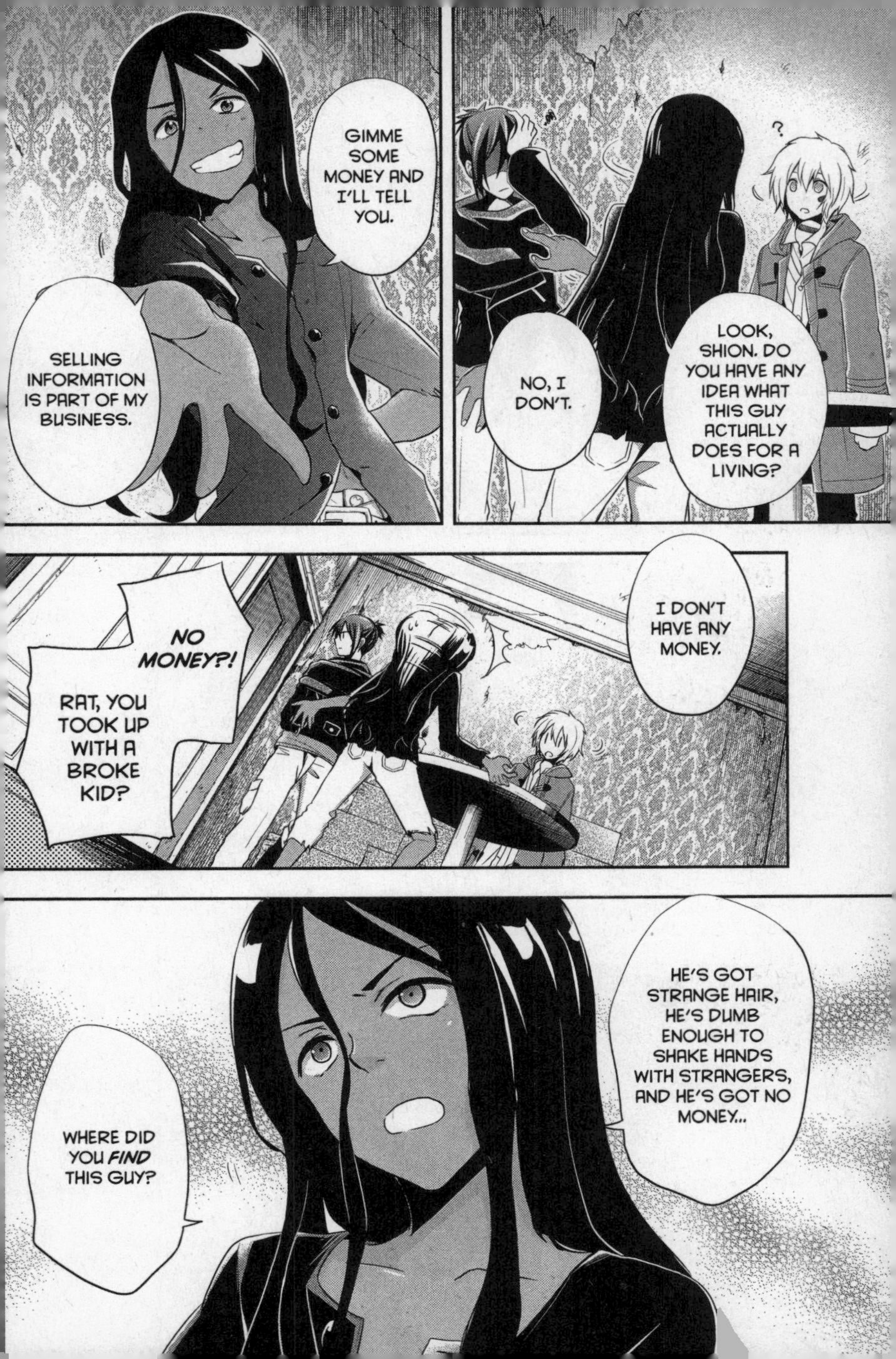
LOOK, SHION. DO YOU HAVE ANY IDEA WHAT THIS GUY ACTUALLY DOES FOR A LIVING?
NO, I DON'T.
GIMME SOME MONEY AND I'LL TELL YOU.
SELLING INFORMATION IS PART OF MY BUSINESS.
I DON'T HAVE ANY MONEY.
NO MONEY?!
RAT, YOU TOOK UP WITH A BROKE KID?
HE'S GOT STRANGE HAIR, HE'S DUMB ENOUGH TO SHAKE HANDS WITH STRANGERS, AND HE'S GOT NO MONEY...
WHERE DID YOU *FIND* THIS GUY?

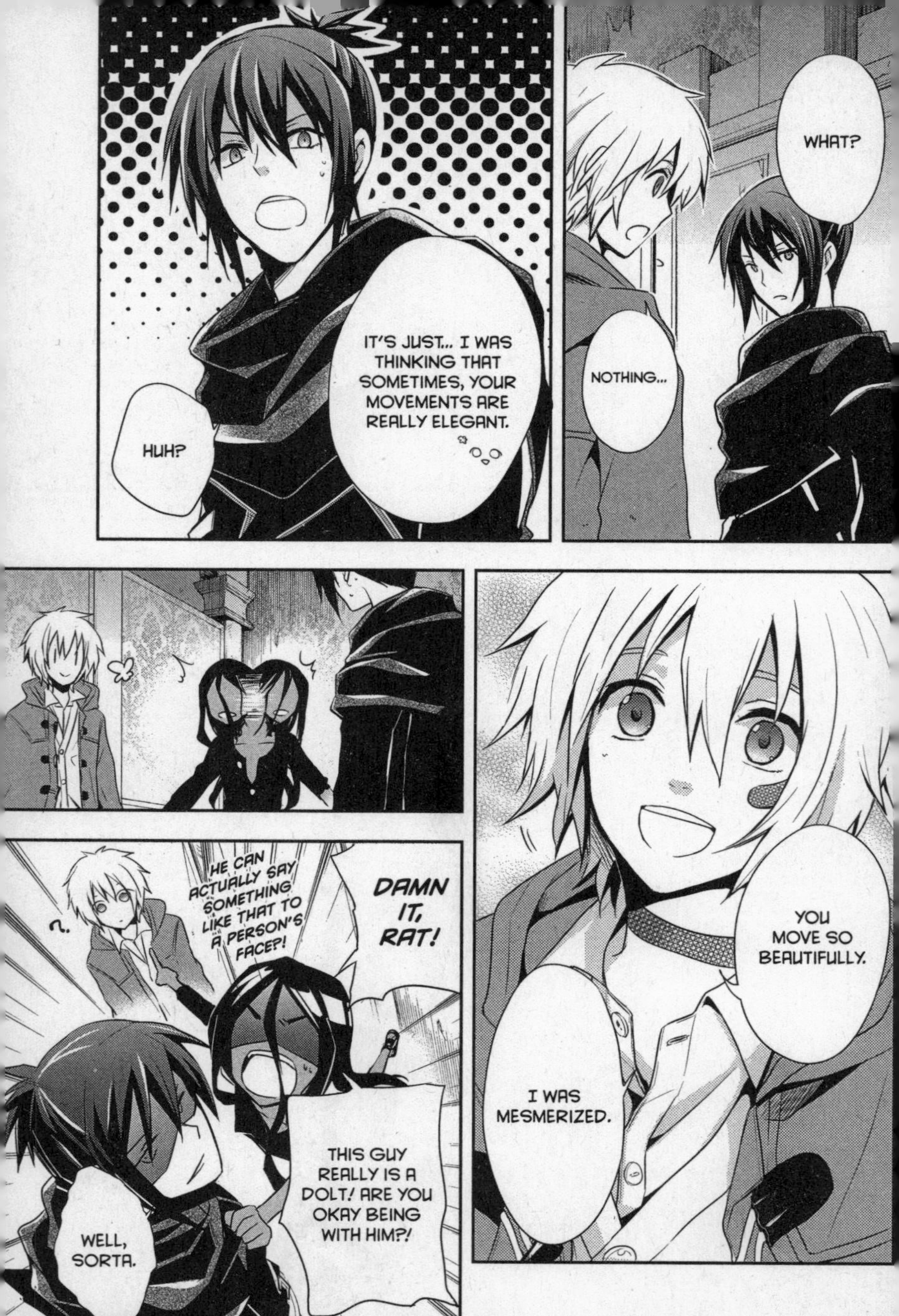
WHAT?
NOTHING...
IT'S JUST... I WAS THINKING THAT SOMETIMES, YOUR MOVEMENTS ARE REALLY ELEGANT.
HUH?
YOU MOVE SO BEAUTIFULLY.
I WAS MESMERIZED.
DAMN IT, RAT!
HE CAN ACTUALLY SAY SOMETHING LIKE THAT TO A PERSON'S FACE?!
THIS GUY REALLY IS A DOLT! ARE YOU OKAY BEING WITH HIM?!
WELL, SORTA.

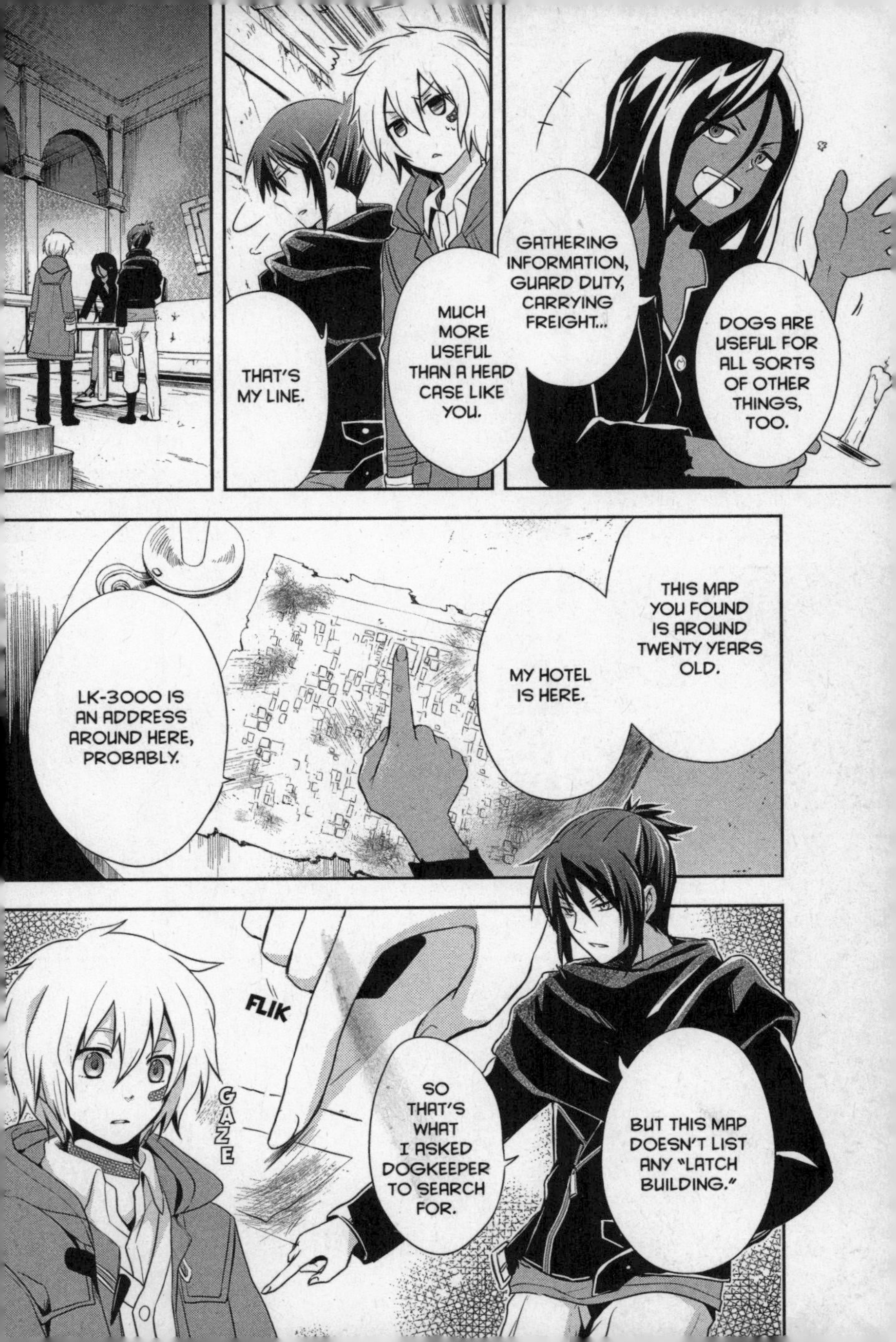
DOGS ARE USEFUL FOR ALL SORTS OF OTHER THINGS, TOO.
GATHERING INFORMATION, GUARD DUTY, CARRYING FREIGHT...
MUCH MORE USEFUL THAN A HEAD CASE LIKE YOU.
THAT'S MY LINE.
THIS MAP YOU FOUND IS AROUND TWENTY YEARS OLD.
MY HOTEL IS HERE.
LK-3000 IS AN ADDRESS AROUND HERE, PROBABLY.
BUT THIS MAP DOESN'T LIST ANY "LATCH BUILDING."
FLIK
SO THAT'S WHAT I ASKED DOGKEEPER TO SEARCH FOR.
GAZE

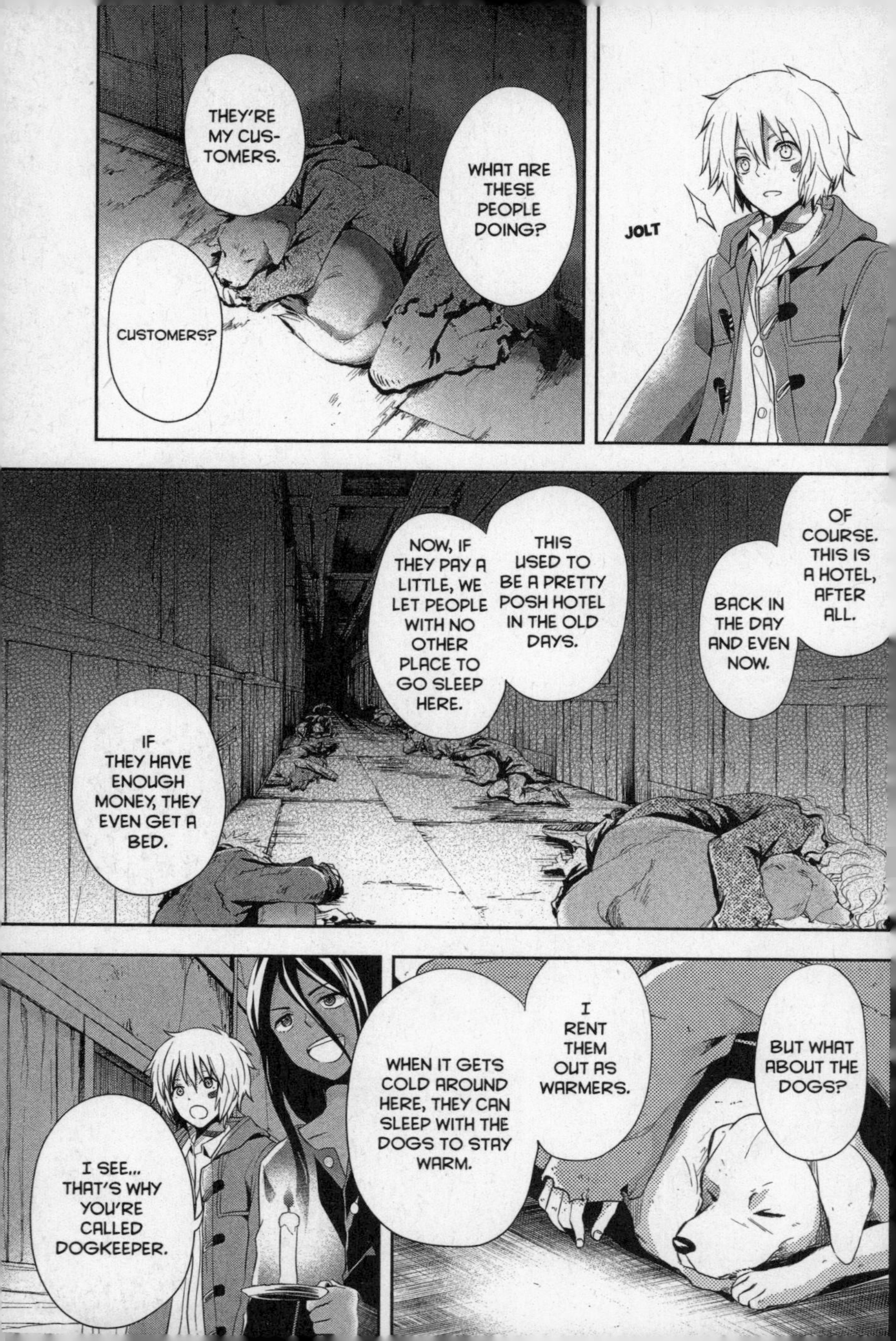
JOLT
WHAT ARE THESE PEOPLE DOING?
THEY'RE MY CUS-TOMERS.
CUSTOMERS?
OF COURSE. THIS IS A HOTEL, AFTER ALL.
BACK IN THE DAY AND EVEN NOW.
THIS USED TO BE A PRETTY POSH HOTEL IN THE OLD DAYS.
NOW, IF THEY PAY A LITTLE, WE LET PEOPLE WITH NO OTHER PLACE TO GO SLEEP HERE.
IF THEY HAVE ENOUGH MONEY, THEY EVEN GET A BED.
BUT WHAT ABOUT THE DOGS?
I RENT THEM OUT AS WARMERS.
WHEN IT GETS COLD AROUND HERE, THEY CAN SLEEP WITH THE DOGS TO STAY WARM.
I SEE... THAT'S WHY YOU'RE CALLED DOGKEEPER.

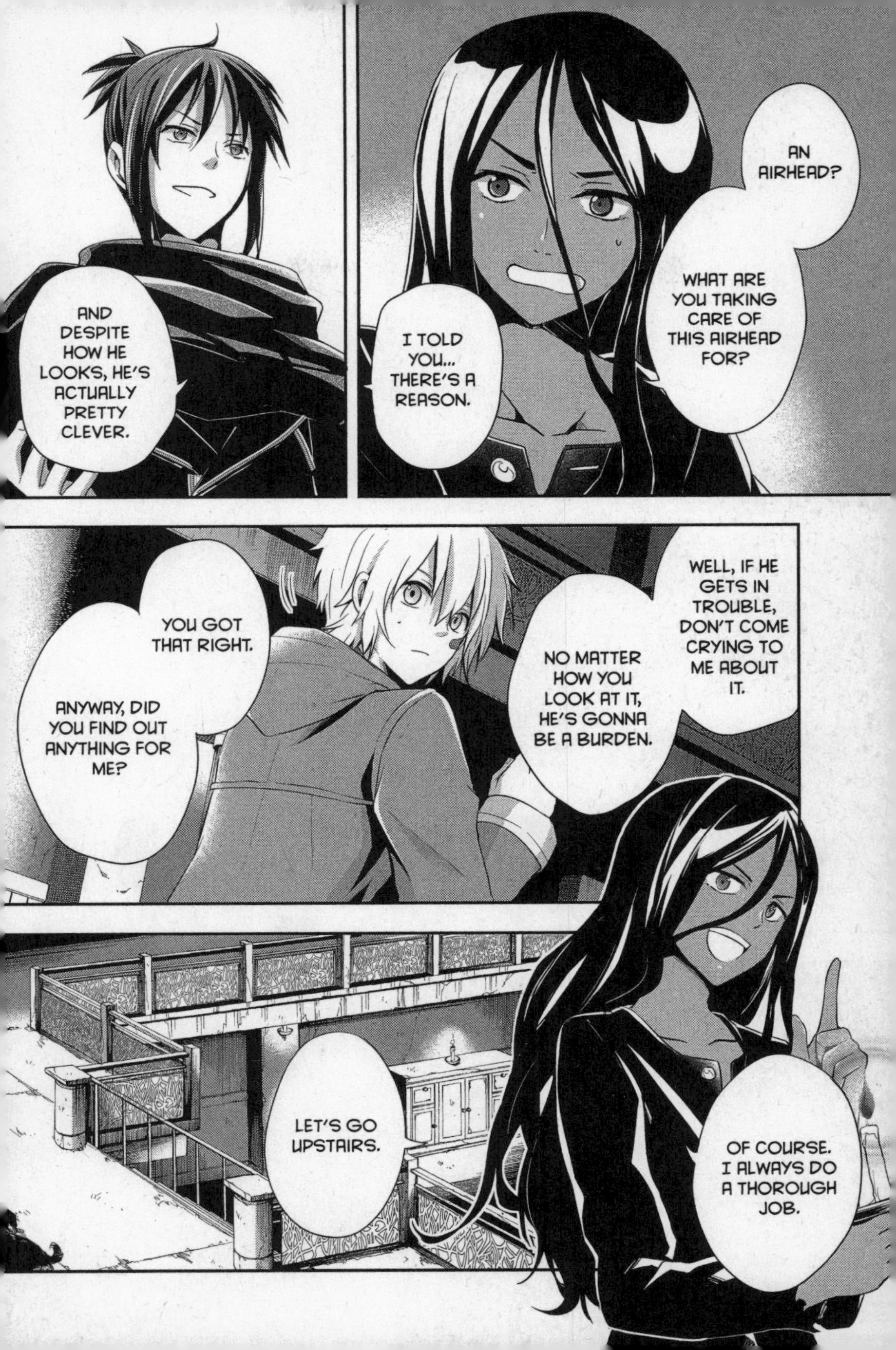
AN AIRHEAD?
WHAT ARE YOU TAKING CARE OF THIS AIRHEAD FOR?
I TOLD YOU... THERE'S A REASON.
AND DESPITE HOW HE LOOKS, HE'S ACTUALLY PRETTY CLEVER.
WELL, IF HE GETS IN TROUBLE, DON'T COME CRYING TO ME ABOUT IT.
NO MATTER HOW YOU LOOK AT IT, HE'S GONNA BE A BURDEN.
YOU GOT THAT RIGHT.
ANYWAY, DID YOU FIND OUT ANYTHING FOR ME?
OF COURSE. I ALWAYS DO A THOROUGH JOB.
LET'S GO UPSTAIRS.

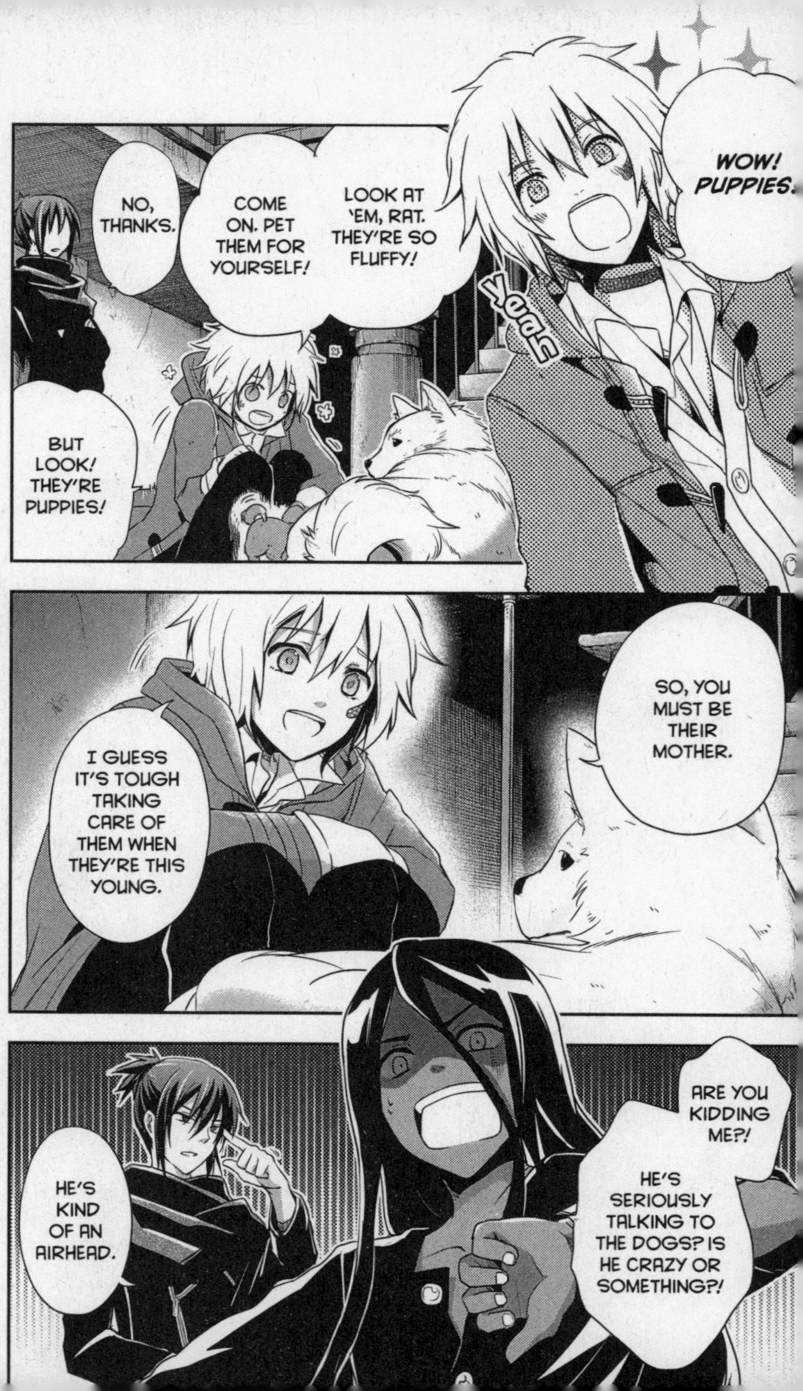
WOW! PUPPIES.
Yeah
LOOK AT 'EM, RAT. THEY'RE SO FLUFFY!
COME ON. PET THEM FOR YOURSELF!
NO, THANKS.
BUT LOOK! THEY'RE PUPPIES!
SO, YOU MUST BE THEIR MOTHER.
I GUESS IT'S TOUGH TAKING CARE OF THEM WHEN THEY'RE THIS YOUNG.
ARE YOU KIDDING ME?!
HE'S SERIOUSLY TALKING TO THE DOGS?! IS HE CRAZY OR SOMETHING?!
HE'S KIND OF AN AIRHEAD.

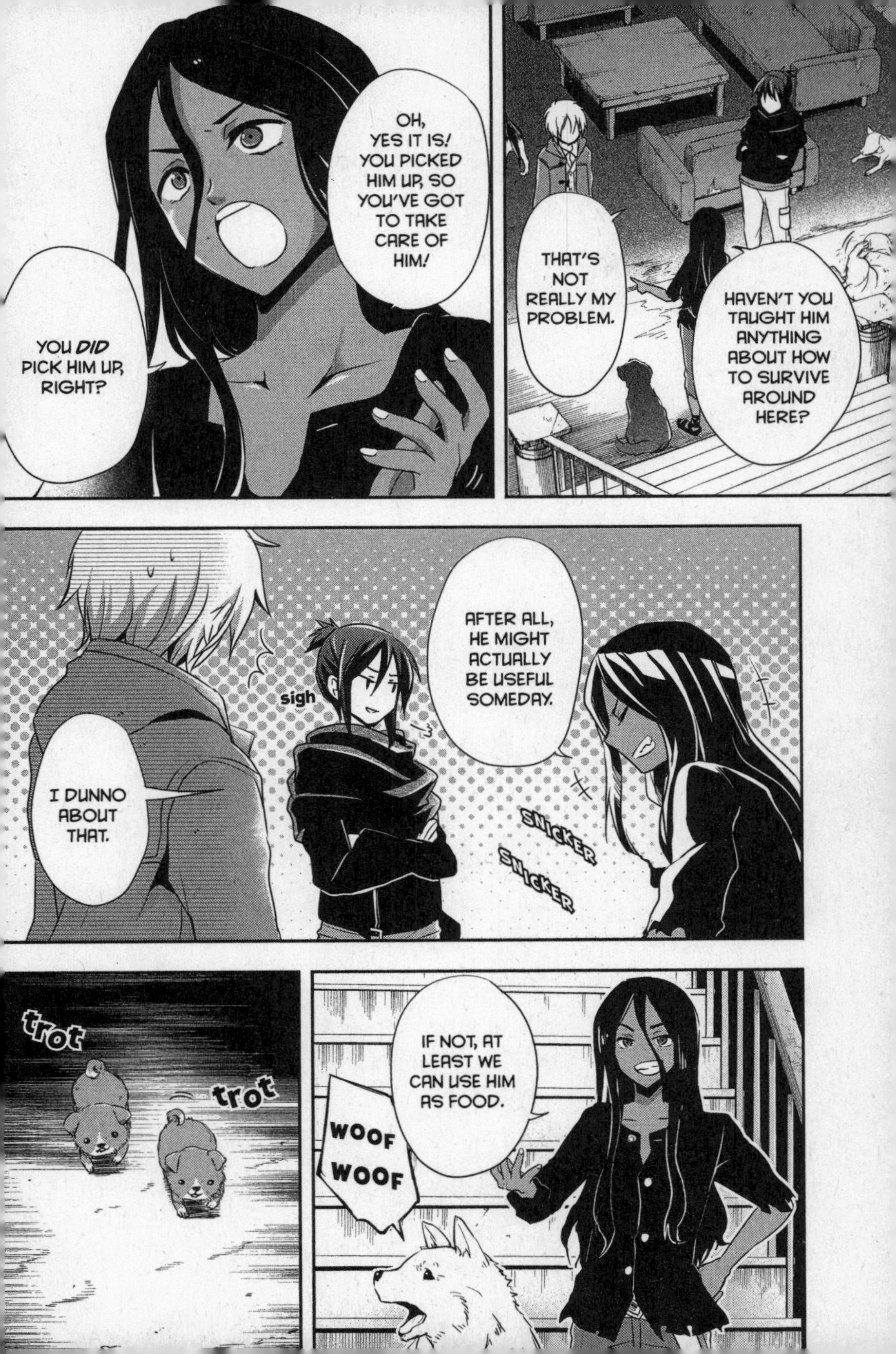
HAVEN'T YOU TAUGHT HIM ANYTHING ABOUT HOW TO SURVIVE AROUND HERE?
THAT'S NOT REALLY MY PROBLEM.
OH, YES IT IS! YOU PICKED HIM UP, SO YOU'VE GOT TO TAKE CARE OF HIM!
YOU *DID* PICK HIM UP, RIGHT?
AFTER ALL, HE MIGHT ACTUALLY BE USEFUL SOMEDAY.
SNICKER
SNICKER
sigh
I DUNNO ABOUT THAT.
IF NOT, AT LEAST WE CAN USE HIM AS FOOD.
WOOF
WOOF
trot
trot

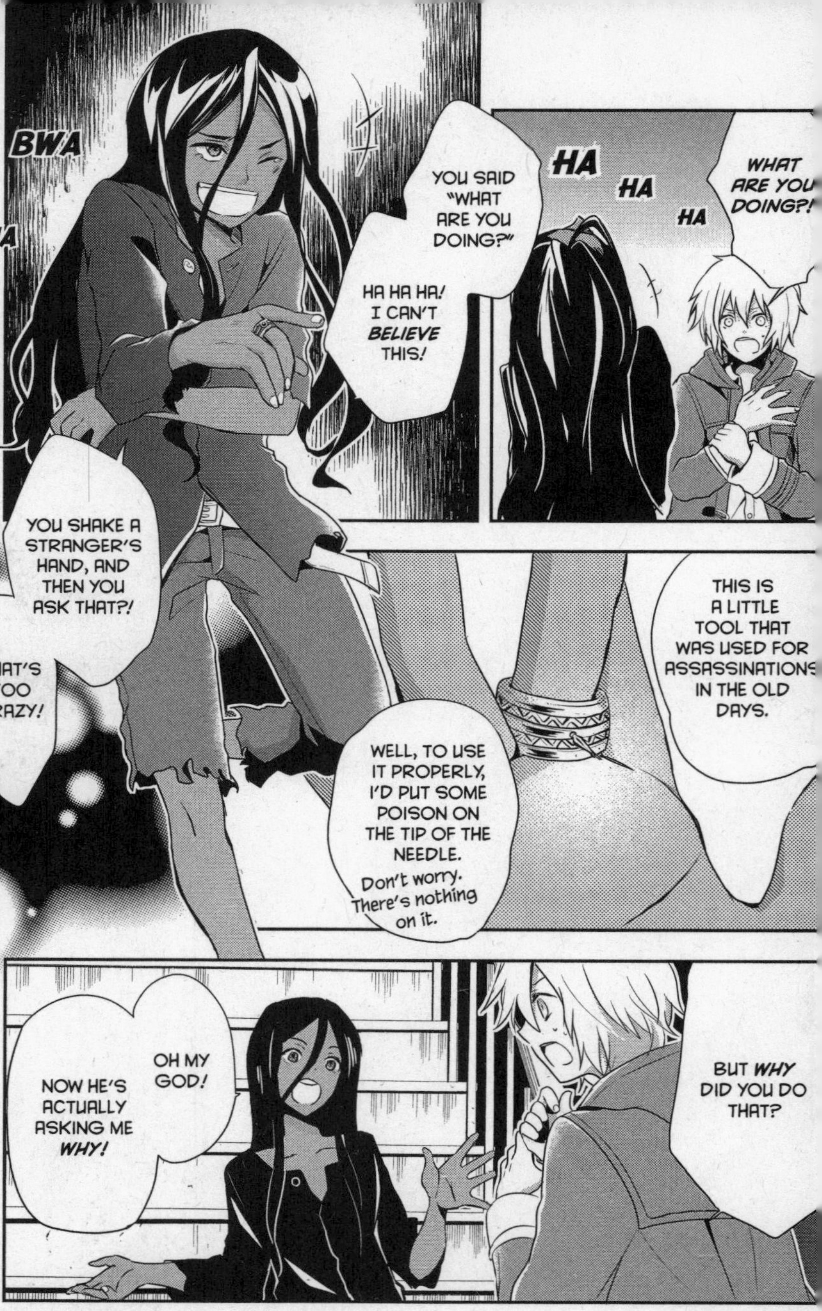
WHAT ARE YOU DOING?!
HA
HA
HA
THIS IS A LITTLE TOOL THAT WAS USED FOR ASSASSINATIONS IN THE OLD DAYS.
WELL, TO USE IT PROPERLY, I'D PUT SOME POISON ON THE TIP OF THE NEEDLE.
Don't worry. There's nothing on it.
BWA
HA
YOU SAID "WHAT ARE YOU DOING?"
HA HA HA! I CAN'T *BELIEVE* THIS!
YOU SHAKE A STRANGER'S HAND, AND THEN YOU ASK THAT?!
THAT'S TOO CRAZY!
BUT *WHY* DID YOU DO THAT?
OH MY GOD!
NOW HE'S ACTUALLY ASKING ME *WHY*!

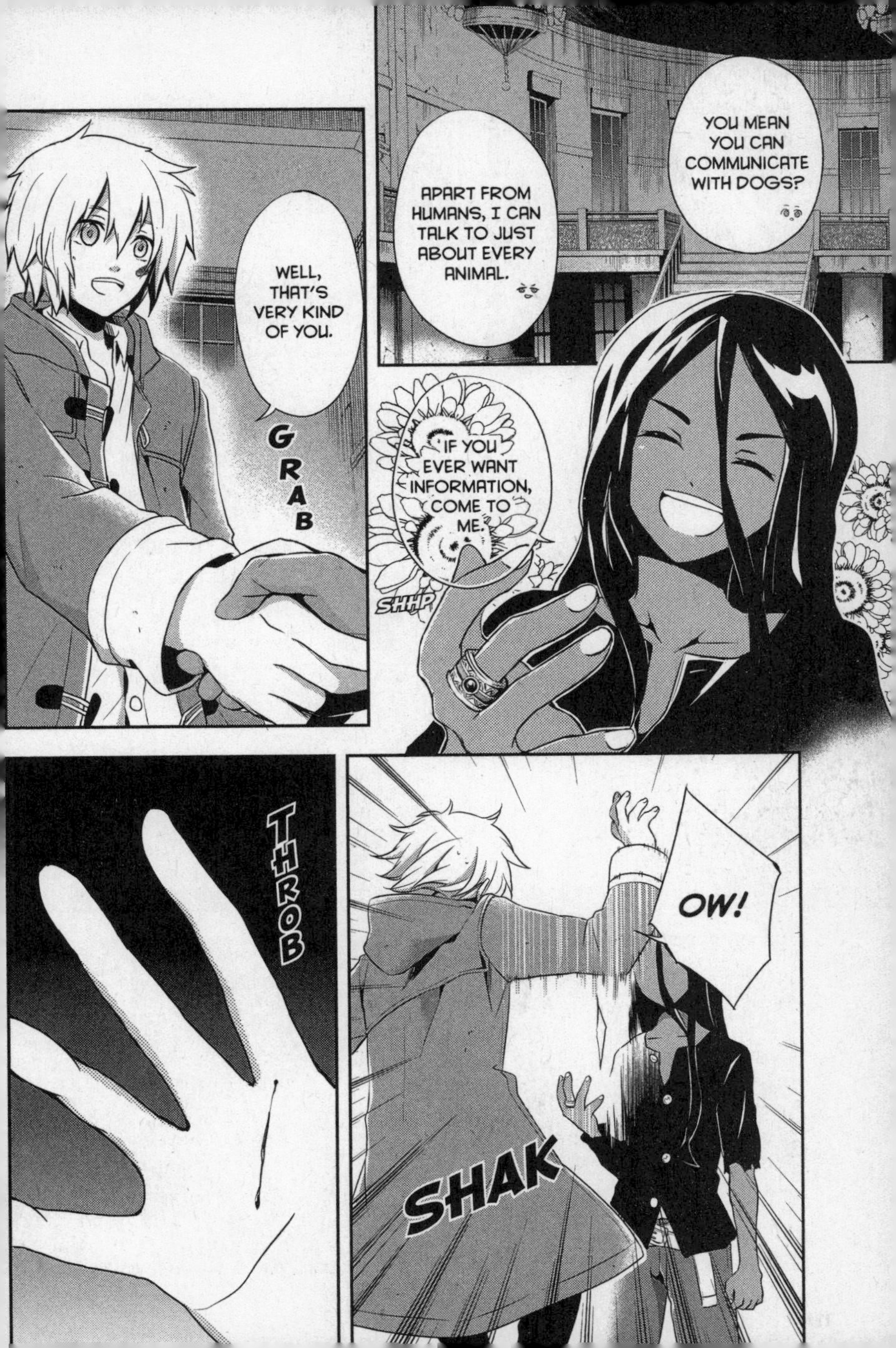
YOU MEAN YOU CAN COMMUNICATE WITH DOGS?
APART FROM HUMANS, I CAN TALK TO JUST ABOUT EVERY ANIMAL.
IF YOU EVER WANT INFORMATION, COME TO ME.
SHHP
WELL, THAT'S VERY KIND OF YOU.
GRAB
OW!
SHAK
THROB

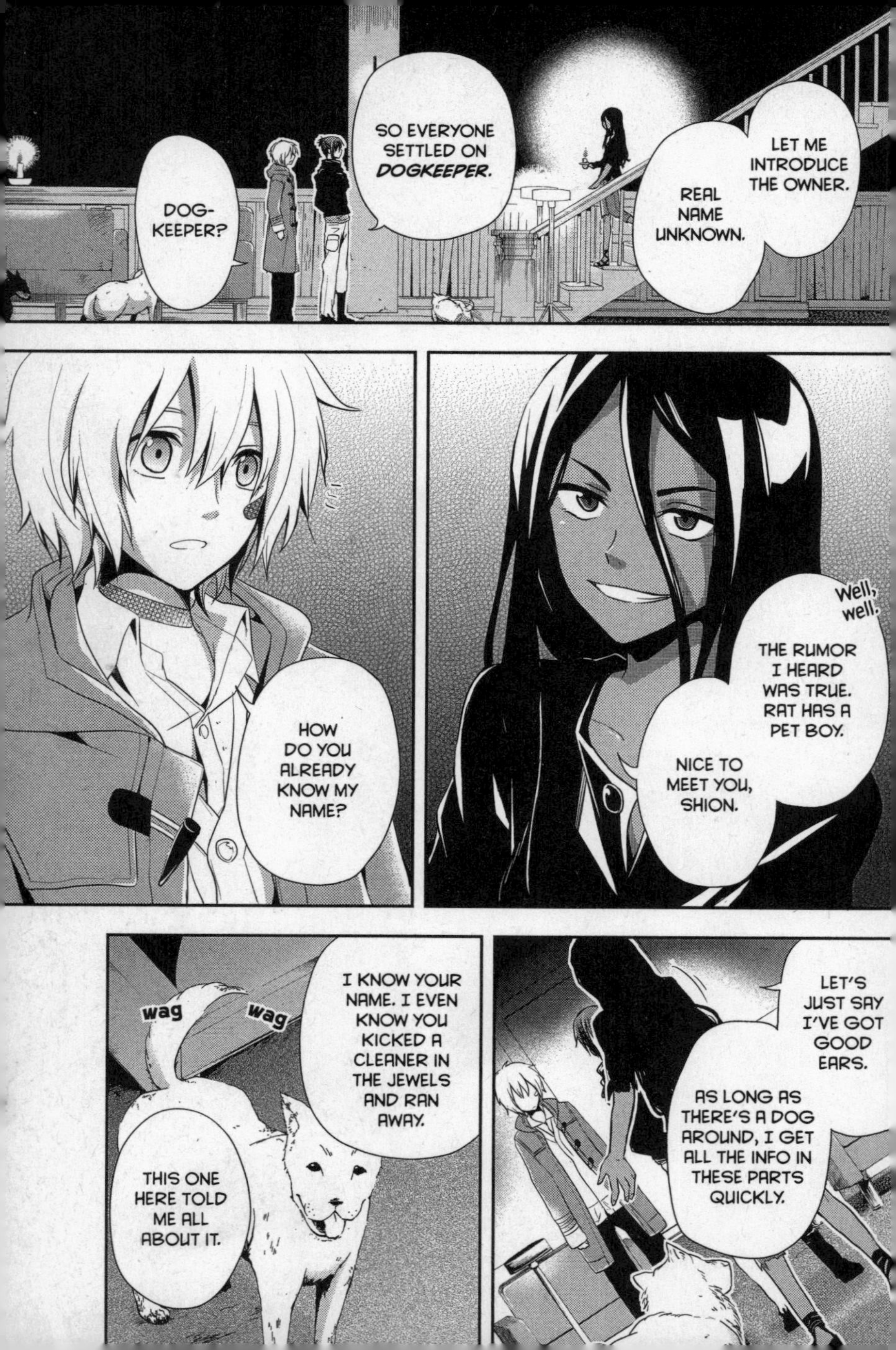

LET ME INTRODUCE THE OWNER.
REAL NAME UNKNOWN.
SO EVERYONE SETTLED ON *DOGKEEPER.*
DOG-KEEPER?
Well, well.
THE RUMOR I HEARD WAS TRUE. RAT HAS A PET BOY.
NICE TO MEET YOU, SHION.
HOW DO YOU ALREADY KNOW MY NAME?
LET'S JUST SAY I'VE GOT GOOD EARS.
AS LONG AS THERE'S A DOG AROUND, I GET ALL THE INFO IN THESE PARTS QUICKLY.
I KNOW YOUR NAME. I EVEN KNOW YOU KICKED A CLEANER IN THE JEWELS AND RAN AWAY.
wag
wag
THIS ONE HERE TOLD ME ALL ABOUT IT.

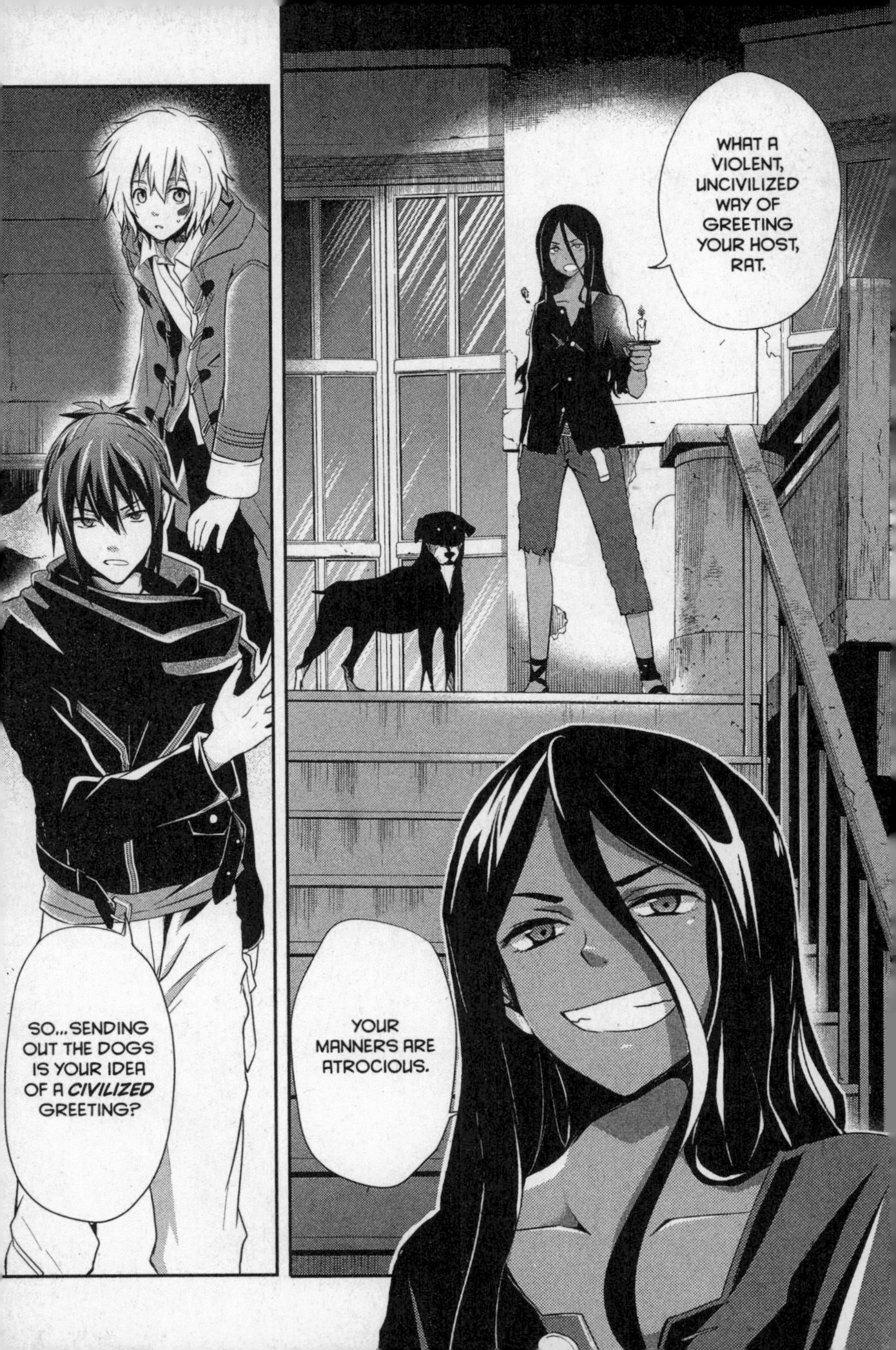
WHAT A VIOLENT, UNCIVILIZED WAY OF GREETING YOUR HOST, RAT.
YOUR MANNERS ARE ATROCIOUS.
SO...SENDING OUT THE DOGS IS YOUR IDEA OF A *CIVILIZED* GREETING?

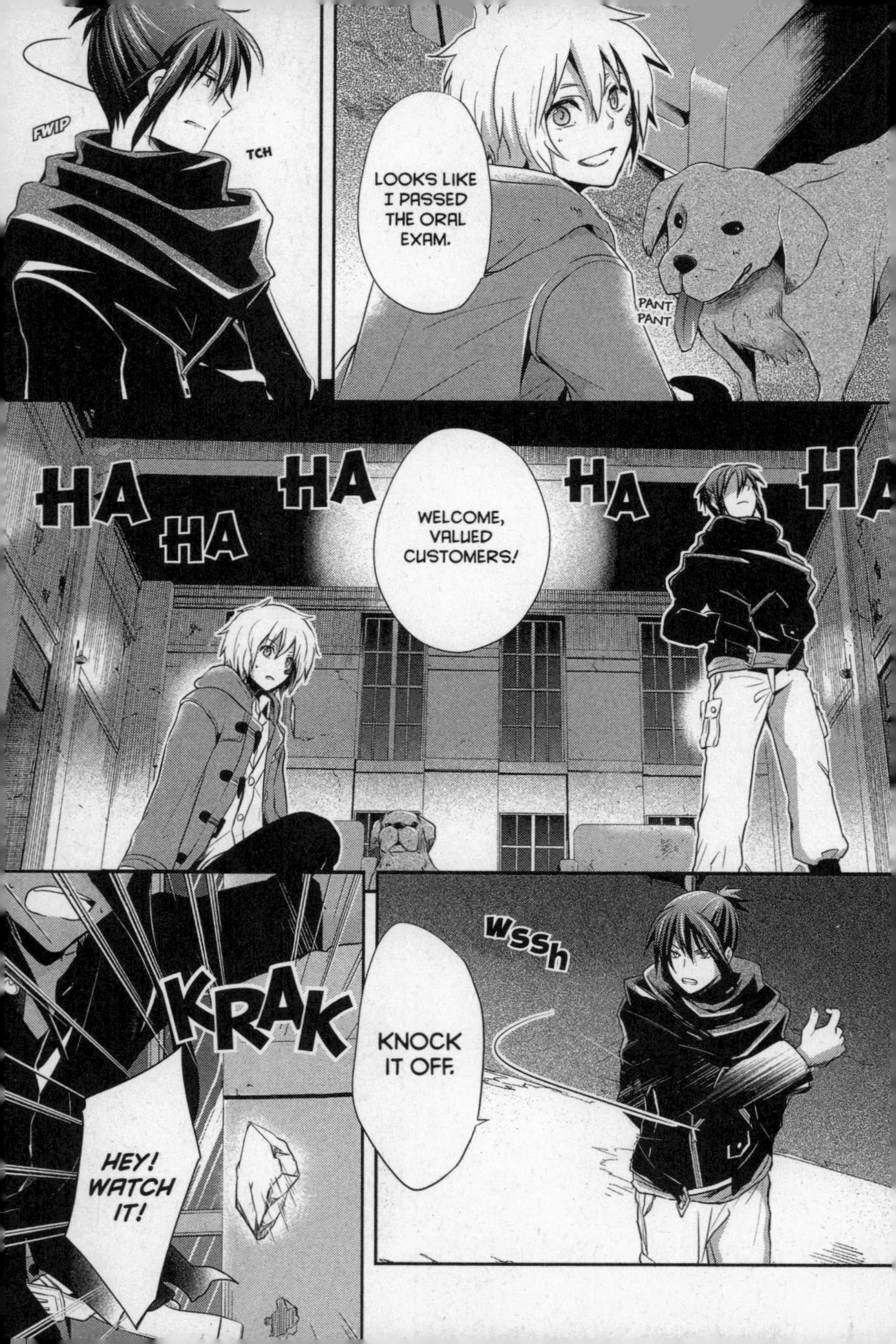
LOOKS LIKE I PASSED THE ORAL EXAM.
PANT PANT
FWIP
TCH
HA
HA
WELCOME, VALUED CUSTOMERS!
HA
HA
HA
WSSH
KNOCK IT OFF.
KRAK
HEY! WATCH IT!

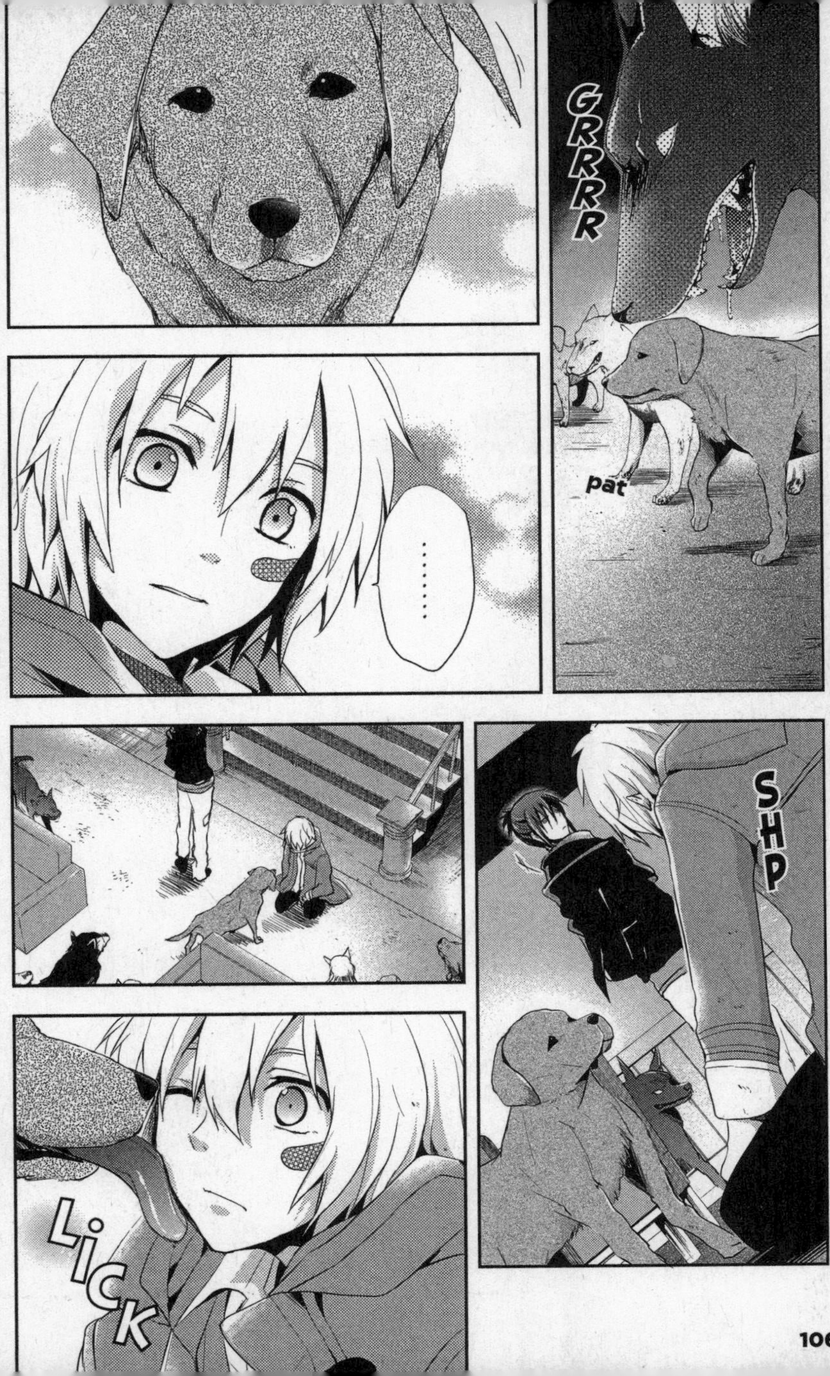
GRRRR
pat
……
SHP
LICK

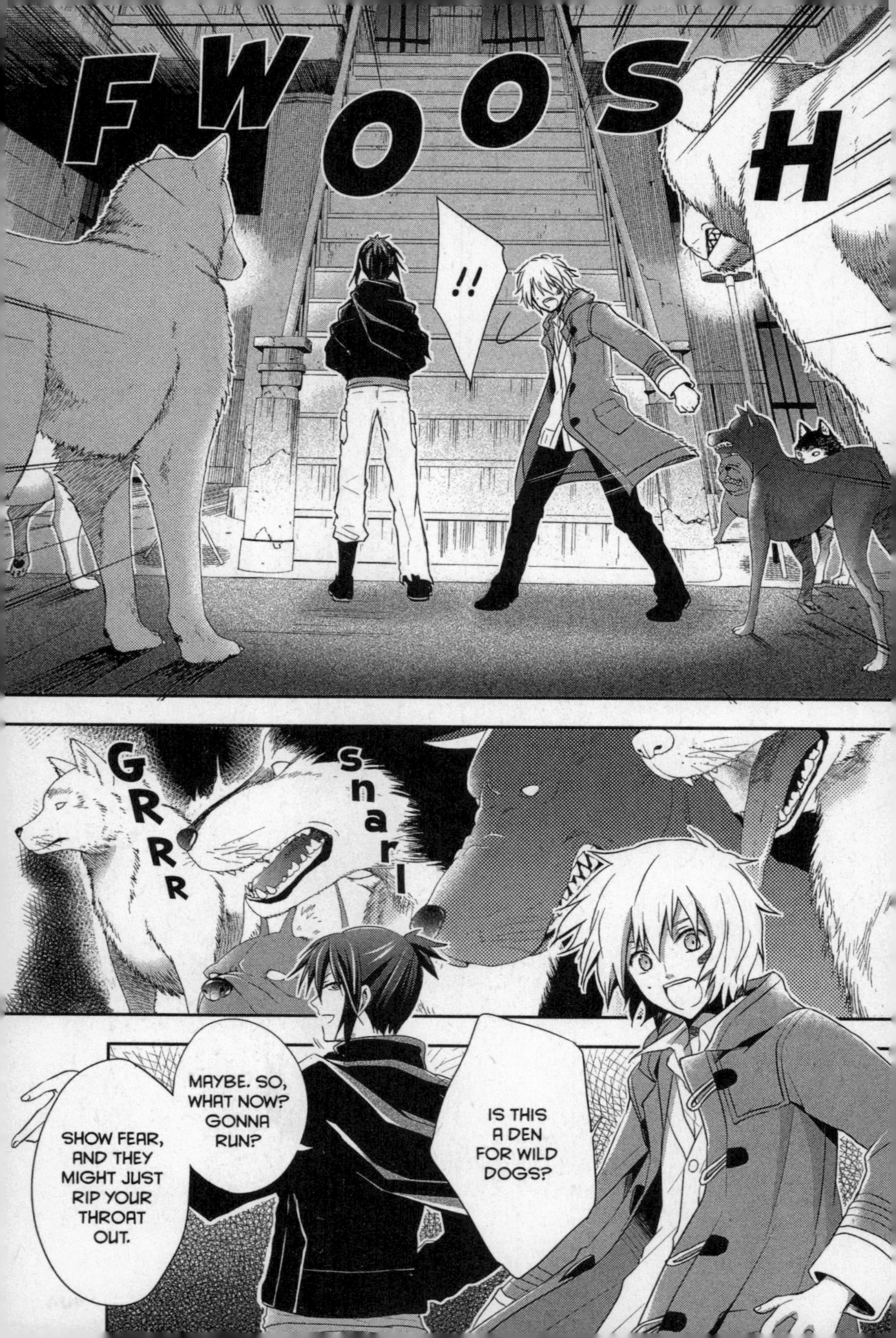
FWOOSH
!!
snarl
GRRR
IS THIS A DEN FOR WILD DOGS?
MAYBE. SO, WHAT NOW? GONNA RUN?
SHOW FEAR, AND THEY MIGHT JUST RIP YOUR THROAT OUT.

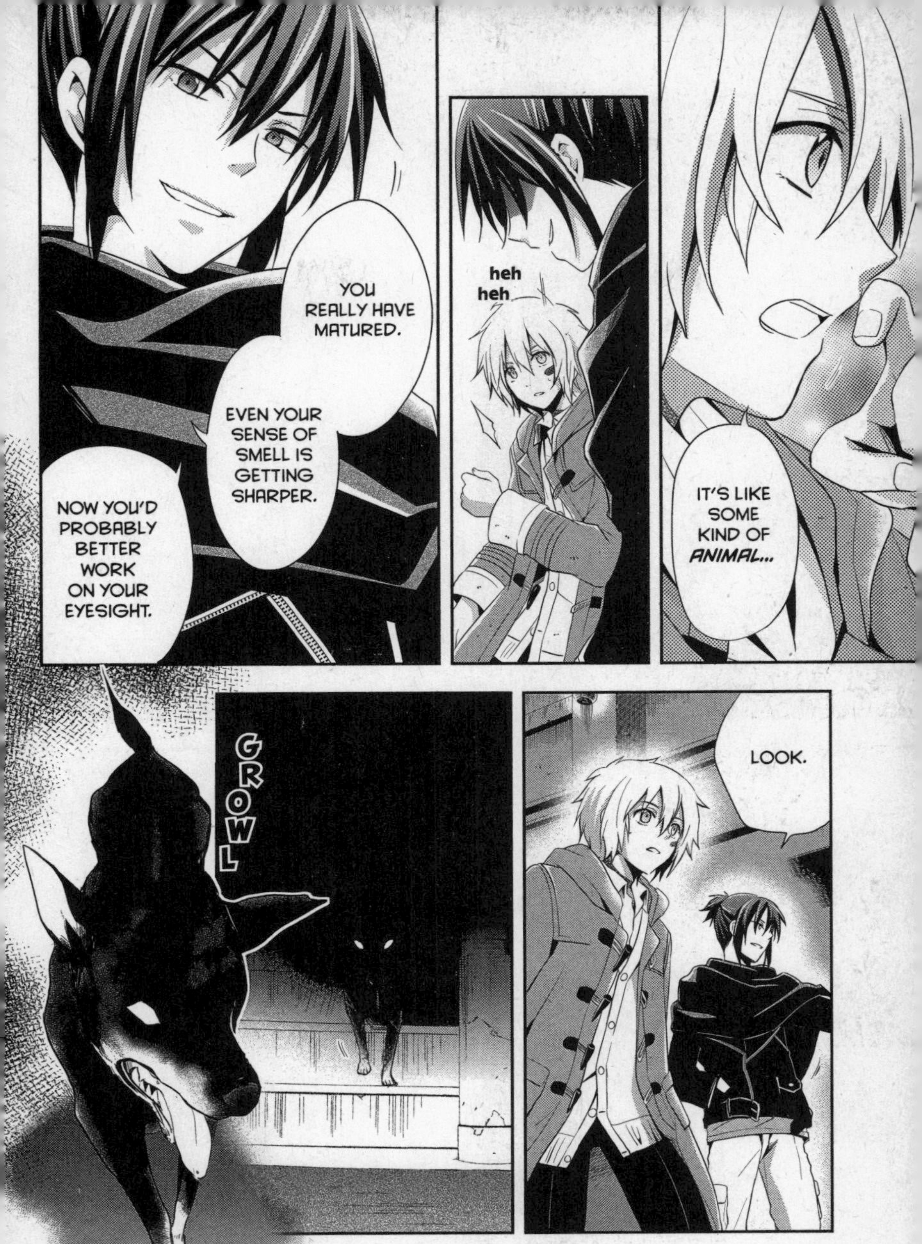

IT'S LIKE SOME KIND OF *ANIMAL...*
heh heh
YOU REALLY HAVE MATURED.
EVEN YOUR SENSE OF SMELL IS GETTING SHARPER.
NOW YOU'D PROBABLY BETTER WORK ON YOUR EYESIGHT.
LOOK.
GROWL

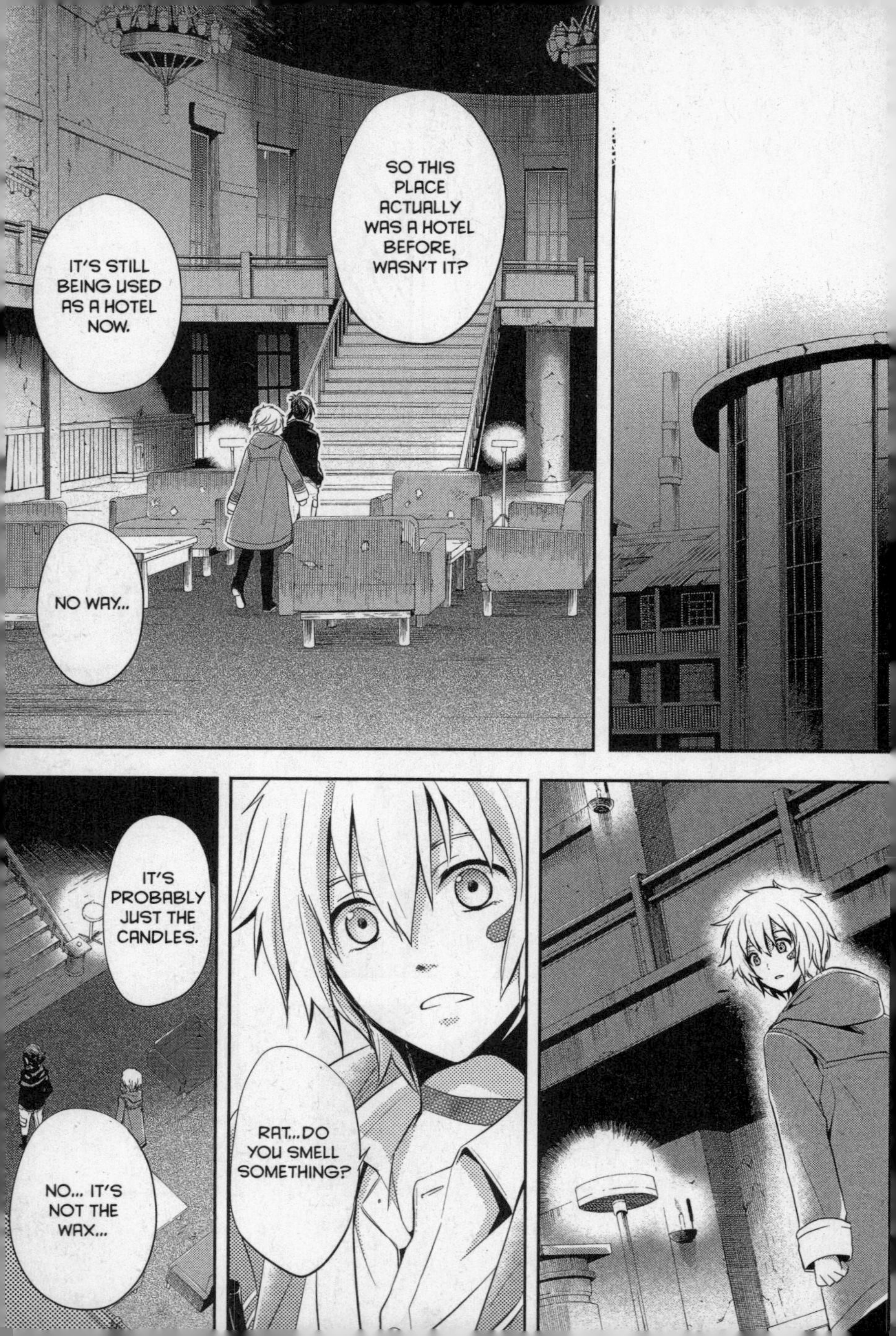
SO THIS PLACE ACTUALLY WAS A HOTEL BEFORE, WASN'T IT?
IT'S STILL BEING USED AS A HOTEL NOW.
NO WAY...
RAT...DO YOU SMELL SOMETHING?
IT'S PROBABLY JUST THE CANDLES.
NO... IT'S NOT THE WAX...

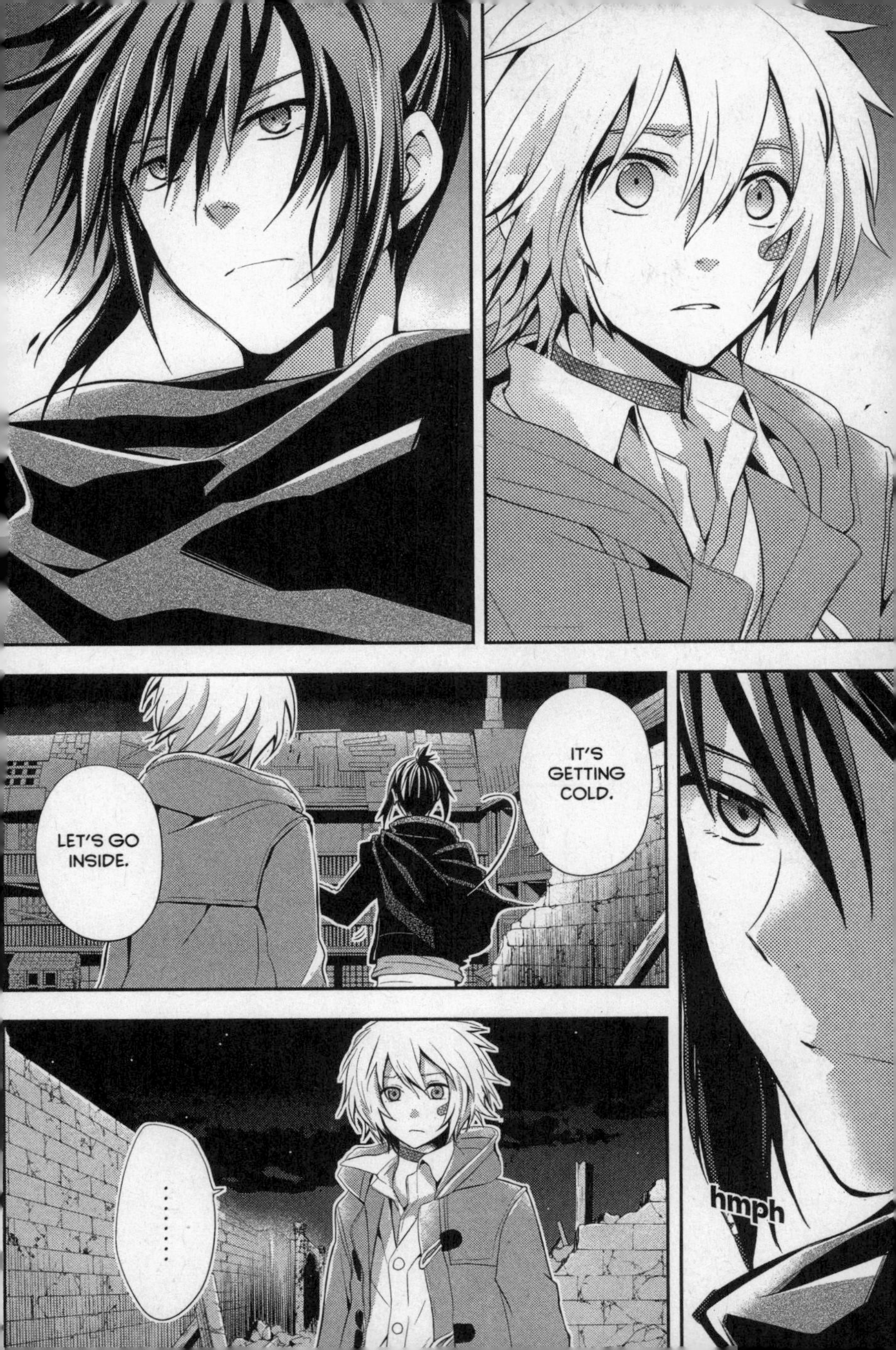
hmph
IT'S GETTING COLD.
LET'S GO INSIDE.
......

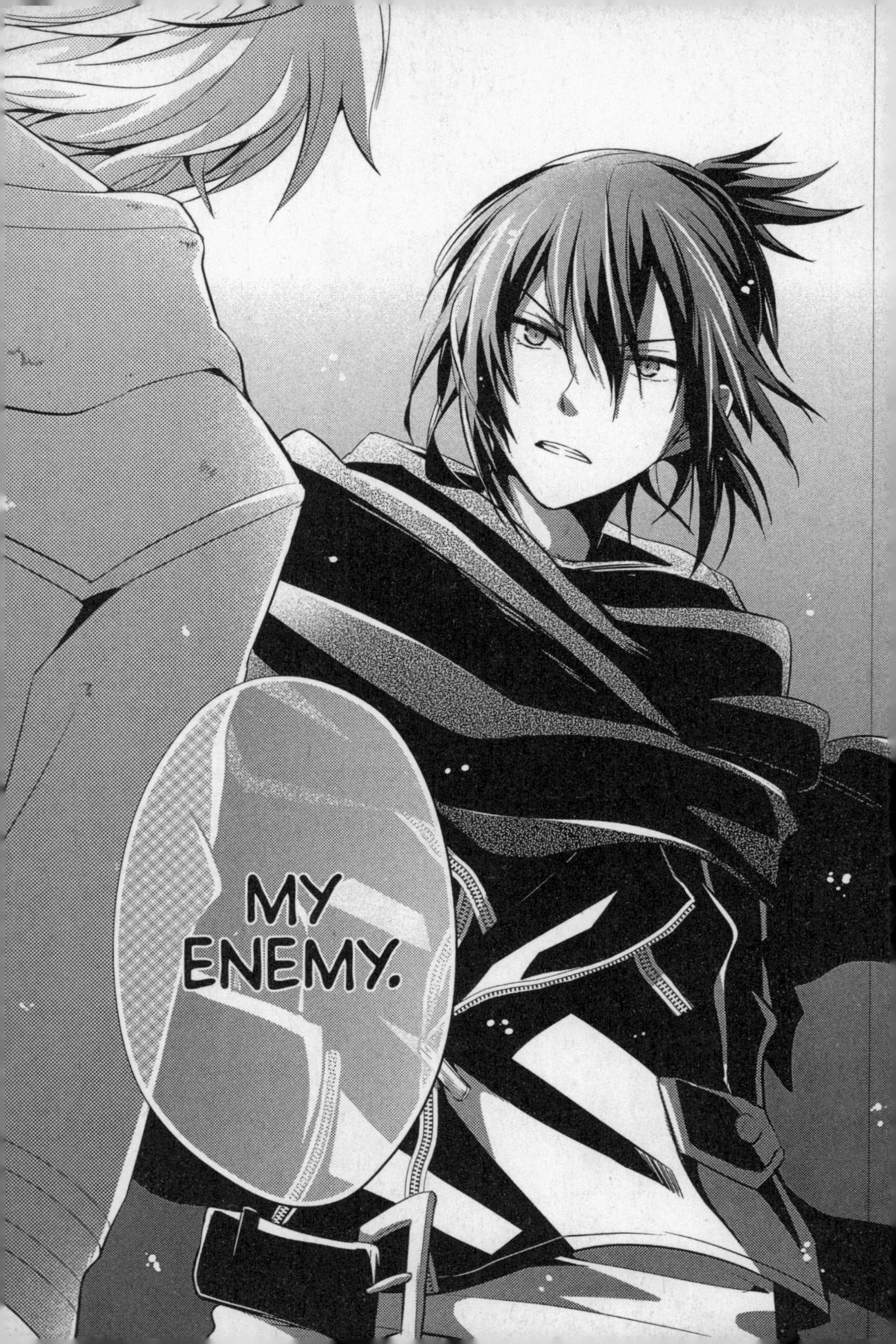
MY ENEMY.

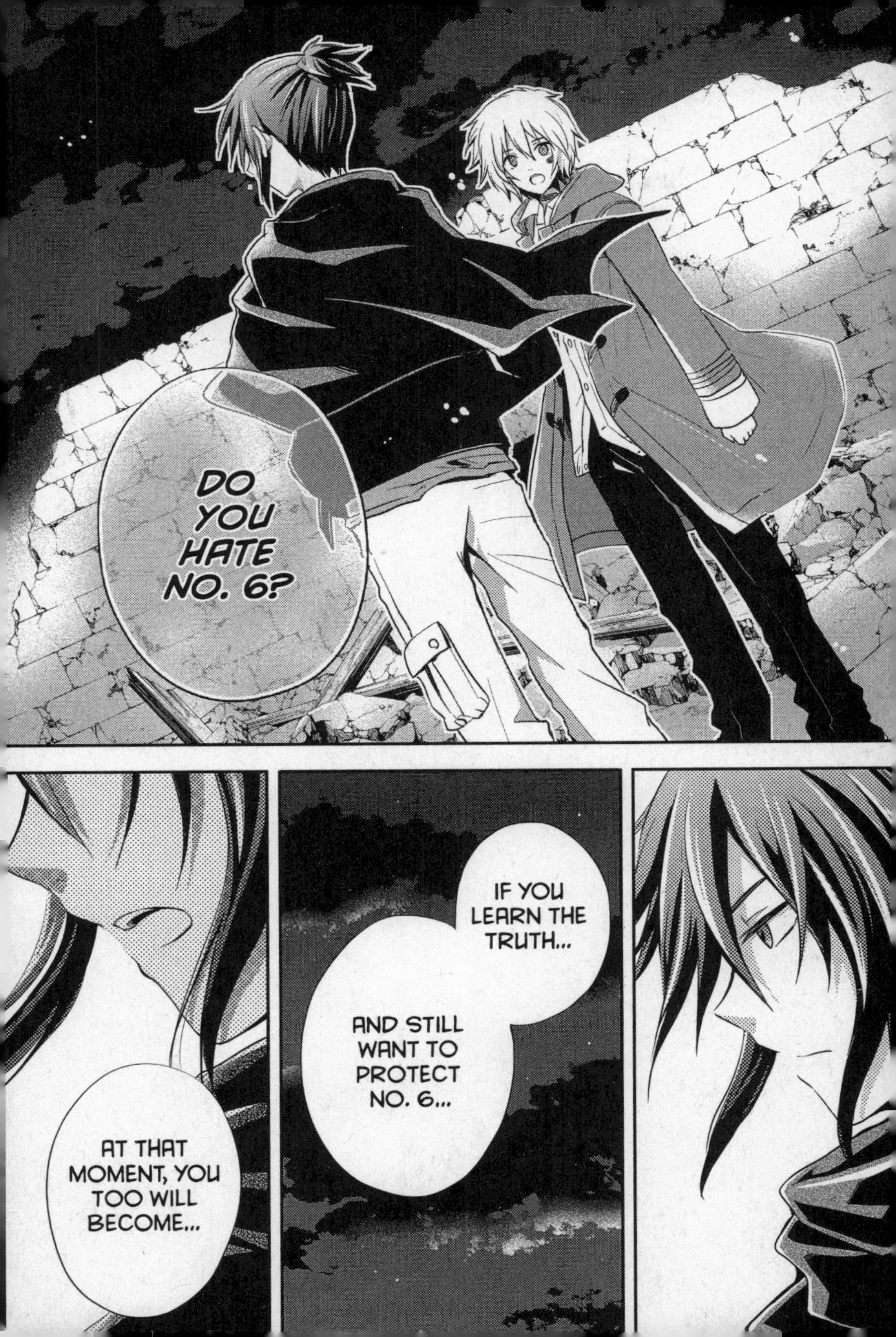
DO YOU HATE NO. 6?
IF YOU LEARN THE TRUTH...
AND STILL WANT TO PROTECT NO. 6...
AT THAT MOMENT, YOU TOO WILL BECOME...

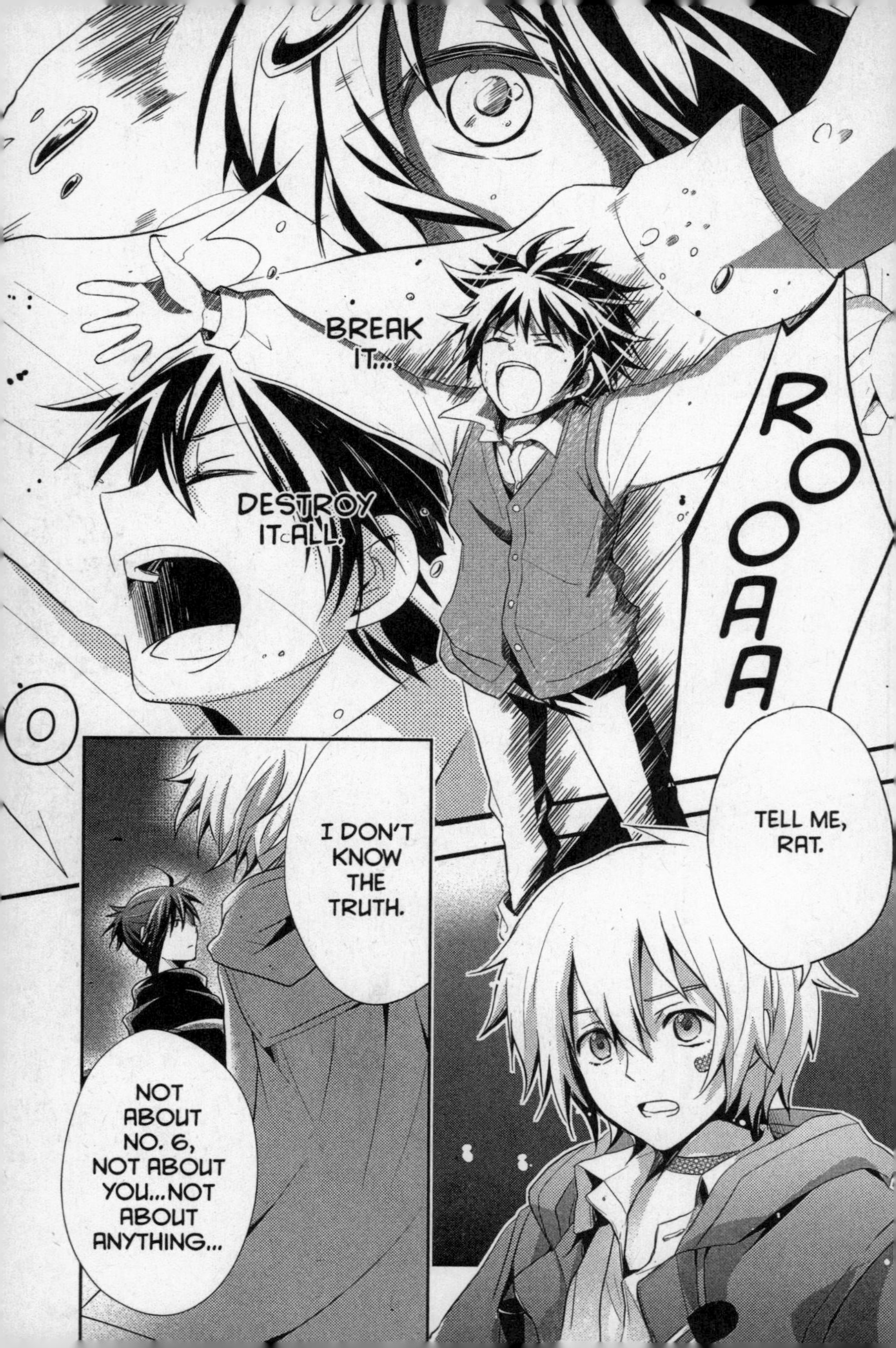
ROOOAAA
BREAK IT...
DESTROY IT ALL.
O
TELL ME, RAT.
I DON'T KNOW THE TRUTH.
NOT ABOUT NO. 6, NOT ABOUT YOU...NOT ABOUT ANYTHING...

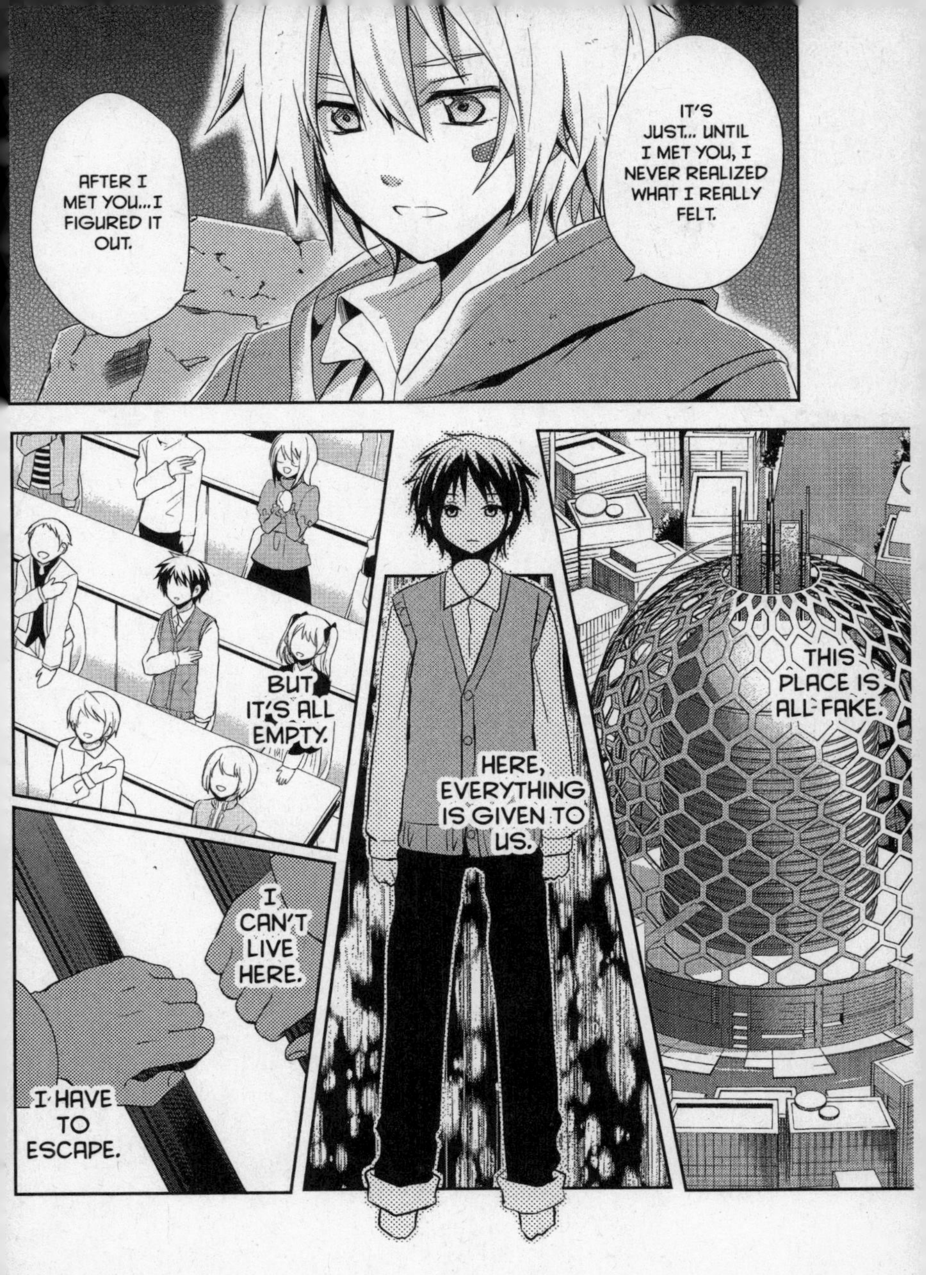
IT'S JUST... UNTIL I MET YOU, I NEVER REALIZED WHAT I REALLY FELT.
AFTER I MET YOU...I FIGURED IT OUT.
THIS PLACE IS ALL FAKE.
HERE, EVERYTHING IS GIVEN TO US.
BUT IT'S ALL EMPTY.
I CAN'T LIVE HERE.
I HAVE TO ESCAPE.

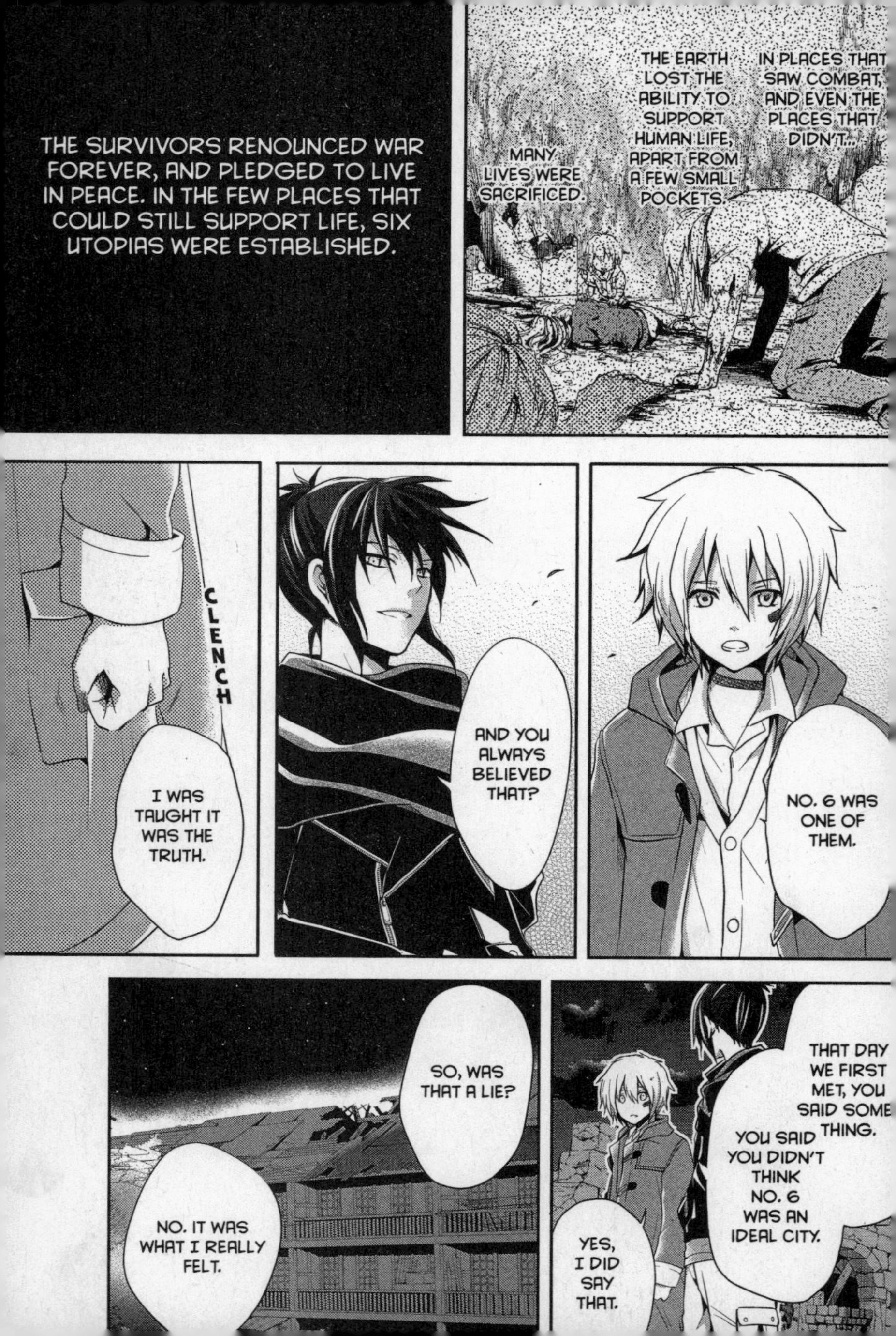
IN PLACES THAT SAW COMBAT, AND EVEN THE PLACES THAT DIDN'T...
THE EARTH LOST THE ABILITY TO SUPPORT HUMAN LIFE, APART FROM A FEW SMALL POCKETS.
MANY LIVES WERE SACRIFICED.
THE SURVIVORS RENOUNCED WAR FOREVER, AND PLEDGED TO LIVE IN PEACE. IN THE FEW PLACES THAT COULD STILL SUPPORT LIFE, SIX UTOPIAS WERE ESTABLISHED.
NO. 6 WAS ONE OF THEM.
AND YOU ALWAYS BELIEVED THAT?
CLENCH
I WAS TAUGHT IT WAS THE TRUTH.
THAT DAY WE FIRST MET, YOU SAID SOME THING.
YOU SAID YOU DIDN'T THINK NO. 6 WAS AN IDEAL CITY.
YES, I DID SAY THAT.
SO, WAS THAT A LIE?
NO. IT WAS WHAT I REALLY FELT.

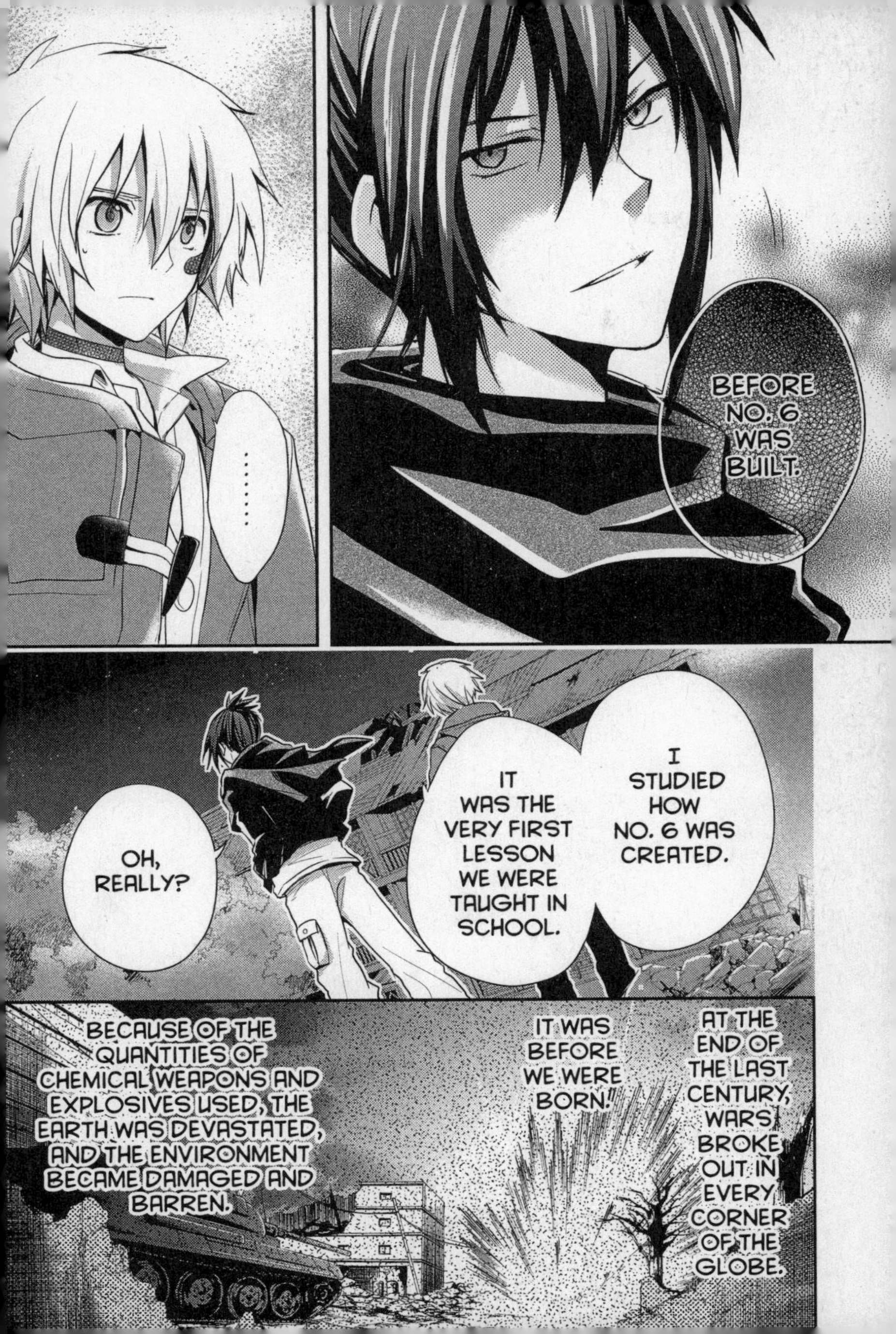
BEFORE NO. 6 WAS BUILT.
……
I STUDIED HOW NO. 6 WAS CREATED.
IT WAS THE VERY FIRST LESSON WE WERE TAUGHT IN SCHOOL.
OH, REALLY?
AT THE END OF THE LAST CENTURY, WARS BROKE OUT IN EVERY CORNER OF THE GLOBE.
IT WAS BEFORE WE WERE BORN.
BECAUSE OF THE QUANTITIES OF CHEMICAL WEAPONS AND EXPLOSIVES USED, THE EARTH WAS DEVASTATED, AND THE ENVIRONMENT BECAME DAMAGED AND BARREN.

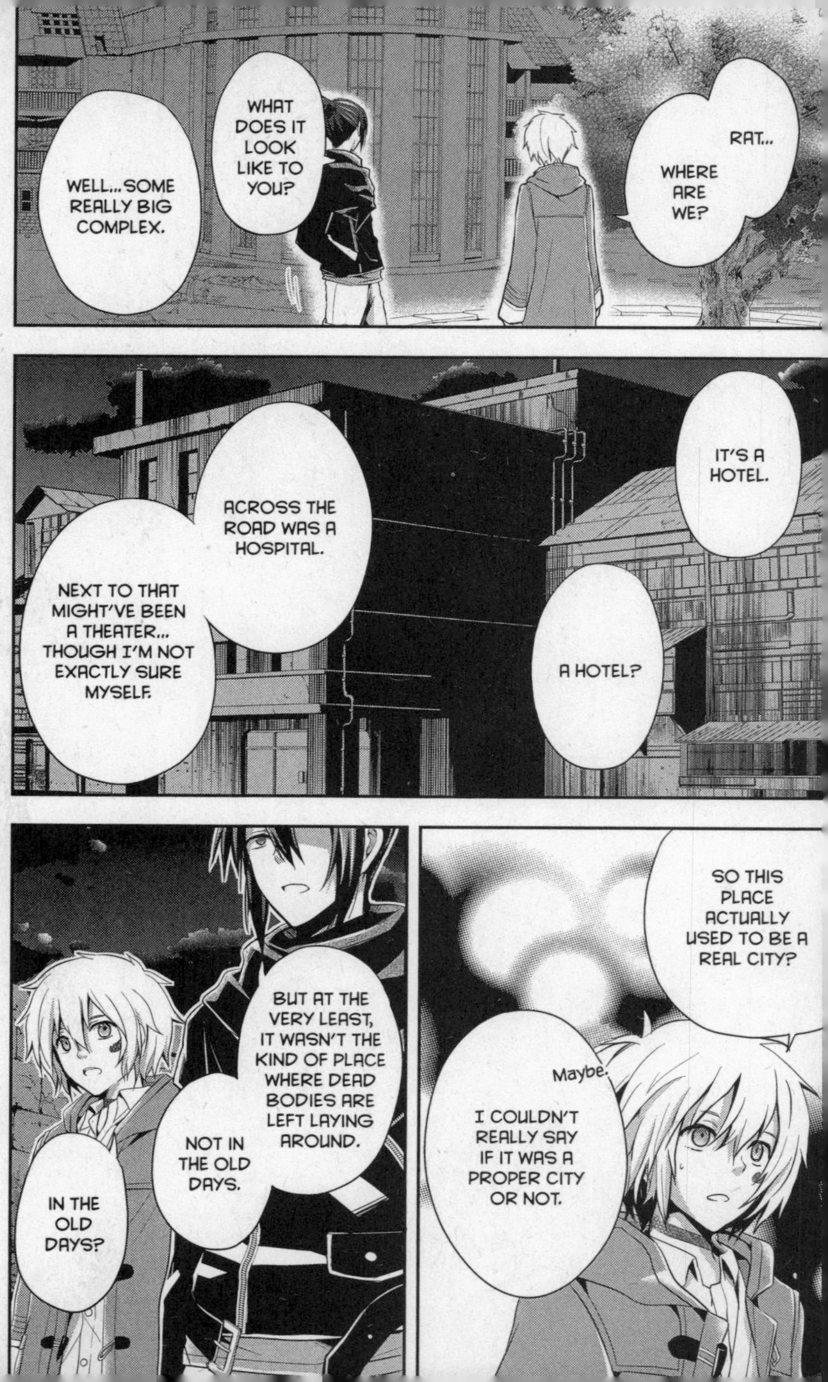
RAT... WHERE ARE WE?
WHAT DOES IT LOOK LIKE TO YOU?
WELL...SOME REALLY BIG COMPLEX.
IT'S A HOTEL.
A HOTEL?
ACROSS THE ROAD WAS A HOSPITAL.
NEXT TO THAT MIGHT'VE BEEN A THEATER... THOUGH I'M NOT EXACTLY SURE MYSELF.
SO THIS PLACE ACTUALLY USED TO BE A REAL CITY?
Maybe.
I COULDN'T REALLY SAY IF IT WAS A PROPER CITY OR NOT.
BUT AT THE VERY LEAST, IT WASN'T THE KIND OF PLACE WHERE DEAD BODIES ARE LEFT LAYING AROUND.
NOT IN THE OLD DAYS.
IN THE OLD DAYS?

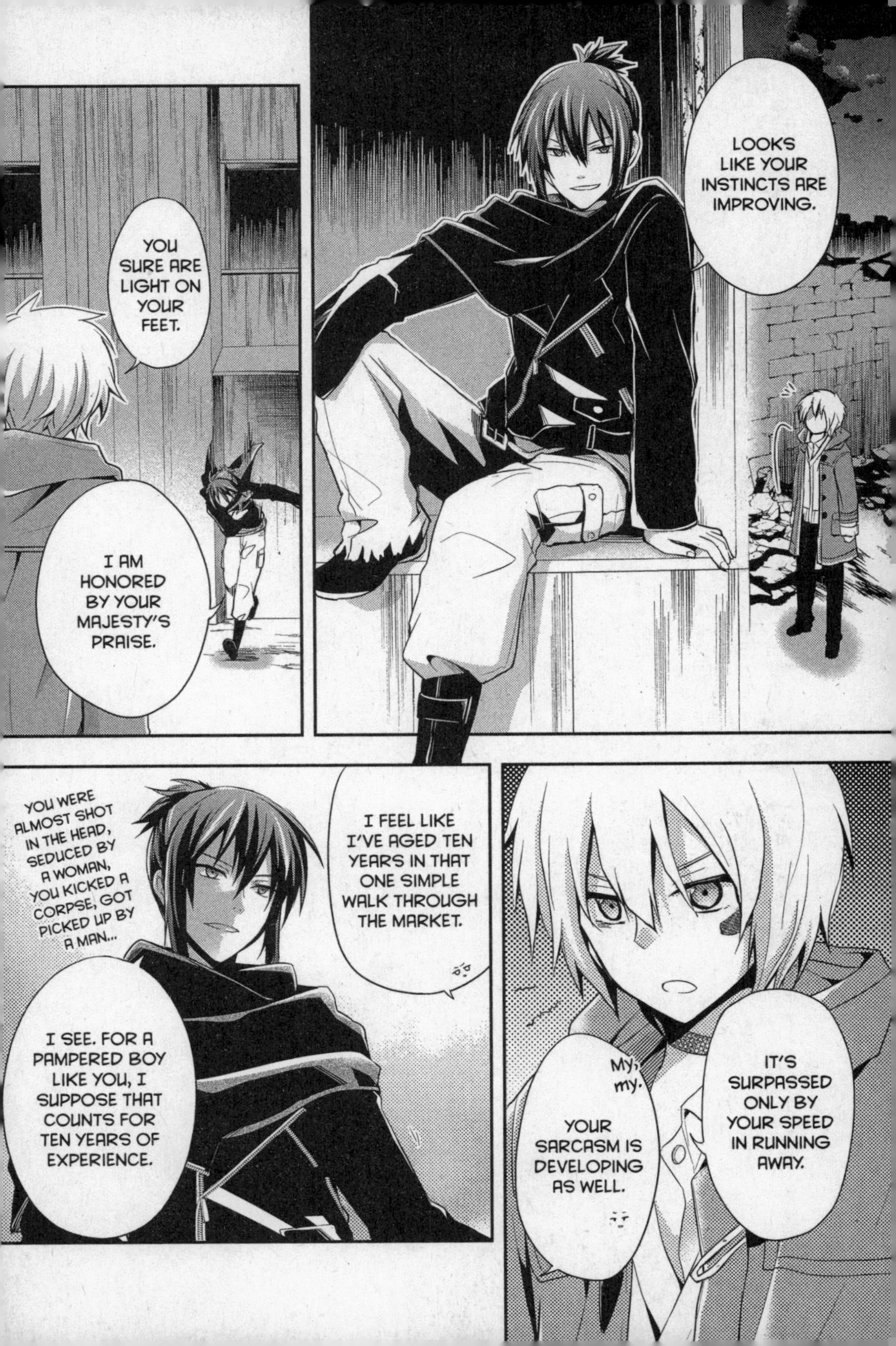
LOOKS LIKE YOUR INSTINCTS ARE IMPROVING.
YOU SURE ARE LIGHT ON YOUR FEET.
I AM HONORED BY YOUR MAJESTY'S PRAISE.
IT'S SURPASSED ONLY BY YOUR SPEED IN RUNNING AWAY.
My, my.
YOUR SARCASM IS DEVELOPING AS WELL.
I FEEL LIKE I'VE AGED TEN YEARS IN THAT ONE SIMPLE WALK THROUGH THE MARKET.
YOU WERE ALMOST SHOT IN THE HEAD, SEDUCED BY A WOMAN, YOU KICKED A CORPSE, GOT PICKED UP BY A MAN...
I SEE. FOR A PAMPERED BOY LIKE YOU, I SUPPOSE THAT COUNTS FOR TEN YEARS OF EXPERIENCE.

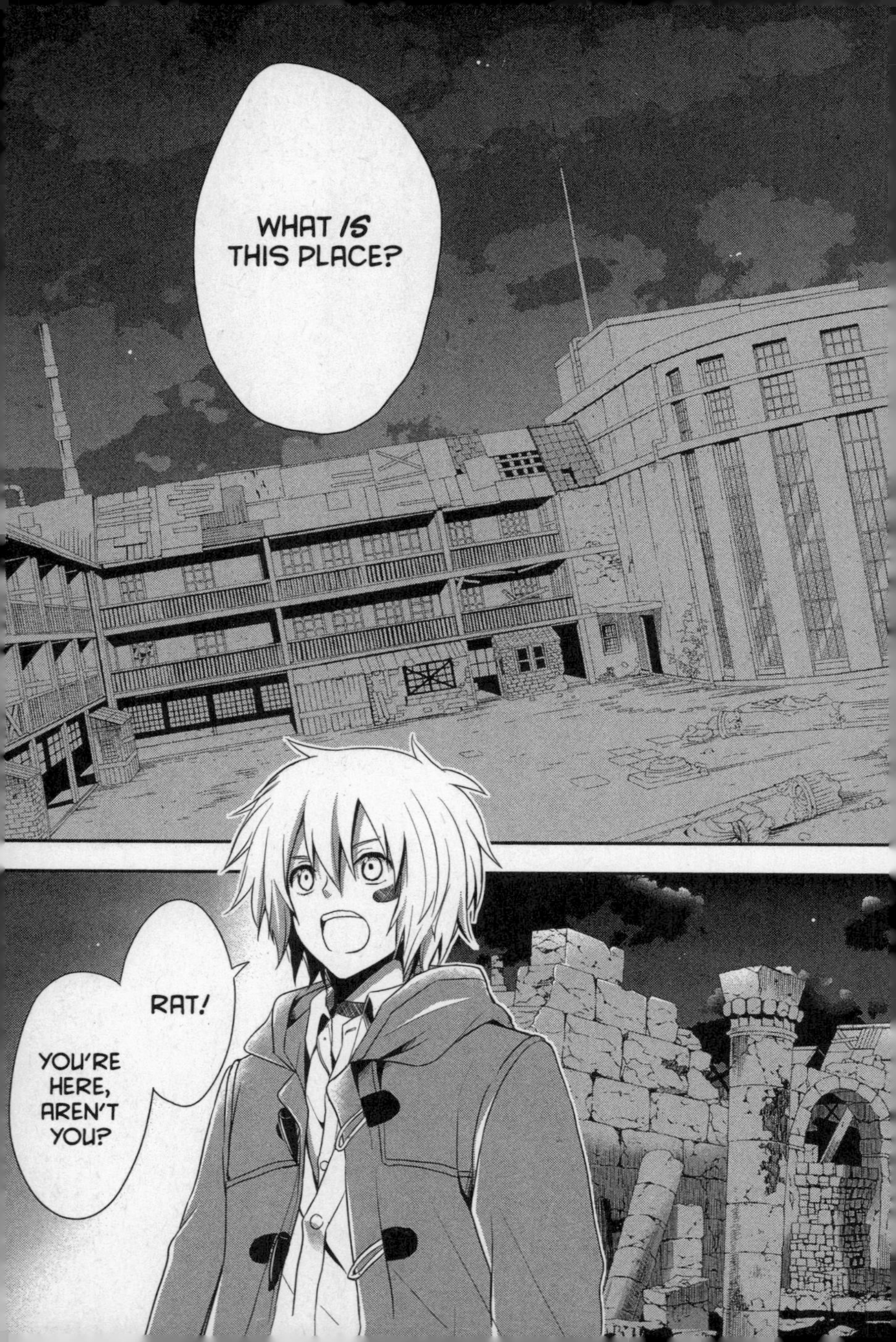
WHAT *IS* THIS PLACE?
RAT!
YOU'RE HERE, AREN'T YOU?

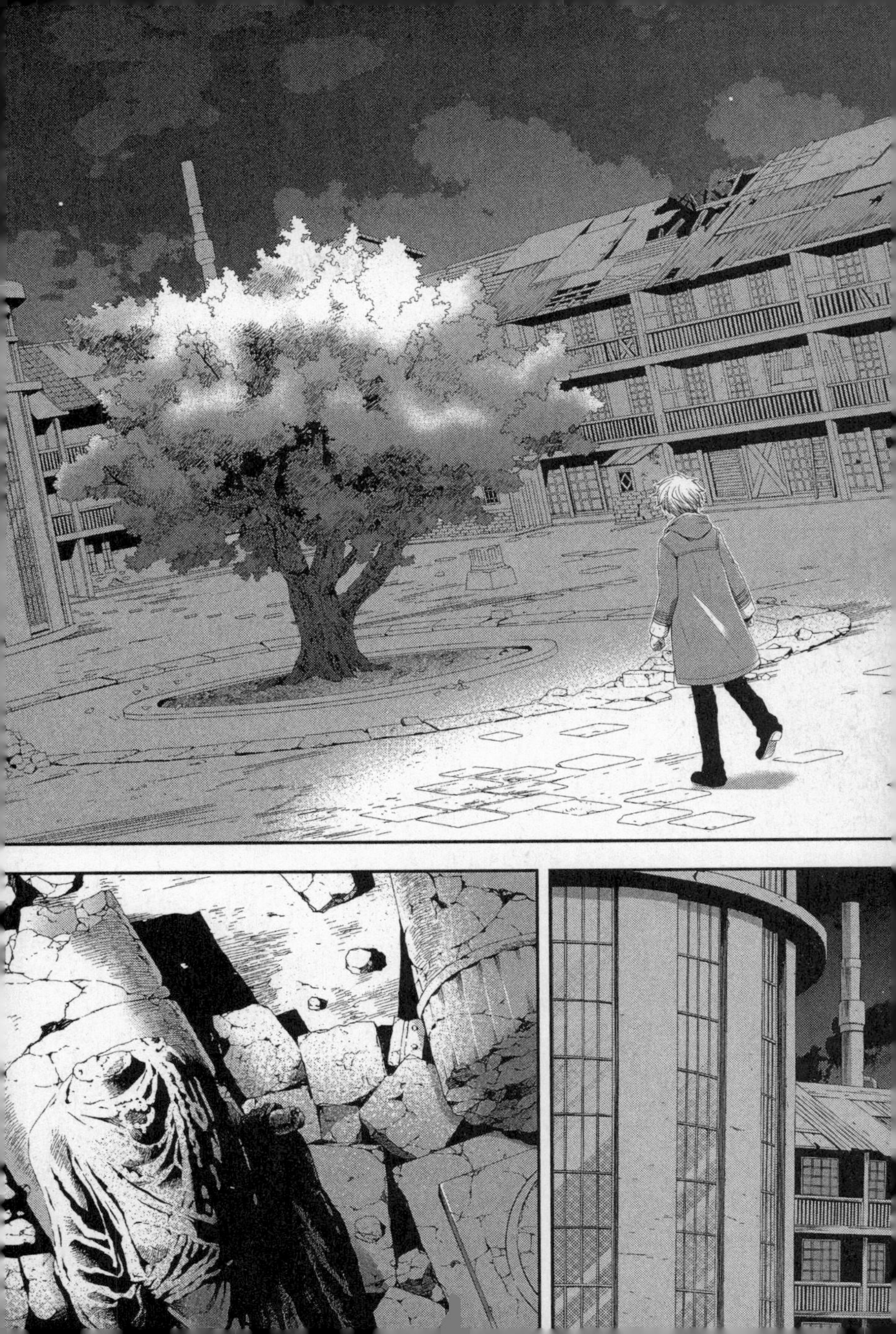

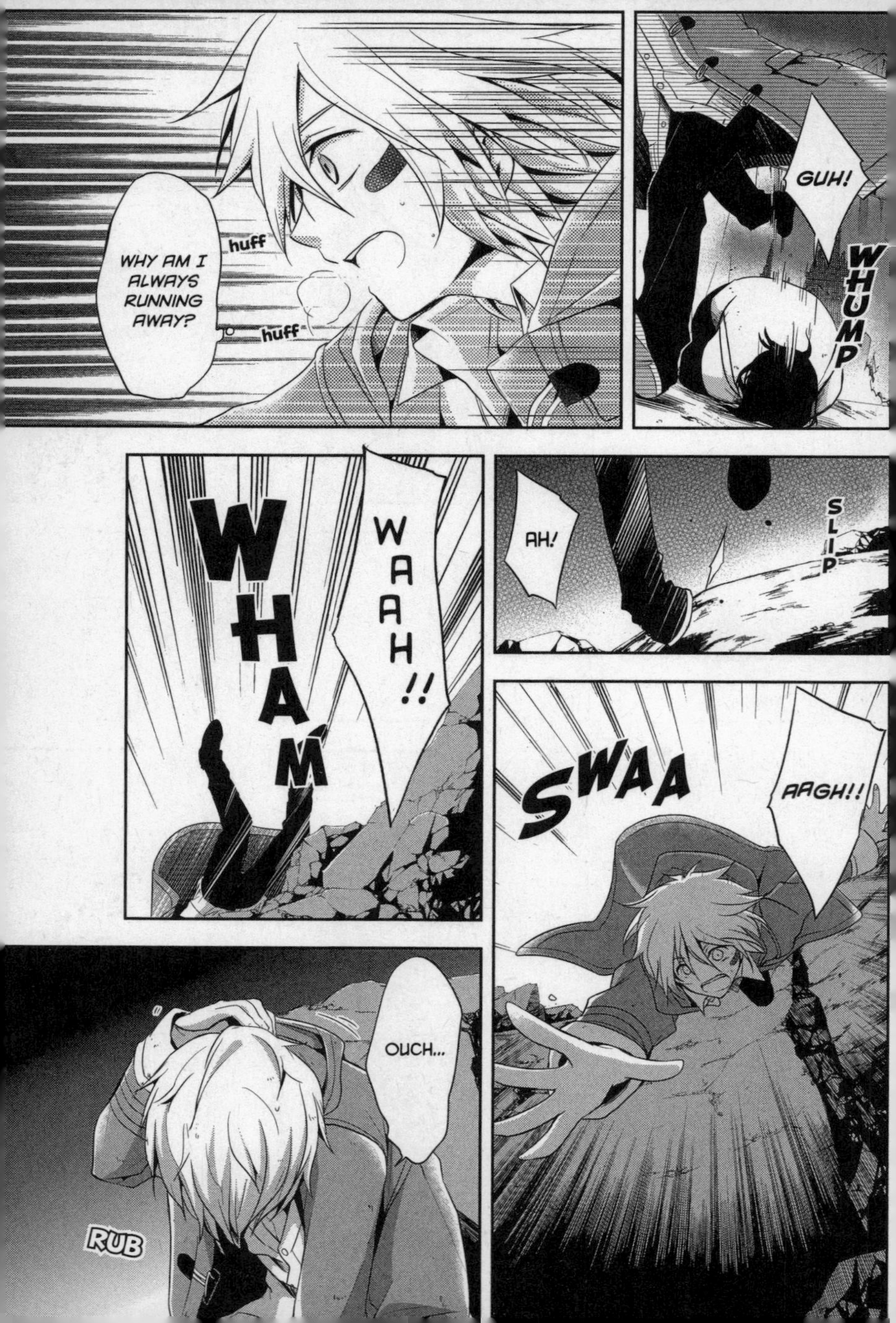
GUH!
WHUMP
huff
WHY AM I ALWAYS RUNNING AWAY?
huff
AH!
SLIP
SWAA
AAGH!!
WHAM
WAAAH!!
OUCH...
RUB

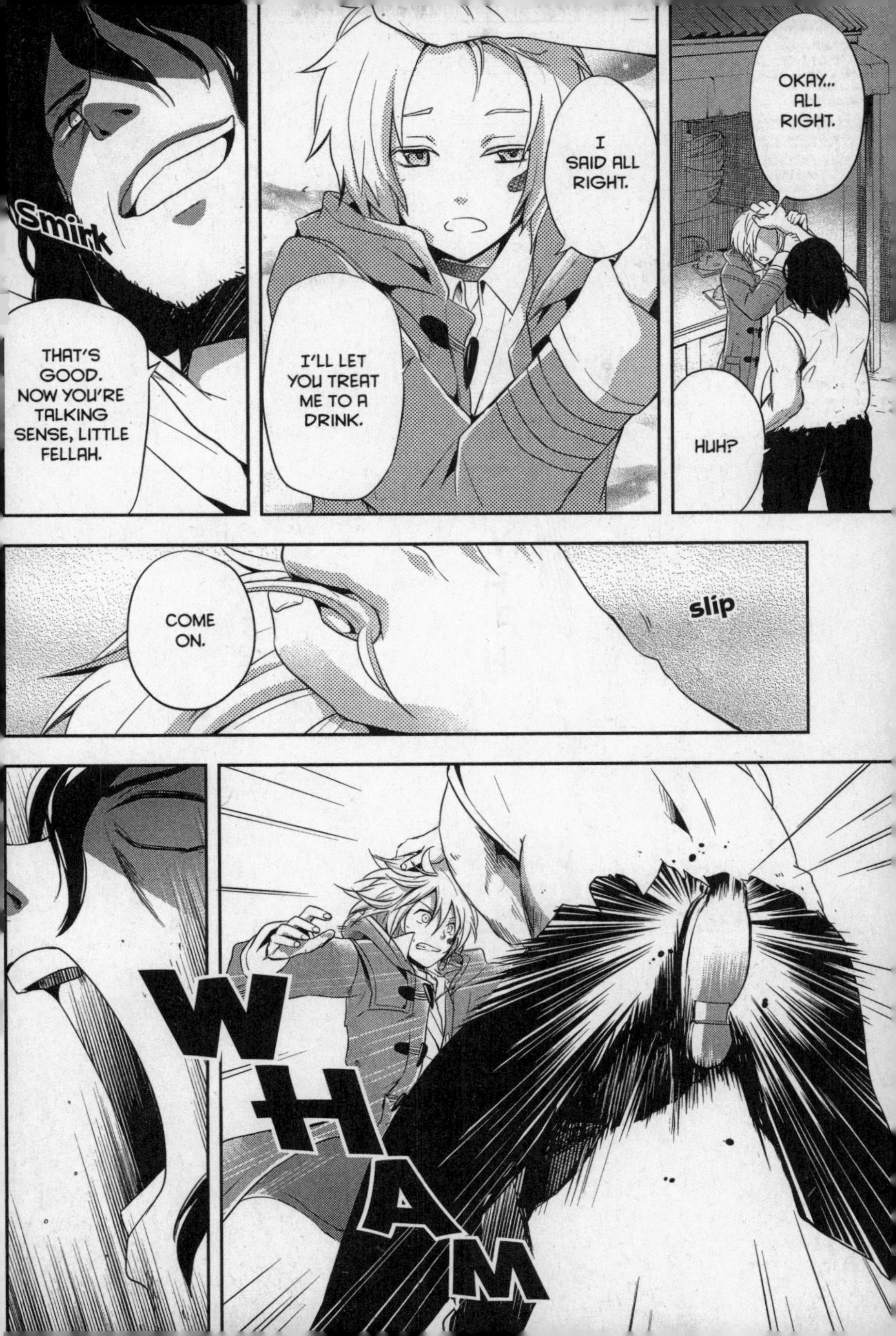
OKAY... ALL RIGHT.
HUH?
I SAID ALL RIGHT.
I'LL LET YOU TREAT ME TO A DRINK.
Smirk
THAT'S GOOD. NOW YOU'RE TALKING SENSE, LITTLE FELLAH.
slip
COME ON.
WHAM

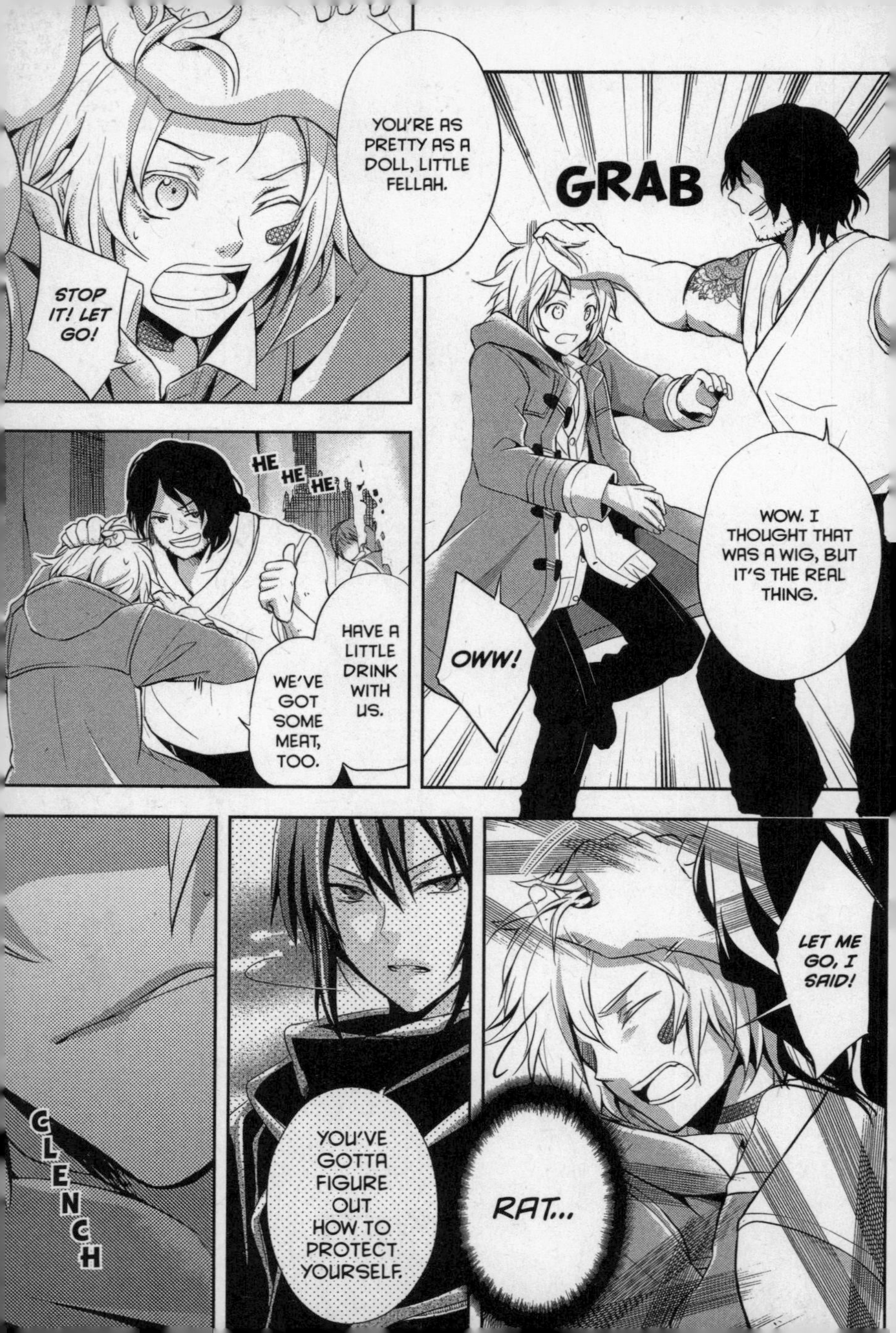
YOU'RE AS PRETTY AS A DOLL, LITTLE FELLAH.
GRAB
WOW. I THOUGHT THAT WAS A WIG, BUT IT'S THE REAL THING.
OWW!
STOP IT! LET GO!
HE HE HE
HAVE A LITTLE DRINK WITH US.
WE'VE GOT SOME MEAT, TOO.
LET ME GO, I SAID!
RAT...
YOU'VE GOTTA FIGURE OUT HOW TO PROTECT YOURSELF.
CLENCH

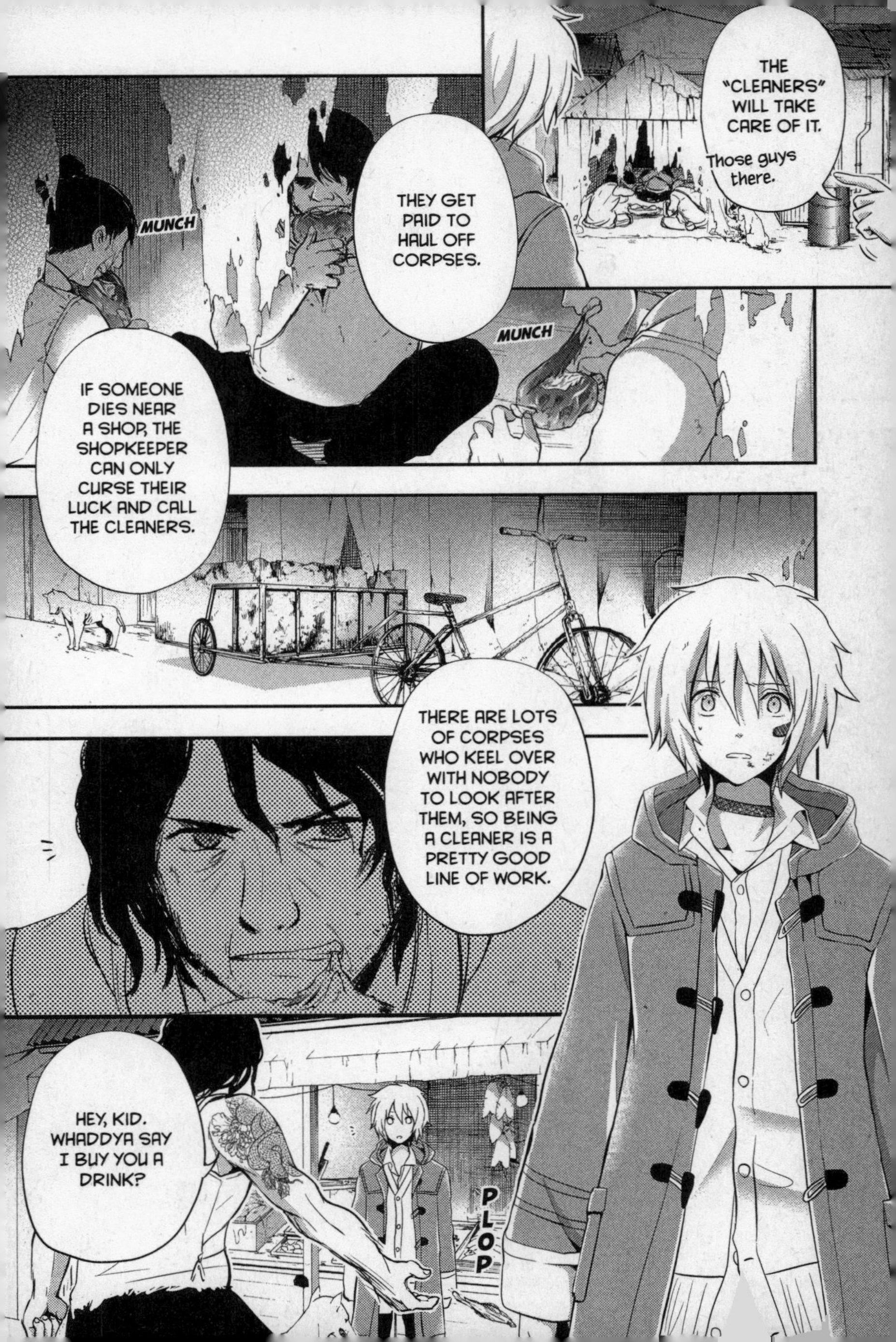
THE "CLEANERS" WILL TAKE CARE OF IT.
Those guys there.
THEY GET PAID TO HAUL OFF CORPSES.
MUNCH
MUNCH
IF SOMEONE DIES NEAR A SHOP, THE SHOPKEEPER CAN ONLY CURSE THEIR LUCK AND CALL THE CLEANERS.
THERE ARE LOTS OF CORPSES WHO KEEL OVER WITH NOBODY TO LOOK AFTER THEM, SO BEING A CLEANER IS A PRETTY GOOD LINE OF WORK.
HEY, KID. WHADDYA SAY I BUY YOU A DRINK?
PLOP

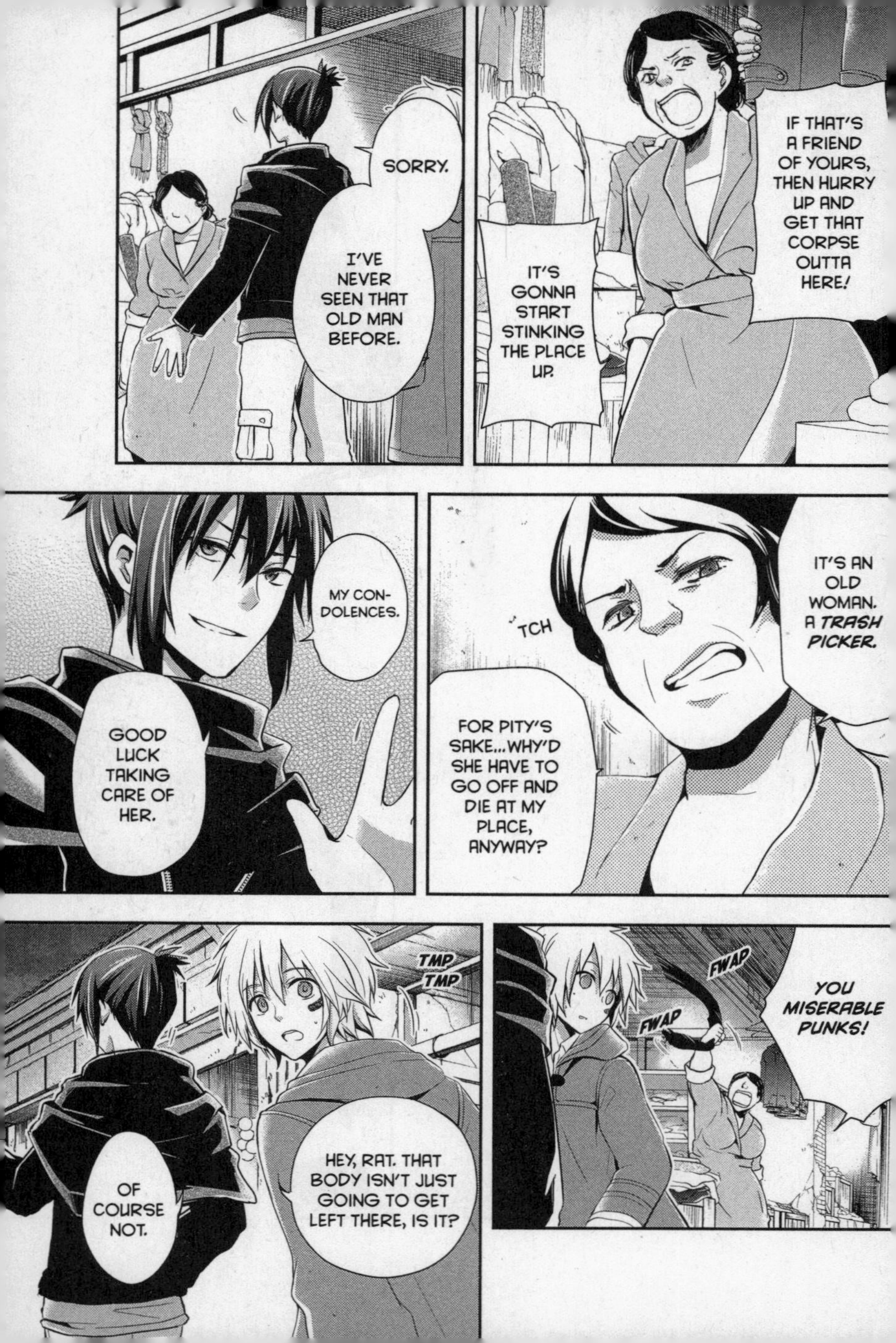
IF THAT'S A FRIEND OF YOURS, THEN HURRY UP AND GET THAT CORPSE OUTTA HERE!
IT'S GONNA START STINKING THE PLACE UP.
SORRY.
I'VE NEVER SEEN THAT OLD MAN BEFORE.
IT'S AN OLD WOMAN. A *TRASH PICKER.*
TCH
FOR PITY'S SAKE...WHY'D SHE HAVE TO GO OFF AND DIE AT MY PLACE, ANYWAY?
MY CON-DOLENCES.
GOOD LUCK TAKING CARE OF HER.
YOU MISERABLE PUNKS!
FWAP
FWAP
TMP TMP
HEY, RAT. THAT BODY ISN'T JUST GOING TO GET LEFT THERE, IS IT?
OF COURSE NOT.

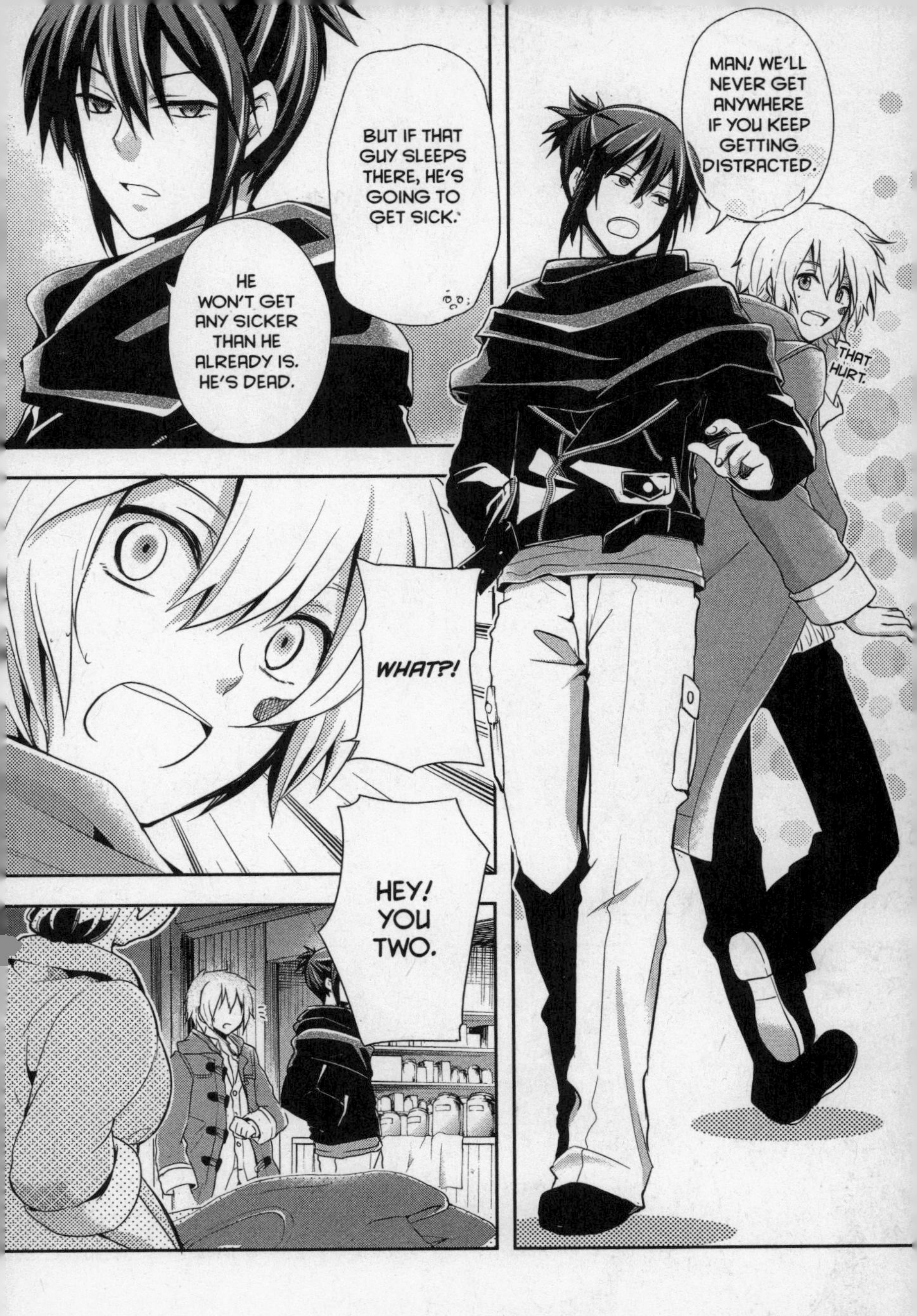
MAN! WE'LL NEVER GET ANYWHERE IF YOU KEEP GETTING DISTRACTED.
THAT HURT.
BUT IF THAT GUY SLEEPS THERE, HE'S GOING TO GET SICK.
HE WON'T GET ANY SICKER THAN HE ALREADY IS. HE'S DEAD.
WHAT?!
HEY! YOU TWO.

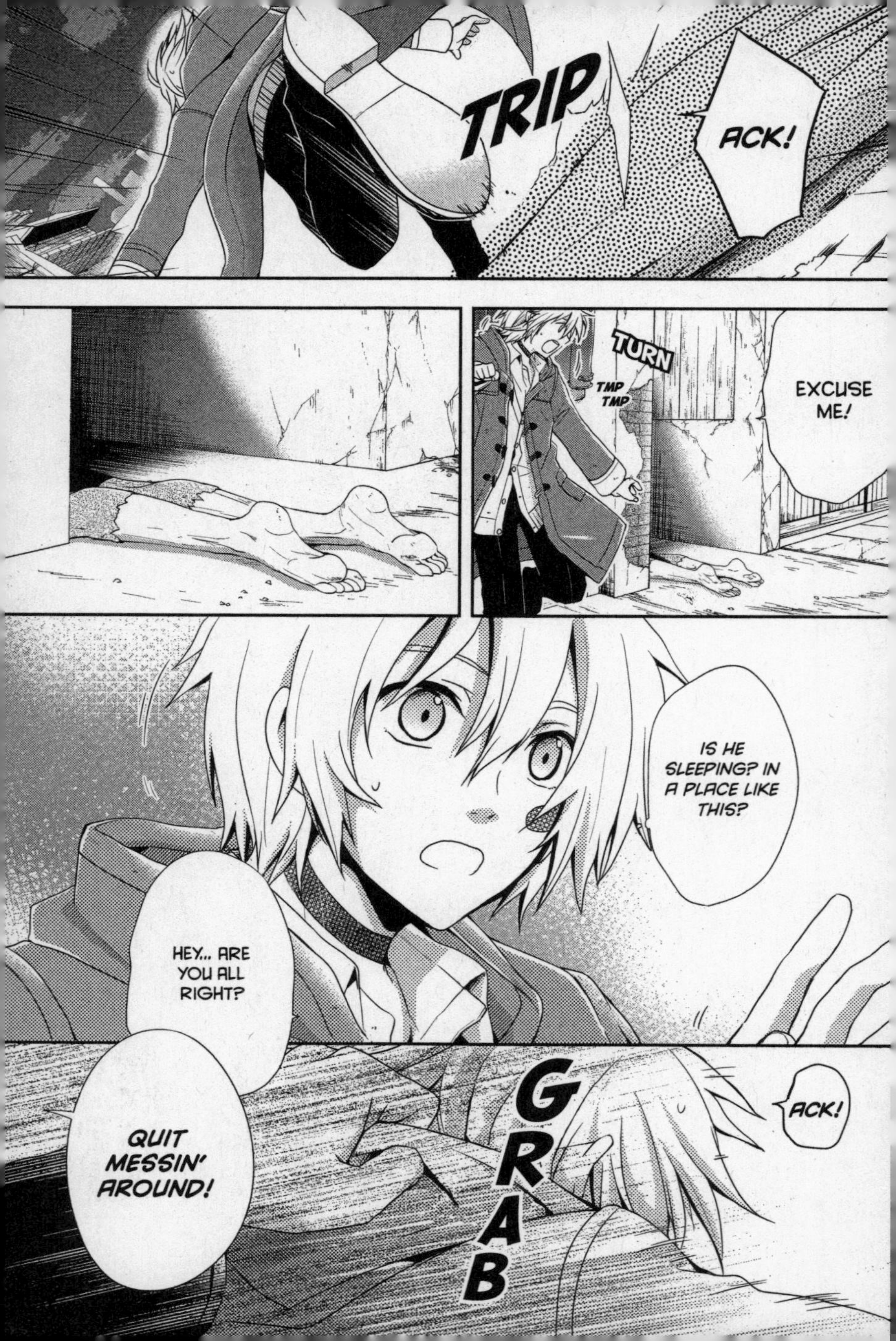
ACK!
TRIP
EXCUSE ME!
TURN
TMP TMP
IS HE SLEEPING? IN A PLACE LIKE THIS?
HEY... ARE YOU ALL RIGHT?
ACK!
GRAB
QUIT MESSIN' AROUND!

NO.6

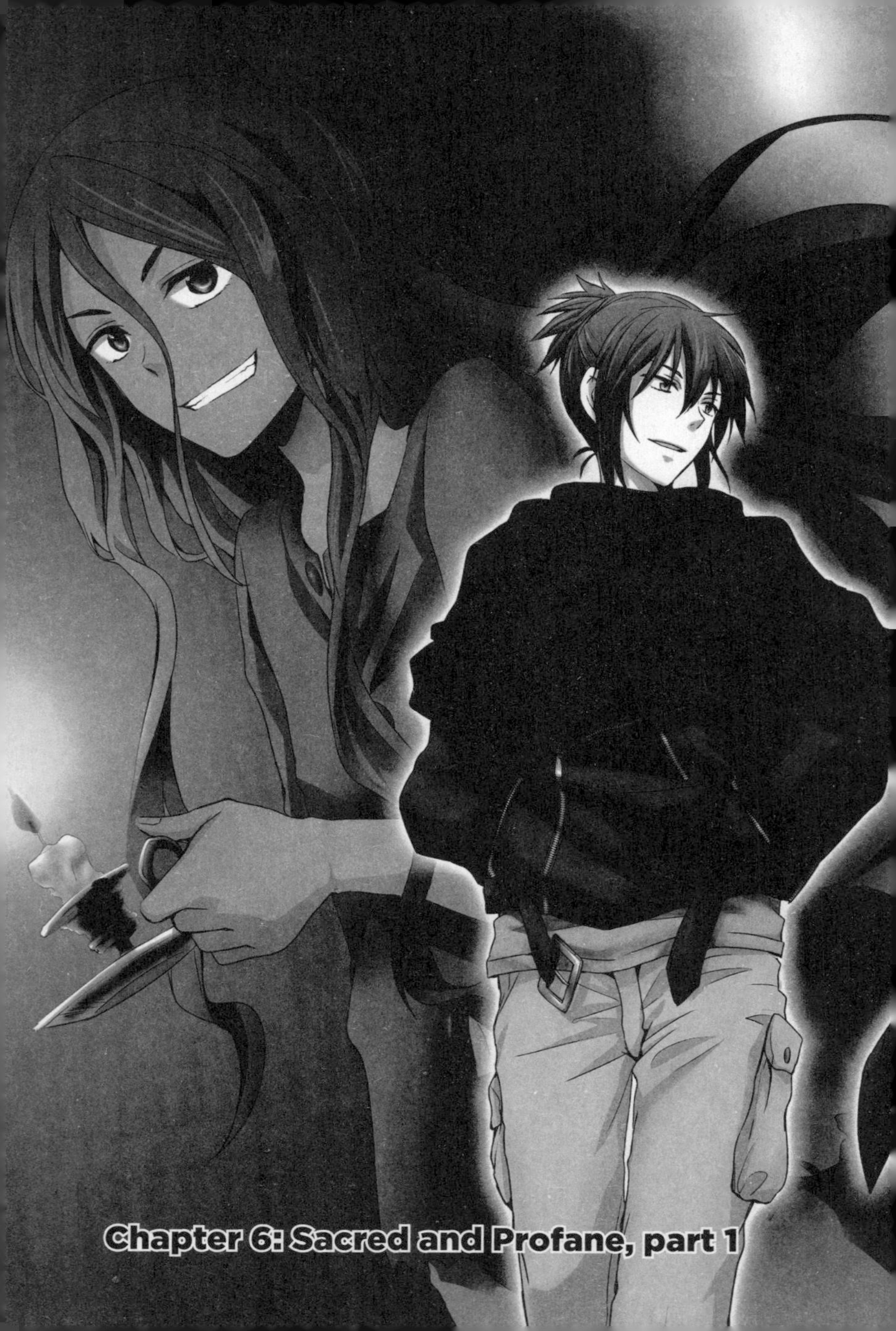
Chapter 6: Sacred and Profane, part 1

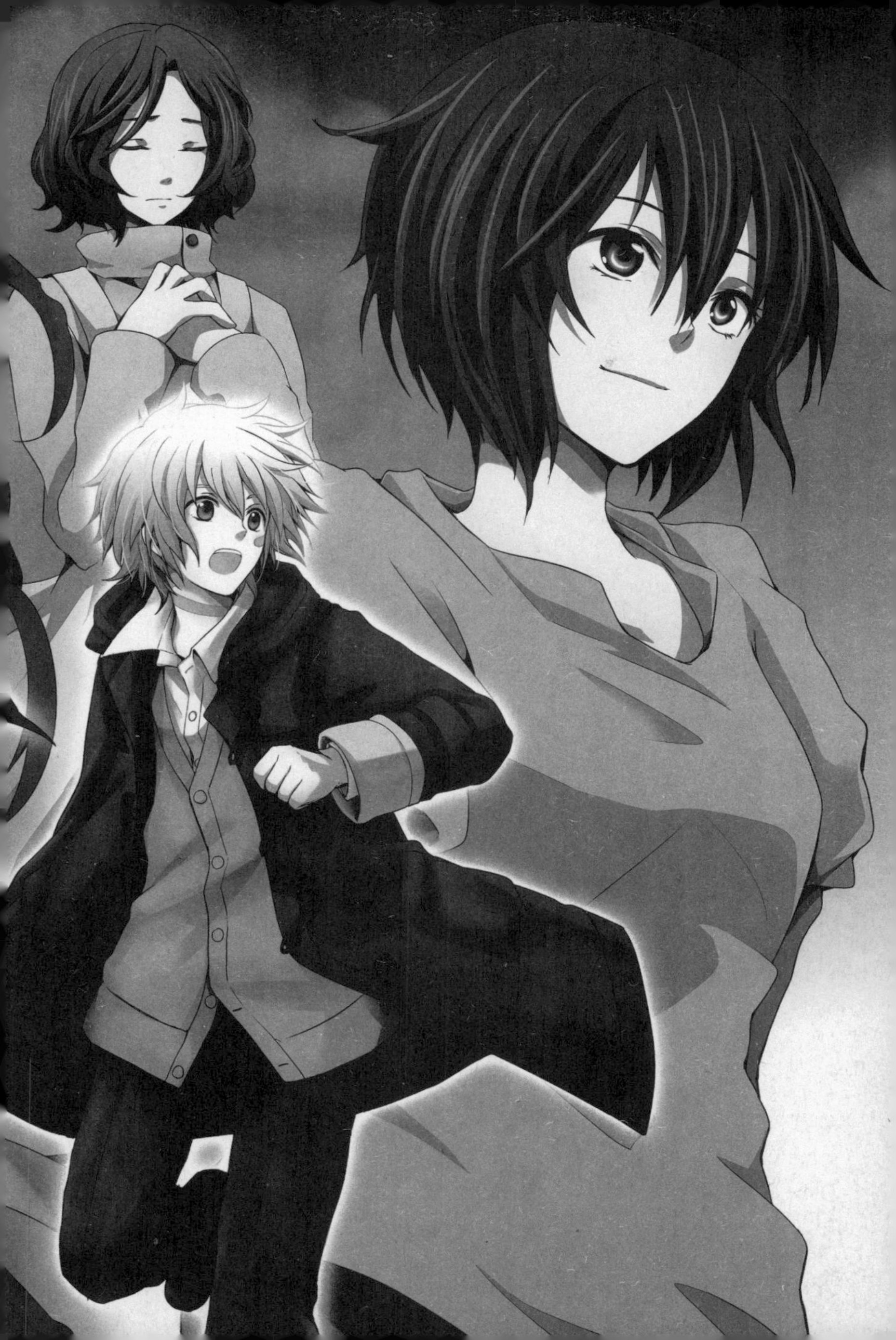

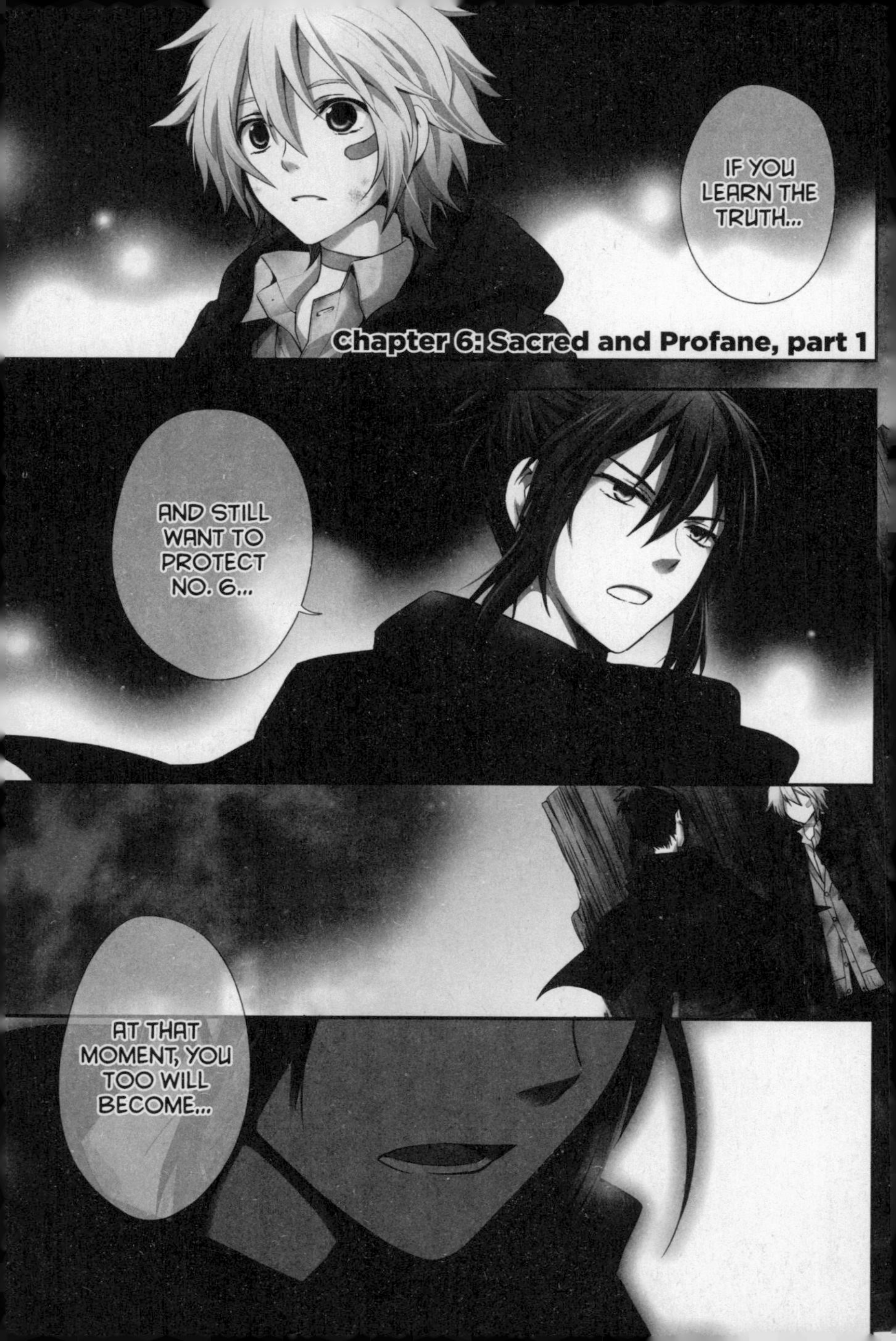
IF YOU LEARN THE TRUTH...
Chapter 6: Sacred and Profane, part 1
AND STILL WANT TO PROTECT NO. 6...
AT THAT MOMENT, YOU TOO WILL BECOME...

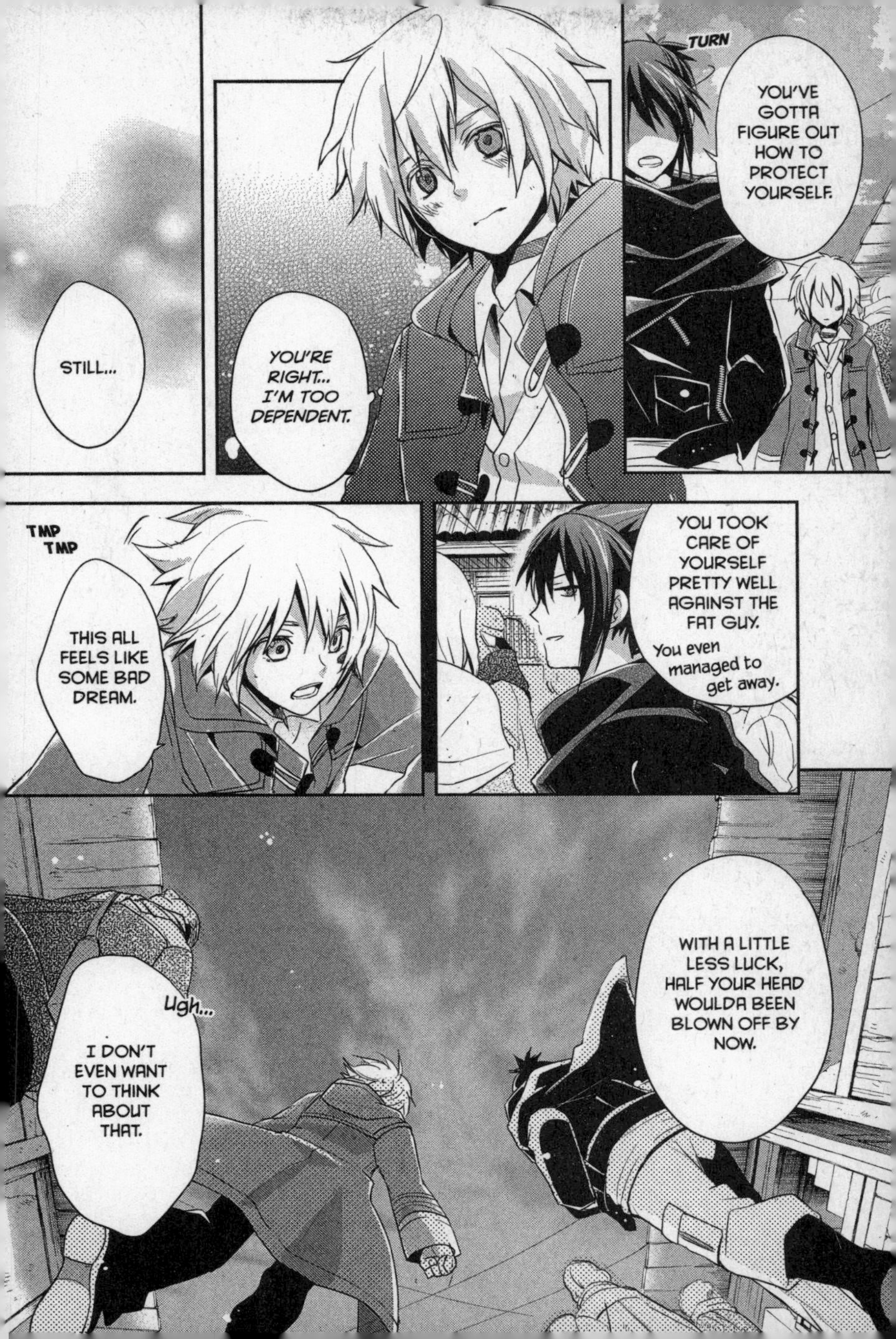
TURN
YOU'VE GOTTA FIGURE OUT HOW TO PROTECT YOURSELF.
YOU'RE RIGHT... I'M TOO DEPENDENT.
STILL...
YOU TOOK CARE OF YOURSELF PRETTY WELL AGAINST THE FAT GUY.
You even managed to get away.
TMP TMP
THIS ALL FEELS LIKE SOME BAD DREAM.
WITH A LITTLE LESS LUCK, HALF YOUR HEAD WOULDA BEEN BLOWN OFF BY NOW.
Ugh...
I DON'T EVEN WANT TO THINK ABOUT THAT.

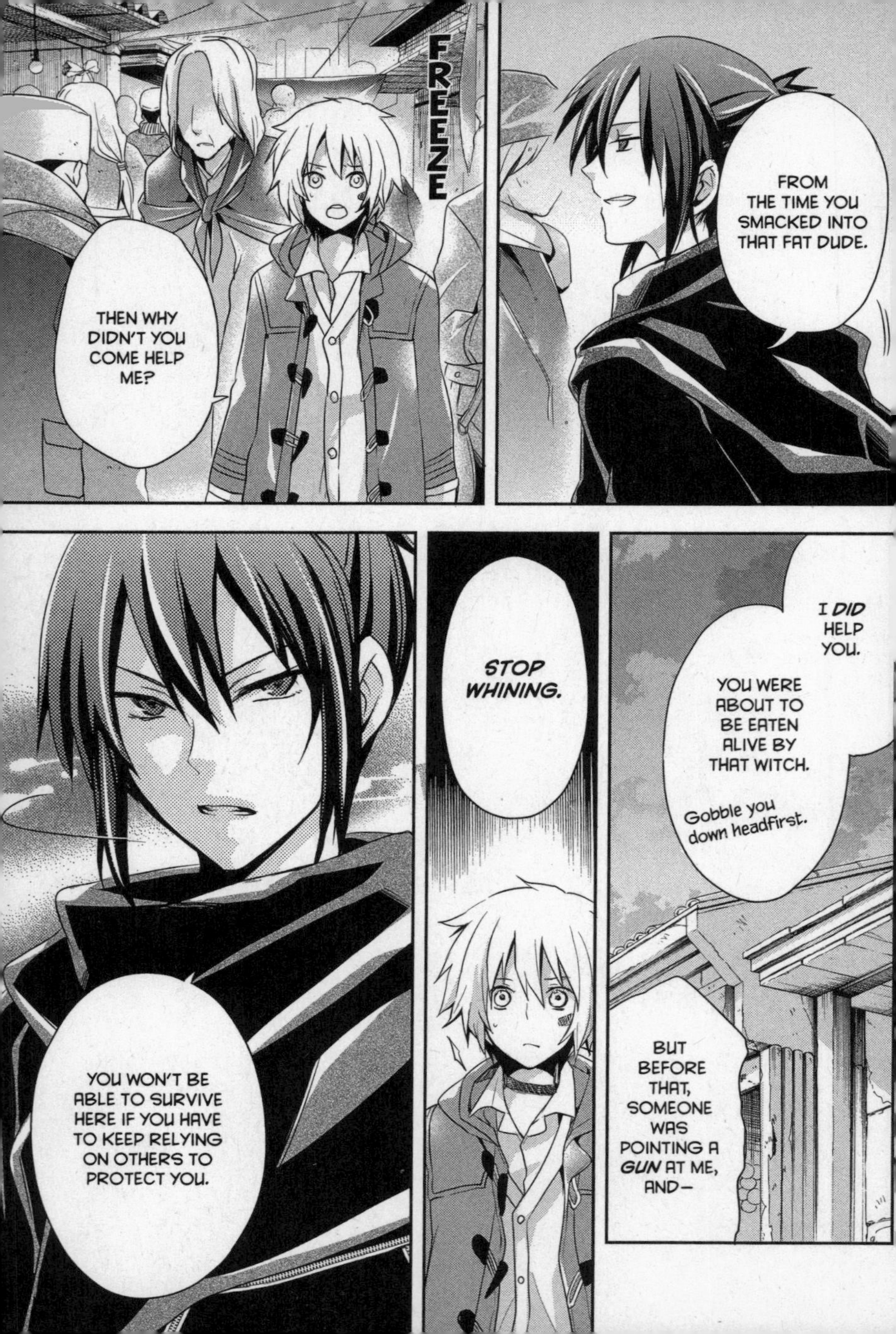
FROM THE TIME YOU SMACKED INTO THAT FAT DUDE.
FREEZE
THEN WHY DIDN'T YOU COME HELP ME?
I DID HELP YOU.
YOU WERE ABOUT TO BE EATEN ALIVE BY THAT WITCH.
Gobble you down headfirst.
BUT BEFORE THAT, SOMEONE WAS POINTING A GUN AT ME, AND—
STOP WHINING.
YOU WON'T BE ABLE TO SURVIVE HERE IF YOU HAVE TO KEEP RELYING ON OTHERS TO PROTECT YOU.

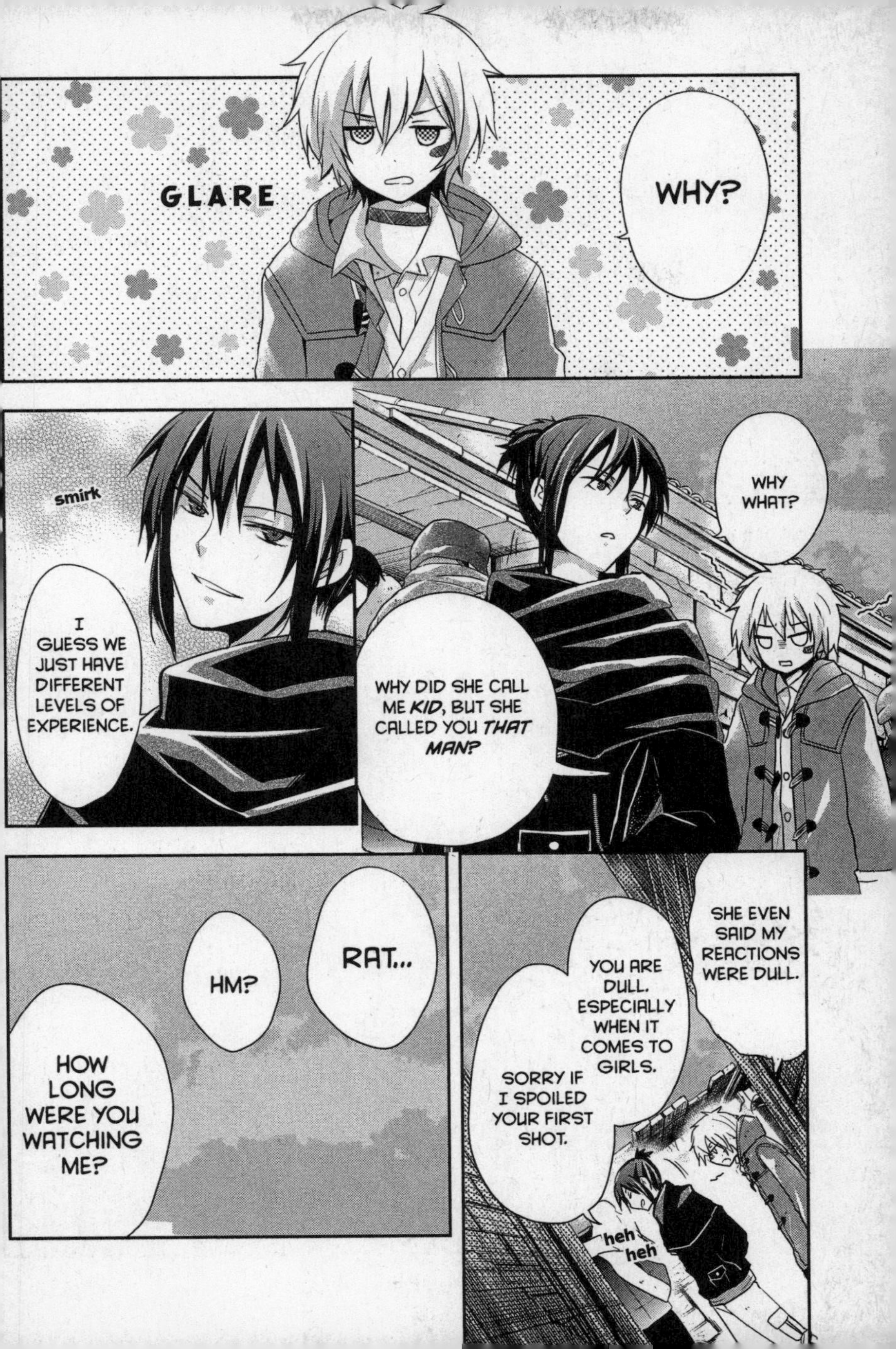
WHY?
GLARE
WHY WHAT?
WHY DID SHE CALL ME *KID*, BUT SHE CALLED YOU *THAT MAN*?
smirk
I GUESS WE JUST HAVE DIFFERENT LEVELS OF EXPERIENCE.
SHE EVEN SAID MY REACTIONS WERE DULL.
YOU ARE DULL. ESPECIALLY WHEN IT COMES TO GIRLS.
SORRY IF I SPOILED YOUR FIRST SHOT.
heh heh
RAT...
HM?
HOW LONG WERE YOU WATCHING ME?

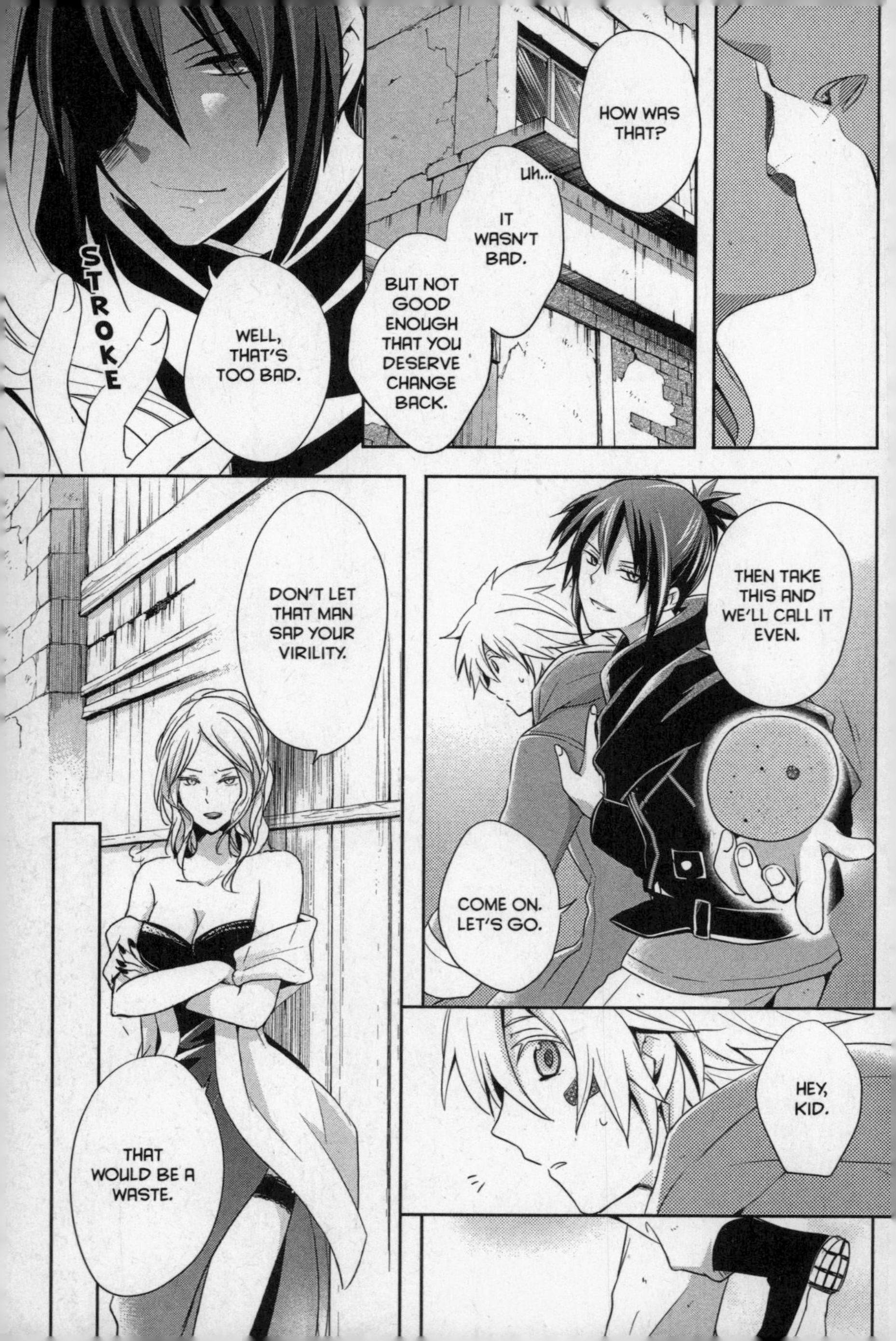
HOW WAS THAT?
Uh...
IT WASN'T BAD.
BUT NOT GOOD ENOUGH THAT YOU DESERVE CHANGE BACK.
STROKE
WELL, THAT'S TOO BAD.
THEN TAKE THIS AND WE'LL CALL IT EVEN.
COME ON. LET'S GO.
HEY, KID.
DON'T LET THAT MAN SAP YOUR VIRILITY.
THAT WOULD BE A WASTE.

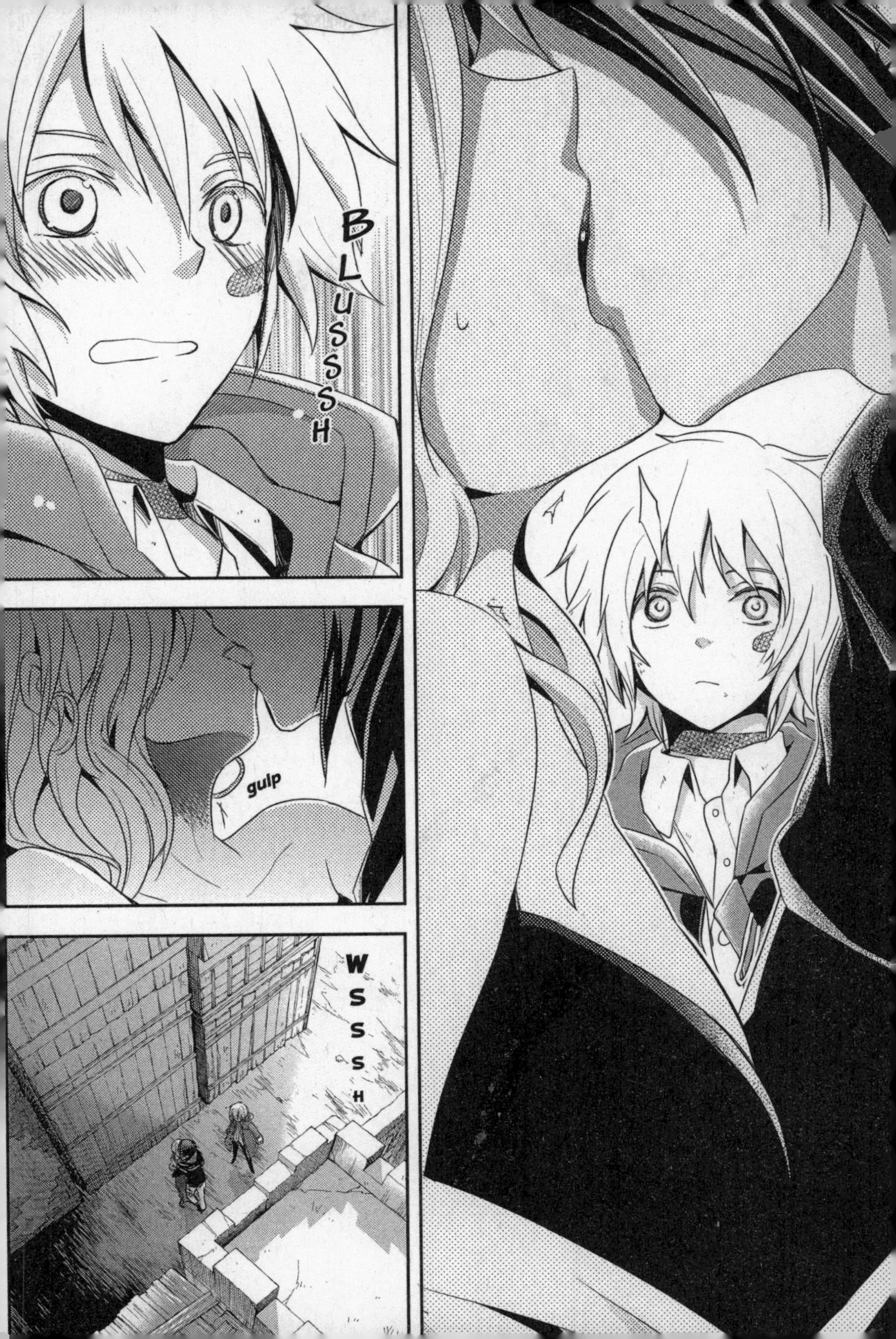
BLUSSSH
gulp
WSSSH

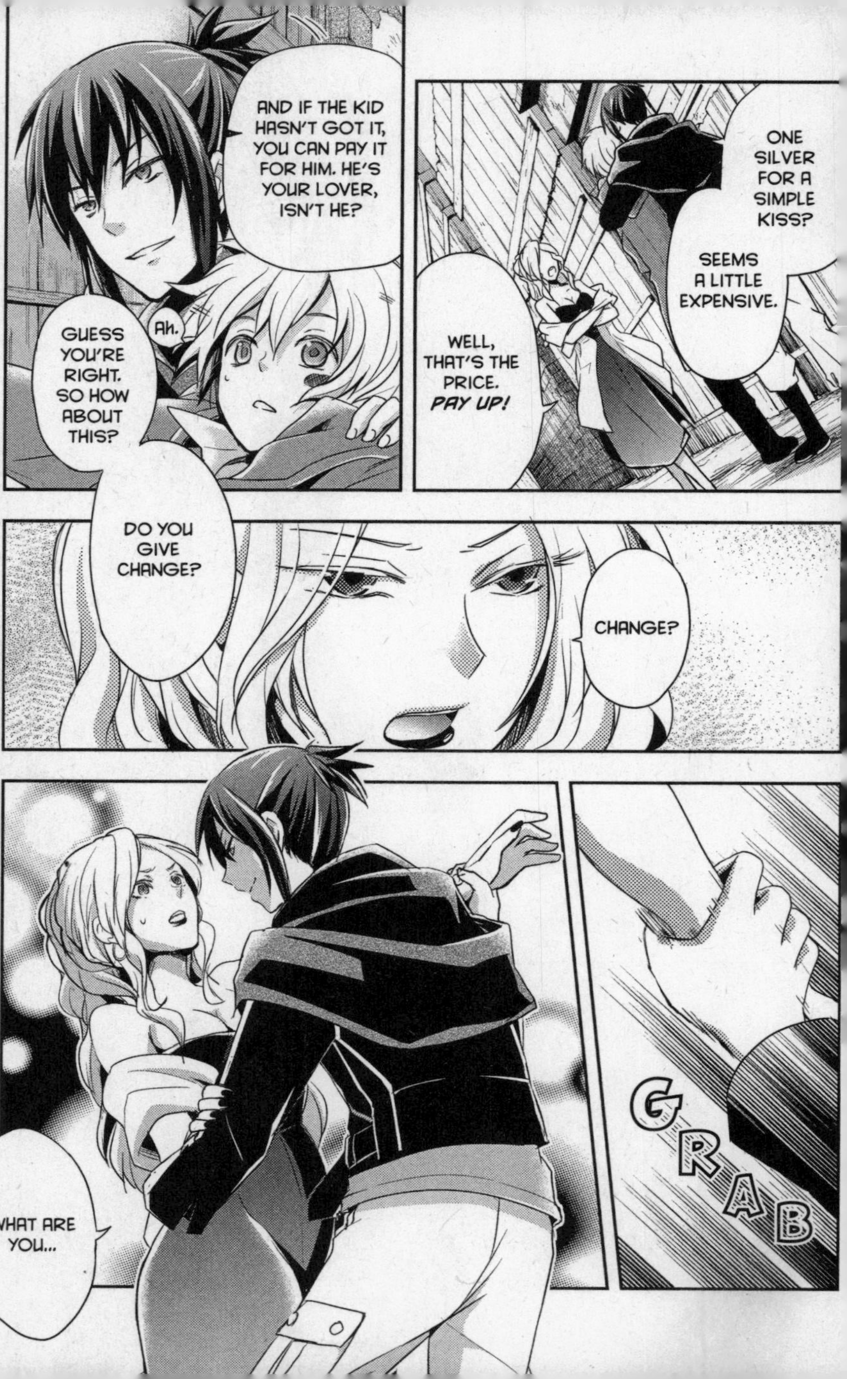
ONE SILVER FOR A SIMPLE KISS?
SEEMS A LITTLE EXPENSIVE.
WELL, THAT'S THE PRICE. *PAY UP!*
AND IF THE KID HASN'T GOT IT, YOU CAN PAY IT FOR HIM. HE'S YOUR LOVER, ISN'T HE?
Ah.
GUESS YOU'RE RIGHT. SO HOW ABOUT THIS?
DO YOU GIVE CHANGE?
CHANGE?
GRAB
WHAT ARE YOU...

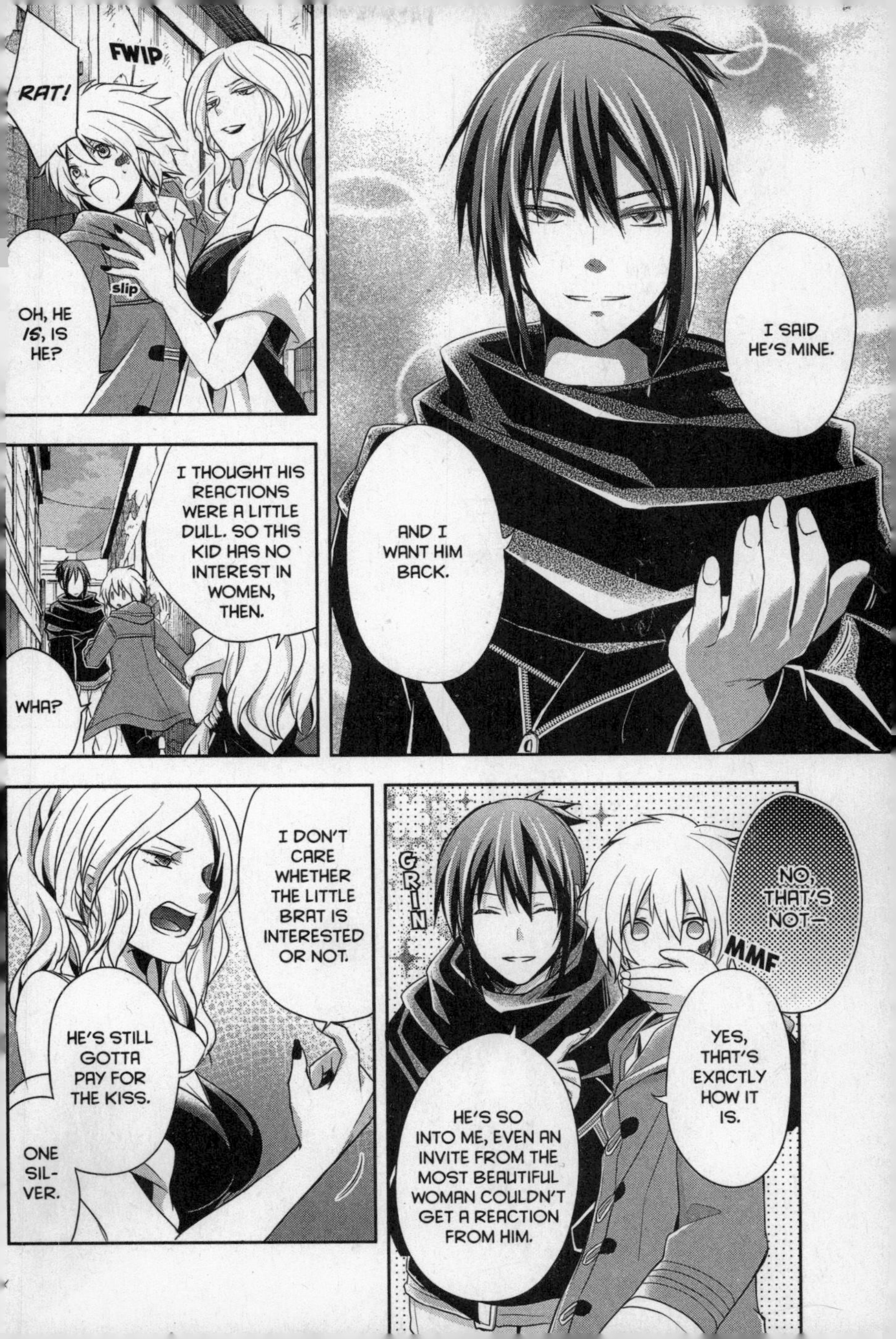
I SAID HE'S MINE.
AND I WANT HIM BACK.
FWIP
RAT!
slip
OH, HE *IS*, IS HE?
I THOUGHT HIS REACTIONS WERE A LITTLE DULL. SO THIS KID HAS NO INTEREST IN WOMEN, THEN.
WHA?
NO, THAT'S NOT—
MMF
YES, THAT'S EXACTLY HOW IT IS.
GRIN
HE'S SO INTO ME, EVEN AN INVITE FROM THE MOST BEAUTIFUL WOMAN COULDN'T GET A REACTION FROM HIM.
I DON'T CARE WHETHER THE LITTLE BRAT IS INTERESTED OR NOT.
HE'S STILL GOTTA PAY FOR THE KISS.
ONE SIL-VER.

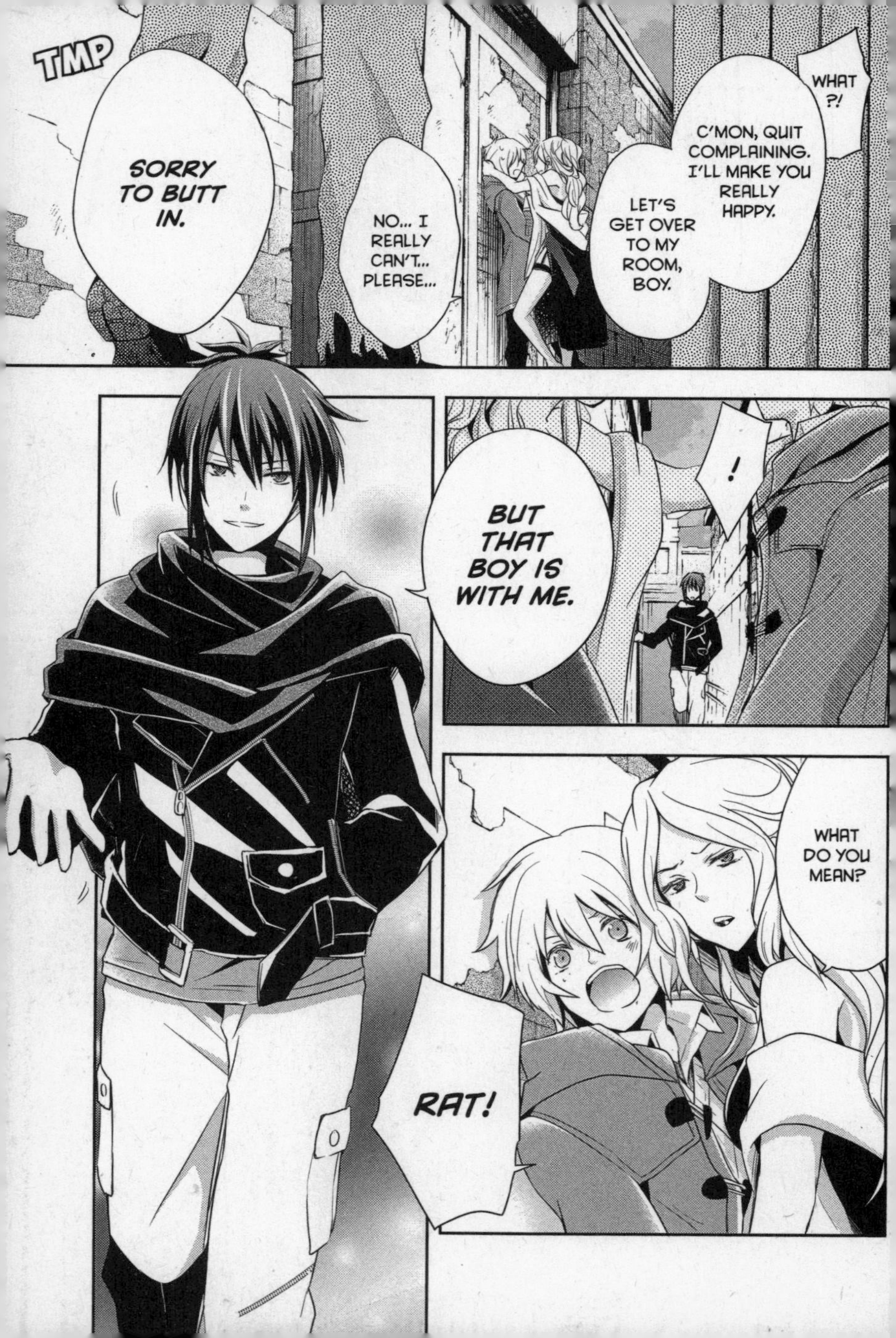
WHAT ?!
C'MON, QUIT COMPLAINING. I'LL MAKE YOU REALLY HAPPY.
LET'S GET OVER TO MY ROOM, BOY.
NO... I REALLY CAN'T... PLEASE...
TMP
SORRY TO BUTT IN.
!
BUT THAT BOY IS WITH ME.
WHAT DO YOU MEAN?
RAT!

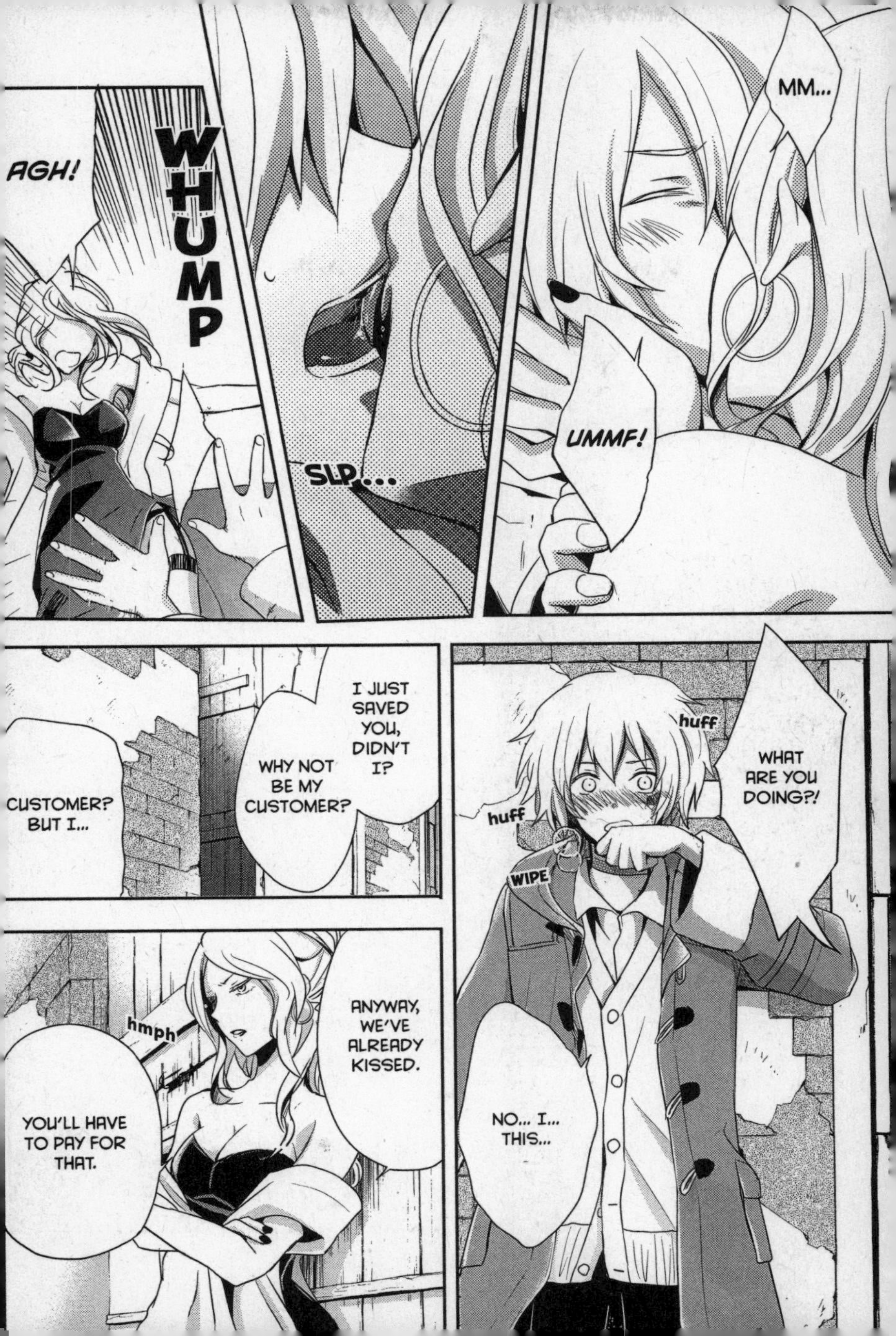
MM...
UMMF!
SLP...
AGH!
WHUMP
WHAT ARE YOU DOING?!
huff
huff
WIPE
NO... I... THIS...
I JUST SAVED YOU, DIDN'T I?
WHY NOT BE MY CUSTOMER?
CUSTOMER? BUT I...
ANYWAY, WE'VE ALREADY KISSED.
hmph
YOU'LL HAVE TO PAY FOR THAT.

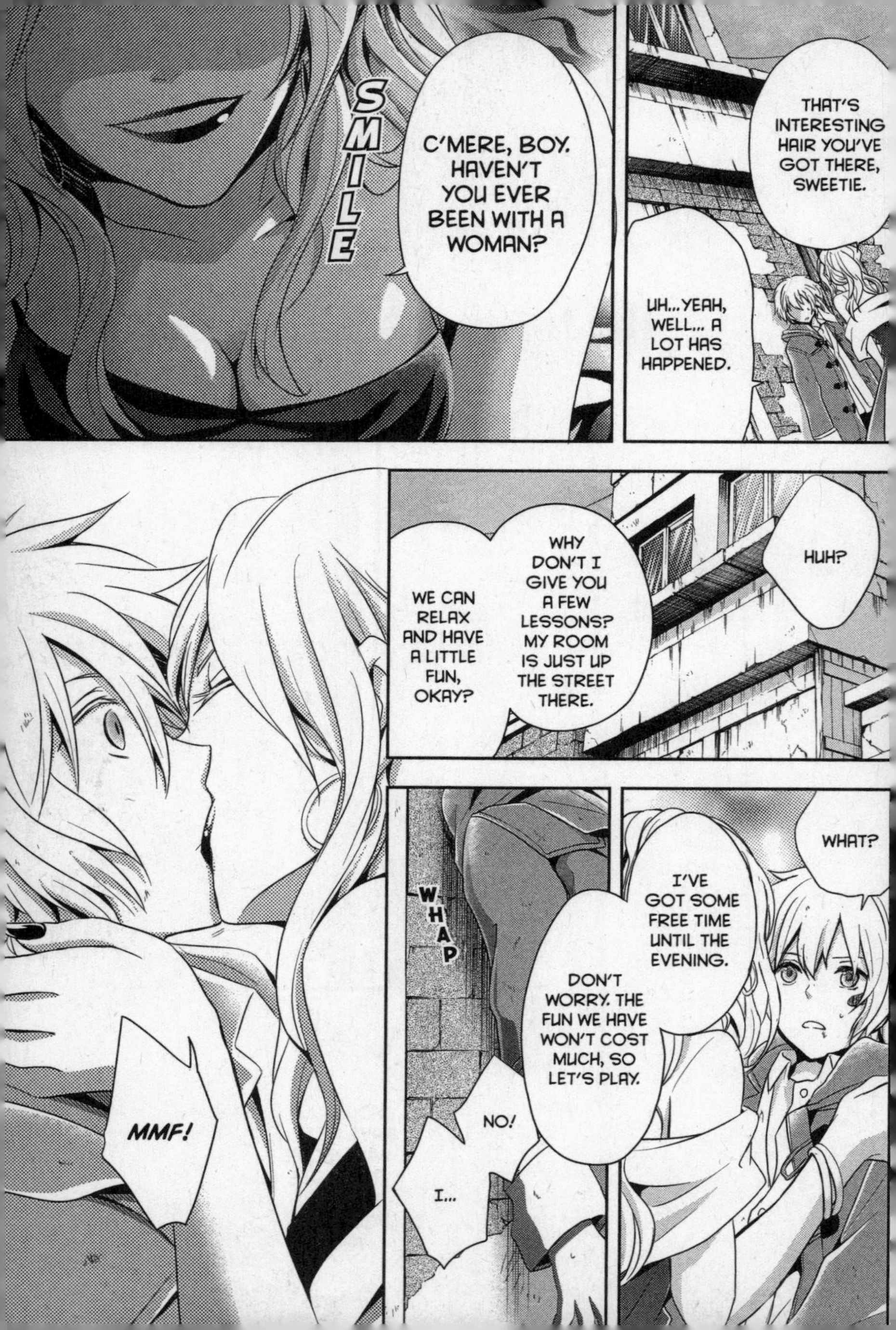
THAT'S INTERESTING HAIR YOU'VE GOT THERE, SWEETIE.
UH...YEAH, WELL... A LOT HAS HAPPENED.
SMILE
C'MERE, BOY. HAVEN'T YOU EVER BEEN WITH A WOMAN?
HUH?
WHY DON'T I GIVE YOU A FEW LESSONS? MY ROOM IS JUST UP THE STREET THERE.
WE CAN RELAX AND HAVE A LITTLE FUN, OKAY?
WHAT?
I'VE GOT SOME FREE TIME UNTIL THE EVENING.
DON'T WORRY. THE FUN WE HAVE WON'T COST MUCH, SO LET'S PLAY.
WHAP
NO!
I...
MMF!

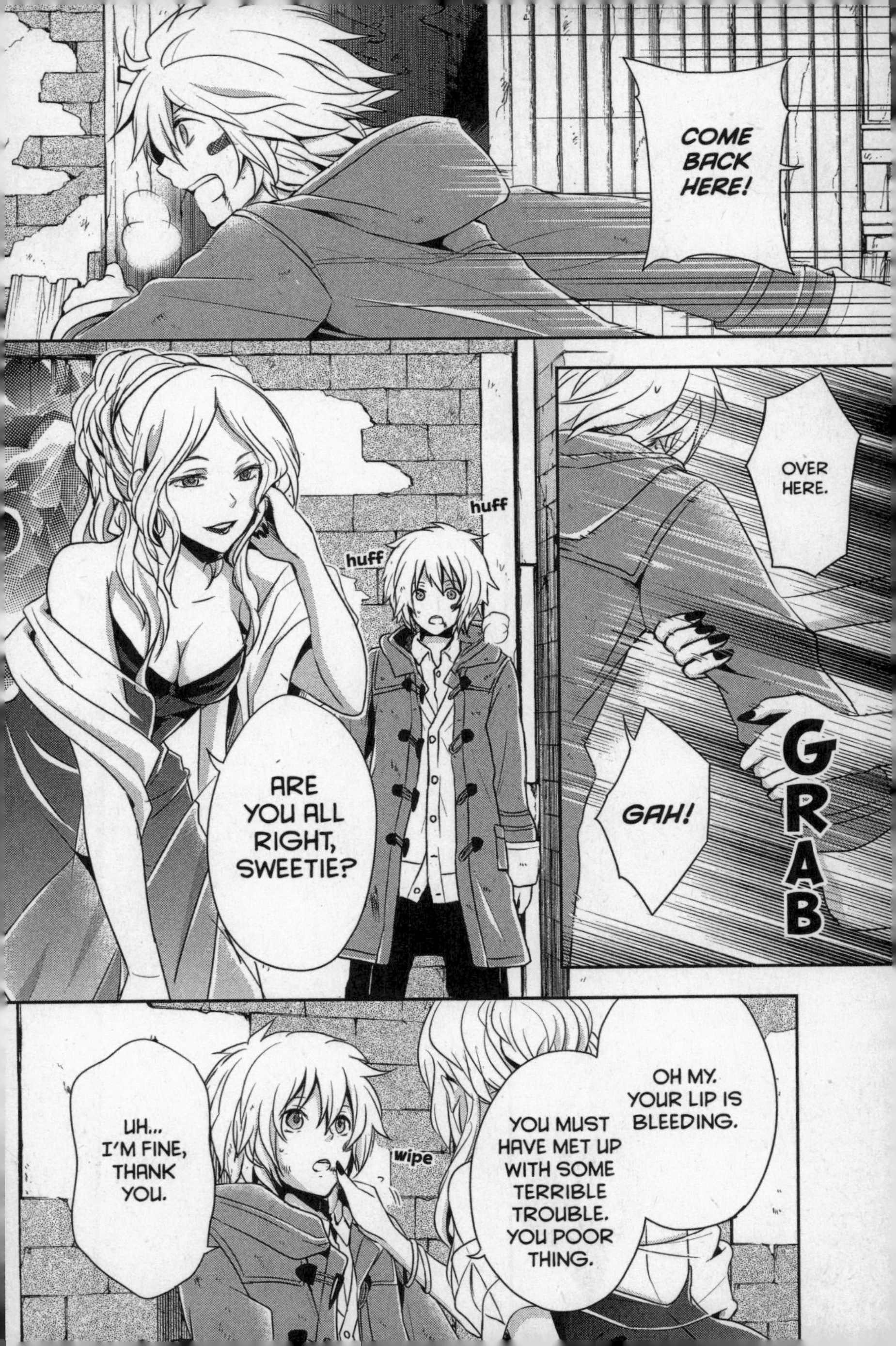
COME BACK HERE!
OVER HERE.
GAH!
GRAB
huff
huff
ARE YOU ALL RIGHT, SWEETIE?
OH MY. YOUR LIP IS BLEEDING.
YOU MUST HAVE MET UP WITH SOME TERRIBLE TROUBLE. YOU POOR THING.
wipe
UH... I'M FINE, THANK YOU.

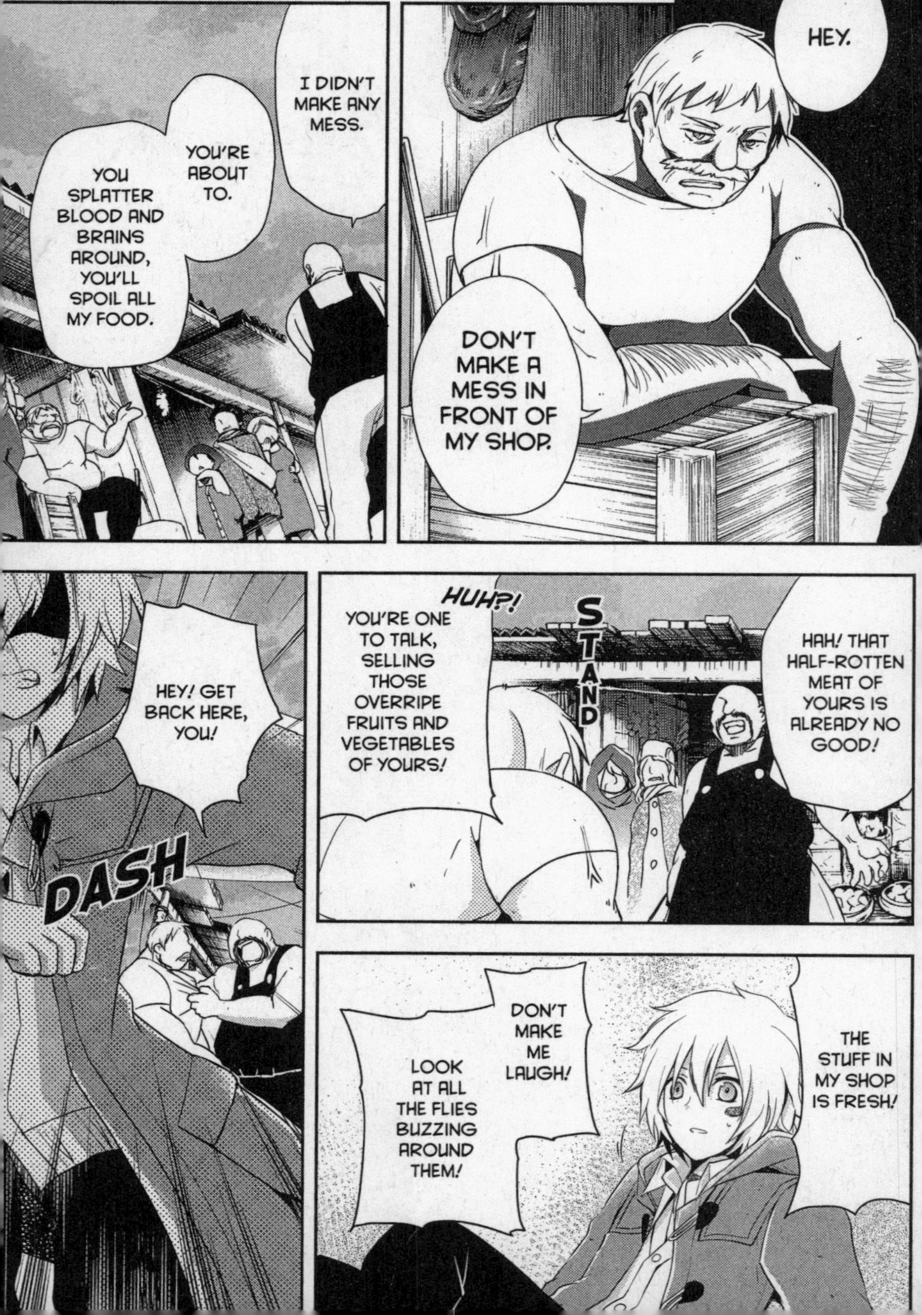
HEY.
DON'T MAKE A MESS IN FRONT OF MY SHOP.
I DIDN'T MAKE ANY MESS.
YOU'RE ABOUT TO.
YOU SPLATTER BLOOD AND BRAINS AROUND, YOU'LL SPOIL ALL MY FOOD.
HAH! THAT HALF-ROTTEN MEAT OF YOURS IS ALREADY NO GOOD!
STAND
HUH?!
YOU'RE ONE TO TALK, SELLING THOSE OVERRIPE FRUITS AND VEGETABLES OF YOURS!
THE STUFF IN MY SHOP IS FRESH!
DON'T MAKE ME LAUGH!
LOOK AT ALL THE FLIES BUZZING AROUND THEM!
HEY! GET BACK HERE, YOU!
DASH

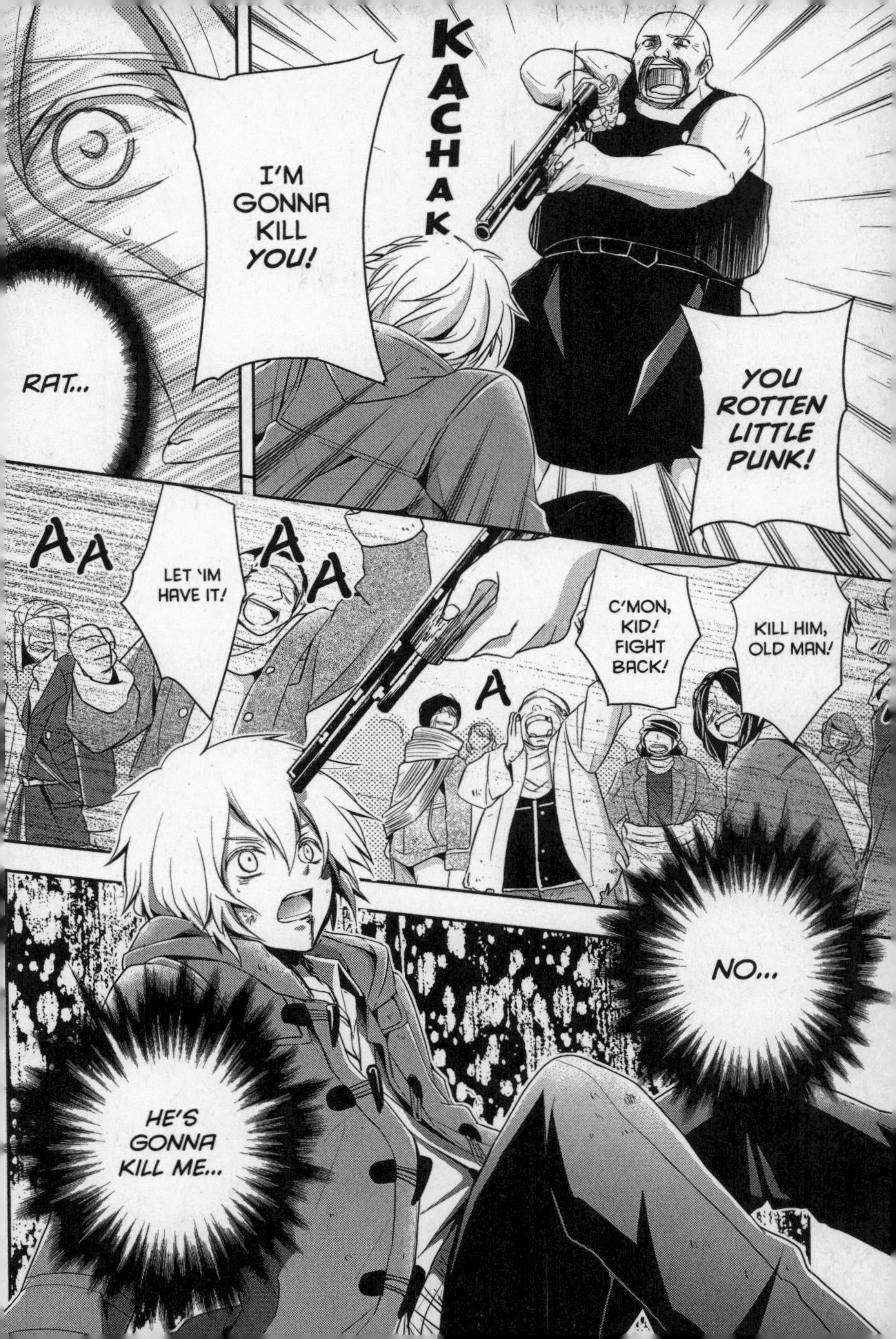
KACHAK
YOU ROTTEN LITTLE PUNK!
I'M GONNA KILL YOU!
RAT...
KILL HIM, OLD MAN!
C'MON, KID! FIGHT BACK!
A
AAA
LET 'IM HAVE IT!
AA
NO...
HE'S GONNA KILL ME...

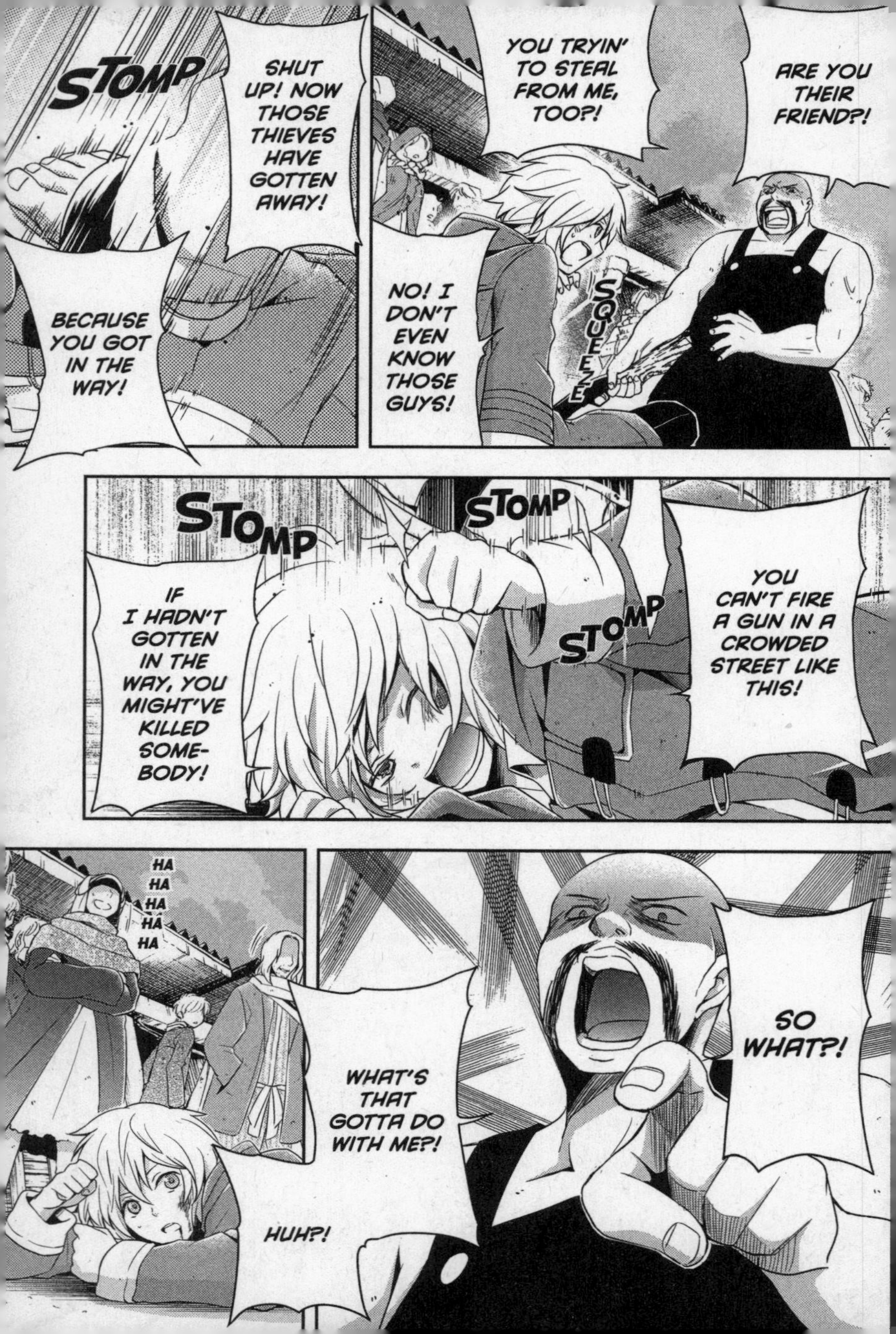
ARE YOU THEIR FRIEND?!
YOU TRYIN' TO STEAL FROM ME, TOO?!
SQUEEZE
NO! I DON'T EVEN KNOW THOSE GUYS!
SHUT UP! NOW THOSE THIEVES HAVE GOTTEN AWAY!
STOMP
BECAUSE YOU GOT IN THE WAY!
YOU CAN'T FIRE A GUN IN A CROWDED STREET LIKE THIS!
STOMP
STOMP
STOMP
IF I HADN'T GOTTEN IN THE WAY, YOU MIGHT'VE KILLED SOME-BODY!
SO WHAT?!
WHAT'S THAT GOTTA DO WITH ME?!
HA HA HA HA HA
HUH?!

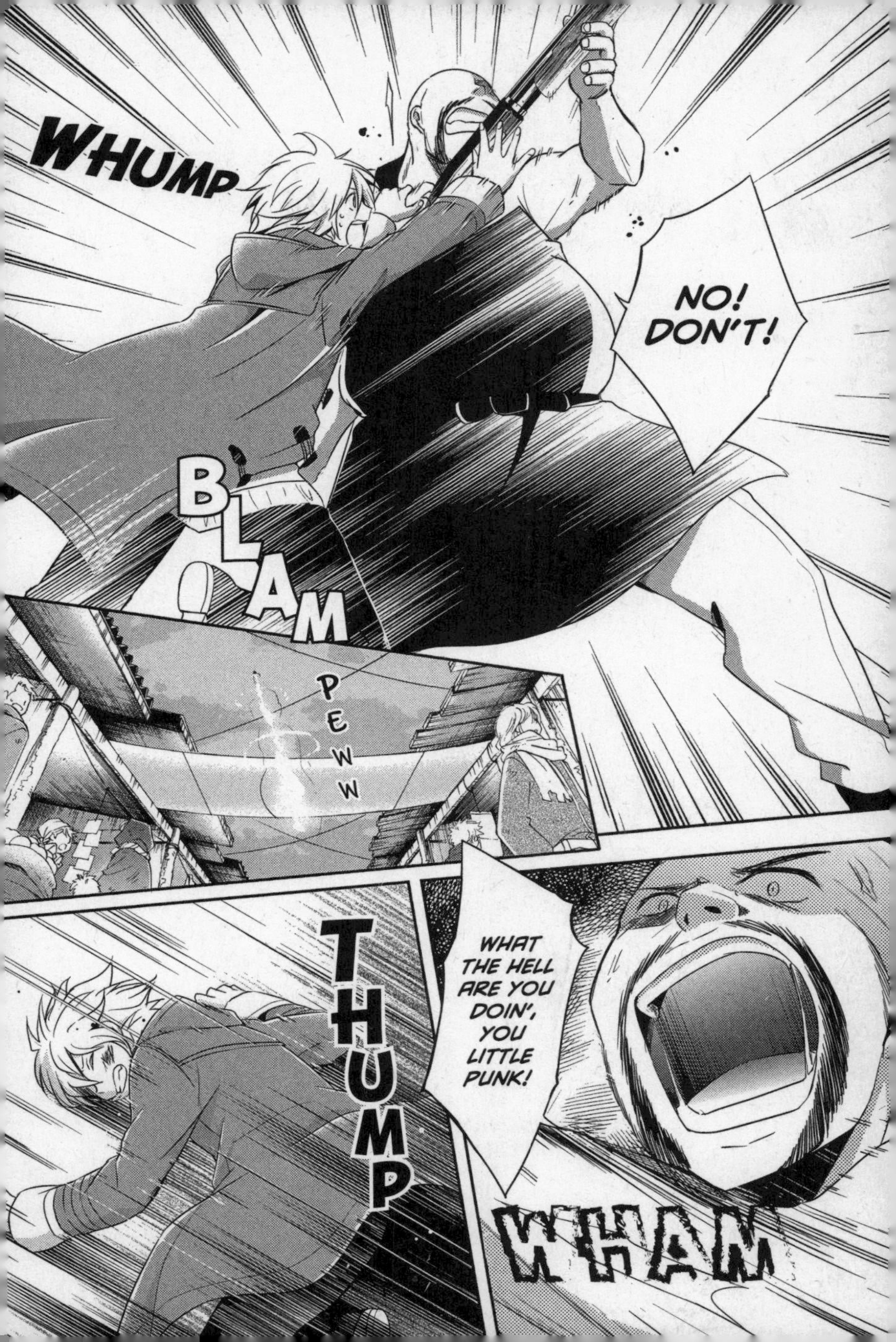
NO! DON'T!
WHUMP
BLAM
PEWW
WHAT THE HELL ARE YOU DOIN', YOU LITTLE PUNK!
WHAM
THUMP

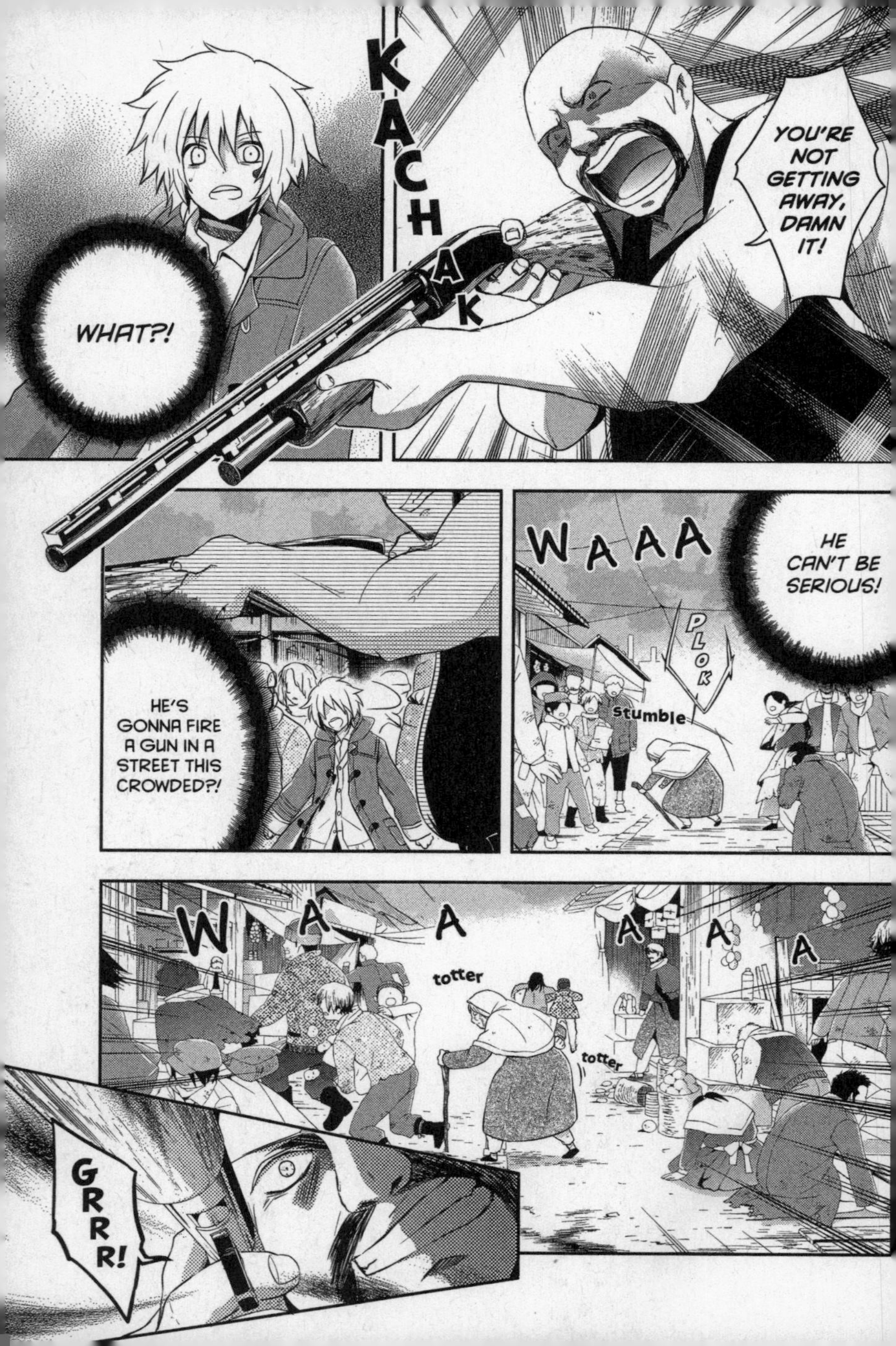
YOU'RE NOT GETTING AWAY, DAMN IT!
KACHAK
WHAT?!
HE CAN'T BE SERIOUS!
WAAA
PLOK
stumble
HE'S GONNA FIRE A GUN IN A STREET THIS CROWDED?!
WAAAAAA
totter
totter
GRRR!

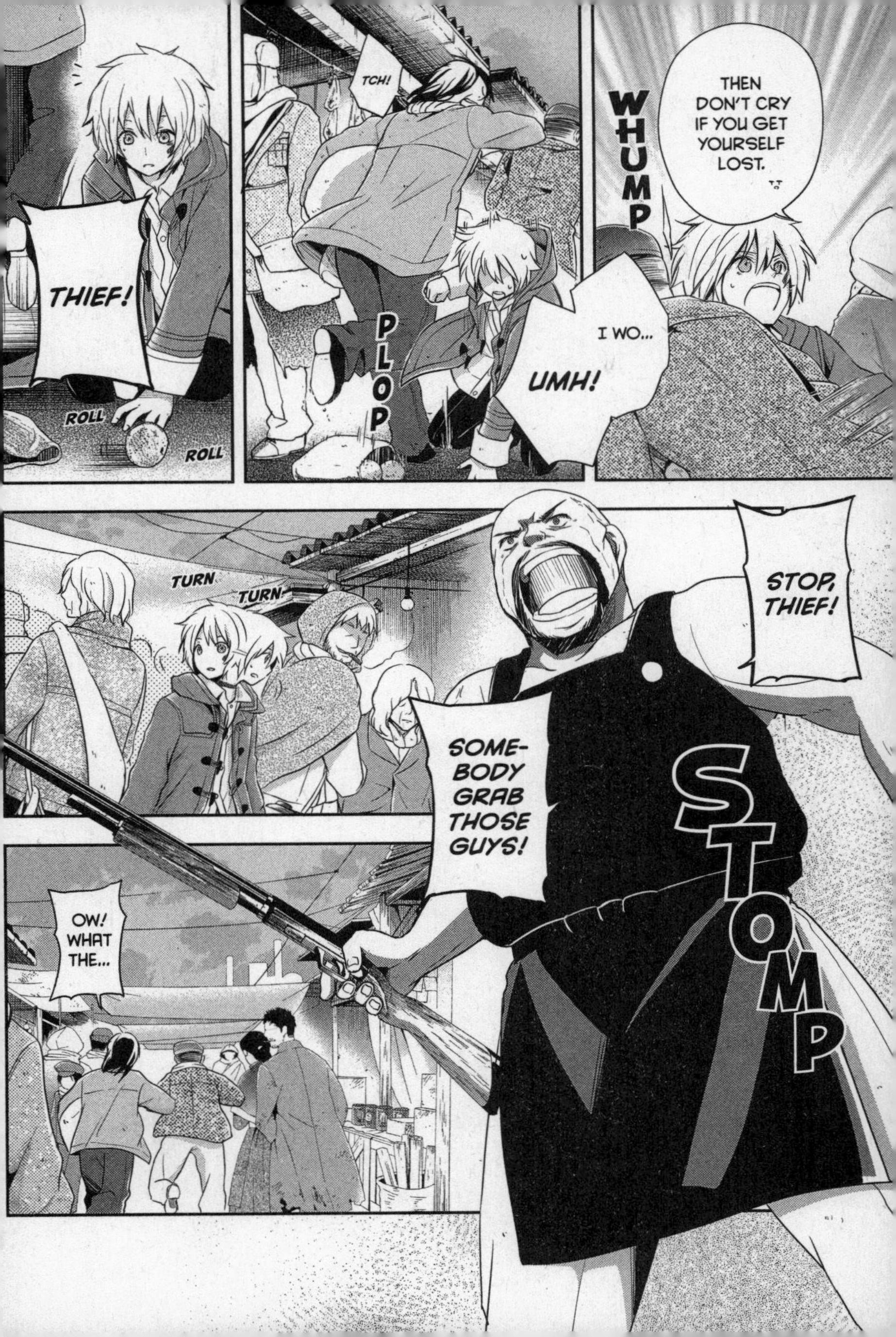
THEN DON'T CRY IF YOU GET YOURSELF LOST.
WHUMP
I WO...
UMH!
TCH!
PLOP
THIEF!
ROLL
ROLL
STOP, THIEF!
SOME-BODY GRAB THOSE GUYS!
STOMP
TURN
TURN
OW! WHAT THE...

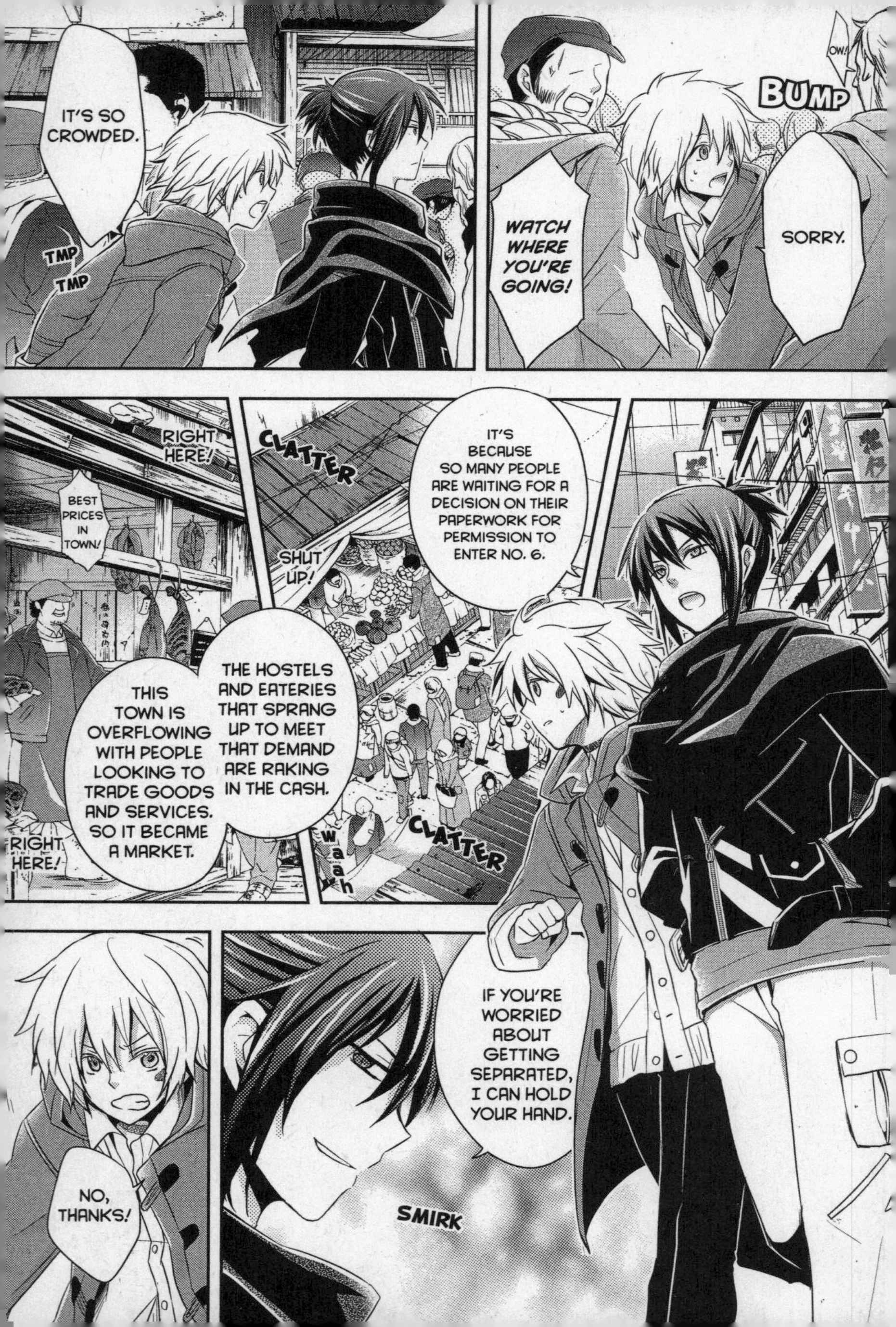
OW!
BUMP
WATCH WHERE YOU'RE GOING!
SORRY.
IT'S SO CROWDED.
TMP
TMP
IT'S BECAUSE SO MANY PEOPLE ARE WAITING FOR A DECISION ON THEIR PAPERWORK FOR PERMISSION TO ENTER NO. 6.
CLATTER
SHUT UP!
CLATTER
waah
THE HOSTELS AND EATERIES THAT SPRANG UP TO MEET THAT DEMAND ARE RAKING IN THE CASH.
THIS TOWN IS OVERFLOWING WITH PEOPLE LOOKING TO TRADE GOODS AND SERVICES. SO IT BECAME A MARKET.
RIGHT HERE!
BEST PRICES IN TOWN!
RIGHT HERE!
IF YOU'RE WORRIED ABOUT GETTING SEPARATED, I CAN HOLD YOUR HAND.
SMIRK
NO, THANKS!

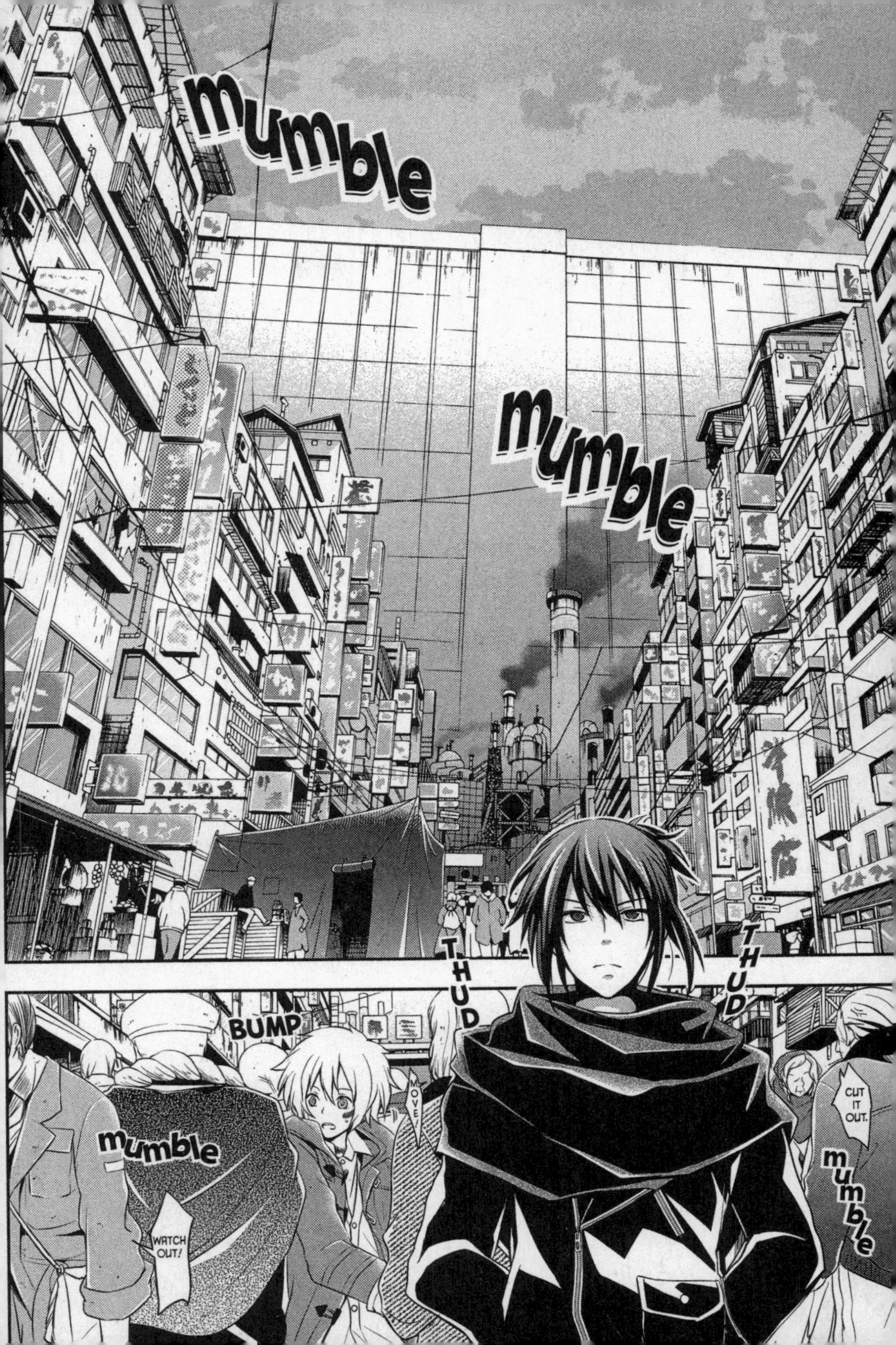
mumble
mumble
THUD
THUD
CUT IT OUT.
mumble
MOVE!
BUMP
mumble
WATCH OUT!

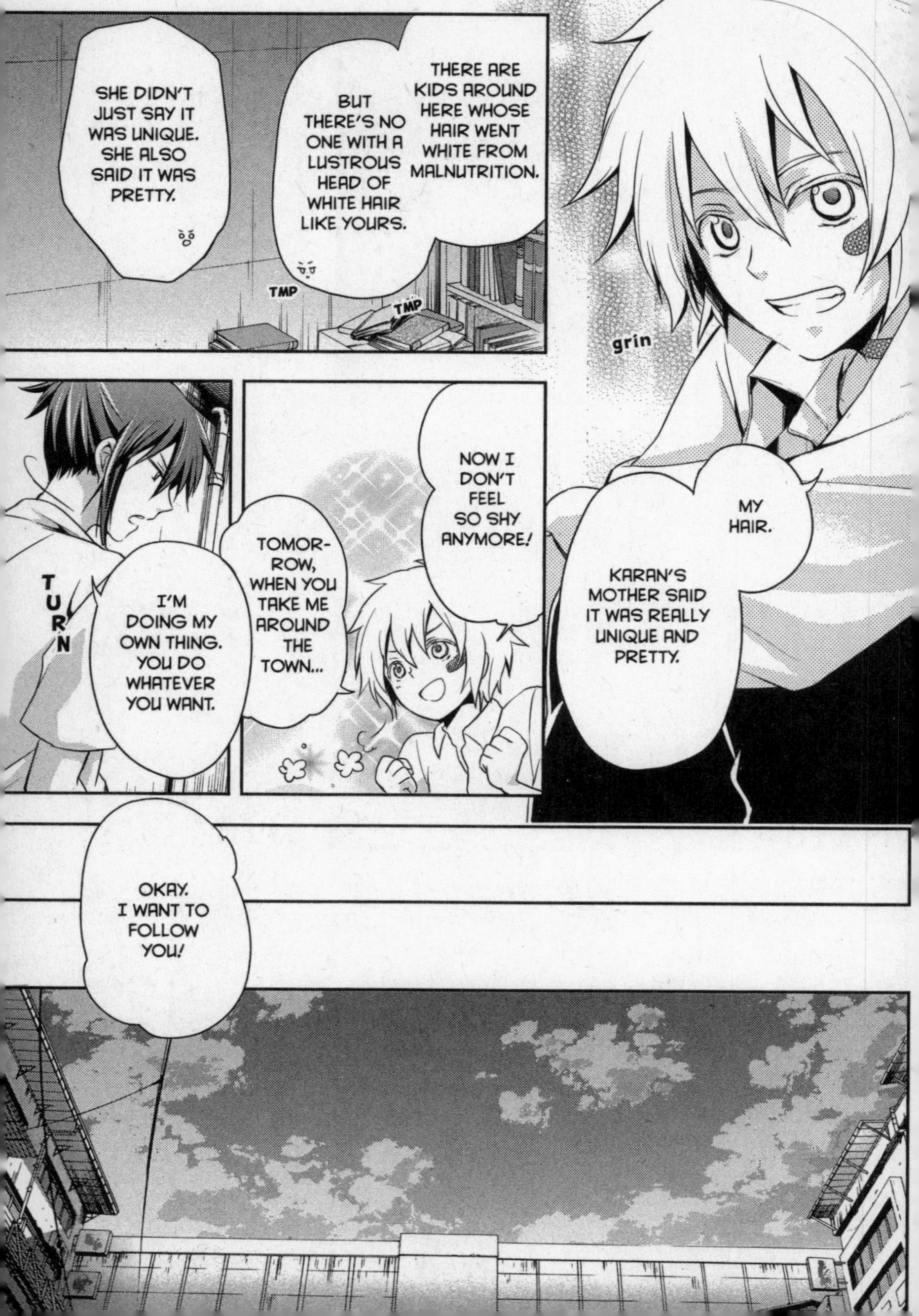

grin
MY HAIR.
KARAN'S MOTHER SAID IT WAS REALLY UNIQUE AND PRETTY.
THERE ARE KIDS AROUND HERE WHOSE HAIR WENT WHITE FROM MALNUTRITION.
BUT THERE'S NO ONE WITH A LUSTROUS HEAD OF WHITE HAIR LIKE YOURS.
TMP
TMP
SHE DIDN'T JUST SAY IT WAS UNIQUE. SHE ALSO SAID IT WAS PRETTY.
NOW I DON'T FEEL SO SHY ANYMORE!
TOMOR-ROW, WHEN YOU TAKE ME AROUND THE TOWN...
I'M DOING MY OWN THING. YOU DO WHATEVER YOU WANT.
TURN
OKAY. I WANT TO FOLLOW YOU!

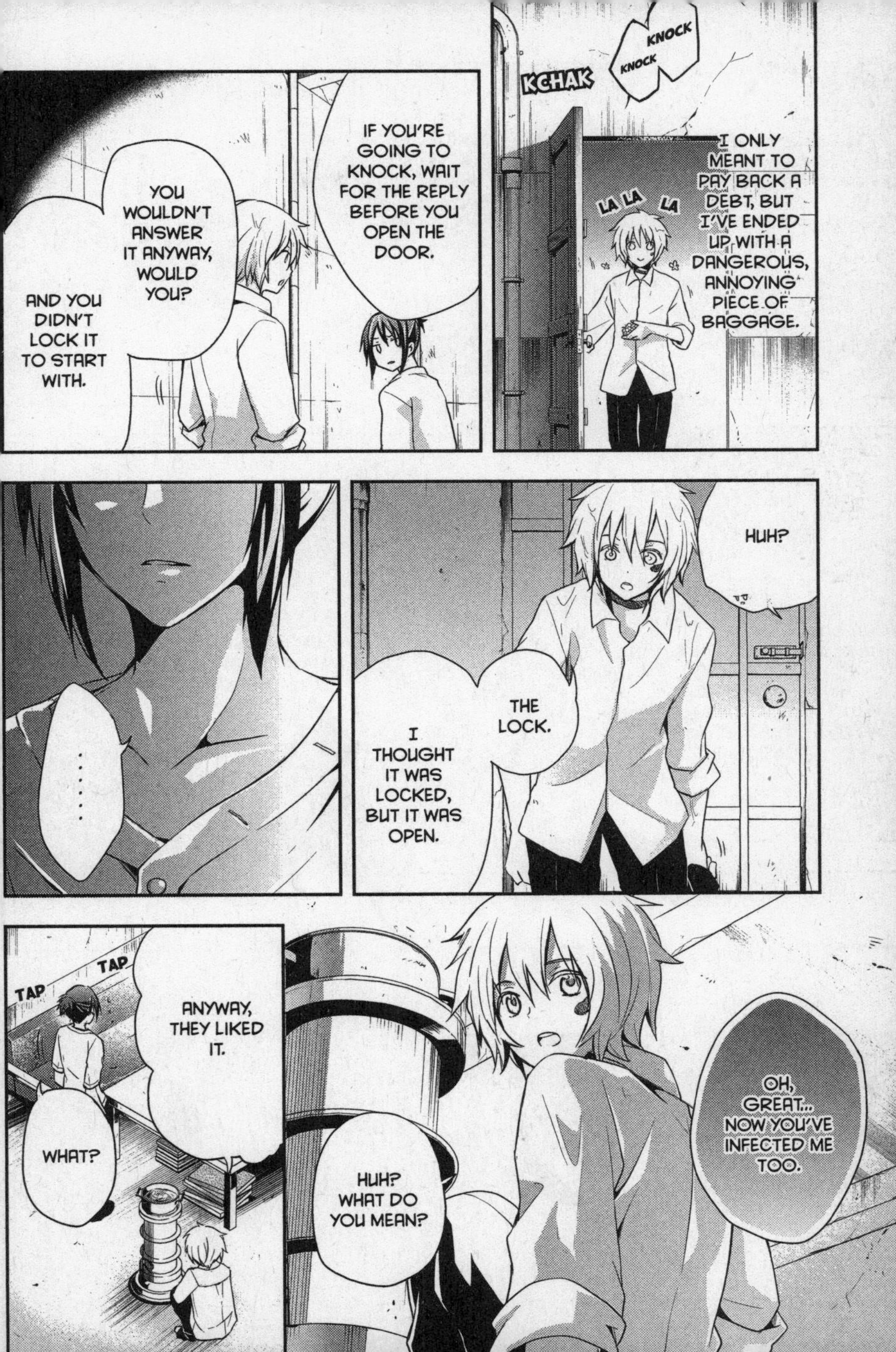
KNOCK KNOCK
KCHAK
LA LA LA
I ONLY MEANT TO PAY BACK A DEBT, BUT I'VE ENDED UP WITH A DANGEROUS, ANNOYING PIECE OF BAGGAGE.
IF YOU'RE GOING TO KNOCK, WAIT FOR THE REPLY BEFORE YOU OPEN THE DOOR.
YOU WOULDN'T ANSWER IT ANYWAY, WOULD YOU?
AND YOU DIDN'T LOCK IT TO START WITH.
HUH?
THE LOCK.
I THOUGHT IT WAS LOCKED, BUT IT WAS OPEN.
......
OH, GREAT... NOW YOU'VE INFECTED ME TOO.
HUH? WHAT DO YOU MEAN?
TAP TAP
ANYWAY, THEY LIKED IT.
WHAT?

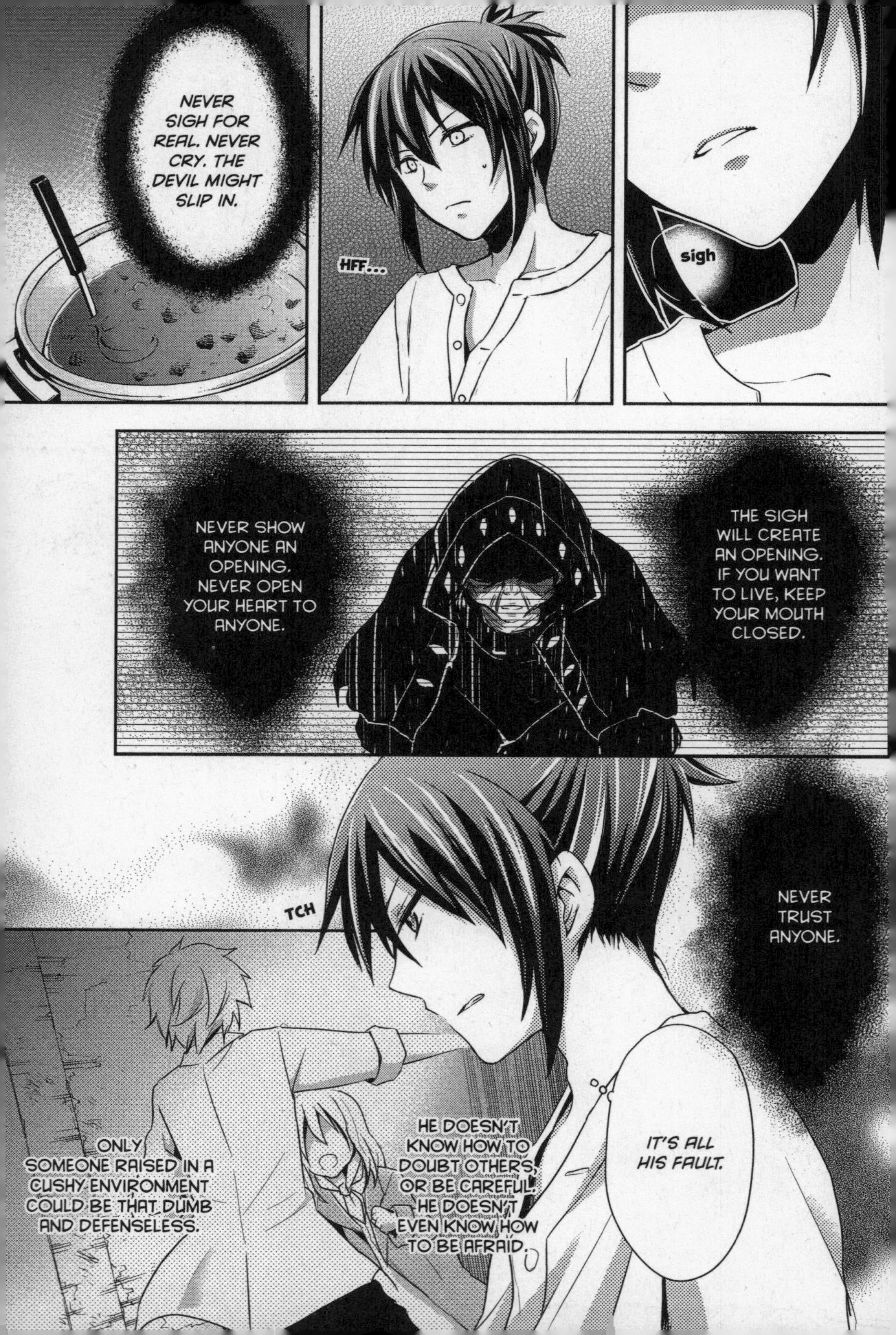
sigh
HFF...
NEVER SIGH FOR REAL. NEVER CRY. THE DEVIL MIGHT SLIP IN.
THE SIGH WILL CREATE AN OPENING. IF YOU WANT TO LIVE, KEEP YOUR MOUTH CLOSED.
NEVER SHOW ANYONE AN OPENING. NEVER OPEN YOUR HEART TO ANYONE.
NEVER TRUST ANYONE.
TCH
IT'S ALL HIS FAULT.
HE DOESN'T KNOW HOW TO DOUBT OTHERS, OR BE CAREFUL. HE DOESN'T EVEN KNOW HOW TO BE AFRAID.
ONLY SOMEONE RAISED IN A CUSHY ENVIRONMENT COULD BE THAT DUMB AND DEFENSELESS.

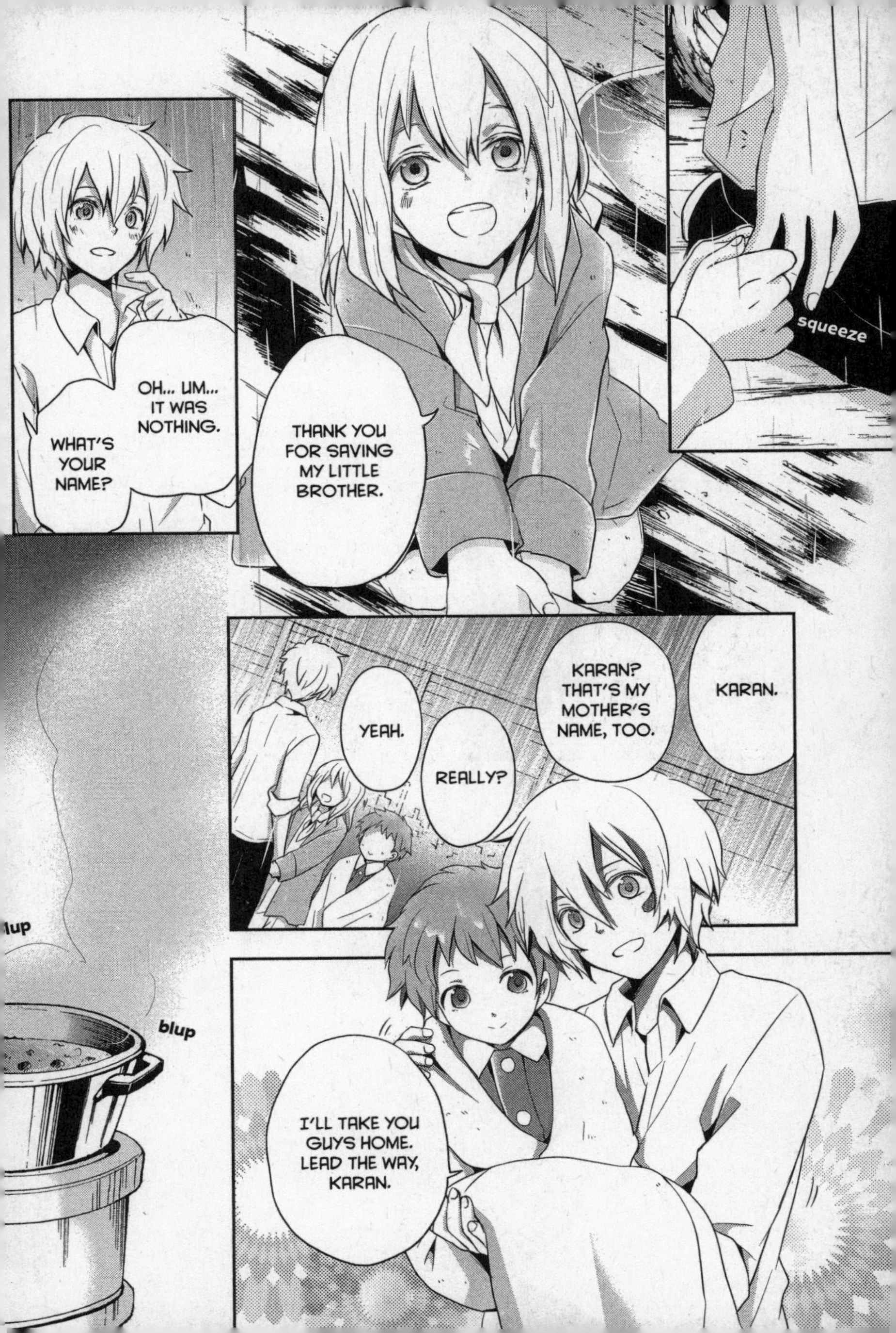
squeeze
THANK YOU FOR SAVING MY LITTLE BROTHER.
OH... UM... IT WAS NOTHING.
WHAT'S YOUR NAME?
KARAN.
KARAN? THAT'S MY MOTHER'S NAME, TOO.
REALLY?
YEAH.
I'LL TAKE YOU GUYS HOME. LEAD THE WAY, KARAN.
blup

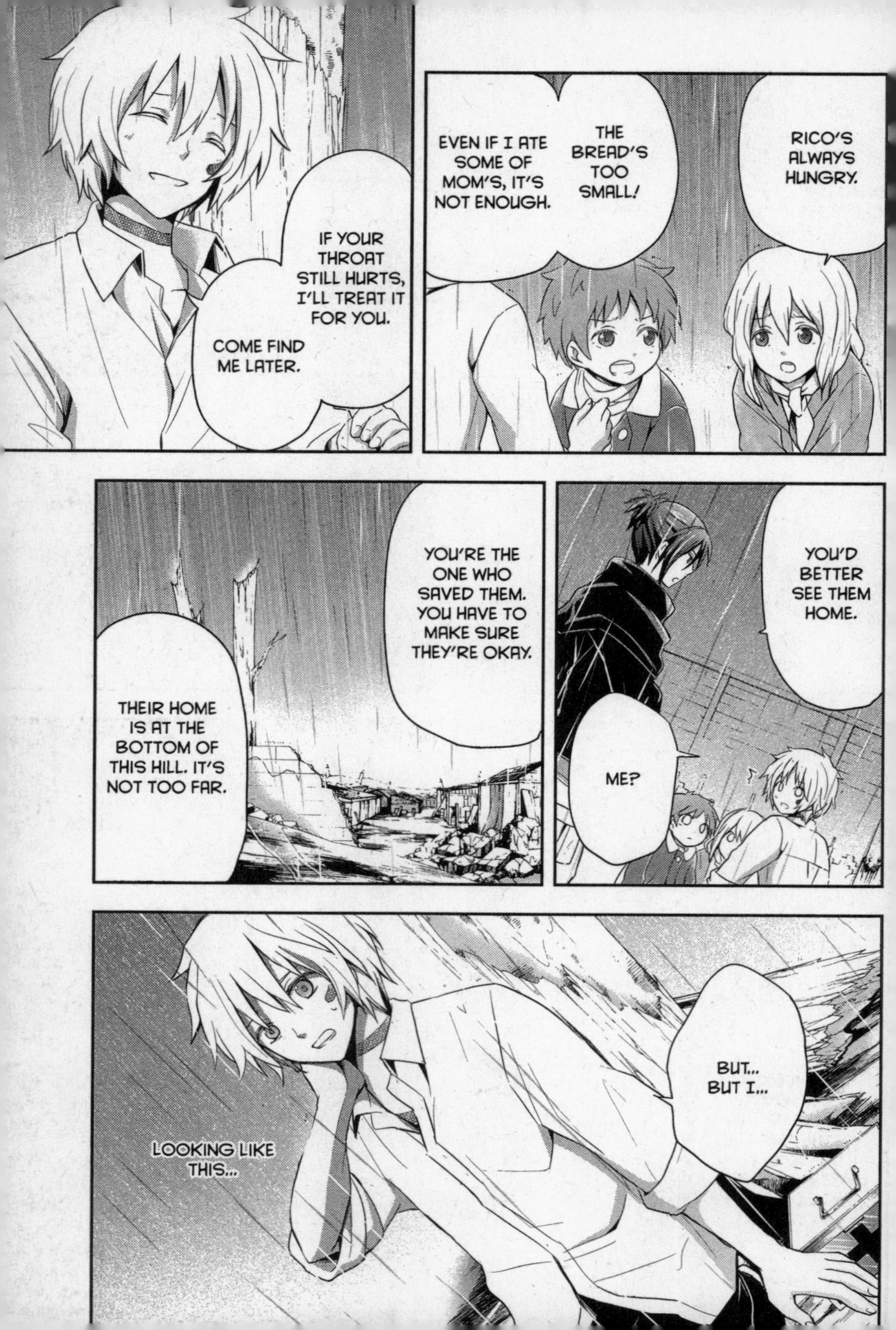
RICO'S ALWAYS HUNGRY.
THE BREAD'S TOO SMALL!
EVEN IF I ATE SOME OF MOM'S, IT'S NOT ENOUGH.
IF YOUR THROAT STILL HURTS, I'LL TREAT IT FOR YOU.
COME FIND ME LATER.
YOU'D BETTER SEE THEM HOME.
ME?
YOU'RE THE ONE WHO SAVED THEM. YOU HAVE TO MAKE SURE THEY'RE OKAY.
THEIR HOME IS AT THE BOTTOM OF THIS HILL. IT'S NOT TOO FAR.
BUT... BUT I...
LOOKING LIKE THIS...

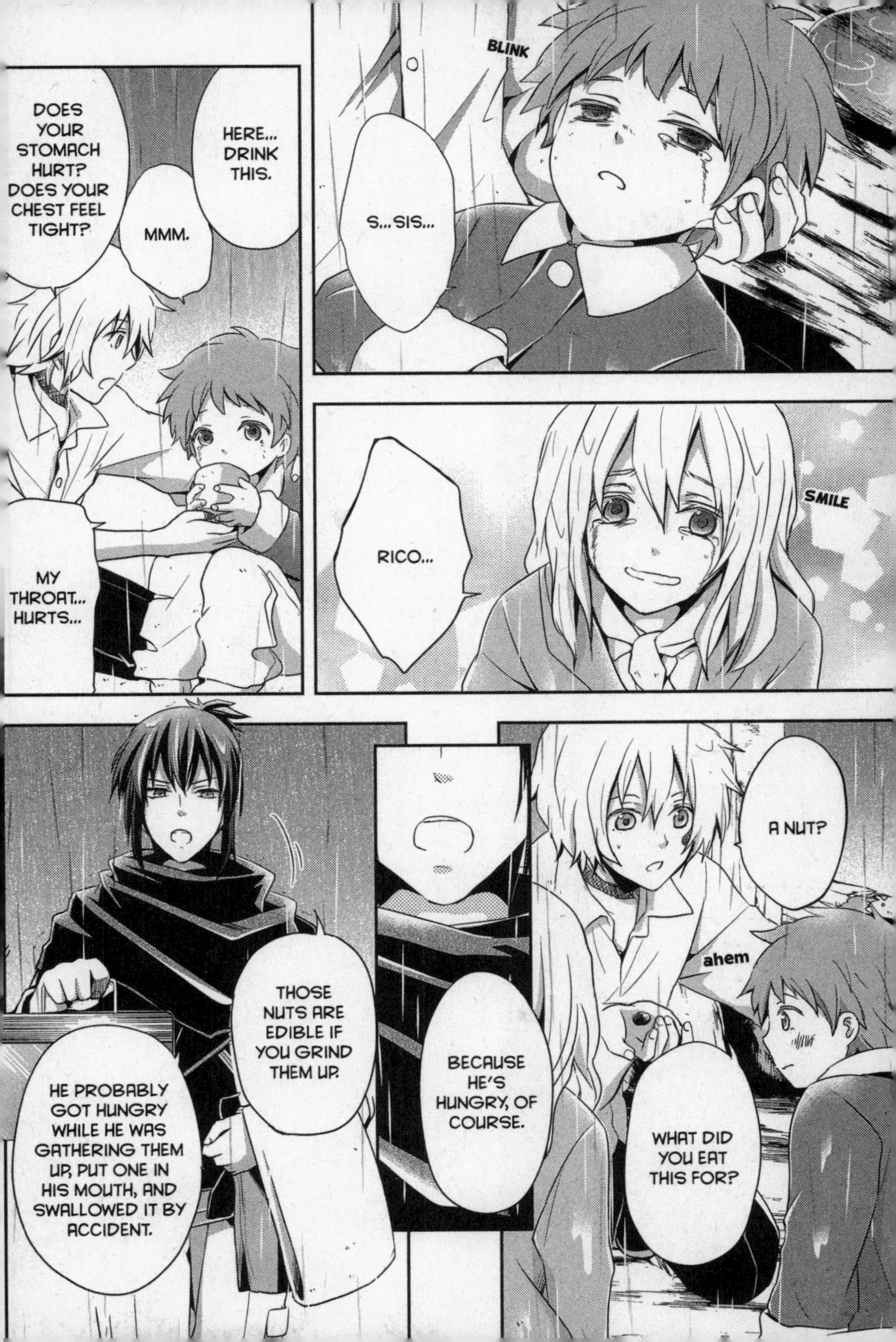
BLINK
S...SIS...
SMILE
RICO...
HERE... DRINK THIS.
DOES YOUR STOMACH HURT? DOES YOUR CHEST FEEL TIGHT?
MMM.
MY THROAT... HURTS...
A NUT?
ahem
WHAT DID YOU EAT THIS FOR?
BECAUSE HE'S HUNGRY, OF COURSE.
THOSE NUTS ARE EDIBLE IF YOU GRIND THEM UP.
HE PROBABLY GOT HUNGRY WHILE HE WAS GATHERING THEM UP, PUT ONE IN HIS MOUTH, AND SWALLOWED IT BY ACCIDENT.

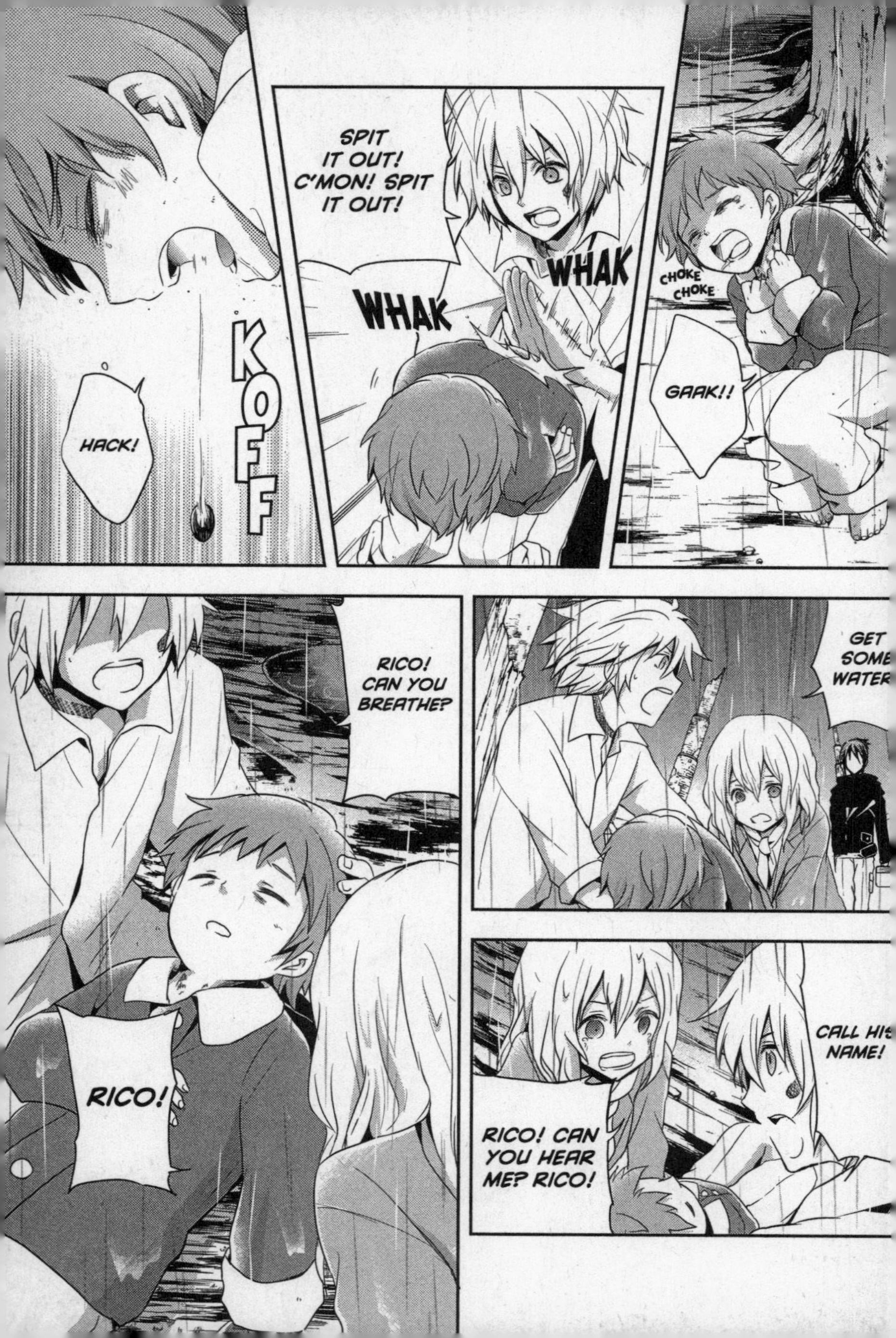
CHOKE CHOKE
GAAK!!
SPIT IT OUT! C'MON! SPIT IT OUT!
WHAK
WHAK
HACK!
KOFF
GET SOME WATER
CALL HIS NAME!
RICO! CAN YOU HEAR ME? RICO!
RICO! CAN YOU BREATHE?
RICO!

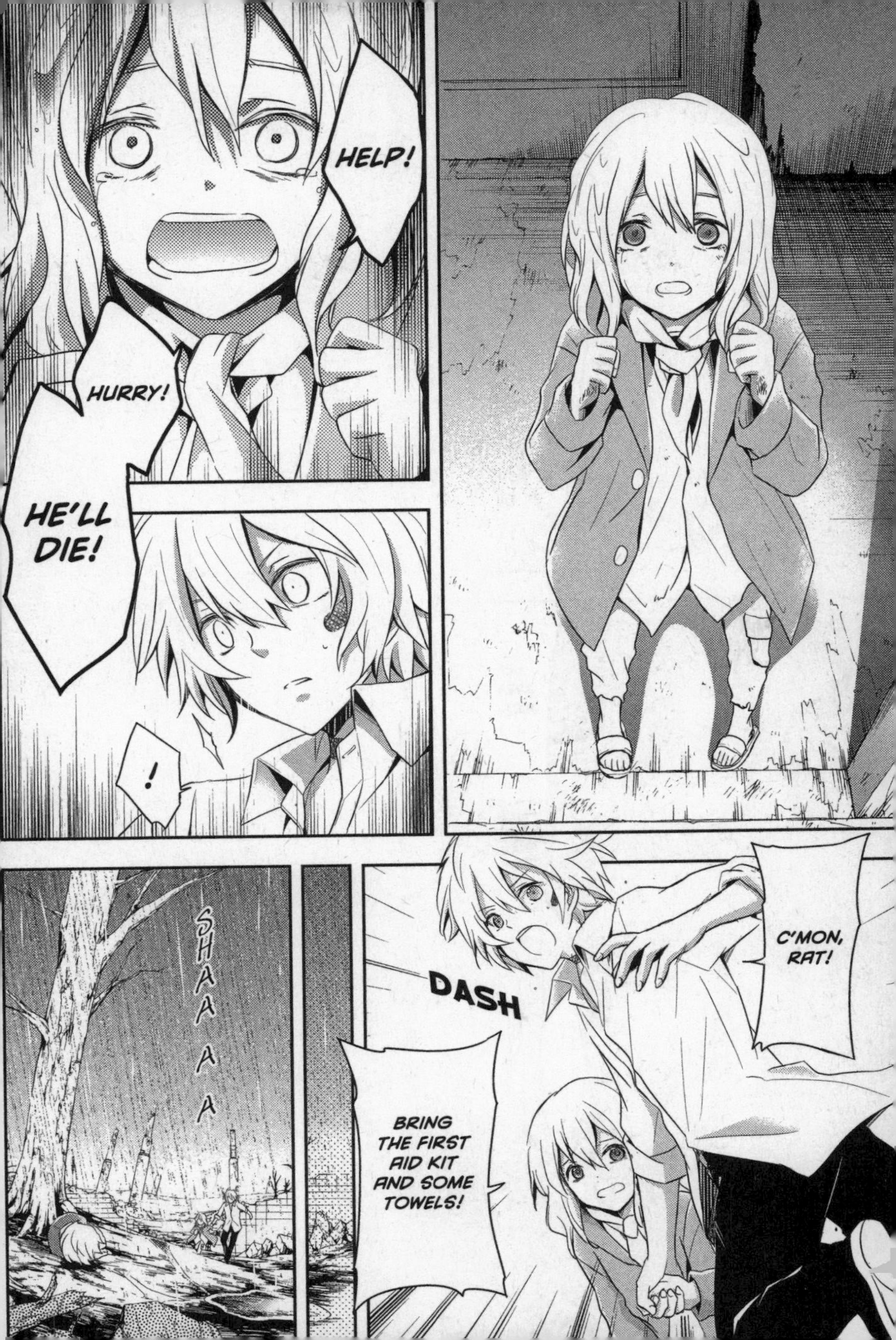
HELP!
HURRY!
HE'LL DIE!
!
C'MON, RAT!
DASH
BRING THE FIRST AID KIT AND SOME TOWELS!
SHAAAAA

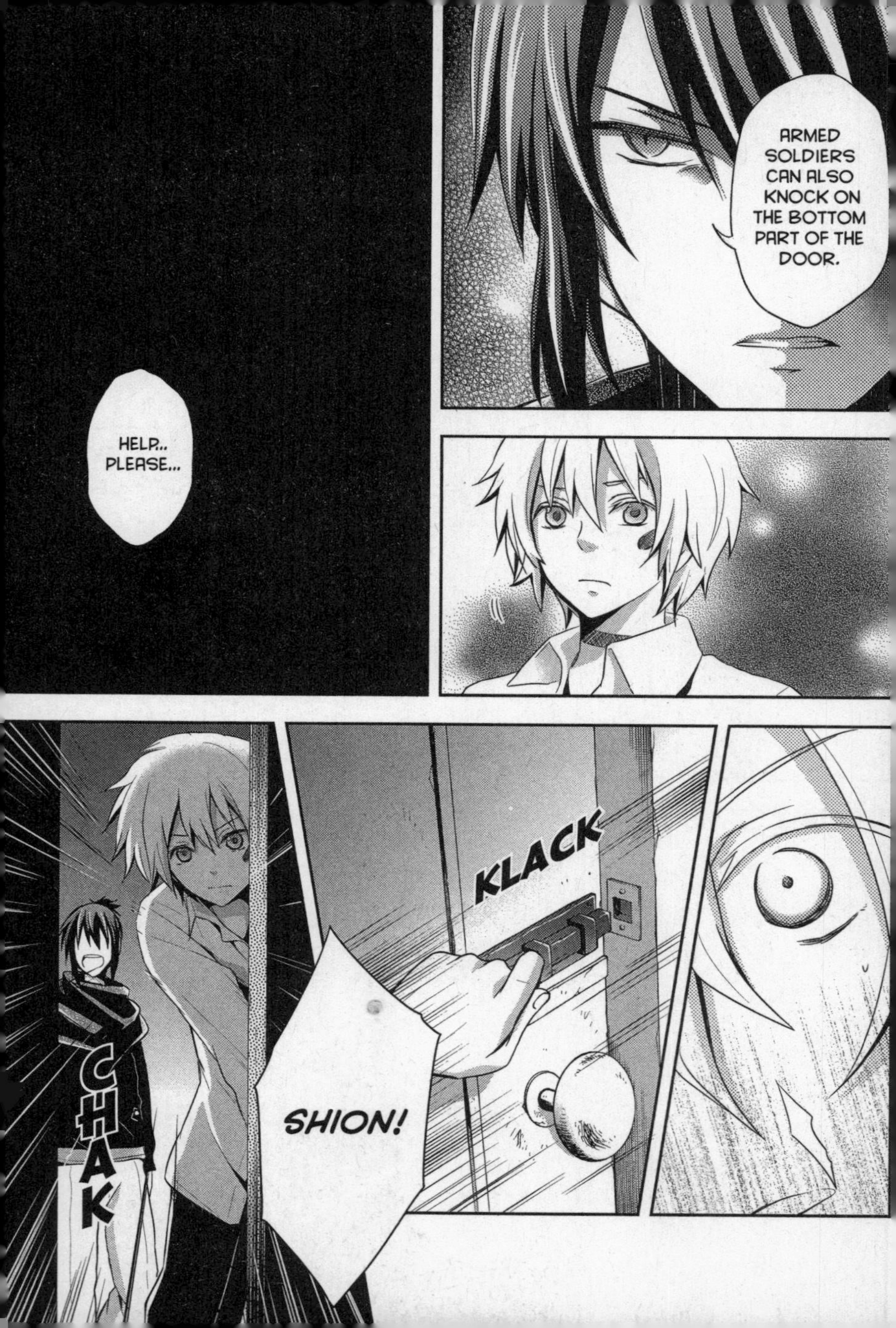
ARMED SOLDIERS CAN ALSO KNOCK ON THE BOTTOM PART OF THE DOOR.
HELP... PLEASE...
KLACK
SHION!
CHAK

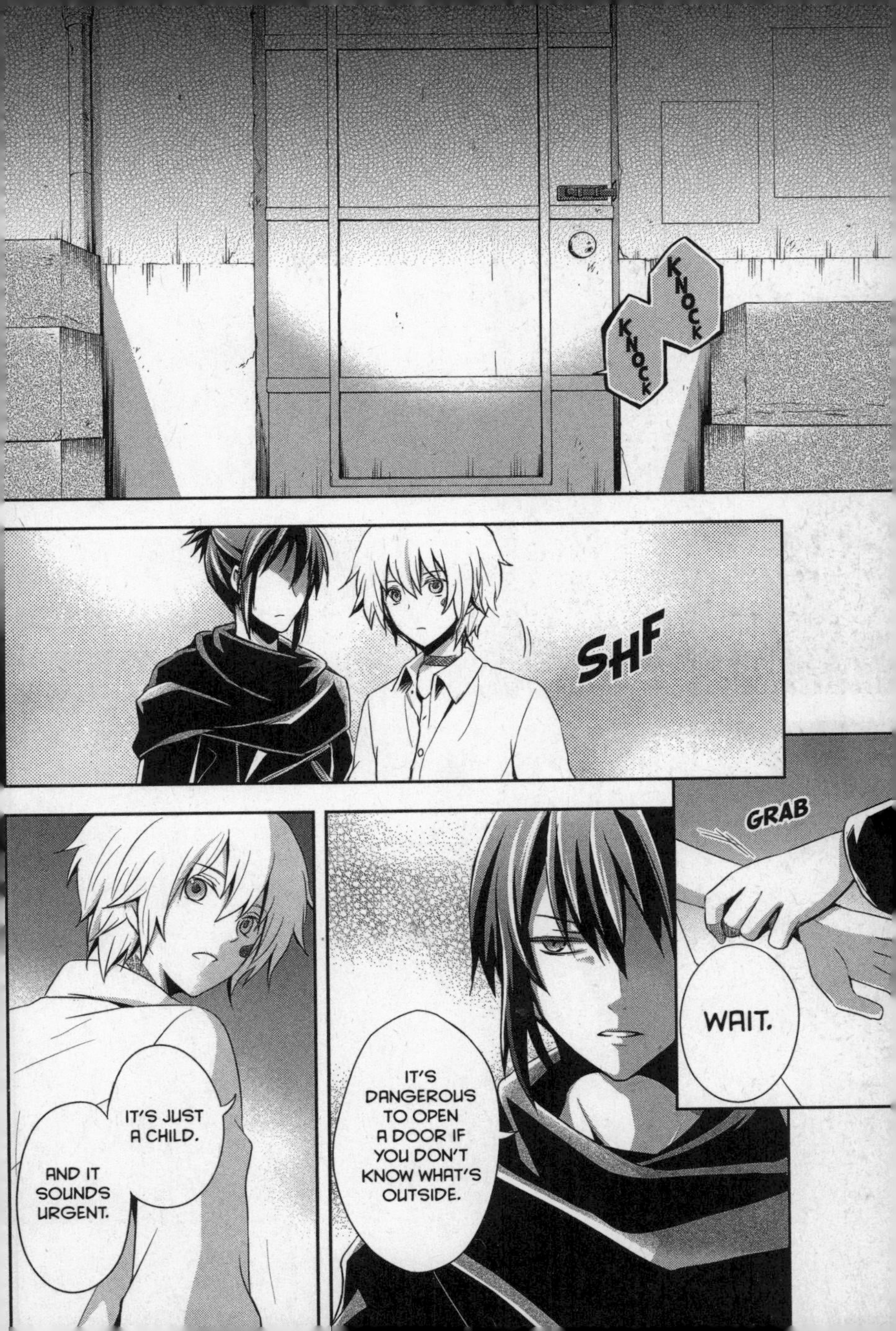
KNOCK KNOCK
SHF
GRAB
WAIT.
IT'S DANGEROUS TO OPEN A DOOR IF YOU DON'T KNOW WHAT'S OUTSIDE.
IT'S JUST A CHILD.
AND IT SOUNDS URGENT.

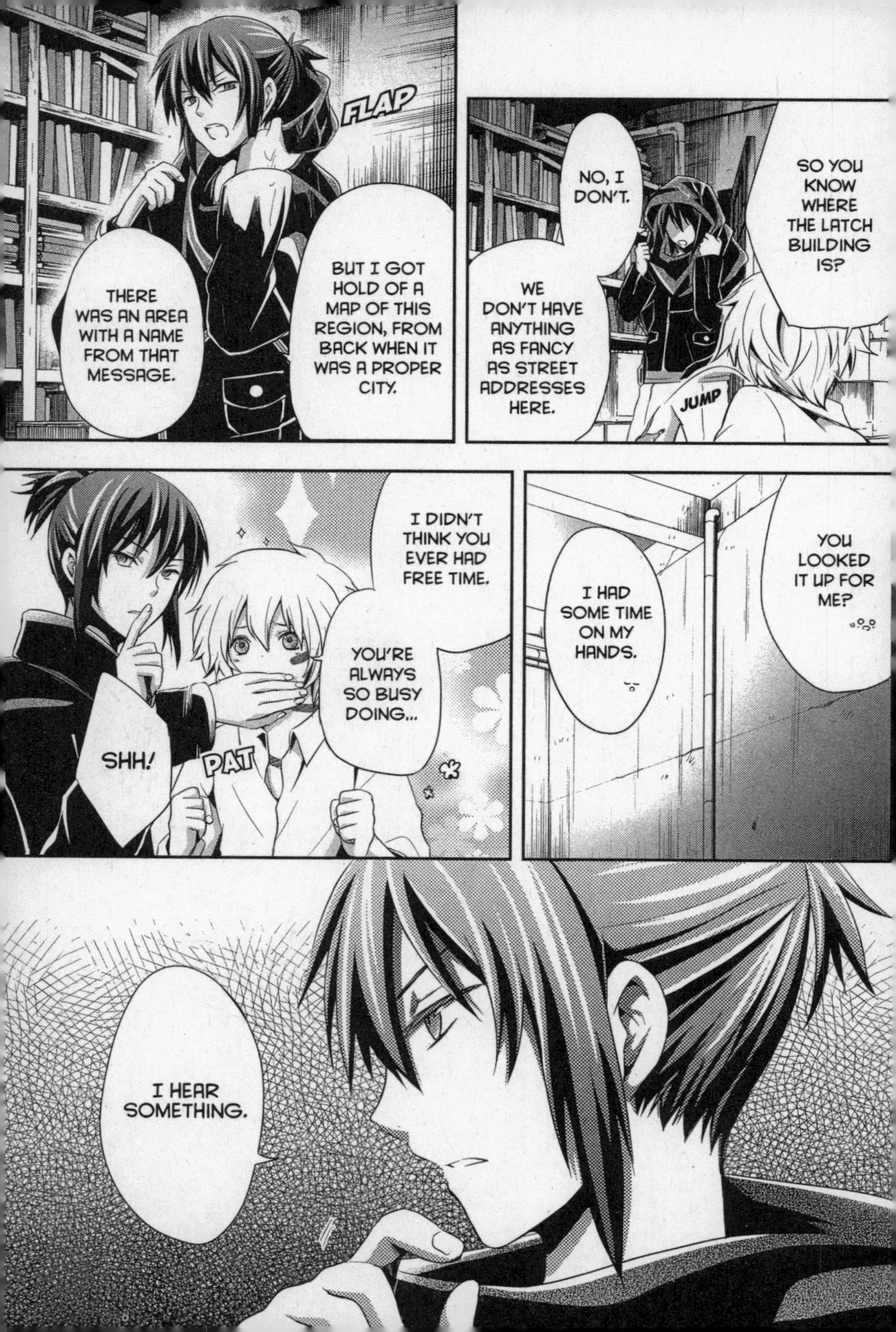
SO YOU KNOW WHERE THE LATCH BUILDING IS?
NO, I DON'T.
WE DON'T HAVE ANYTHING AS FANCY AS STREET ADDRESSES HERE.
JUMP
FLAP
BUT I GOT HOLD OF A MAP OF THIS REGION, FROM BACK WHEN IT WAS A PROPER CITY.
THERE WAS AN AREA WITH A NAME FROM THAT MESSAGE.
YOU LOOKED IT UP FOR ME?
I HAD SOME TIME ON MY HANDS.
I DIDN'T THINK YOU EVER HAD FREE TIME.
YOU'RE ALWAYS SO BUSY DOING...
PAT
SHH!
I HEAR SOMETHING.

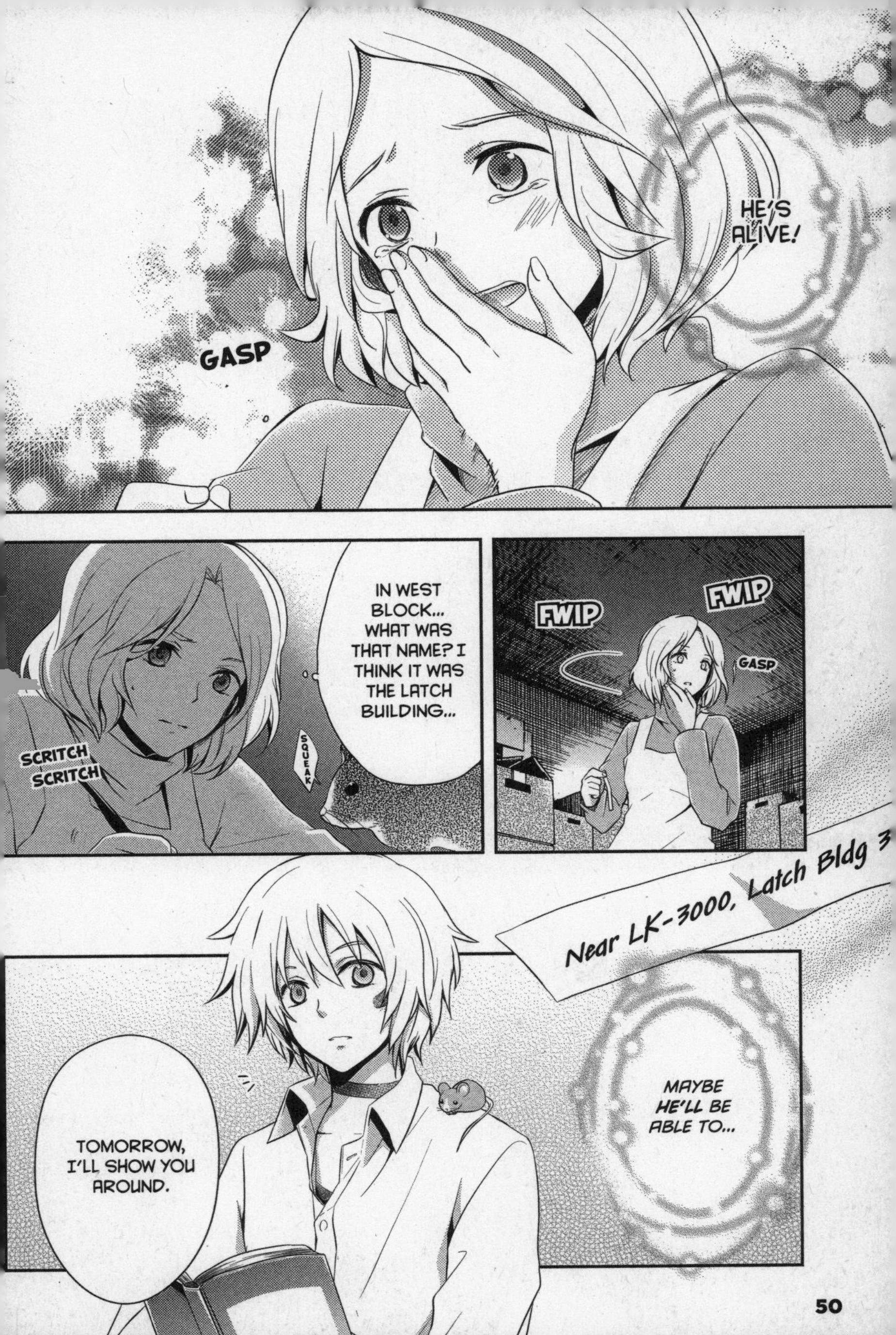
HE'S ALIVE!
GASP
FWIP
FWIP
GASP
IN WEST BLOCK... WHAT WAS THAT NAME? I THINK IT WAS THE LATCH BUILDING...
SQUEAK
SCRITCH SCRITCH
Near LK-3000, Latch Bldg 3
MAYBE HE'LL BE ABLE TO...
TOMORROW, I'LL SHOW YOU AROUND.

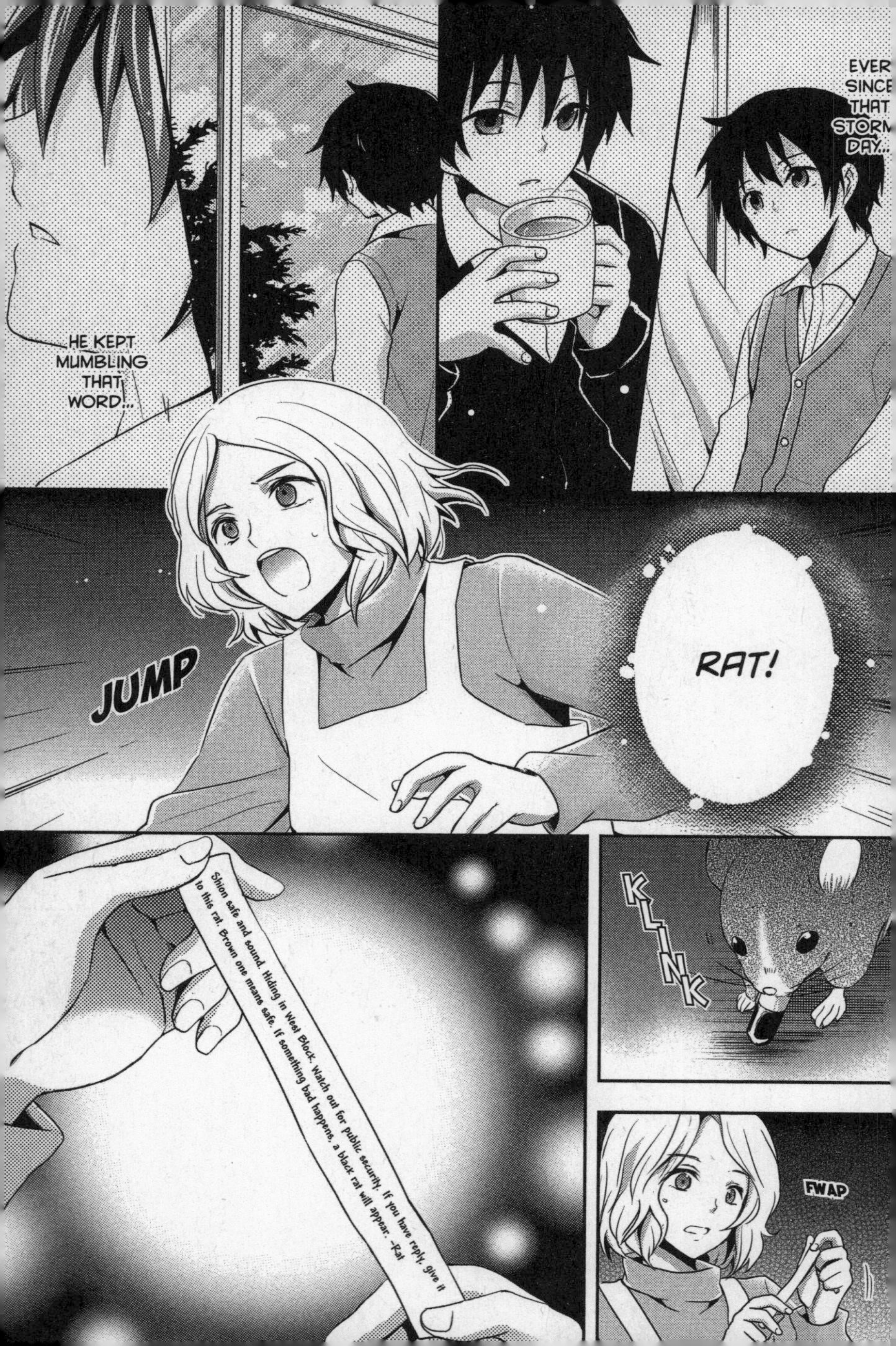
EVER SINCE THAT STORM DAY...
HE KEPT MUMBLING THAT WORD...
RAT!
JUMP
KLINK
FWAP
Shion safe and sound. Hiding in West Block. Watch out for public security. If you have reply, give it to this rat. Brown one means safe. If something bad happens, a black rat will appear. -Rat

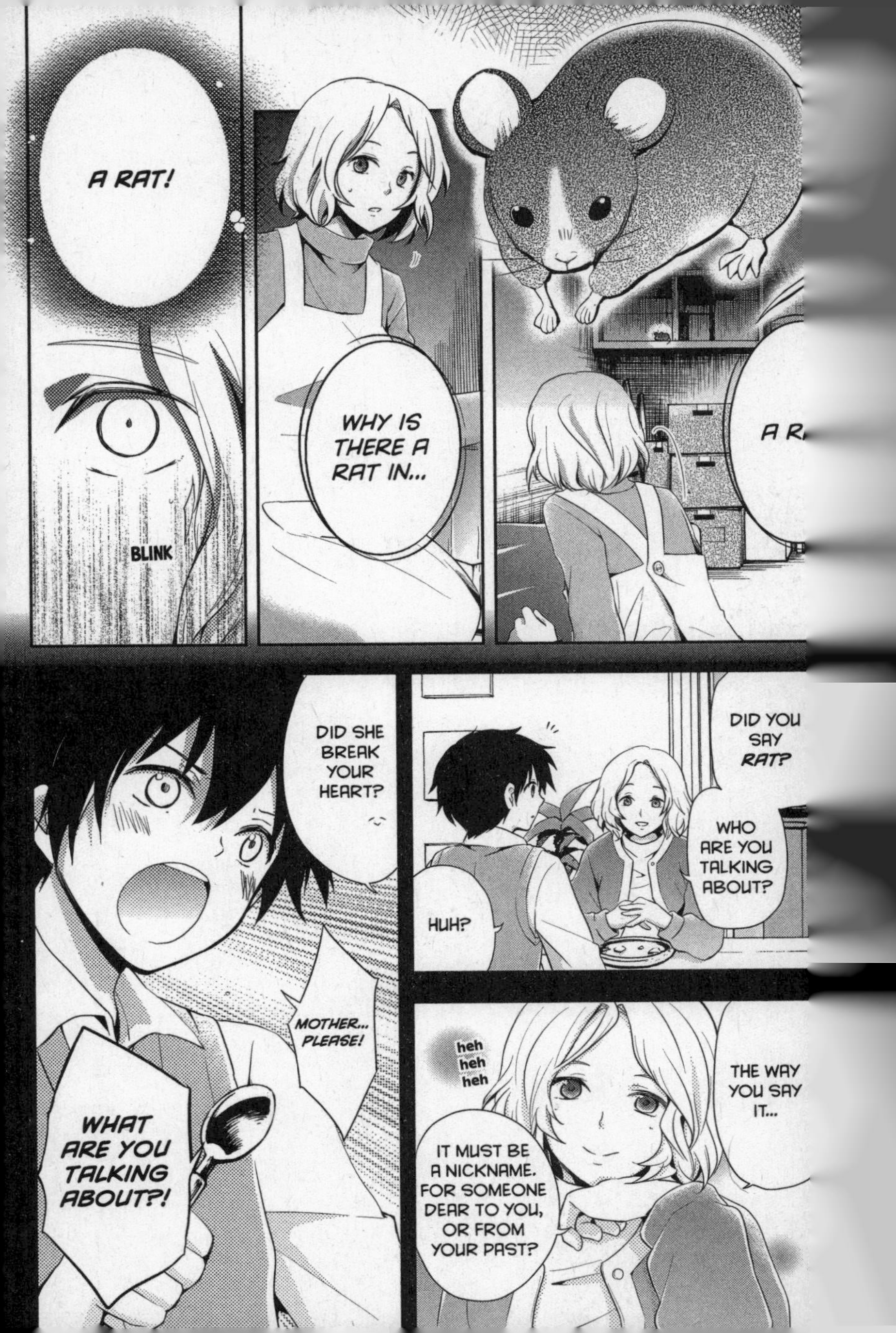
A R
WHY IS THERE A RAT IN...
A RAT!
BLINK
DID YOU SAY RAT?
WHO ARE YOU TALKING ABOUT?
HUH?
THE WAY YOU SAY IT...
heh heh heh
IT MUST BE A NICKNAME. FOR SOMEONE DEAR TO YOU, OR FROM YOUR PAST?
DID SHE BREAK YOUR HEART?
MOTHER... PLEASE!
WHAT ARE YOU TALKING ABOUT?!

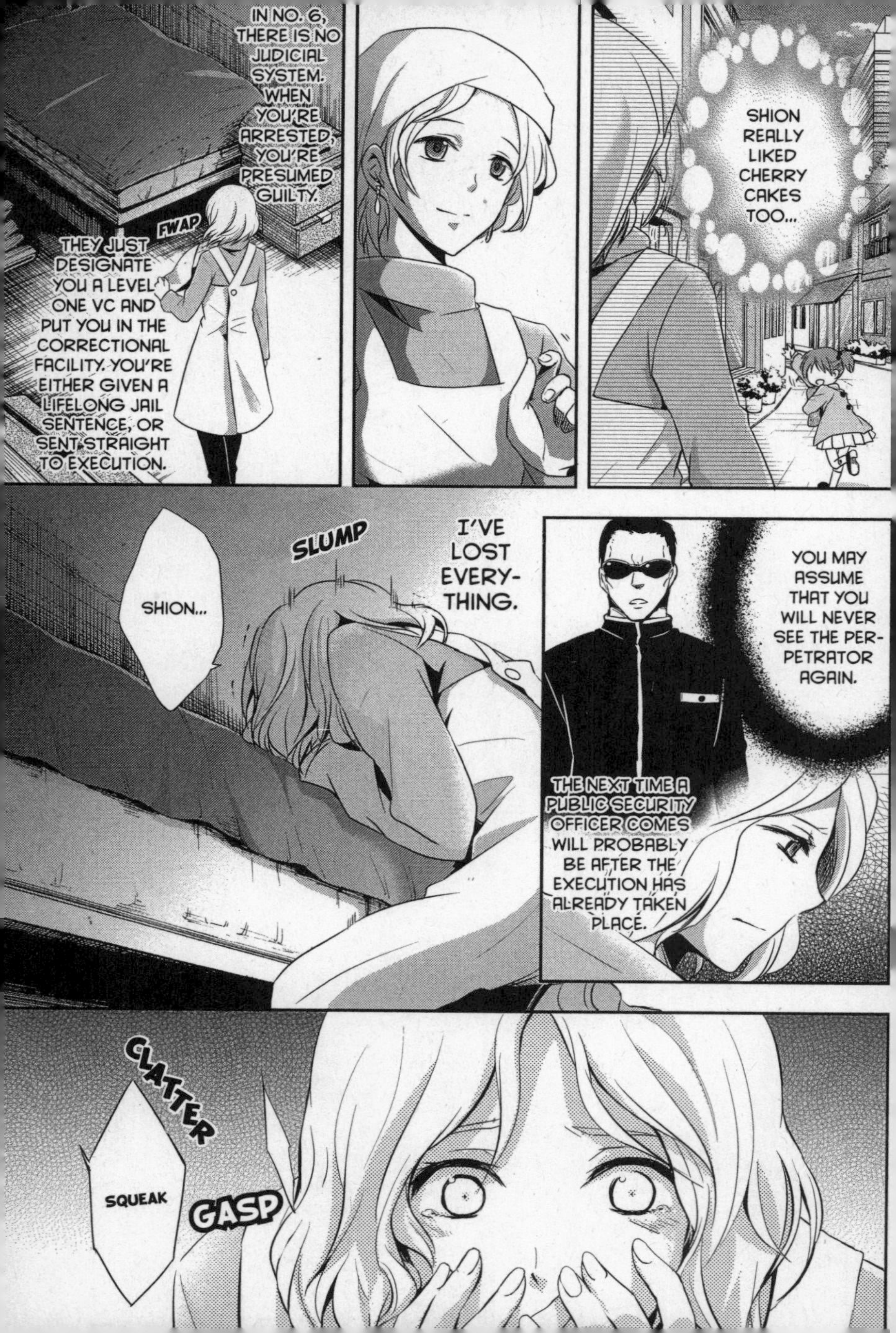
SHION REALLY LIKED CHERRY CAKES TOO...
IN NO. 6, THERE IS NO JUDICIAL SYSTEM. WHEN YOU'RE ARRESTED, YOU'RE PRESUMED GUILTY.
FWAP
THEY JUST DESIGNATE YOU A LEVEL ONE VC AND PUT YOU IN THE CORRECTIONAL FACILITY. YOU'RE EITHER GIVEN A LIFELONG JAIL SENTENCE, OR SENT STRAIGHT TO EXECUTION.
YOU MAY ASSUME THAT YOU WILL NEVER SEE THE PER-PETRATOR AGAIN.
THE NEXT TIME A PUBLIC SECURITY OFFICER COMES WILL PROBABLY BE AFTER THE EXECUTION HAS ALREADY TAKEN PLACE.
I'VE LOST EVERY-THING.
SLUMP
SHION...
CLATTER
GASP
SQUEAK

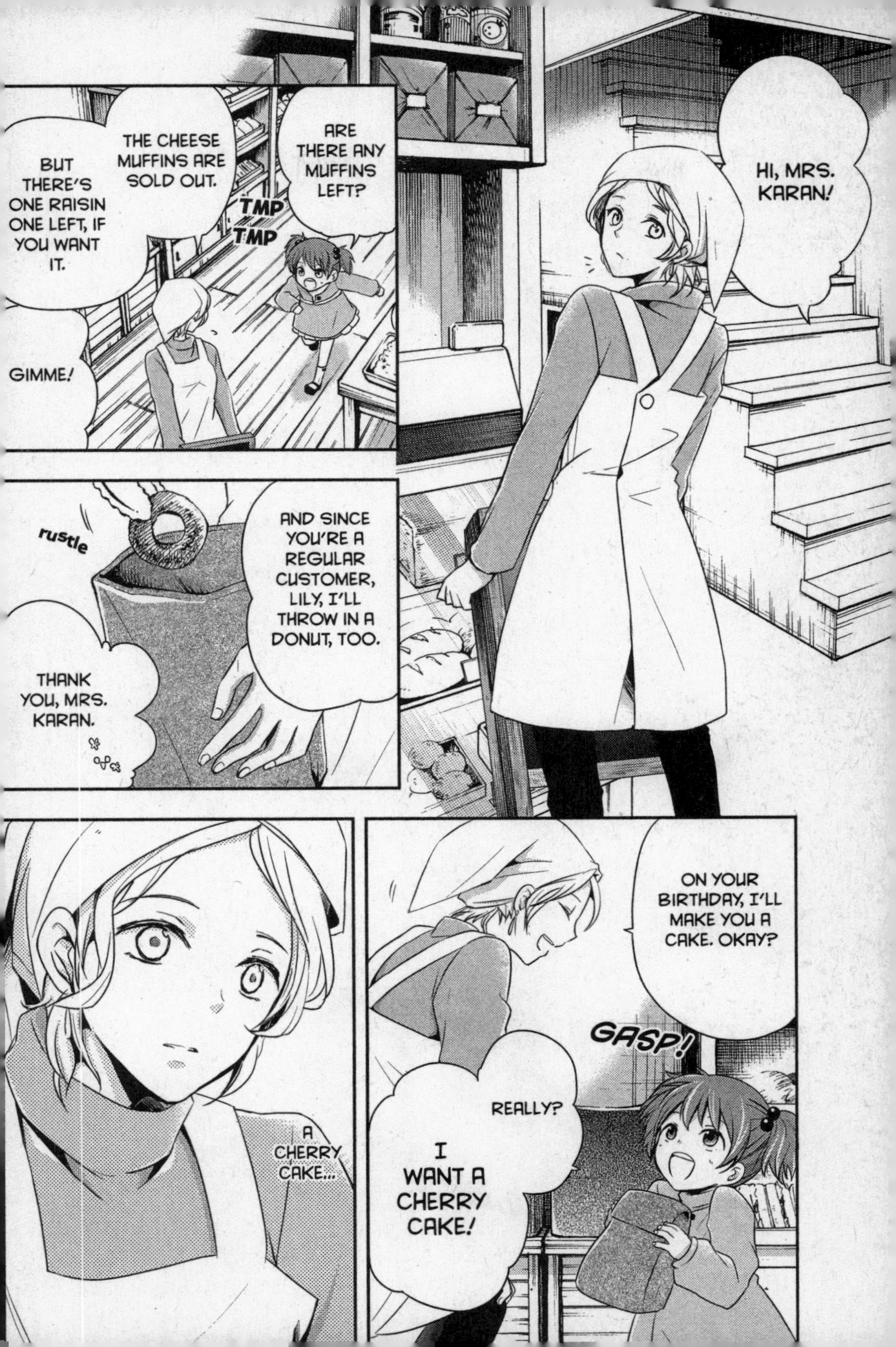
HI, MRS. KARAN!
ARE THERE ANY MUFFINS LEFT?
TMP
TMP
THE CHEESE MUFFINS ARE SOLD OUT.
BUT THERE'S ONE RAISIN ONE LEFT, IF YOU WANT IT.
GIMME!
AND SINCE YOU'RE A REGULAR CUSTOMER, LILY, I'LL THROW IN A DONUT, TOO.
rustle
THANK YOU, MRS. KARAN.
ON YOUR BIRTHDAY, I'LL MAKE YOU A CAKE. OKAY?
GASP!
REALLY?
I WANT A CHERRY CAKE!
A CHERRY CAKE...

Chapter 5: Place of the Gods

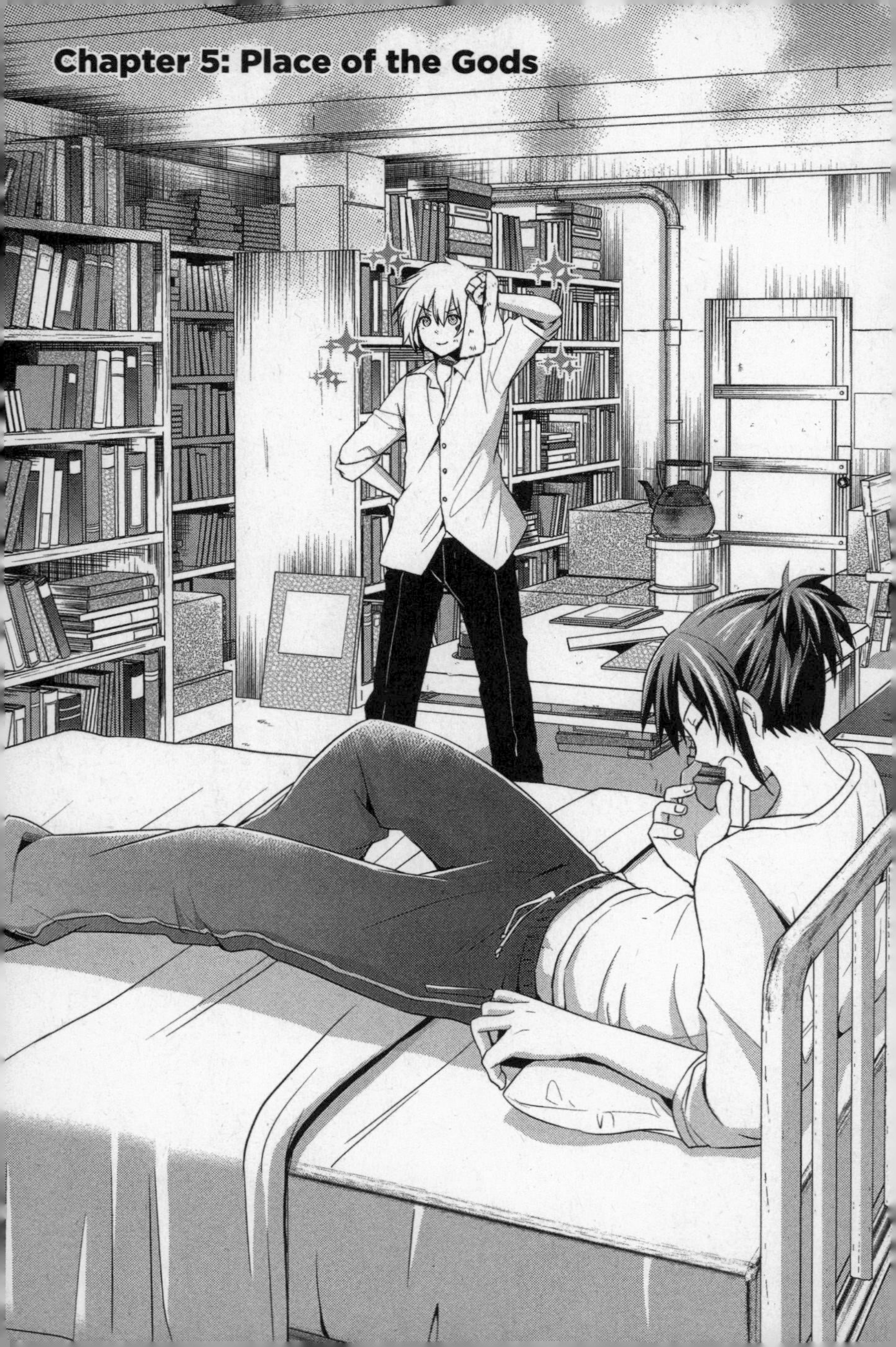

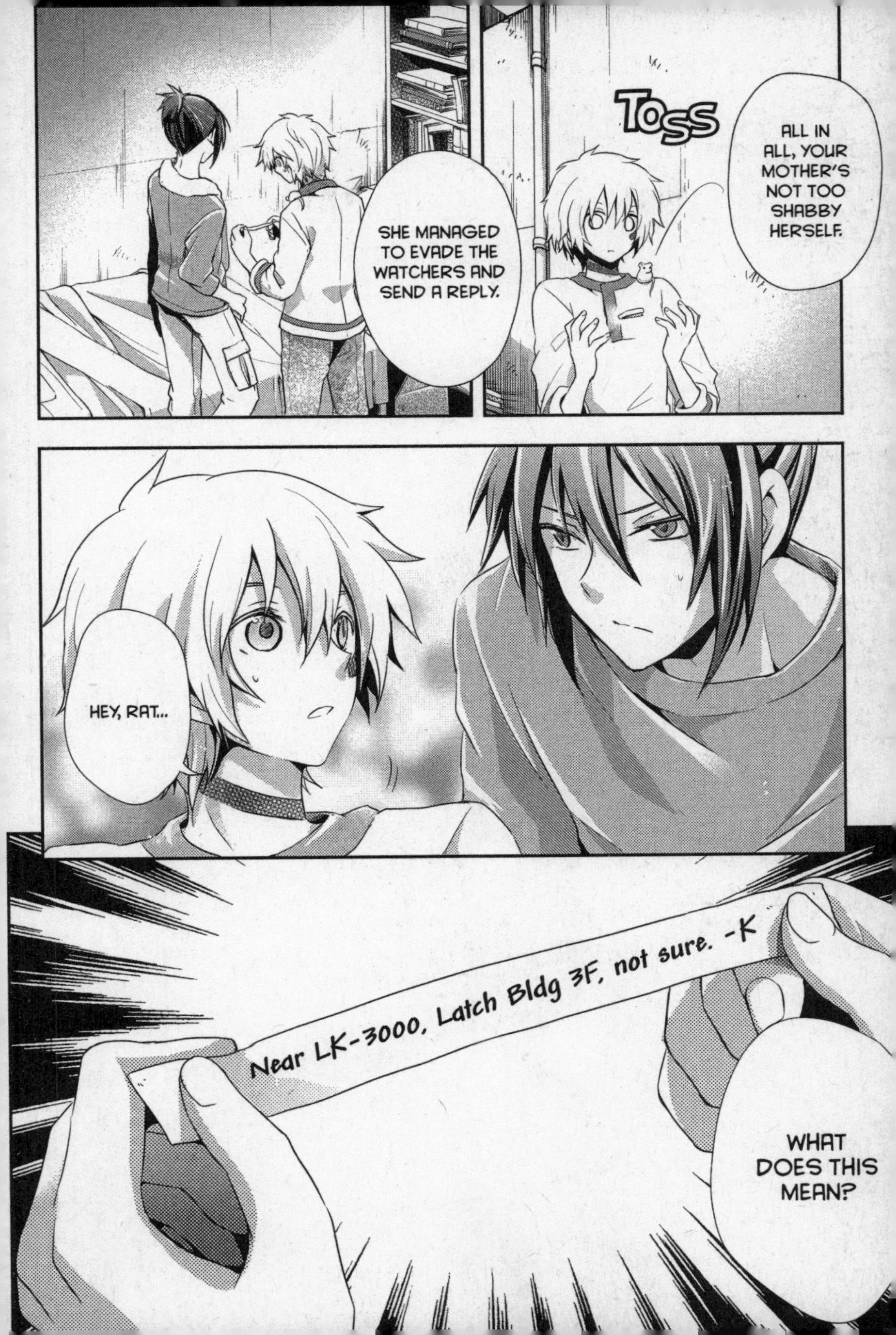
TOSS
ALL IN ALL, YOUR MOTHER'S NOT TOO SHABBY HERSELF.
SHE MANAGED TO EVADE THE WATCHERS AND SEND A REPLY.
HEY, RAT...
Near LK-3000, Latch Bldg 3F, not sure. -K
WHAT DOES THIS MEAN?

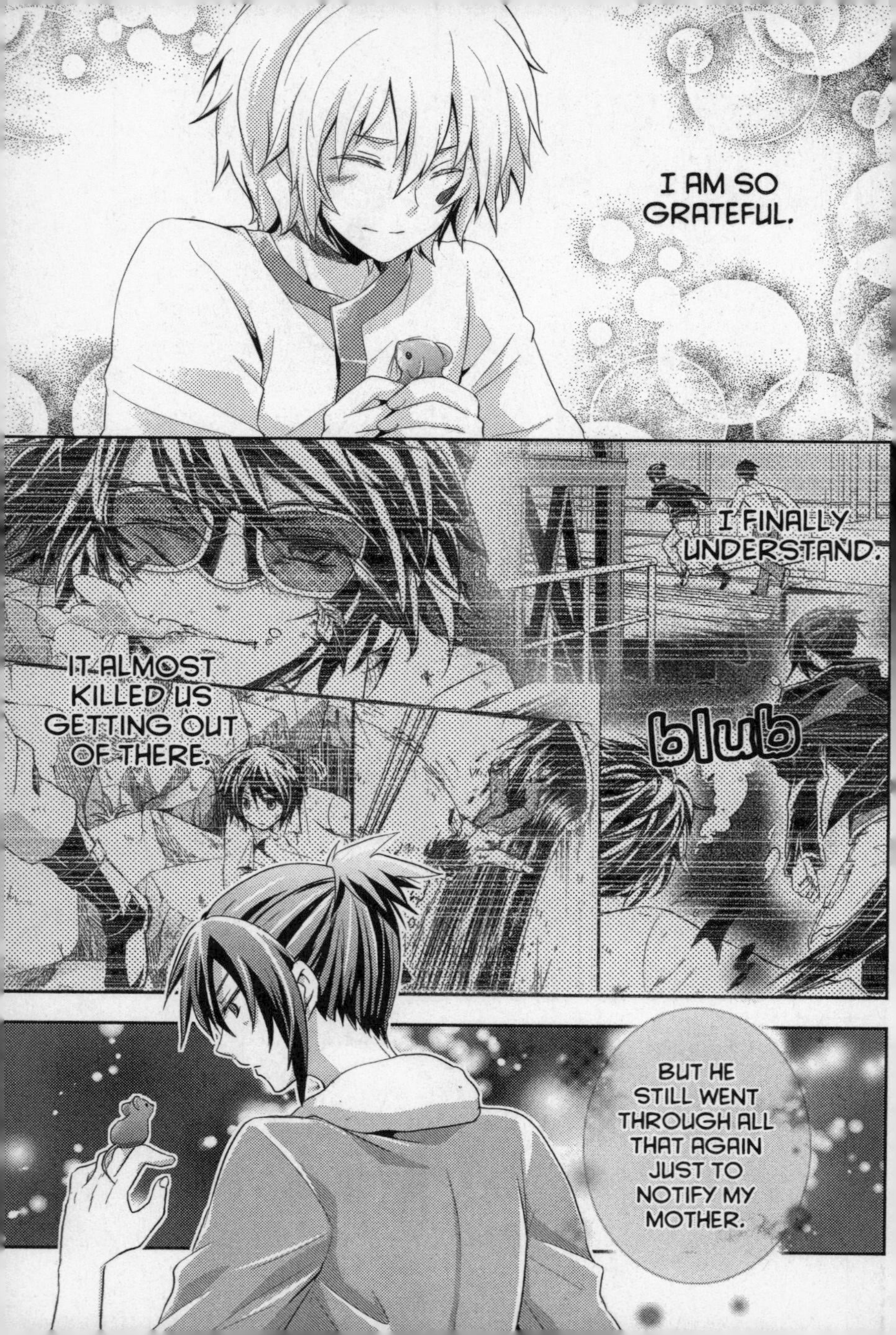
I AM SO GRATEFUL.
I FINALLY UNDERSTAND.
blub
IT ALMOST KILLED US GETTING OUT OF THERE.
BUT HE STILL WENT THROUGH ALL THAT AGAIN JUST TO NOTIFY MY MOTHER.

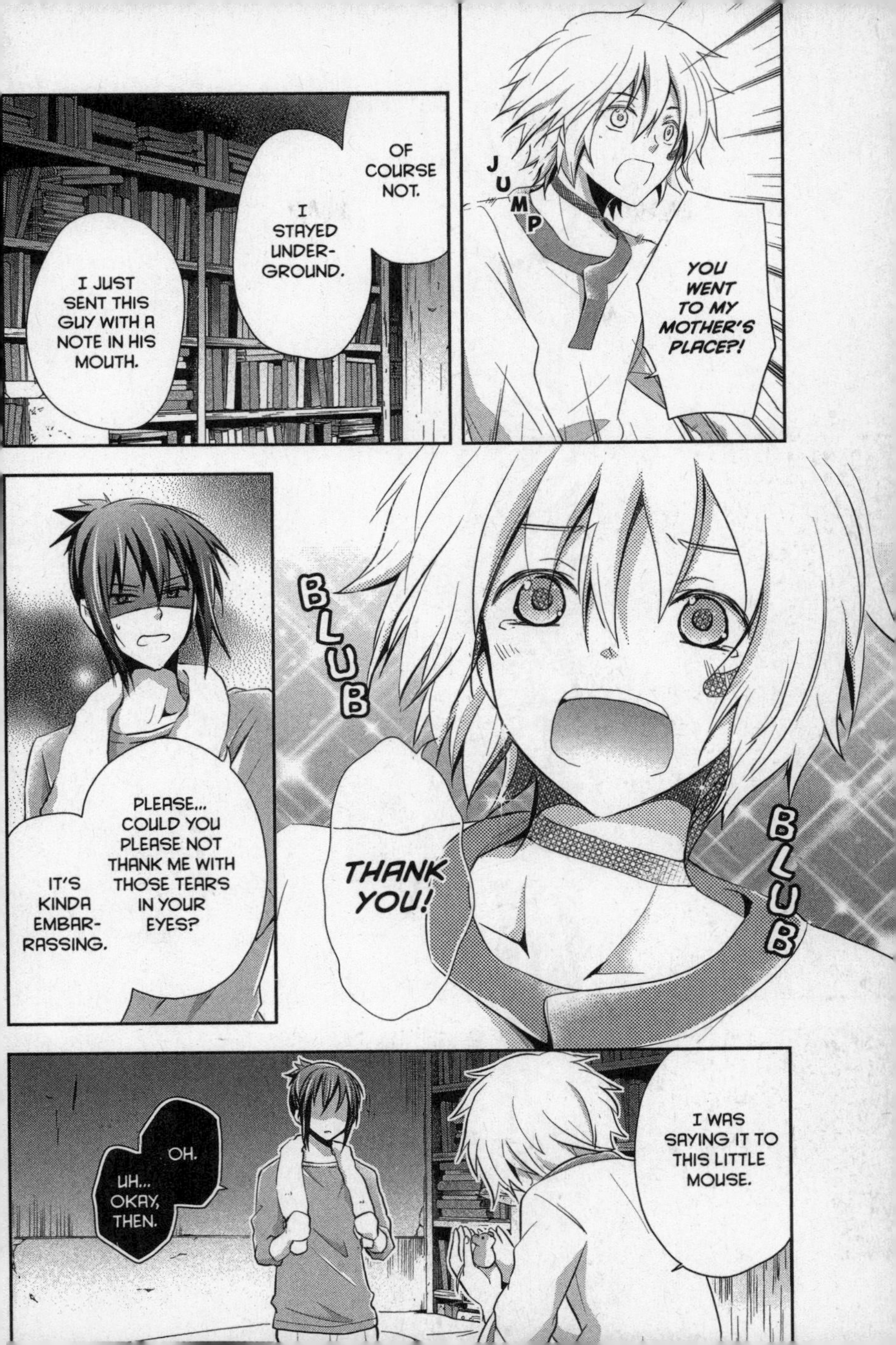
JUMP
YOU WENT TO MY MOTHER'S PLACE?!
OF COURSE NOT.
I STAYED UNDER-GROUND.
I JUST SENT THIS GUY WITH A NOTE IN HIS MOUTH.
BLUB
BLUB
THANK YOU!
PLEASE... COULD YOU PLEASE NOT THANK ME WITH THOSE TEARS IN YOUR EYES?
IT'S KINDA EMBAR-RASSING.
I WAS SAYING IT TO THIS LITTLE MOUSE.
OH.
UH... OKAY, THEN.

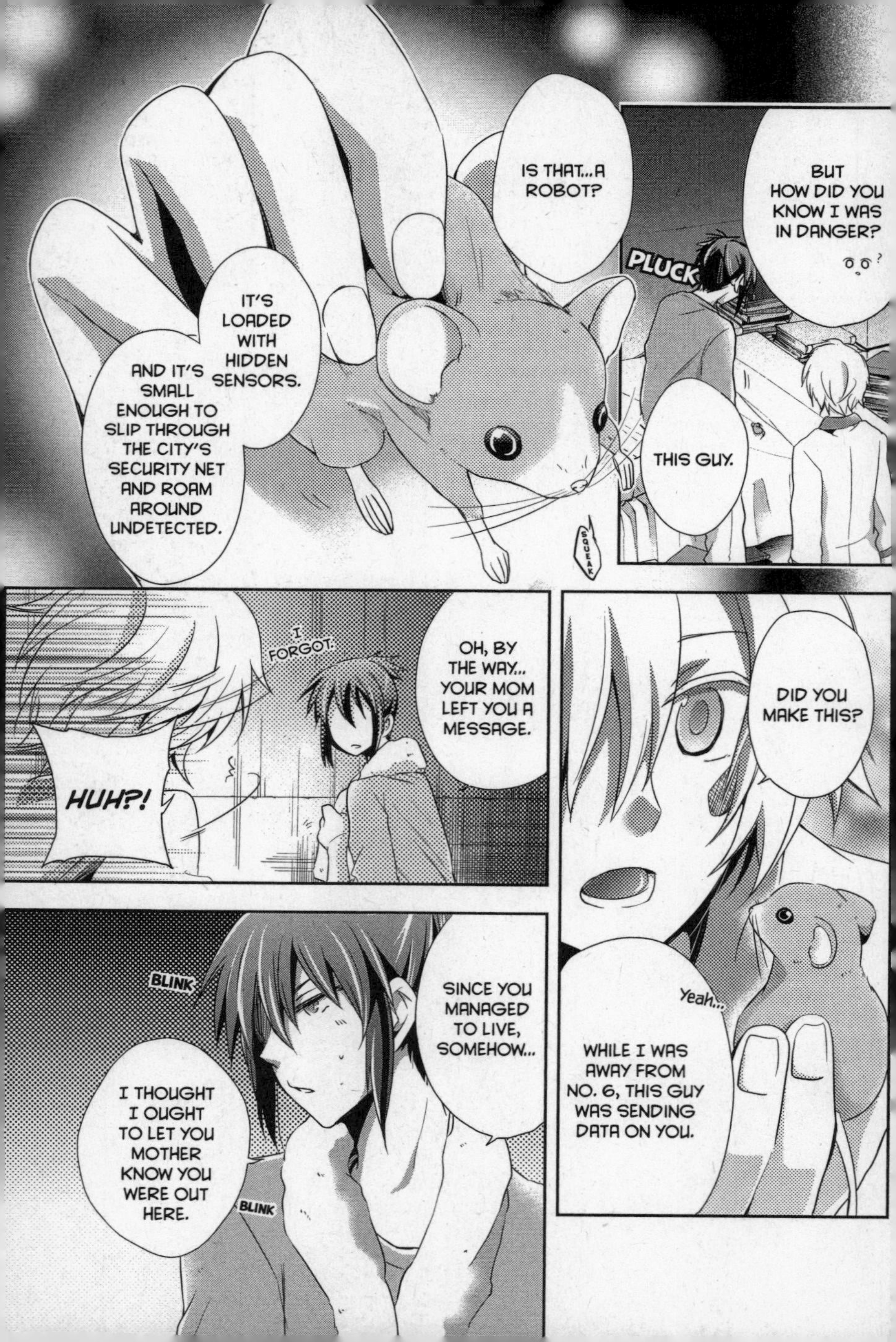
BUT HOW DID YOU KNOW I WAS IN DANGER?
PLUCK
THIS GUY.
IS THAT...A ROBOT?
IT'S LOADED WITH HIDDEN SENSORS.
AND IT'S SMALL ENOUGH TO SLIP THROUGH THE CITY'S SECURITY NET AND ROAM AROUND UNDETECTED.
SQUEAK
DID YOU MAKE THIS?
Yeah...
WHILE I WAS AWAY FROM NO. 6, THIS GUY WAS SENDING DATA ON YOU.
OH, BY THE WAY... YOUR MOM LEFT YOU A MESSAGE.
I FORGOT.
HUH?!
SINCE YOU MANAGED TO LIVE, SOMEHOW...
BLINK
I THOUGHT I OUGHT TO LET YOU MOTHER KNOW YOU WERE OUT HERE.
BLINK

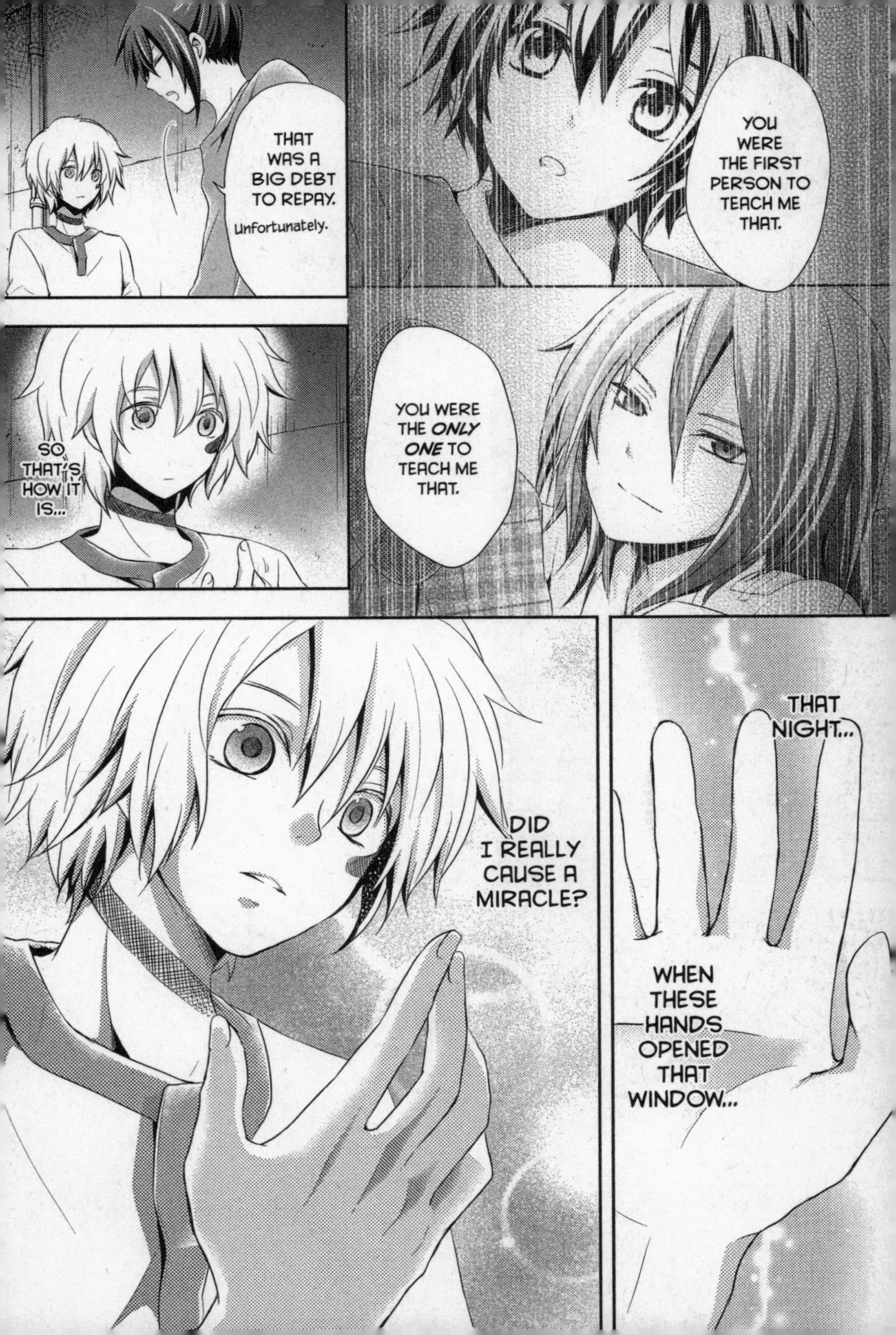
YOU WERE THE FIRST PERSON TO TEACH ME THAT.
THAT WAS A BIG DEBT TO REPAY.
Unfortunately.
YOU WERE THE *ONLY ONE* TO TEACH ME THAT.
SO THAT'S HOW IT IS...
THAT NIGHT...
WHEN THESE HANDS OPENED THAT WINDOW...
DID I REALLY CAUSE A MIRACLE?

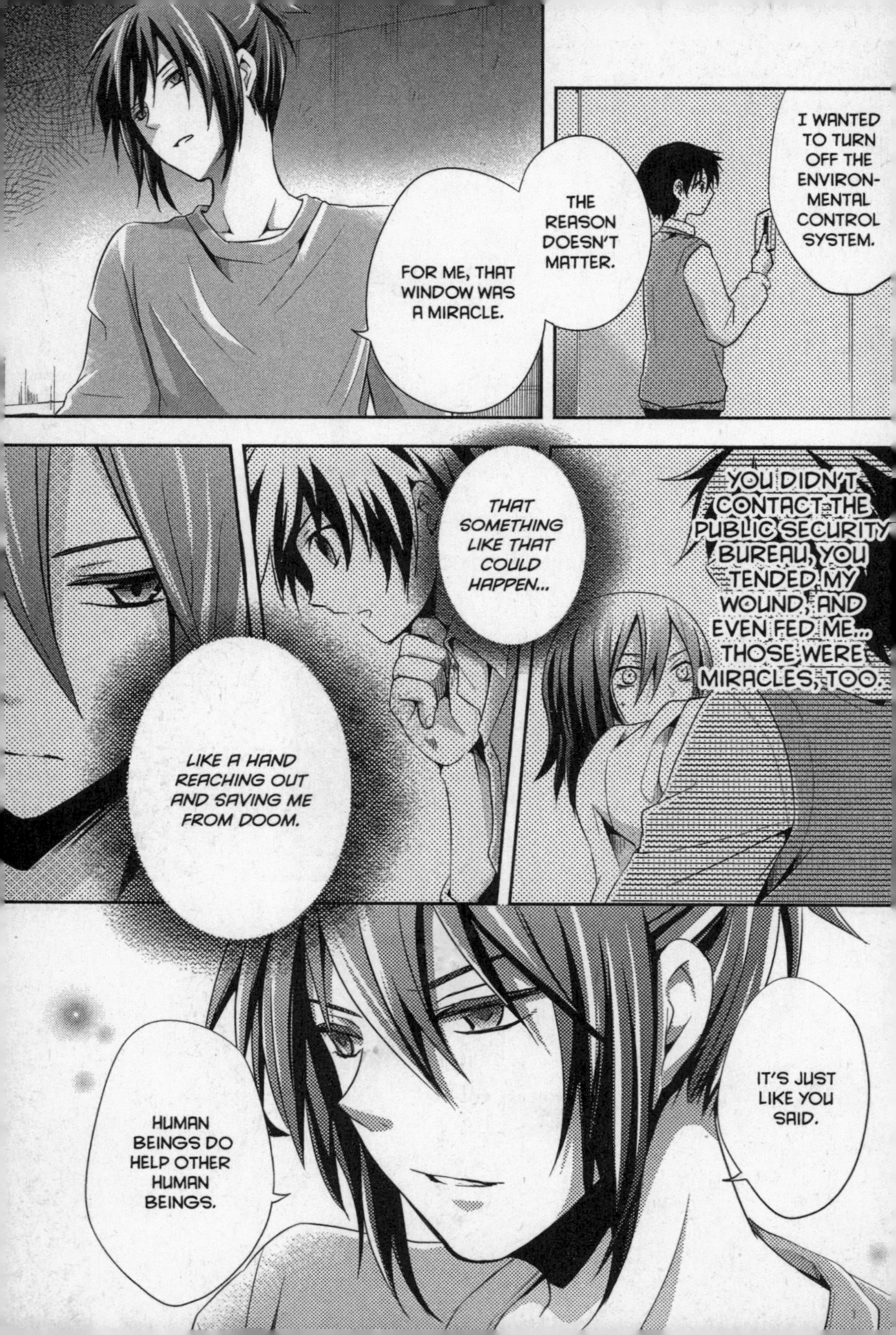
I WANTED TO TURN OFF THE ENVIRON-MENTAL CONTROL SYSTEM.
THE REASON DOESN'T MATTER.
FOR ME, THAT WINDOW WAS A MIRACLE.
YOU DIDN'T CONTACT THE PUBLIC SECURITY BUREAU, YOU TENDED MY WOUND, AND EVEN FED ME... THOSE WERE MIRACLES, TOO.
THAT SOMETHING LIKE THAT COULD HAPPEN...
LIKE A HAND REACHING OUT AND SAVING ME FROM DOOM.
IT'S JUST LIKE YOU SAID.
HUMAN BEINGS DO HELP OTHER HUMAN BEINGS.

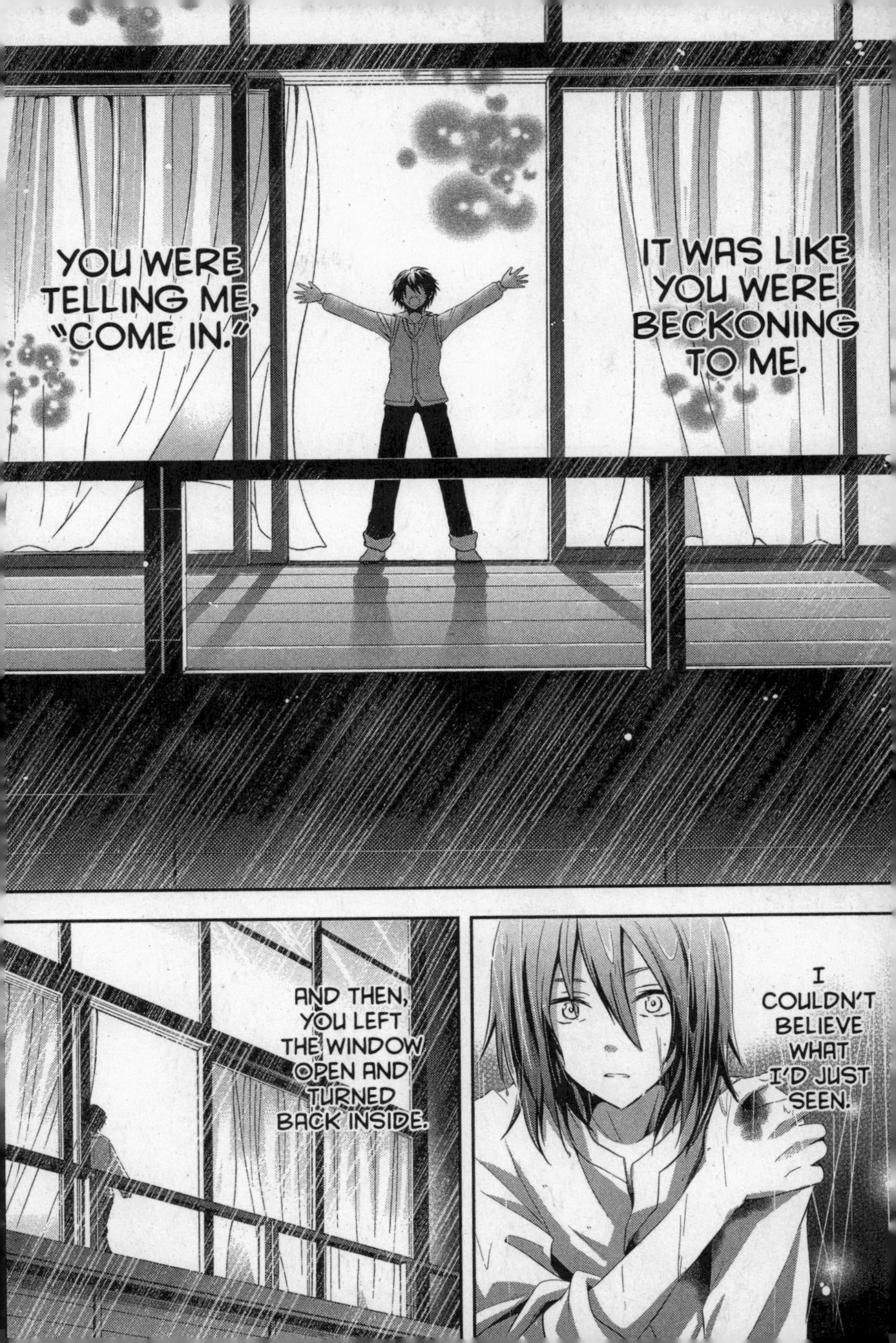
IT WAS LIKE YOU WERE BECKONING TO ME.
YOU WERE TELLING ME, "COME IN."
I COULDN'T BELIEVE WHAT I'D JUST SEEN.
AND THEN, YOU LEFT THE WINDOW OPEN AND TURNED BACK INSIDE.

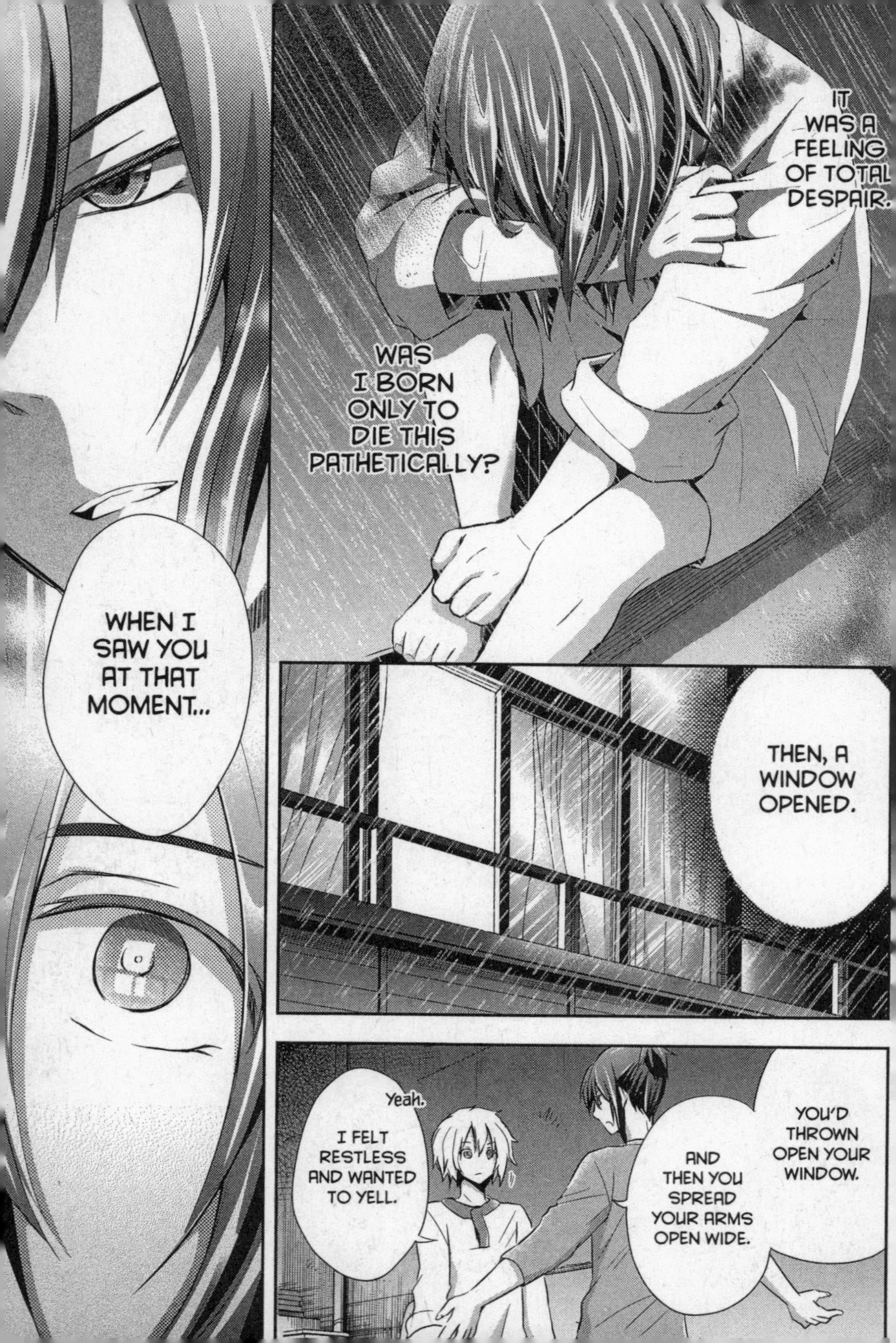
IT WAS A FEELING OF TOTAL DESPAIR.
WAS I BORN ONLY TO DIE THIS PATHETICALLY?
THEN, A WINDOW OPENED.
YOU'D THROWN OPEN YOUR WINDOW.
AND THEN YOU SPREAD YOUR ARMS OPEN WIDE.
Yeah.
I FELT RESTLESS AND WANTED TO YELL.
WHEN I SAW YOU AT THAT MOMENT...

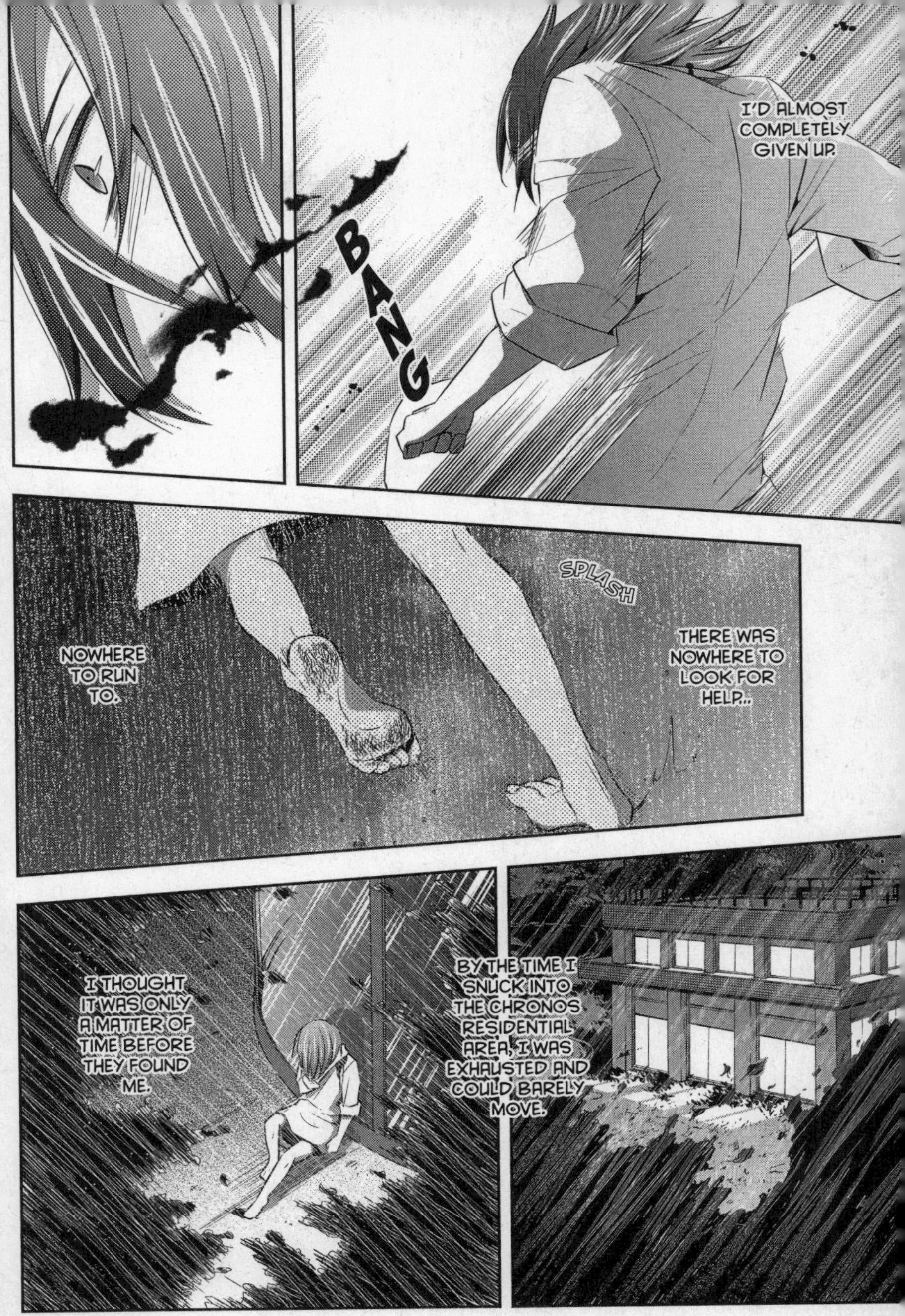
I'D ALMOST COMPLETELY GIVEN UP.
BANG
SPLASH
THERE WAS NOWHERE TO LOOK FOR HELP...
NOWHERE TO RUN TO.
BY THE TIME I SNUCK INTO THE CHRONOS RESIDENTIAL AREA, I WAS EXHAUSTED AND COULD BARELY MOVE.
I THOUGHT IT WAS ONLY A MATTER OF TIME BEFORE THEY FOUND ME.

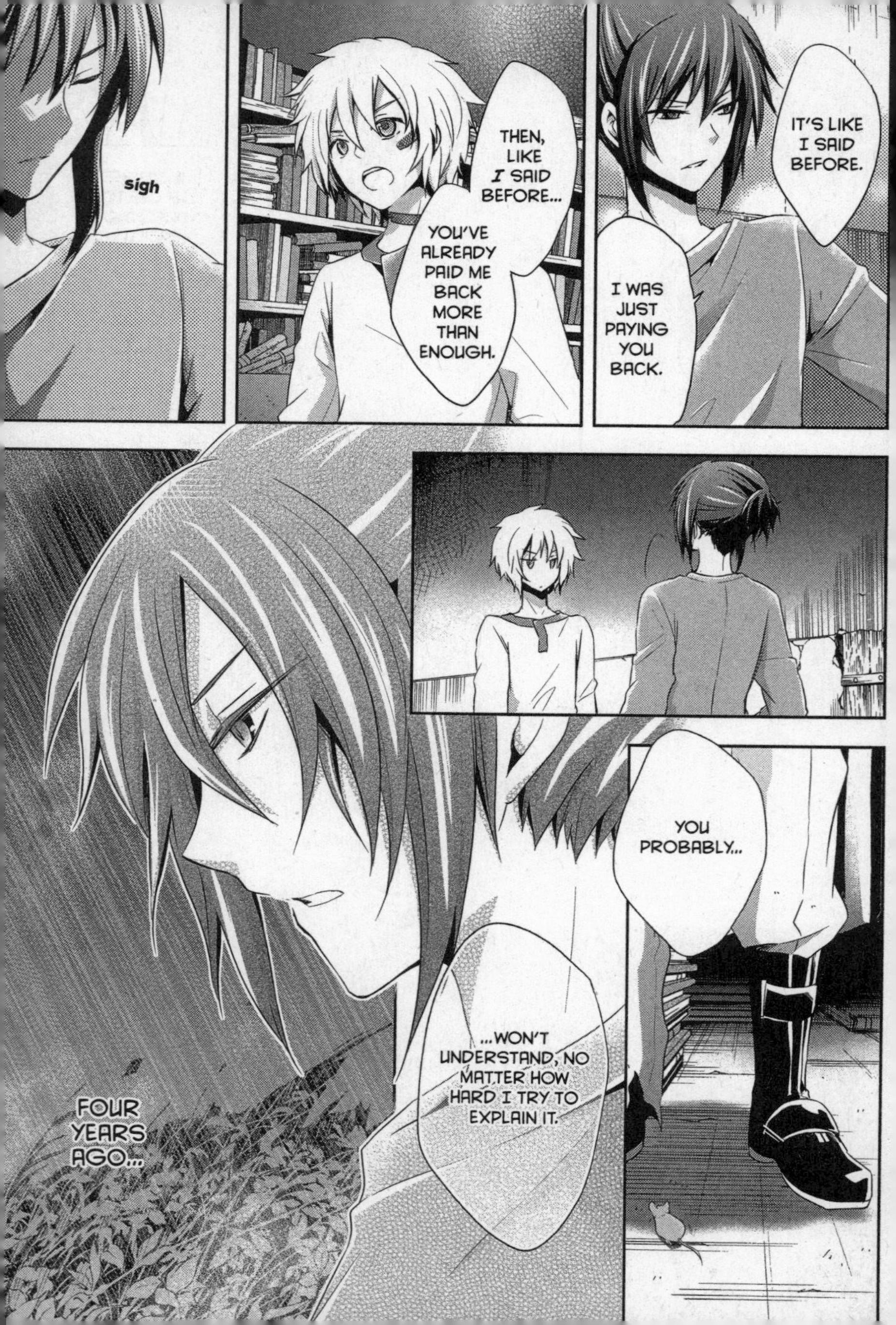
IT'S LIKE I SAID BEFORE.
I WAS JUST PAYING YOU BACK.
THEN, LIKE *I* SAID BEFORE...
YOU'VE ALREADY PAID ME BACK MORE THAN ENOUGH.
sigh
YOU PROBABLY...
...WON'T UNDERSTAND, NO MATTER HOW HARD I TRY TO EXPLAIN IT.
FOUR YEARS AGO...

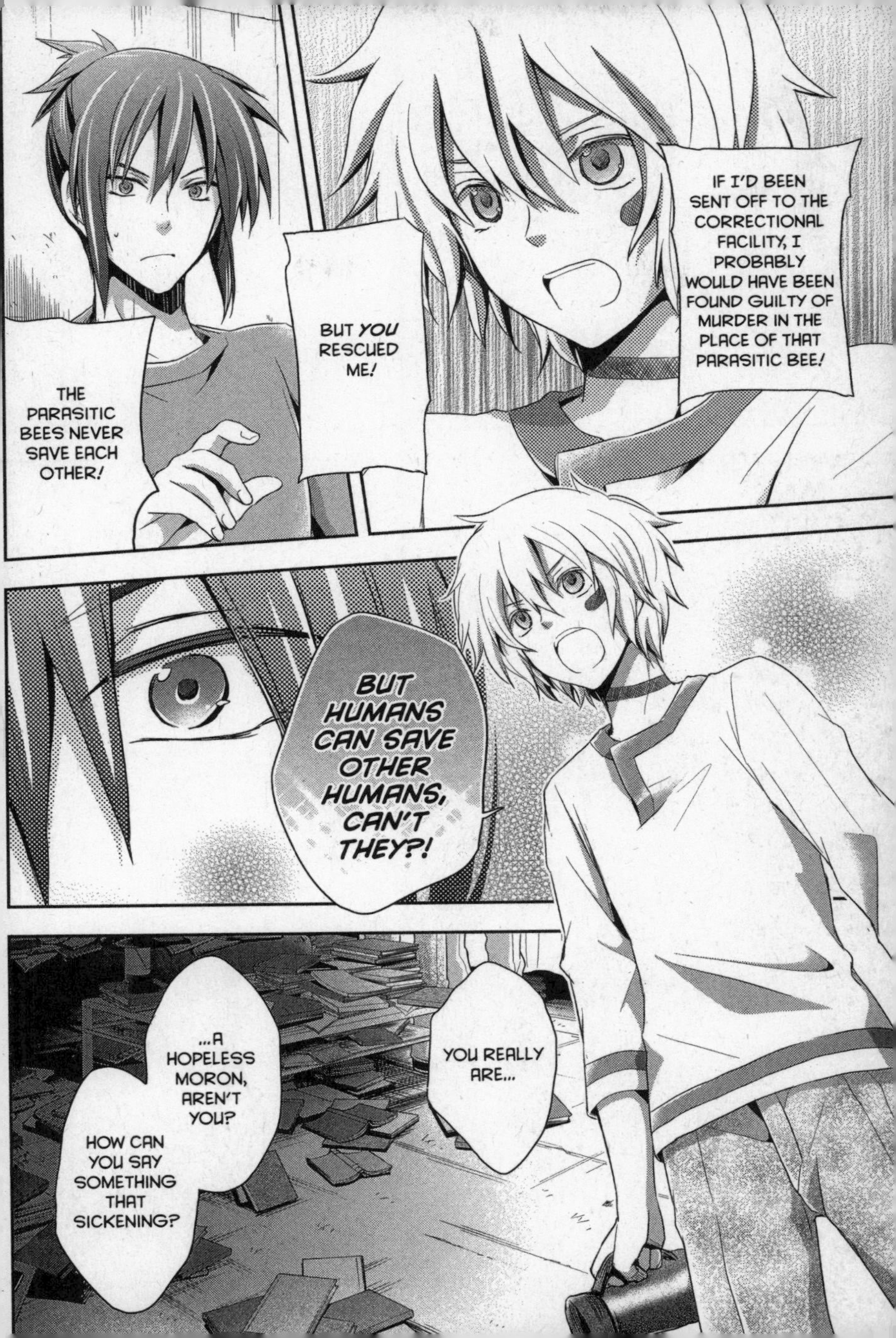
IF I'D BEEN SENT OFF TO THE CORRECTIONAL FACILITY, I PROBABLY WOULD HAVE BEEN FOUND GUILTY OF MURDER IN THE PLACE OF THAT PARASITIC BEE!
BUT *YOU* RESCUED ME!
THE PARASITIC BEES NEVER SAVE EACH OTHER!
BUT HUMANS CAN SAVE OTHER HUMANS, CAN'T THEY?!
YOU REALLY ARE...
...A HOPELESS MORON, AREN'T YOU?
HOW CAN YOU SAY SOMETHING THAT SICKENING?

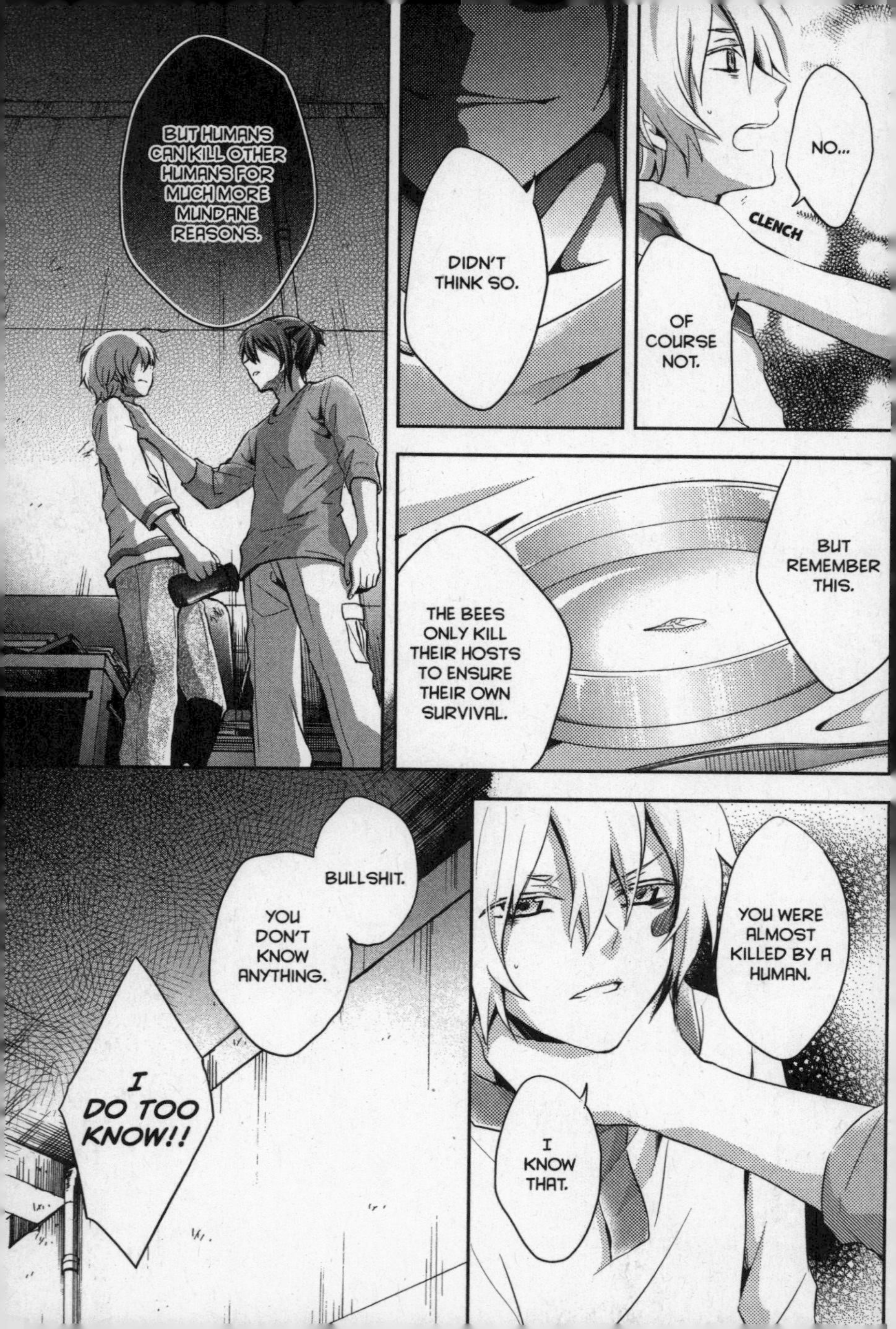
NO...
CLENCH
OF COURSE NOT.
DIDN'T THINK SO.
BUT REMEMBER THIS.
THE BEES ONLY KILL THEIR HOSTS TO ENSURE THEIR OWN SURVIVAL.
BUT HUMANS CAN KILL OTHER HUMANS FOR MUCH MORE MUNDANE REASONS.
YOU WERE ALMOST KILLED BY A HUMAN.
I KNOW THAT.
BULLSHIT.
YOU DON'T KNOW ANYTHING.
I DO TOO KNOW!!

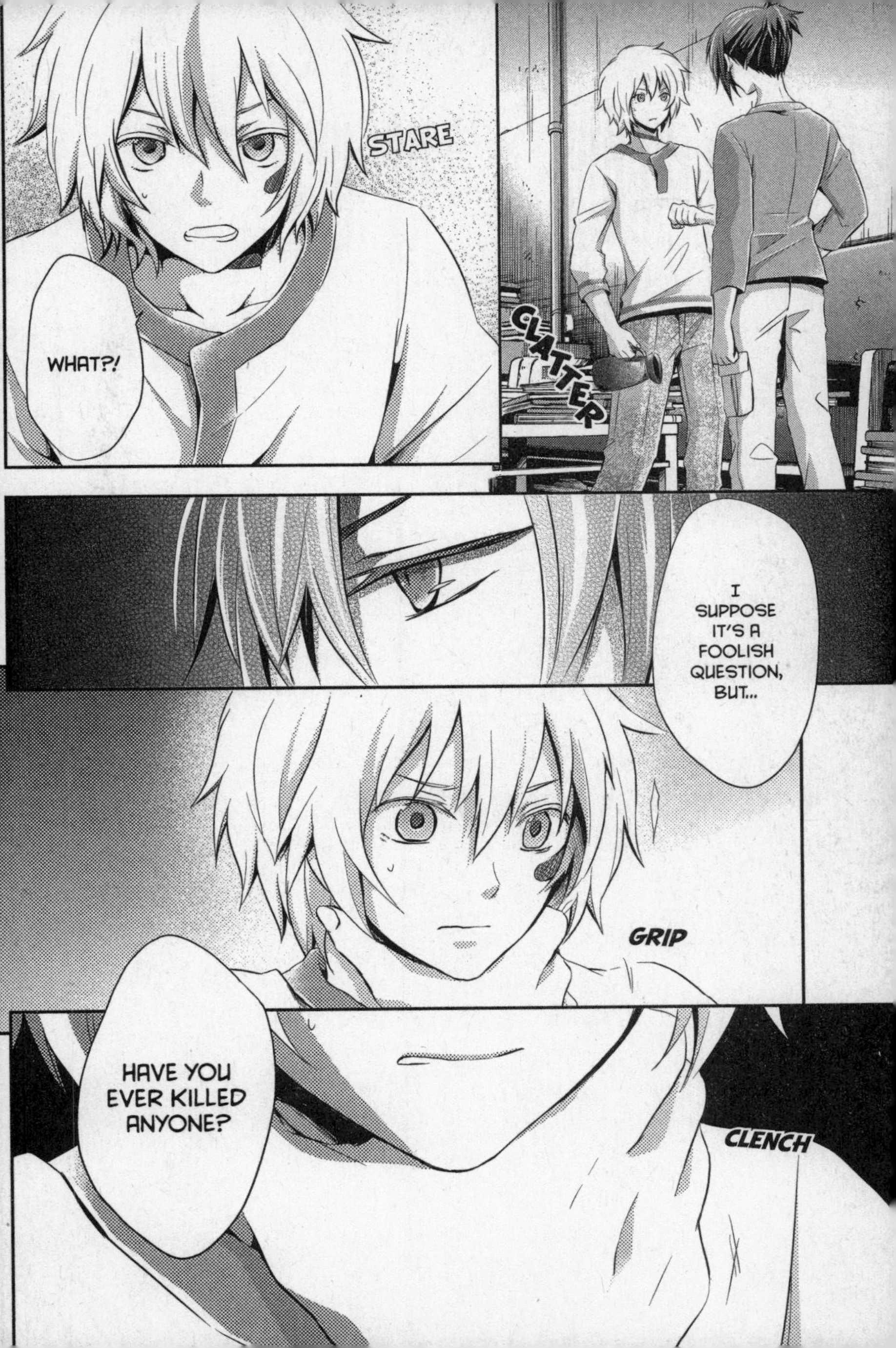
CLATTER
STARE
WHAT?!
I SUPPOSE IT'S A FOOLISH QUESTION, BUT...
GRIP
HAVE YOU EVER KILLED ANYONE?
CLENCH

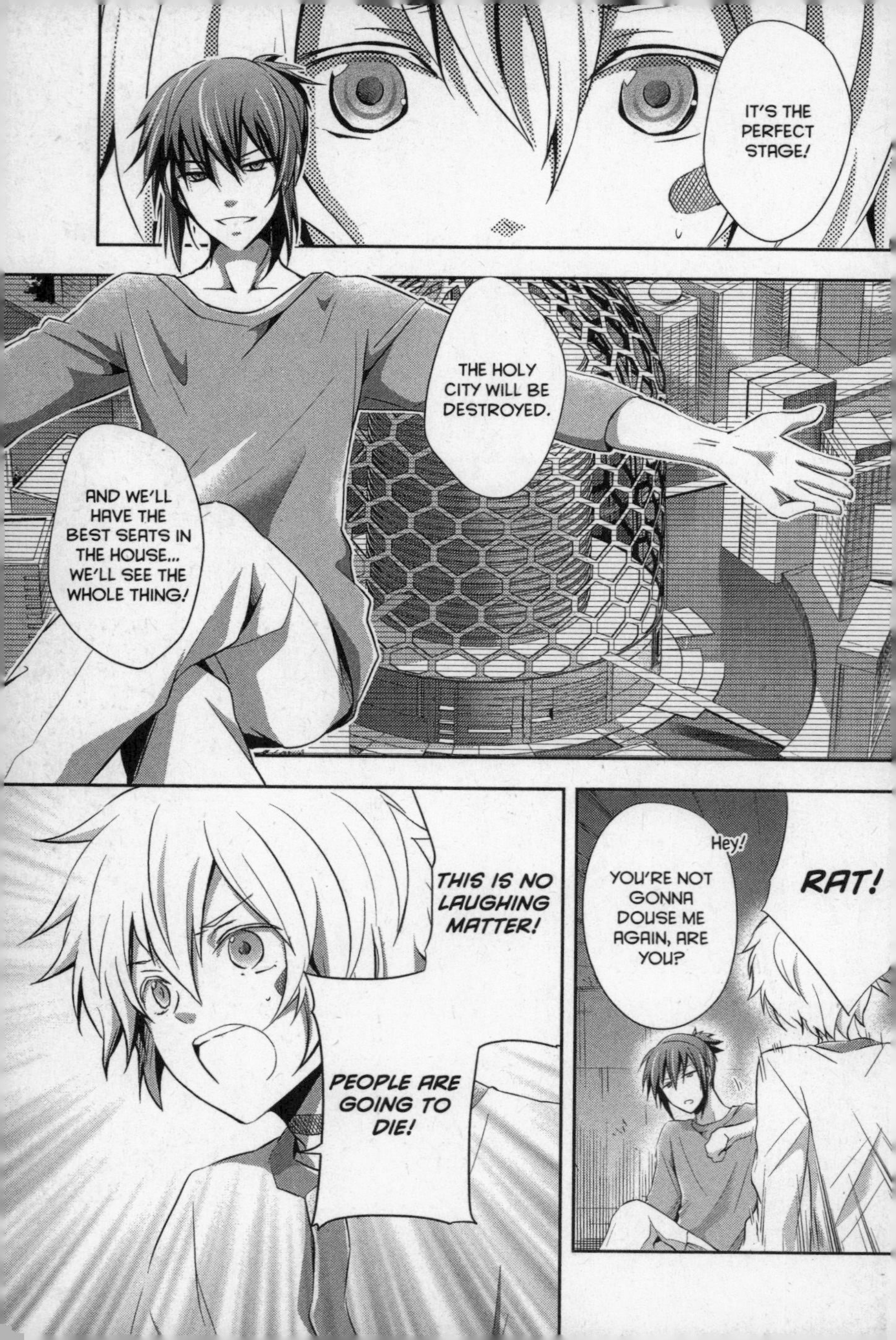
IT'S THE PERFECT STAGE!
THE HOLY CITY WILL BE DESTROYED.
AND WE'LL HAVE THE BEST SEATS IN THE HOUSE... WE'LL SEE THE WHOLE THING!
RAT!
Hey!
YOU'RE NOT GONNA DOUSE ME AGAIN, ARE YOU?
THIS IS NO LAUGHING MATTER!
PEOPLE ARE GOING TO DIE!

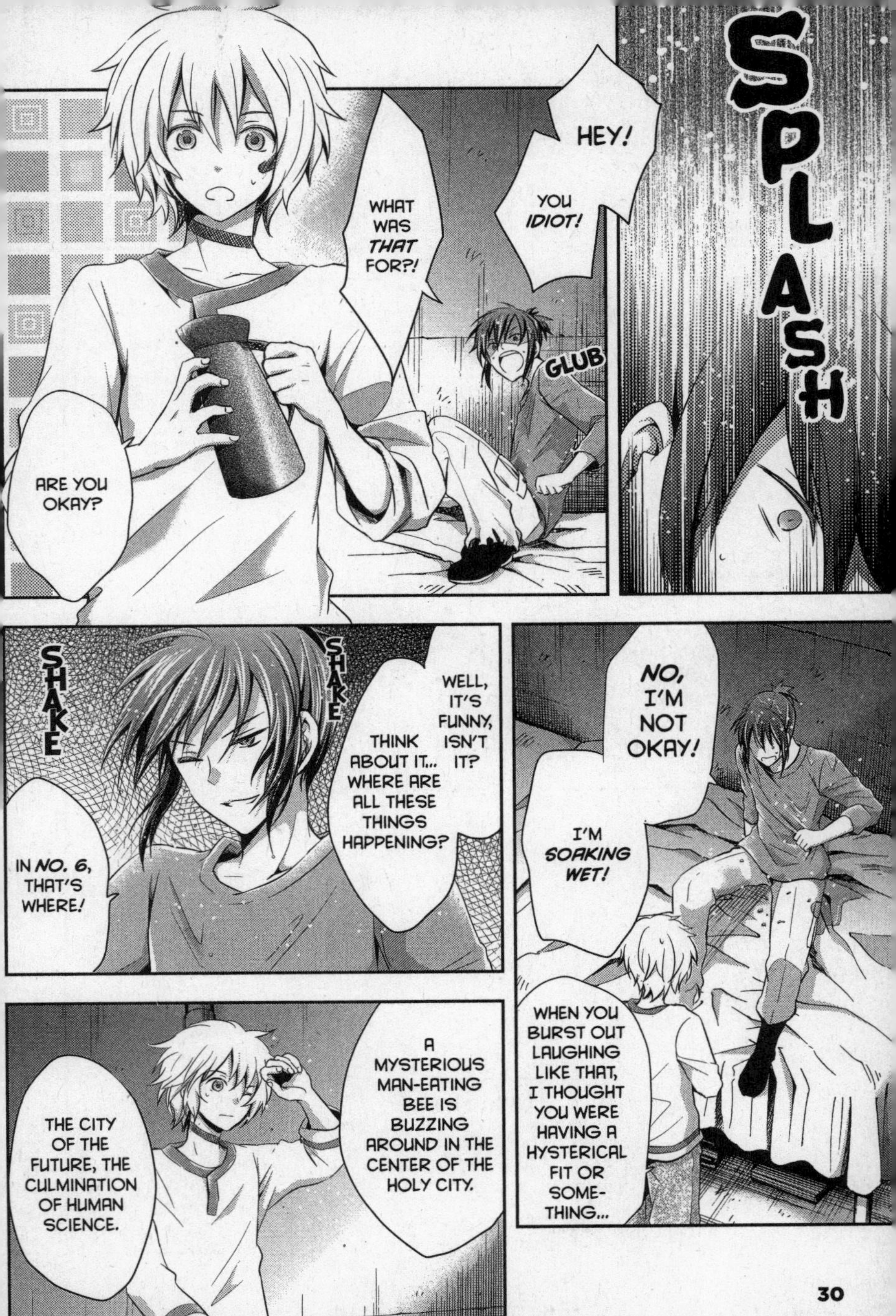
SPLASH
HEY!
YOU *IDIOT!*
GLUB
WHAT WAS *THAT* FOR?!
ARE YOU OKAY?
NO, I'M NOT OKAY!
I'M *SOAKING WET!*
WHEN YOU BURST OUT LAUGHING LIKE THAT, I THOUGHT YOU WERE HAVING A HYSTERICAL FIT OR SOME-THING...
SHAKE
SHAKE
WELL, IT'S FUNNY, ISN'T IT?
THINK ABOUT IT... WHERE ARE ALL THESE THINGS HAPPENING?
IN *NO. 6,* THAT'S WHERE!
A MYSTERIOUS MAN-EATING BEE IS BUZZING AROUND IN THE CENTER OF THE HOLY CITY.
THE CITY OF THE FUTURE, THE CULMINATION OF HUMAN SCIENCE.

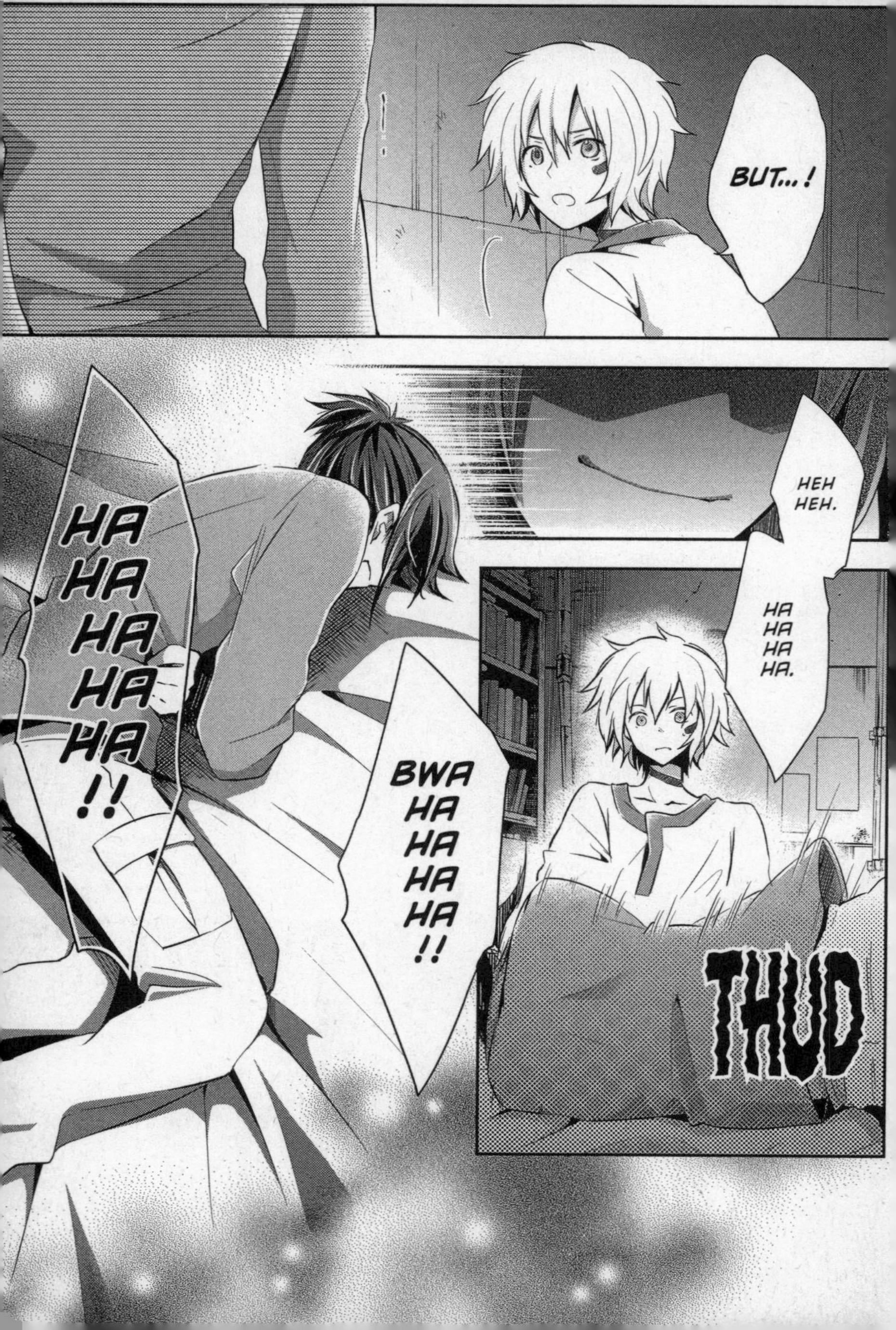
BUT...!
HEH HEH.
HA HA HA HA.
THUD
BWA HA HA HA HA!!
HA HA HA HA HA!!

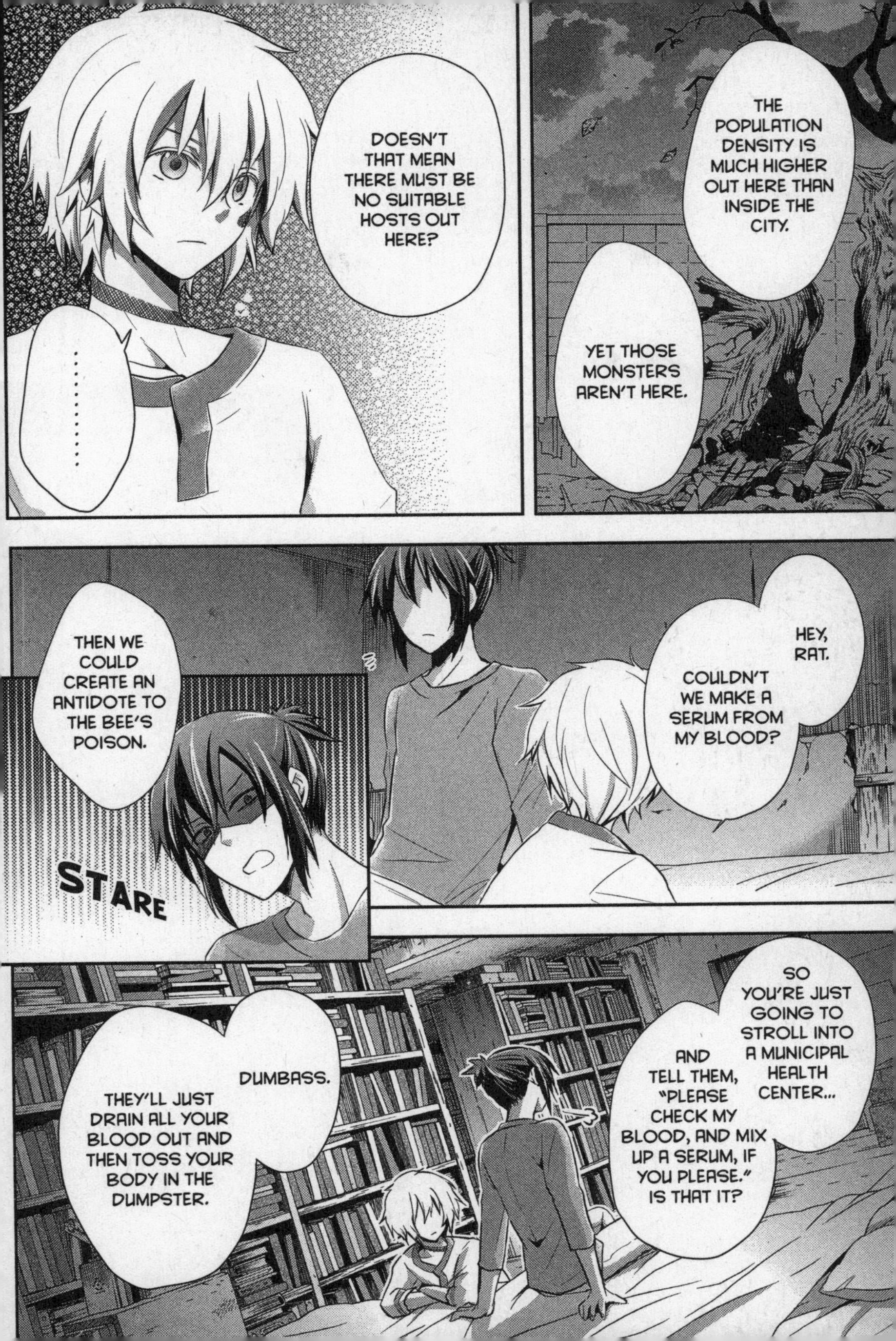
THE POPULATION DENSITY IS MUCH HIGHER OUT HERE THAN INSIDE THE CITY.
YET THOSE MONSTERS AREN'T HERE.
DOESN'T THAT MEAN THERE MUST BE NO SUITABLE HOSTS OUT HERE?
......
HEY, RAT.
COULDN'T WE MAKE A SERUM FROM MY BLOOD?
THEN WE COULD CREATE AN ANTIDOTE TO THE BEE'S POISON.
STARE
SO YOU'RE JUST GOING TO STROLL INTO A MUNICIPAL HEALTH CENTER...
AND TELL THEM, "PLEASE CHECK MY BLOOD, AND MIX UP A SERUM, IF YOU PLEASE." IS THAT IT?
DUMBASS.
THEY'LL JUST DRAIN ALL YOUR BLOOD OUT AND THEN TOSS YOUR BODY IN THE DUMPSTER.

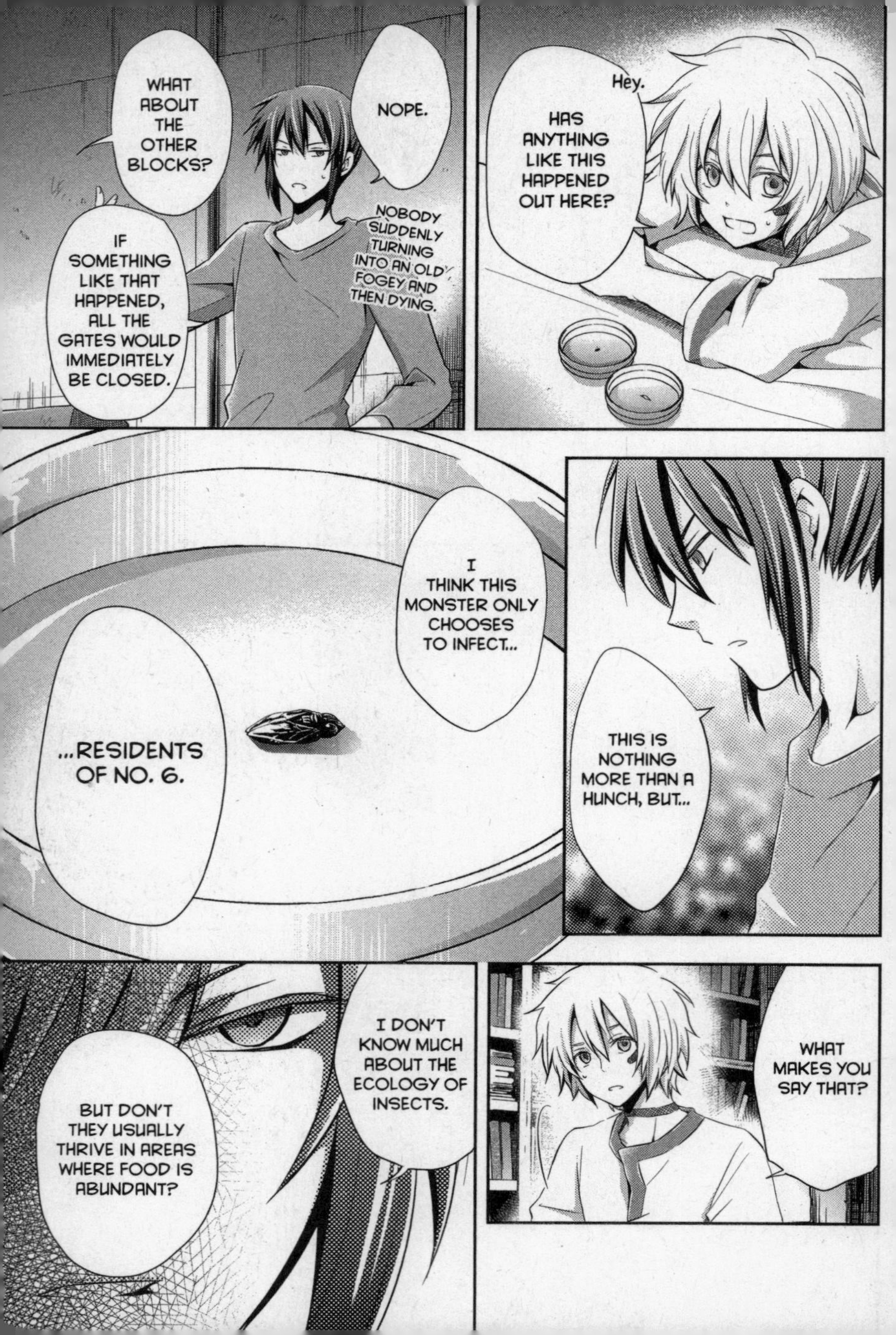
Hey.
HAS ANYTHING LIKE THIS HAPPENED OUT HERE?
NOPE.
NOBODY SUDDENLY TURNING INTO AN OLD FOGEY AND THEN DYING.
WHAT ABOUT THE OTHER BLOCKS?
IF SOMETHING LIKE THAT HAPPENED, ALL THE GATES WOULD IMMEDIATELY BE CLOSED.
THIS IS NOTHING MORE THAN A HUNCH, BUT...
I THINK THIS MONSTER ONLY CHOOSES TO INFECT...
...RESIDENTS OF NO. 6.
WHAT MAKES YOU SAY THAT?
I DON'T KNOW MUCH ABOUT THE ECOLOGY OF INSECTS.
BUT DON'T THEY USUALLY THRIVE IN AREAS WHERE FOOD IS ABUNDANT?

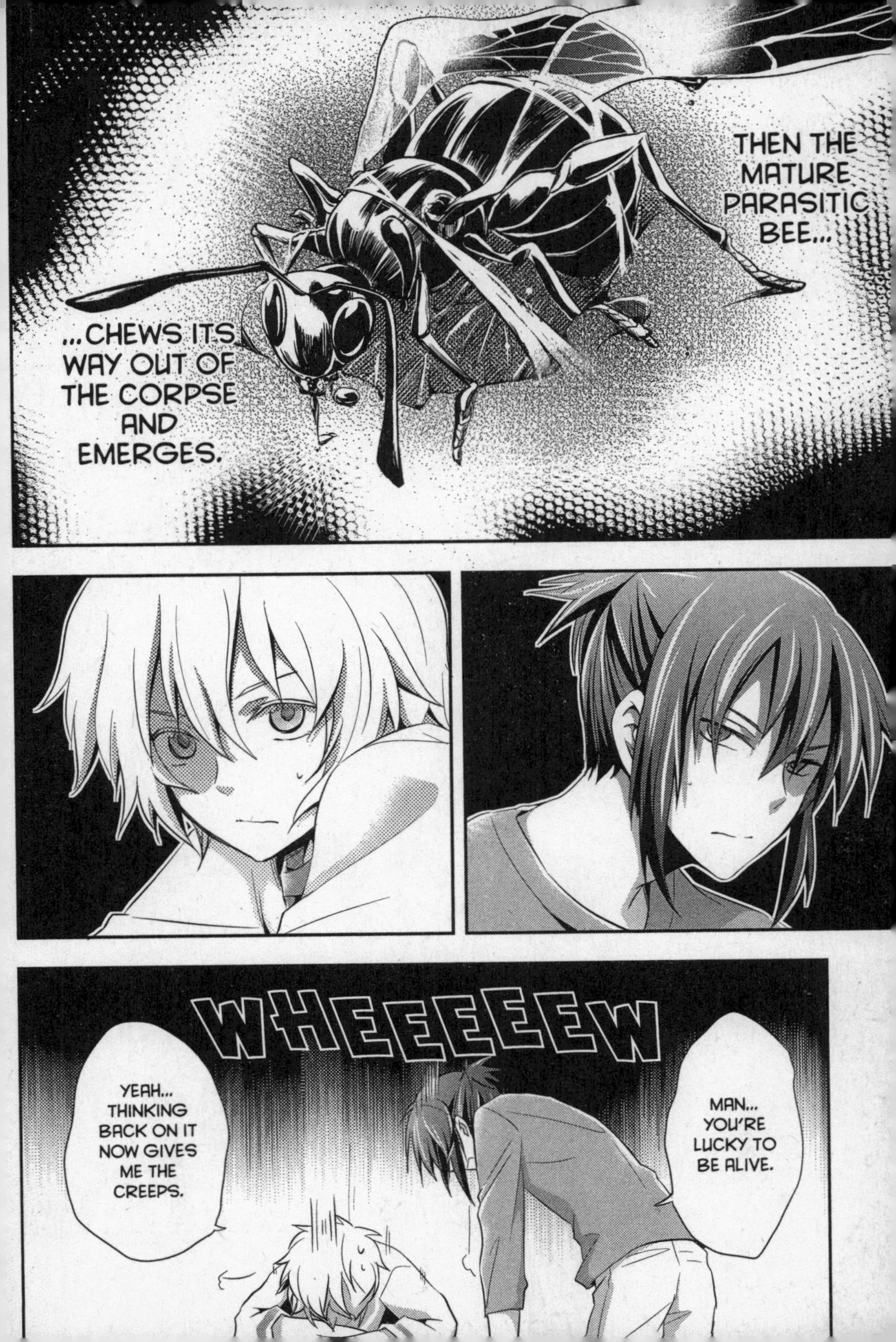
THEN THE MATURE PARASITIC BEE...
...CHEWS ITS WAY OUT OF THE CORPSE AND EMERGES.
WHEEEEEEW
MAN... YOU'RE LUCKY TO BE ALIVE.
YEAH... THINKING BACK ON IT NOW GIVES ME THE CREEPS.

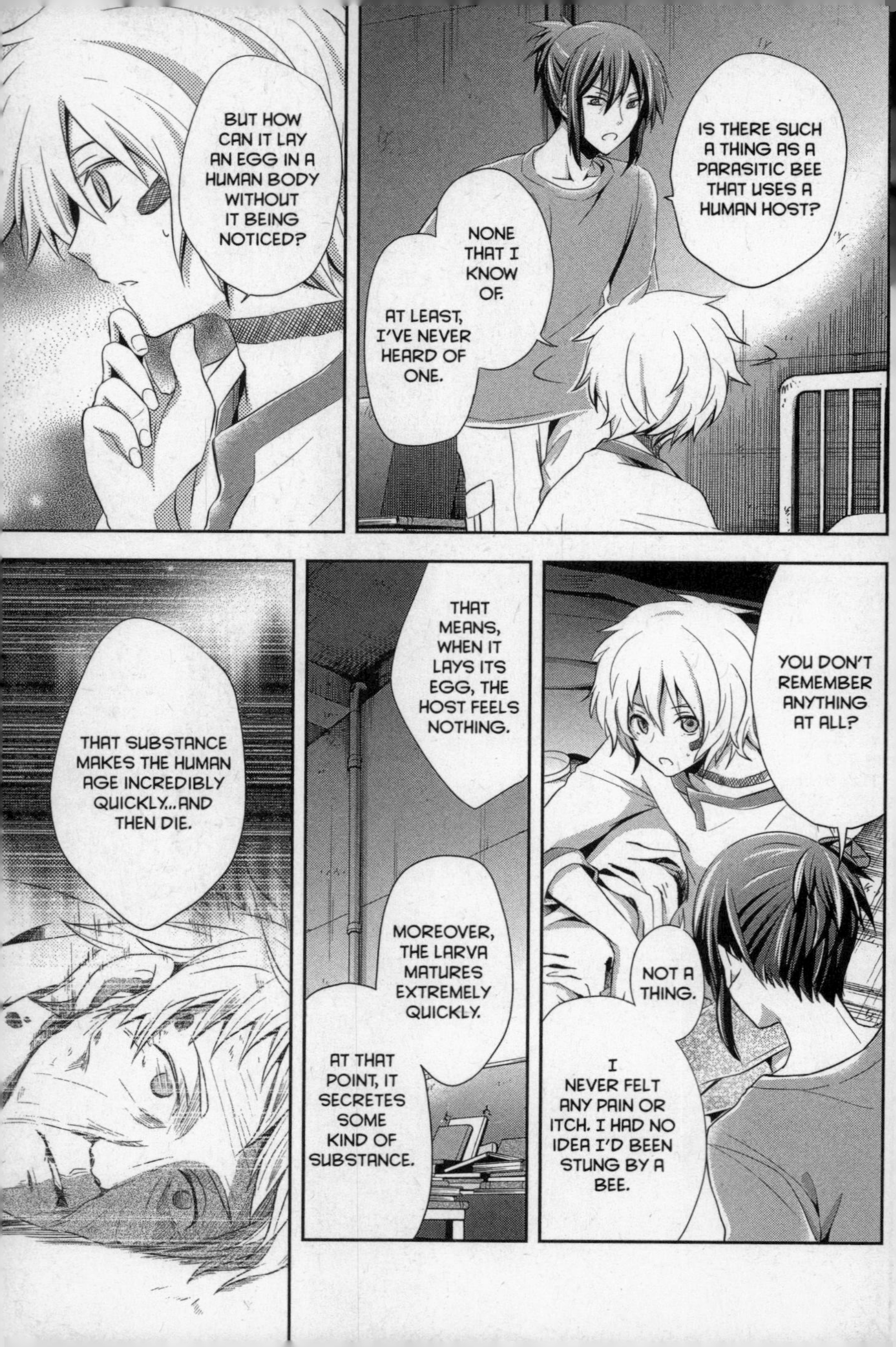
IS THERE SUCH A THING AS A PARASITIC BEE THAT USES A HUMAN HOST?
NONE THAT I KNOW OF.
AT LEAST, I'VE NEVER HEARD OF ONE.
BUT HOW CAN IT LAY AN EGG IN A HUMAN BODY WITHOUT IT BEING NOTICED?
YOU DON'T REMEMBER ANYTHING AT ALL?
NOT A THING.
I NEVER FELT ANY PAIN OR ITCH. I HAD NO IDEA I'D BEEN STUNG BY A BEE.
THAT MEANS, WHEN IT LAYS ITS EGG, THE HOST FEELS NOTHING.
MOREOVER, THE LARVA MATURES EXTREMELY QUICKLY.
AT THAT POINT, IT SECRETES SOME KIND OF SUBSTANCE.
THAT SUBSTANCE MAKES THE HUMAN AGE INCREDIBLY QUICKLY...AND THEN DIE.

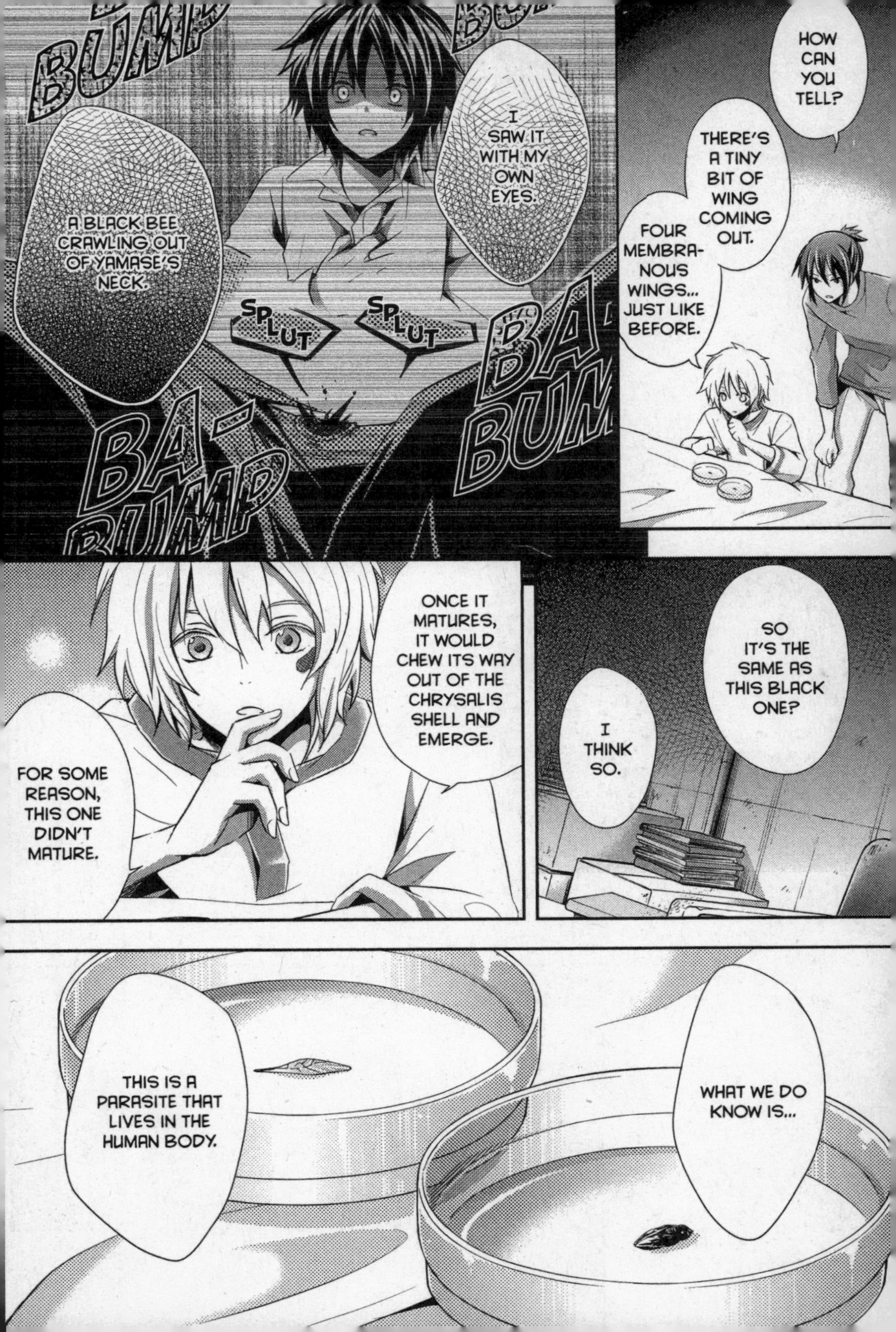
HOW CAN YOU TELL?
THERE'S A TINY BIT OF WING COMING OUT.
FOUR MEMBRA-NOUS WINGS... JUST LIKE BEFORE.
BUMP
I SAW IT WITH MY OWN EYES.
A BLACK BEE CRAWLING OUT OF YAMASE'S NECK.
SPLUT
SPLUT
BA-BUMP
BA-BUMP
SO IT'S THE SAME AS THIS BLACK ONE?
I THINK SO.
ONCE IT MATURES, IT WOULD CHEW ITS WAY OUT OF THE CHRYSALIS SHELL AND EMERGE.
FOR SOME REASON, THIS ONE DIDN'T MATURE.
WHAT WE DO KNOW IS...
THIS IS A PARASITE THAT LIVES IN THE HUMAN BODY.

DELICIOUS!

IT'S THE BEST THING I'VE EVER TASTED IN MY LIFE!

YOU DO ME TOO GREAT AN HONOR, MY LORD.

GULP

SHAKE

SHAKE

PLOK

IT'S THE THING I EXTRACTED FROM YOUR BODY.

WHAT'S THIS?

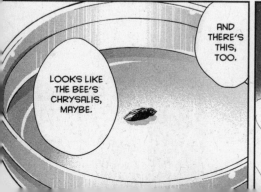

AND THERE'S THIS, TOO.

LOOKS LIKE THE BEE'S CHRYSALIS, MAYBE.

A... WING?

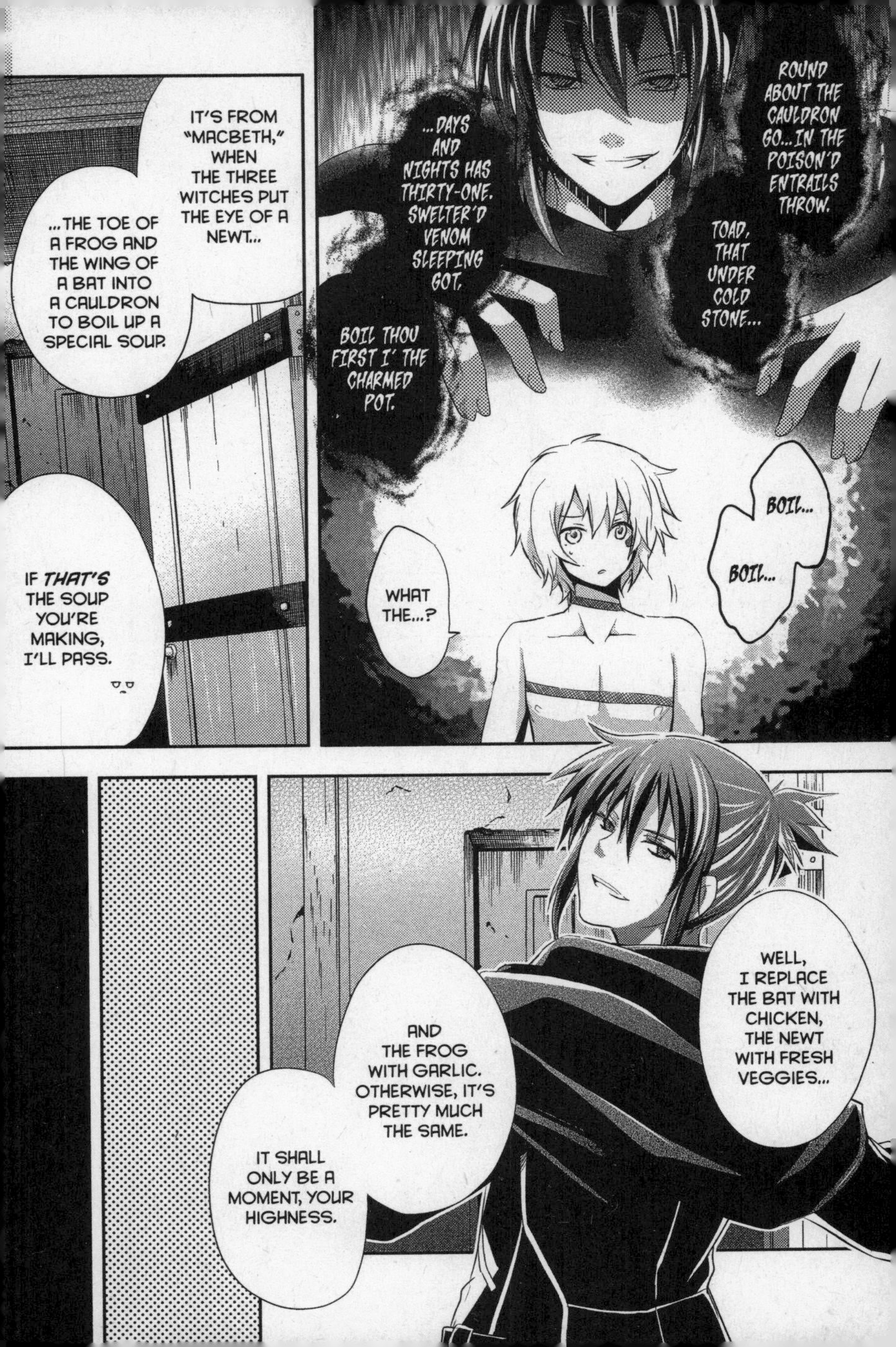
ROUND ABOUT THE CAULDRON GO...IN THE POISON'D ENTRAILS THROW.
TOAD, THAT UNDER COLD STONE...
...DAYS AND NIGHTS HAS THIRTY-ONE. SWELTER'D VENOM SLEEPING GOT,
BOIL THOU FIRST I' THE CHARMED POT.
BOIL... BOIL...
WHAT THE...?
IT'S FROM "MACBETH," WHEN THE THREE WITCHES PUT THE EYE OF A NEWT...
...THE TOE OF A FROG AND THE WING OF A BAT INTO A CAULDRON TO BOIL UP A SPECIAL SOUP.
IF *THAT'S* THE SOUP YOU'RE MAKING, I'LL PASS.
WELL, I REPLACE THE BAT WITH CHICKEN, THE NEWT WITH FRESH VEGGIES...
AND THE FROG WITH GARLIC. OTHERWISE, IT'S PRETTY MUCH THE SAME.
IT SHALL ONLY BE A MOMENT, YOUR HIGHNESS.

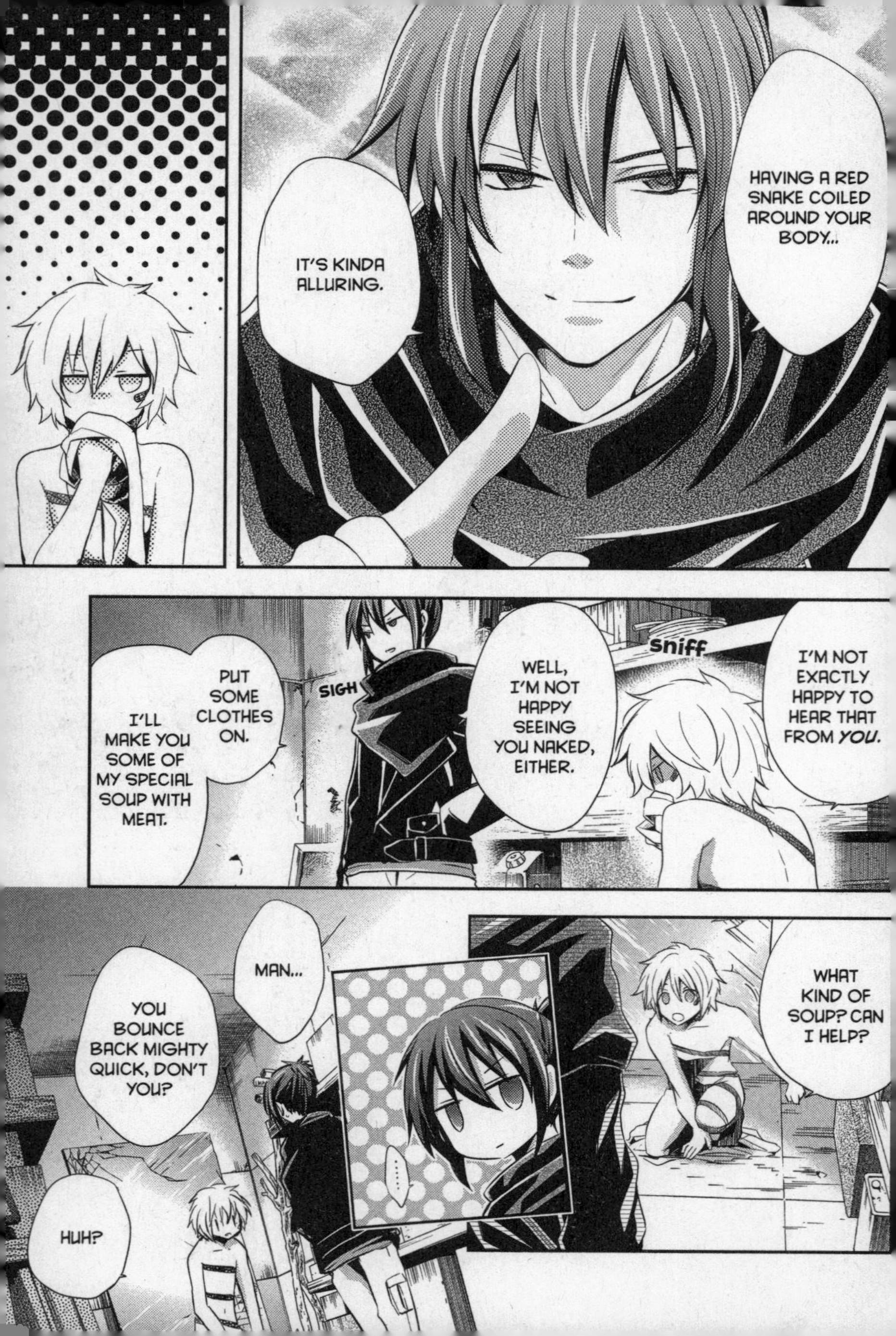
HAVING A RED SNAKE COILED AROUND YOUR BODY...
IT'S KINDA ALLURING.
I'M NOT EXACTLY HAPPY TO HEAR THAT FROM *YOU*.
sniff
WELL, I'M NOT HAPPY SEEING YOU NAKED, EITHER.
SIGH
PUT SOME CLOTHES ON.
I'LL MAKE YOU SOME OF MY SPECIAL SOUP WITH MEAT.
WHAT KIND OF SOUP? CAN I HELP?
......
MAN...
YOU BOUNCE BACK MIGHTY QUICK, DON'T YOU?
HUH?

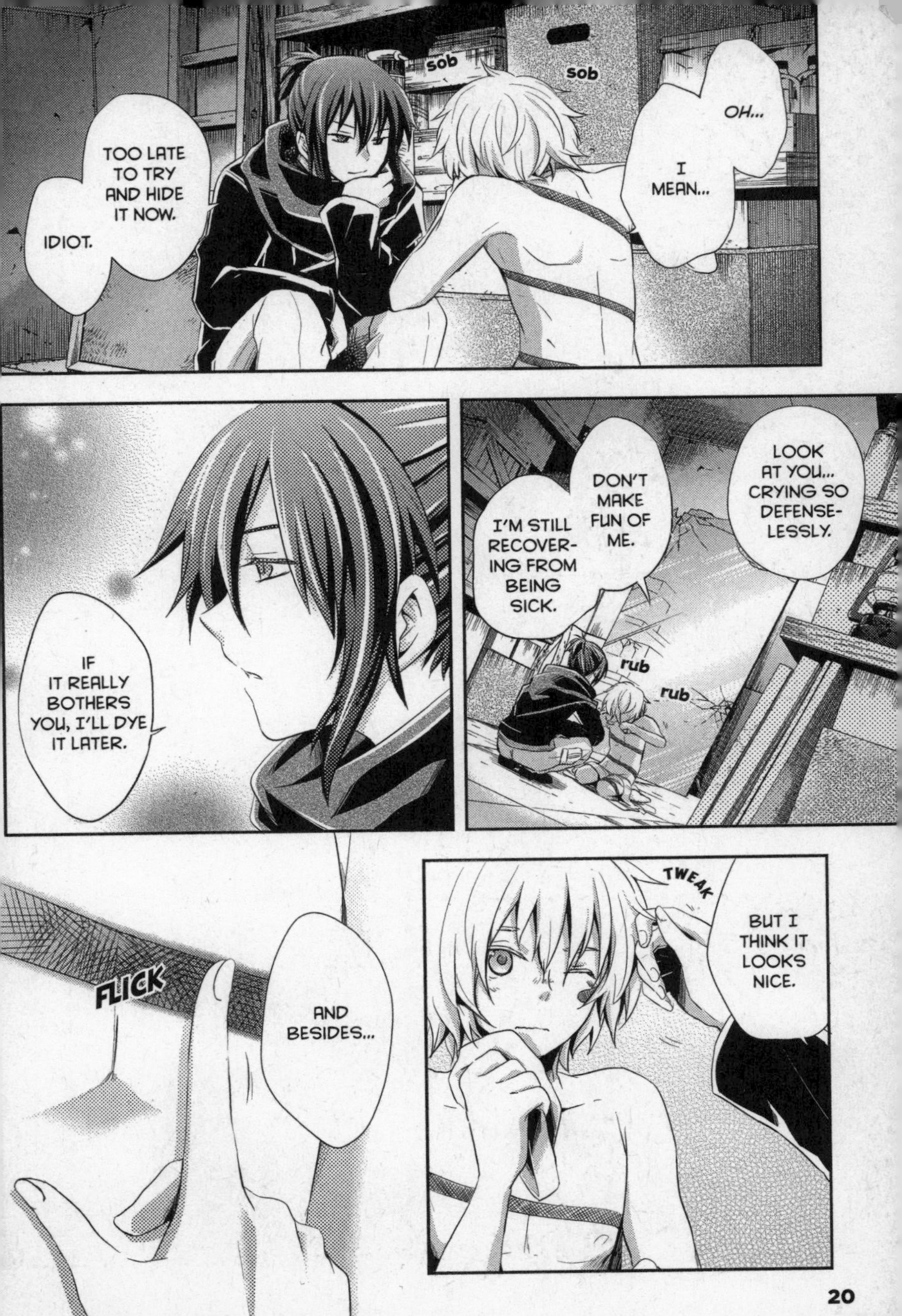
sob
sob
OH...
I MEAN...
TOO LATE TO TRY AND HIDE IT NOW.
IDIOT.
LOOK AT YOU... CRYING SO DEFENSE-LESSLY.
DON'T MAKE FUN OF ME.
I'M STILL RECOVER-ING FROM BEING SICK.
rub
rub
IF IT REALLY BOTHERS YOU, I'LL DYE IT LATER.
TWEAK
BUT I THINK IT LOOKS NICE.
AND BESIDES...
FLICK

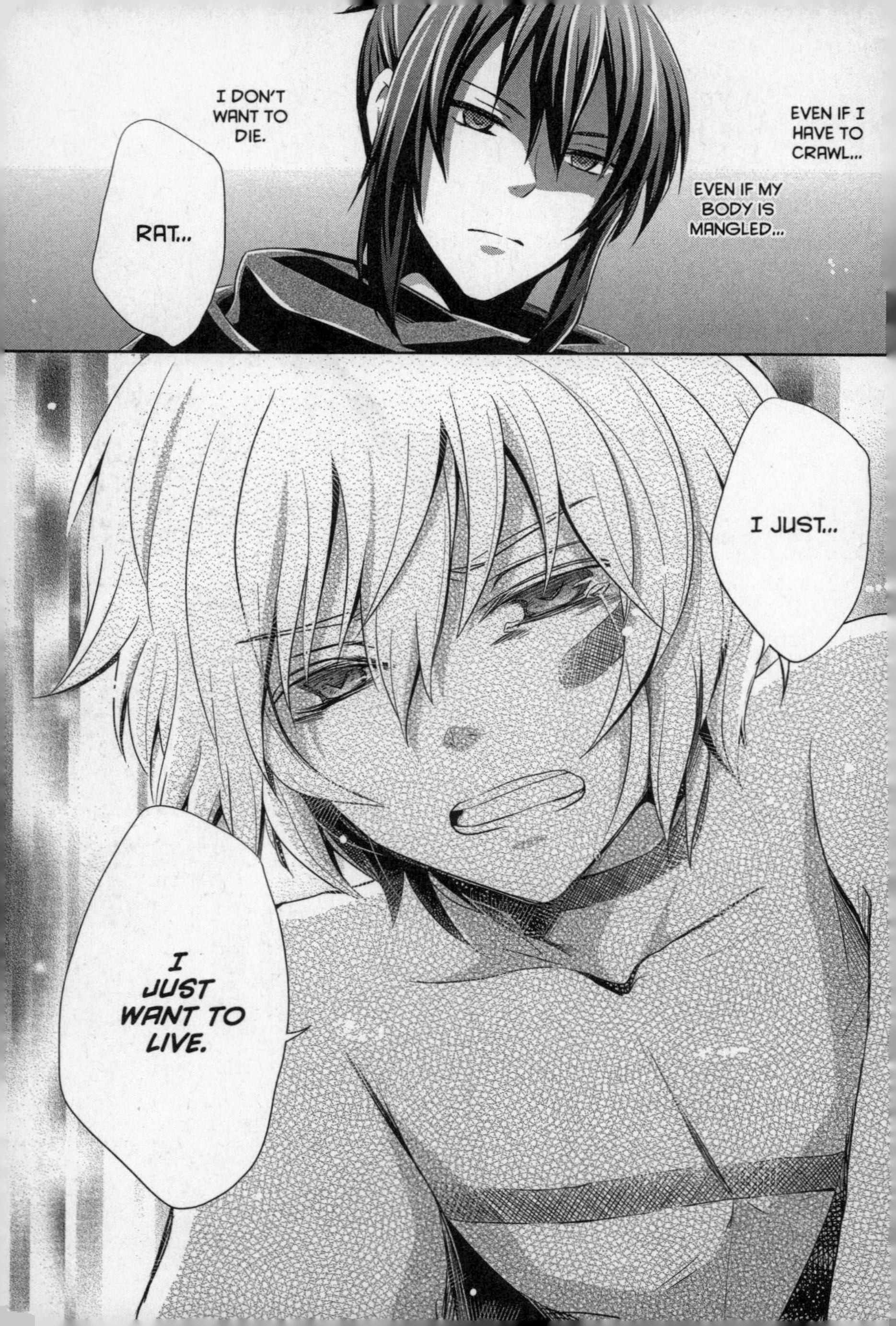
EVEN IF I HAVE TO CRAWL...
EVEN IF MY BODY IS MANGLED...
I DON'T WANT TO DIE.
RAT...
I JUST...
I JUST WANT TO LIVE.

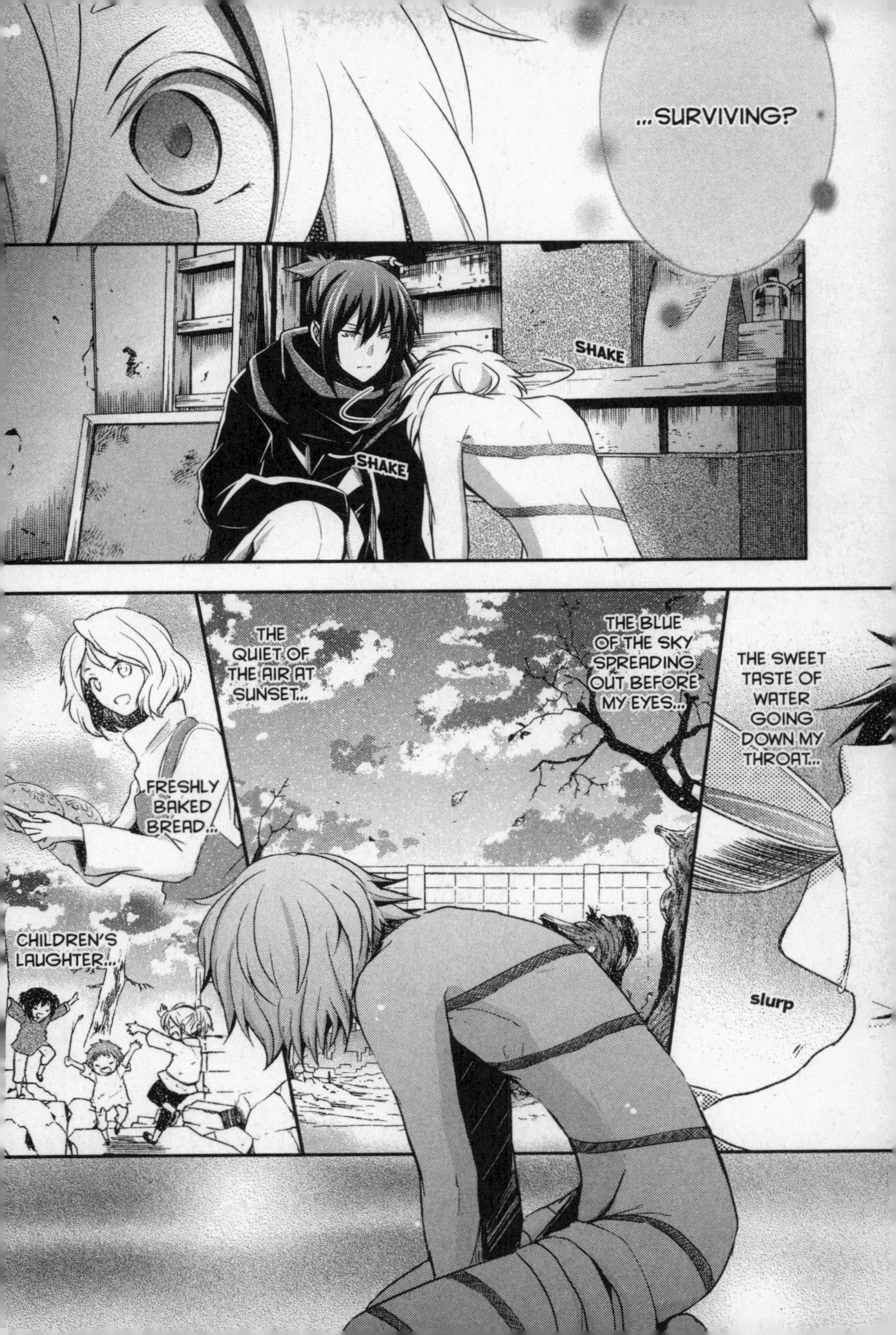
...SURVIVING?
SHAKE
SHAKE
THE SWEET TASTE OF WATER GOING DOWN MY THROAT...
slurp
THE BLUE OF THE SKY SPREADING OUT BEFORE MY EYES...
THE QUIET OF THE AIR AT SUNSET...
FRESHLY BAKED BREAD...
CHILDREN'S LAUGHTER...

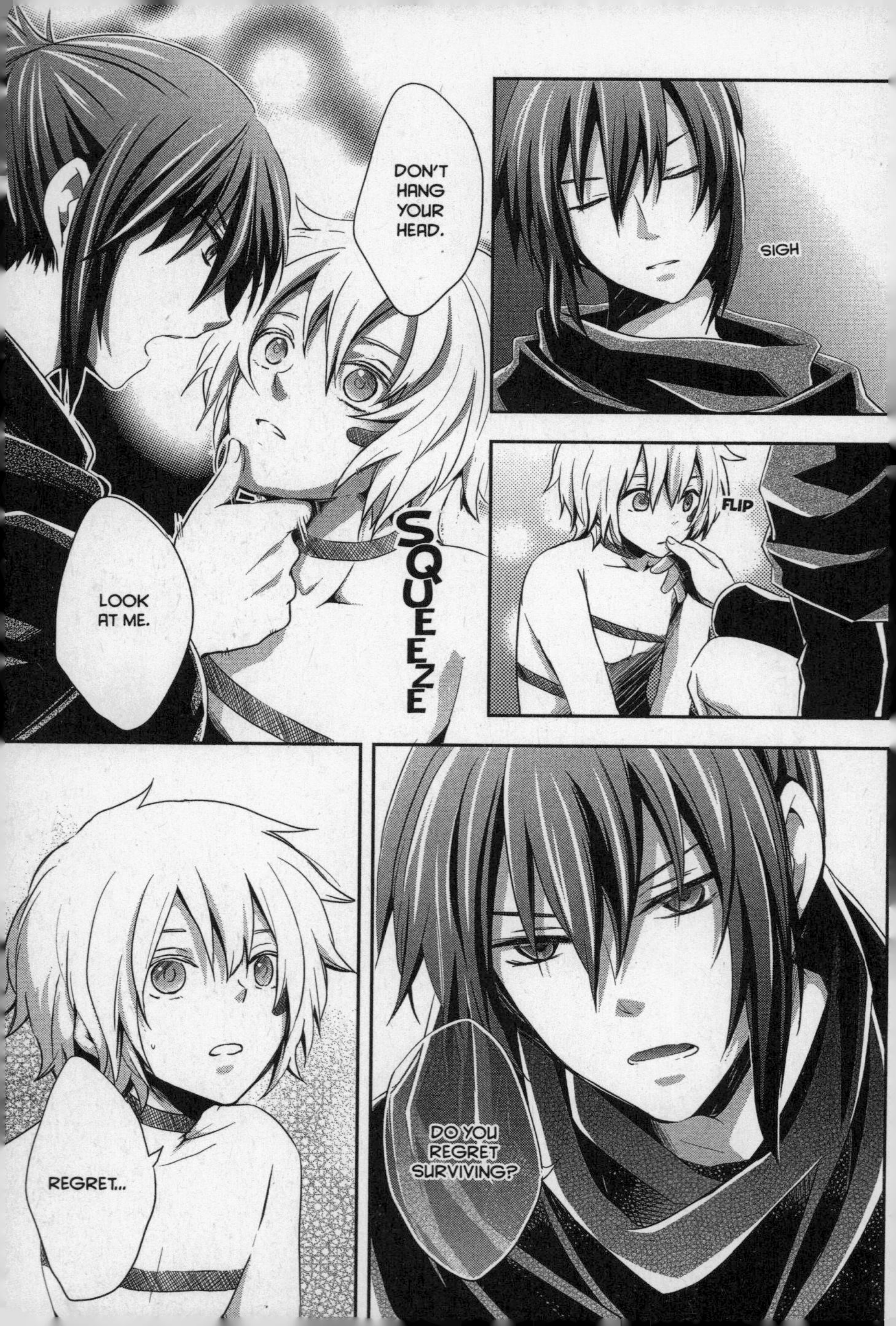
SIGH
FLIP
DON'T HANG YOUR HEAD.
SQUEEZE
LOOK AT ME.
DO YOU REGRET SURVIVING?
REGRET...

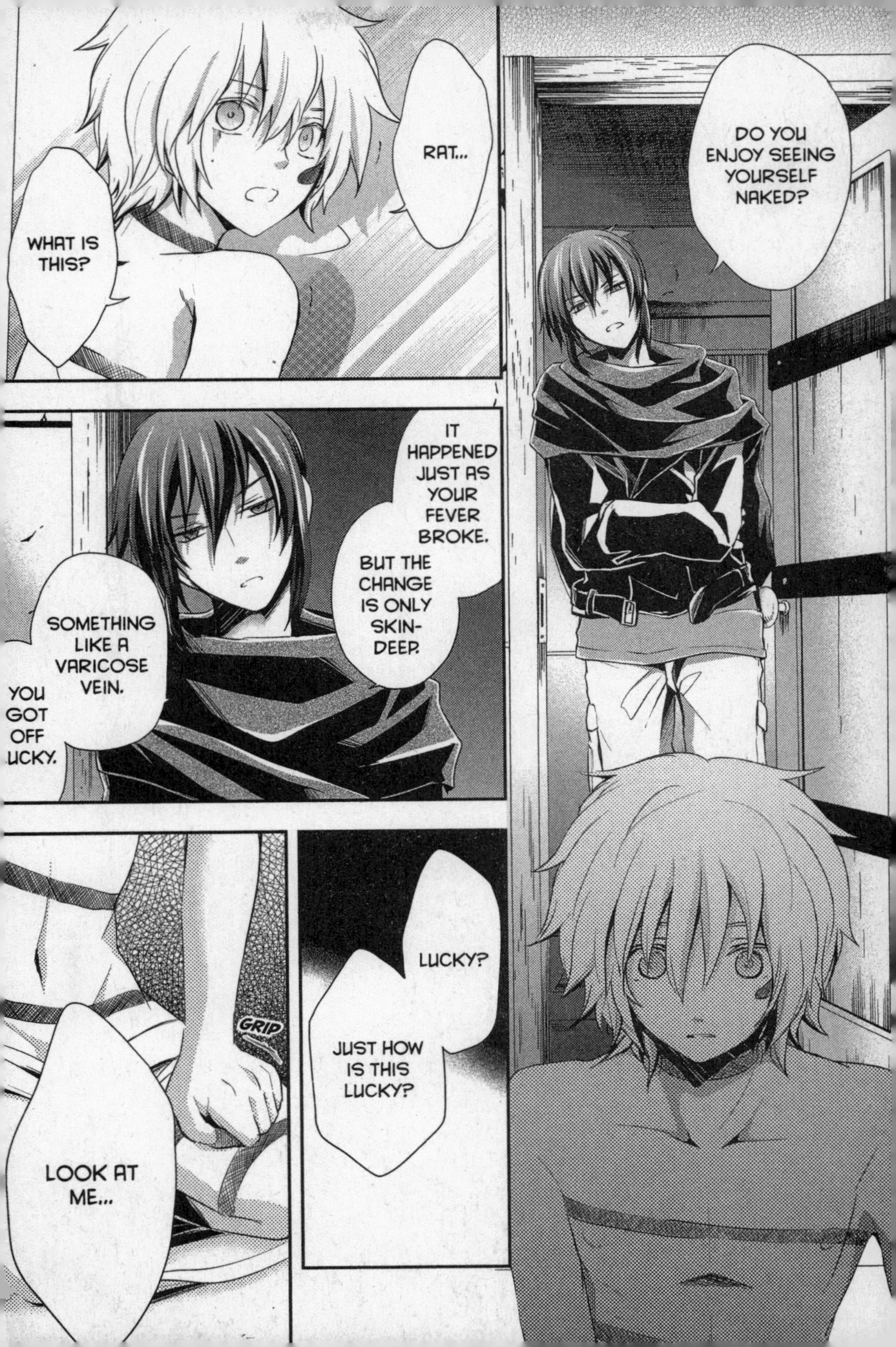
DO YOU ENJOY SEEING YOURSELF NAKED?
RAT...
WHAT IS THIS?
IT HAPPENED JUST AS YOUR FEVER BROKE.
BUT THE CHANGE IS ONLY SKIN-DEEP.
SOMETHING LIKE A VARICOSE VEIN.
YOU GOT OFF LUCKY.
LUCKY?
JUST HOW IS THIS LUCKY?
GRIP
LOOK AT ME...

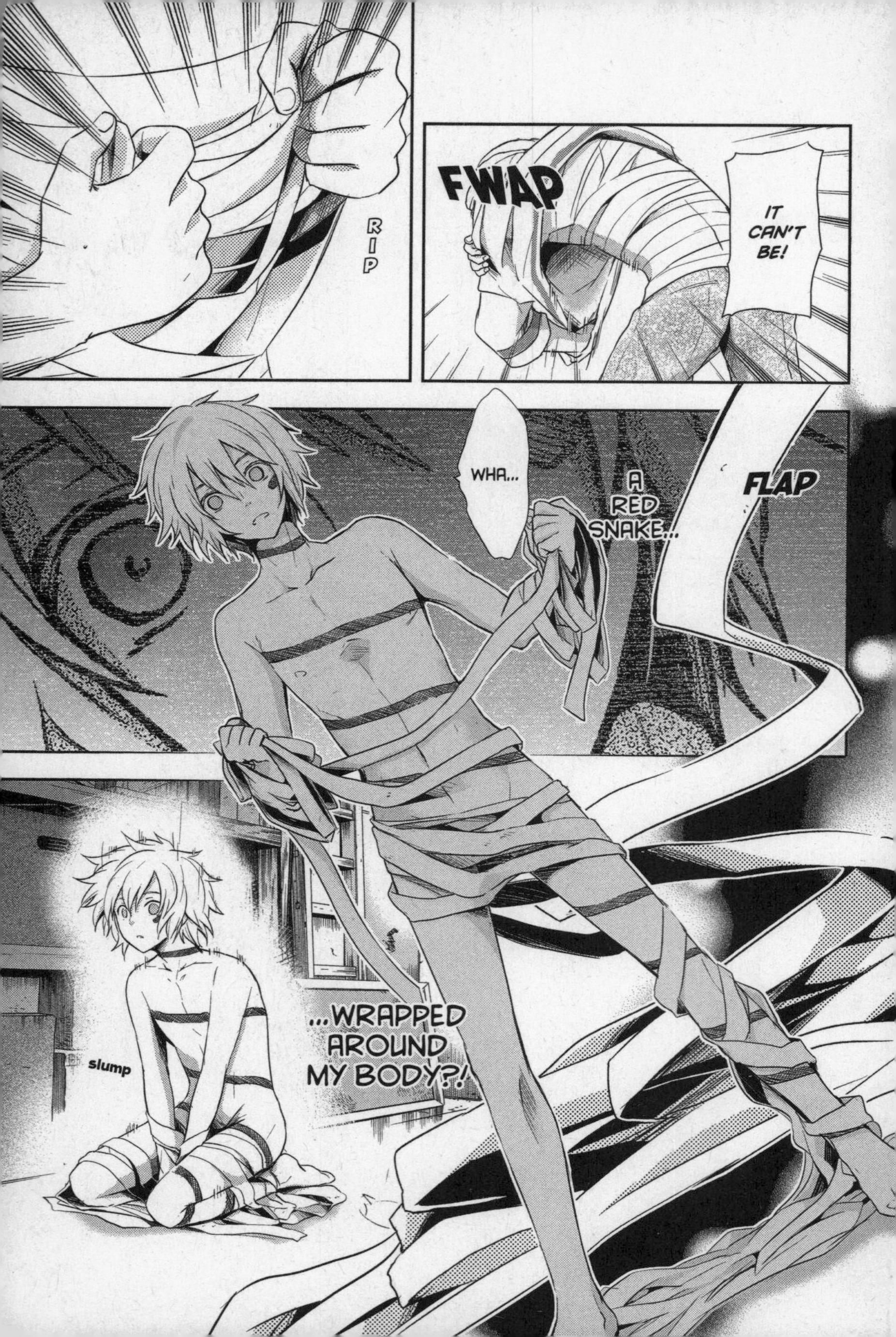
IT CAN'T BE!
FWAP
RIP
FLAP
A RED SNAKE...
WHA...
...WRAPPED AROUND MY BODY?!
slump

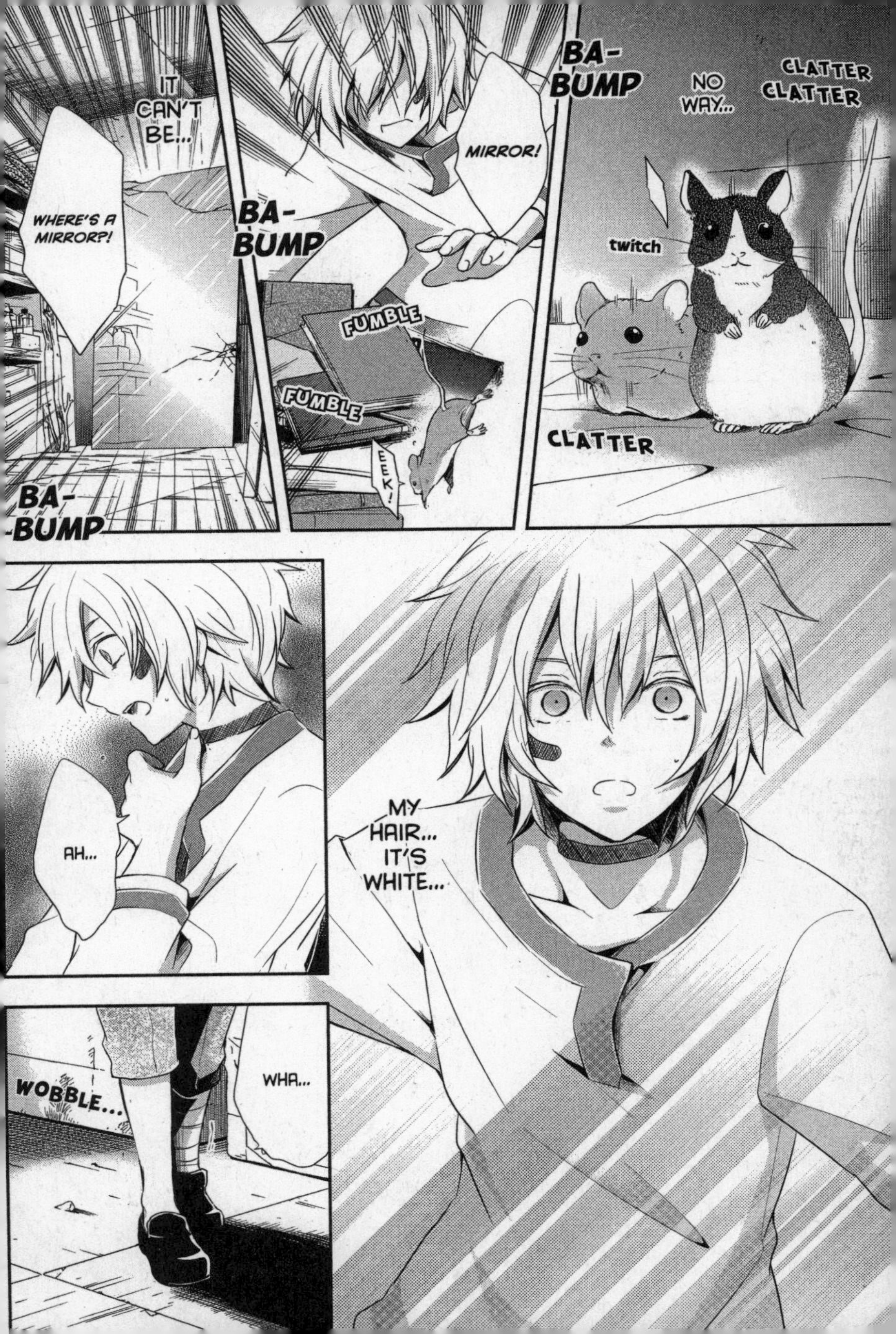
CLATTER CLATTER
NO WAY...
BA-BUMP
twitch
CLATTER
MIRROR!
BA-BUMP
FUMBLE
FUMBLE
EEK!
IT CAN'T BE...
WHERE'S A MIRROR?!
BA-BUMP
MY HAIR... IT'S WHITE...
AH...
WHA...
WOBBLE...

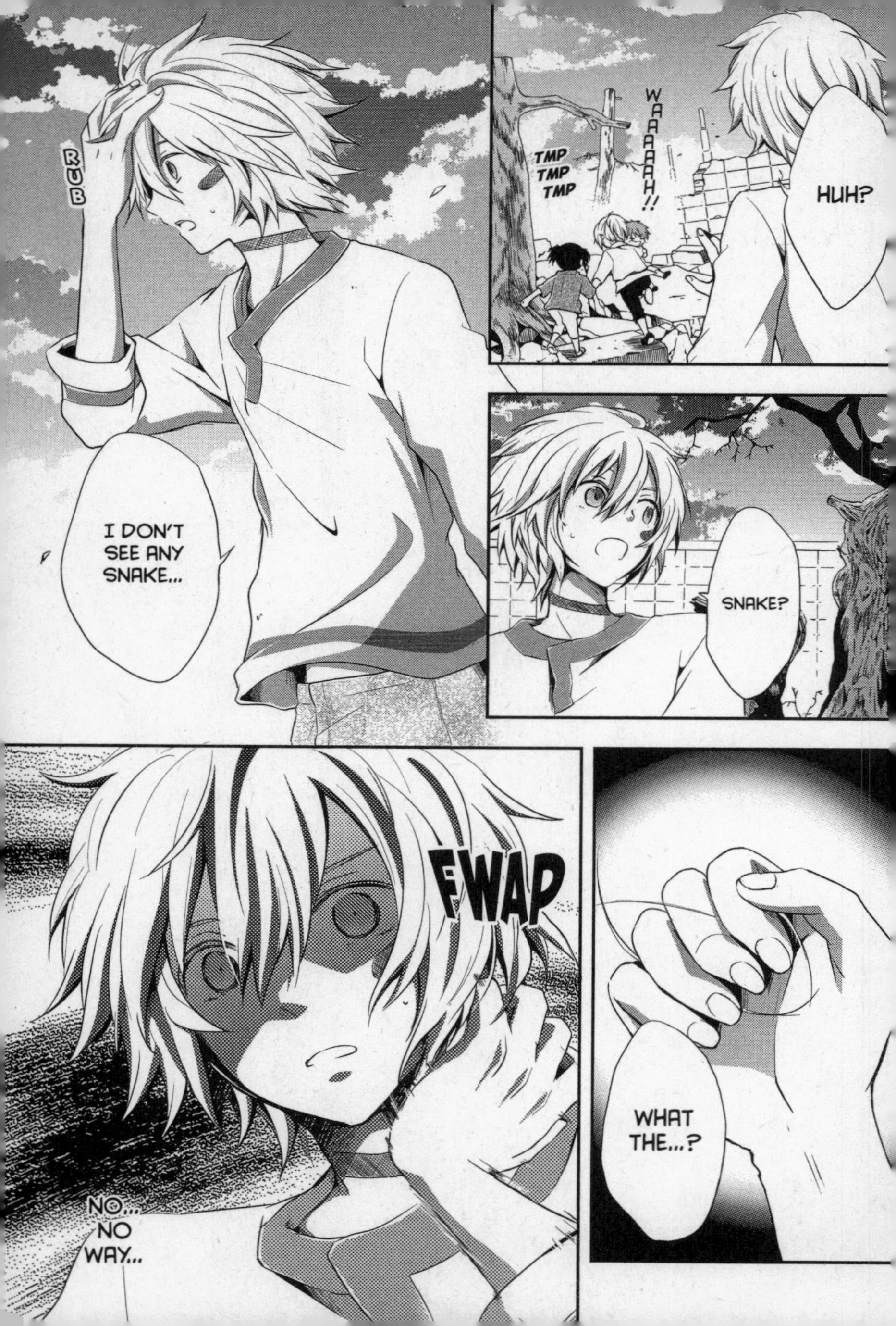
HUH?
WAAAAAAH!!
TMP TMP TMP
SNAKE?
RUB
I DON'T SEE ANY SNAKE...
WHAT THE...?
FWAP
NO... NO WAY...

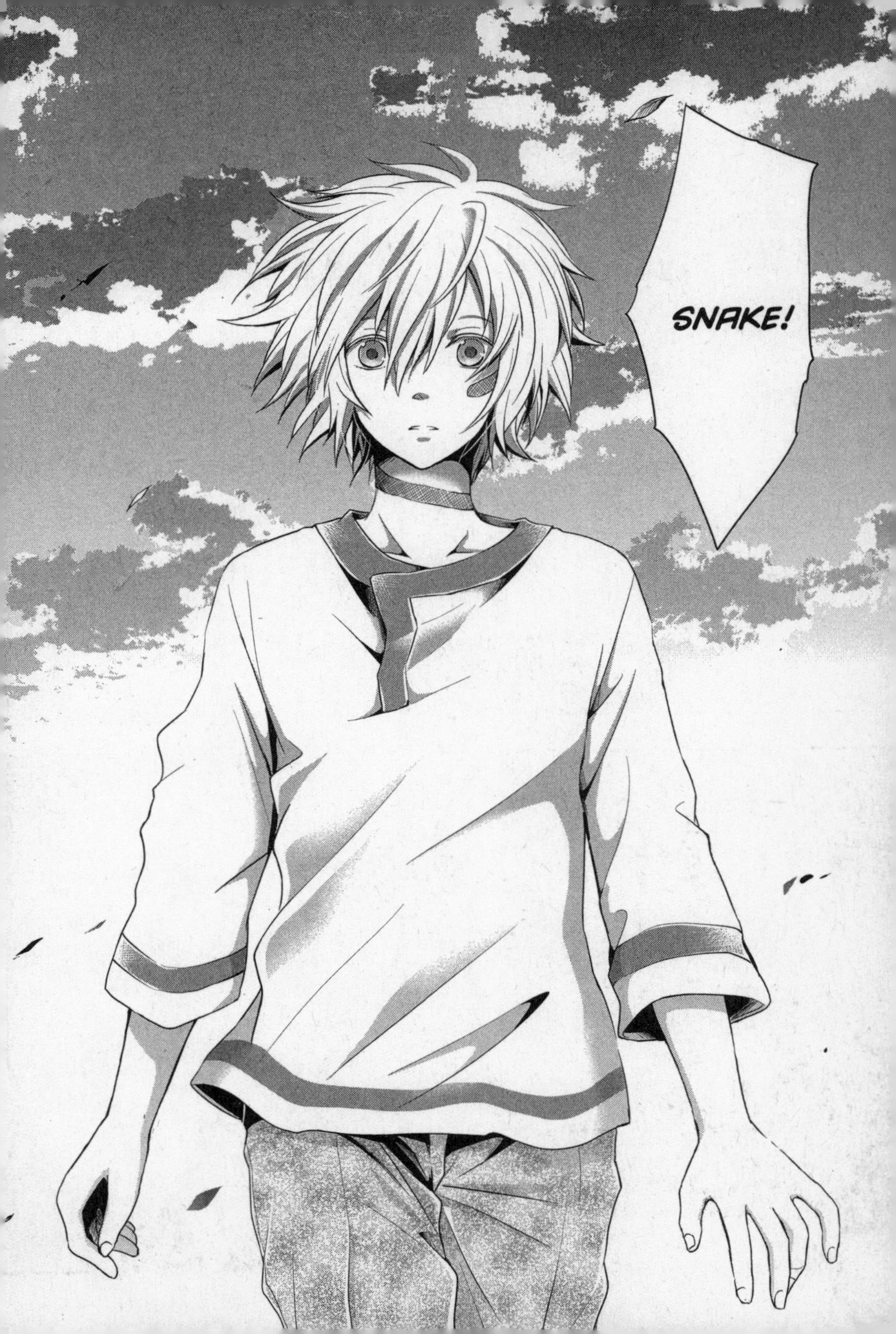
SNAKE!

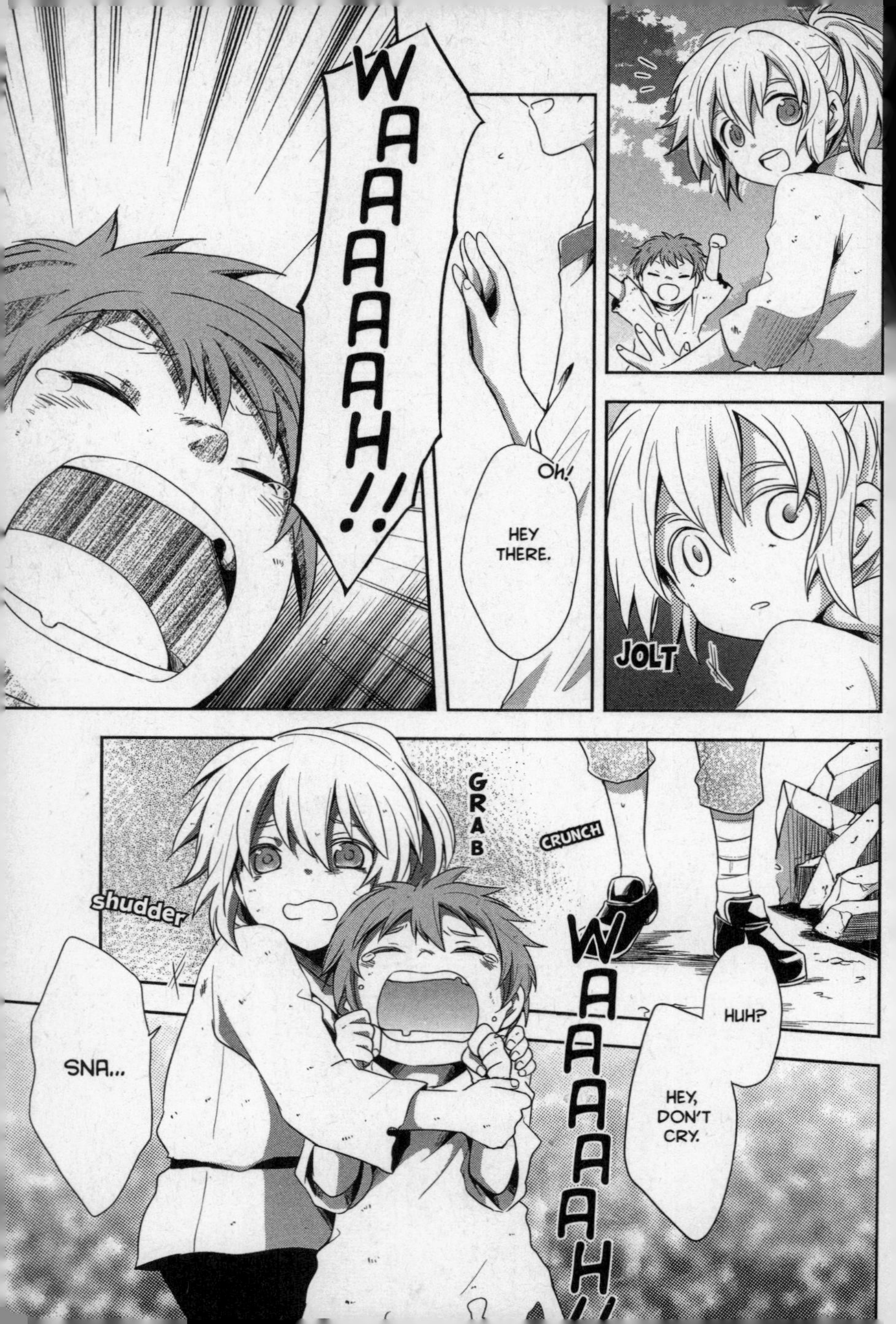
JOLT
Oh!
HEY THERE.
WAAAAAH!!
HUH?
HEY, DON'T CRY.
WAAAAAH!!
CRUNCH
GRAB
shudder
SNA...

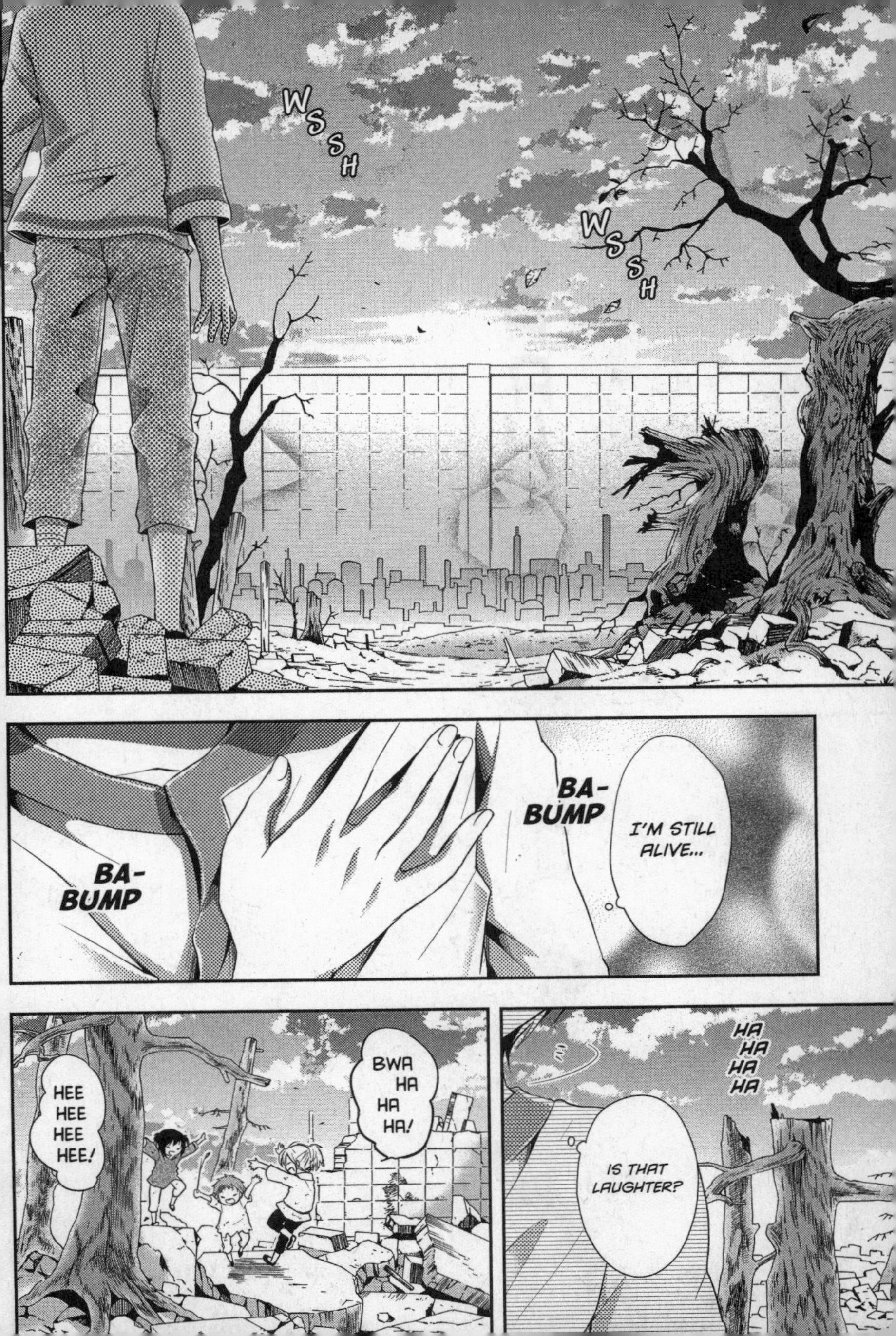
WSSH
WSSH
I'M STILL ALIVE...
BA-BUMP
BA-BUMP
HA HA HA HA
IS THAT LAUGHTER?
BWA HA HA HA!
HEE HEE HEE HEE!

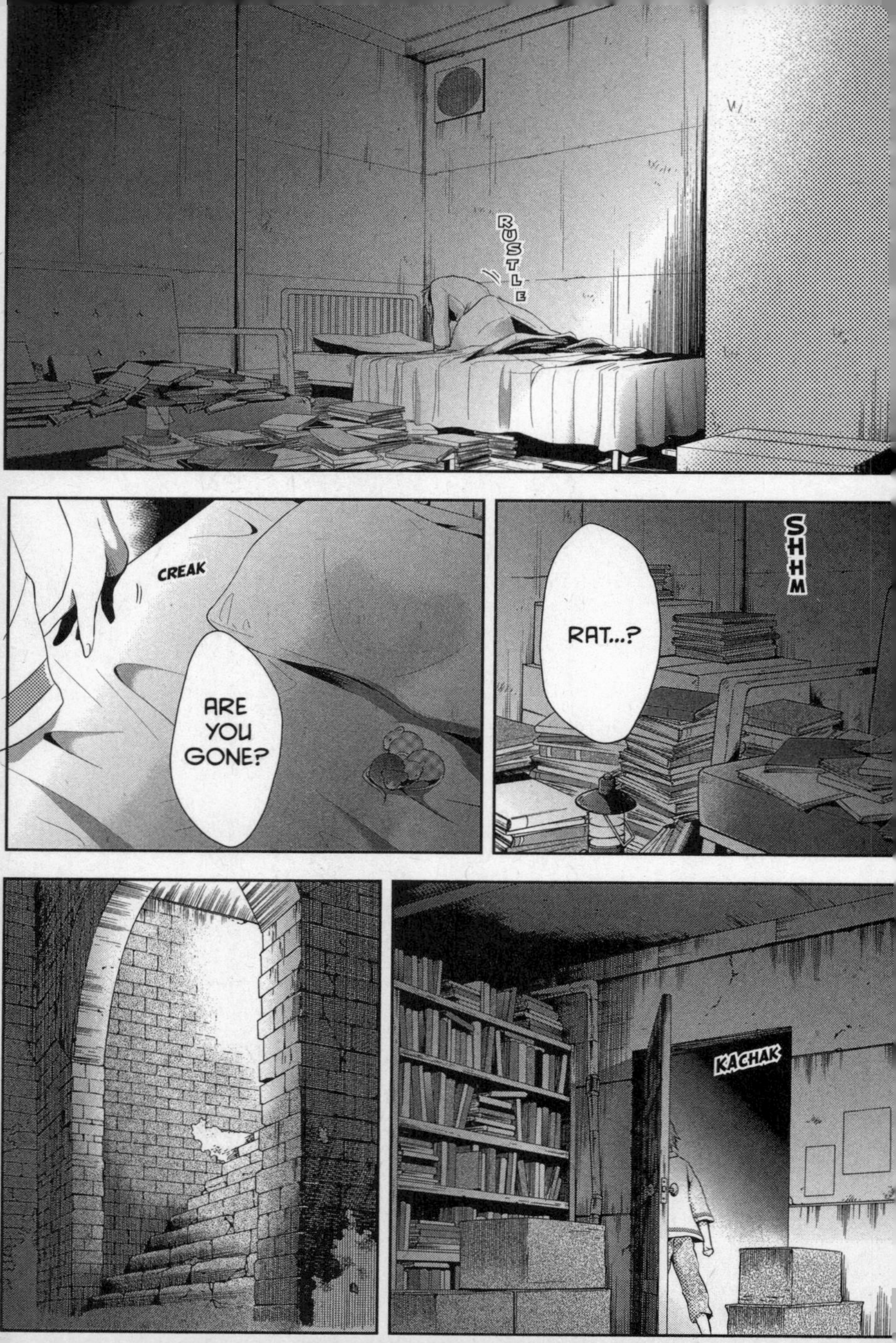
RUSTLE
SHHM
RAT...?
CREAK
ARE YOU GONE?
KACHAK

NO.6

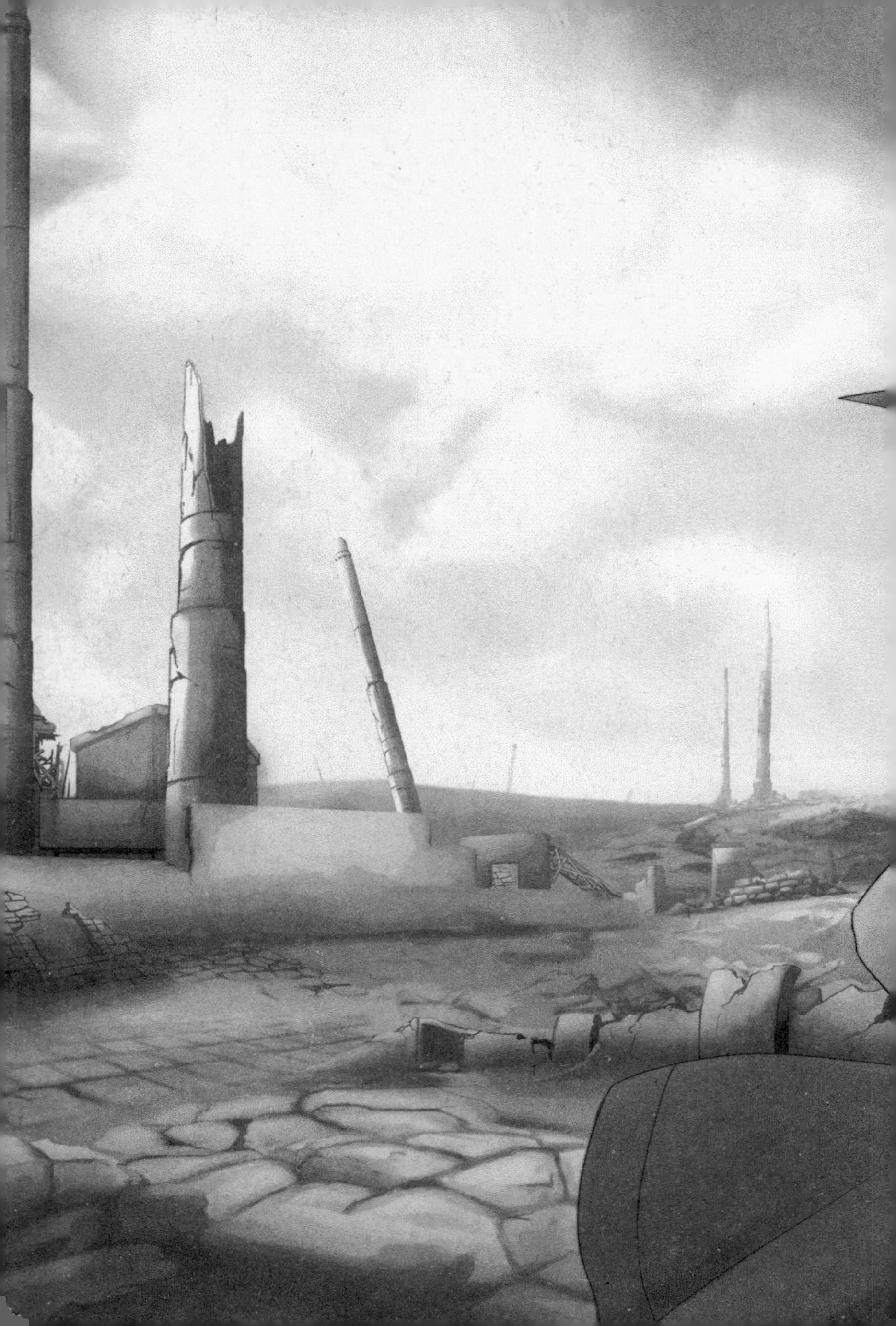

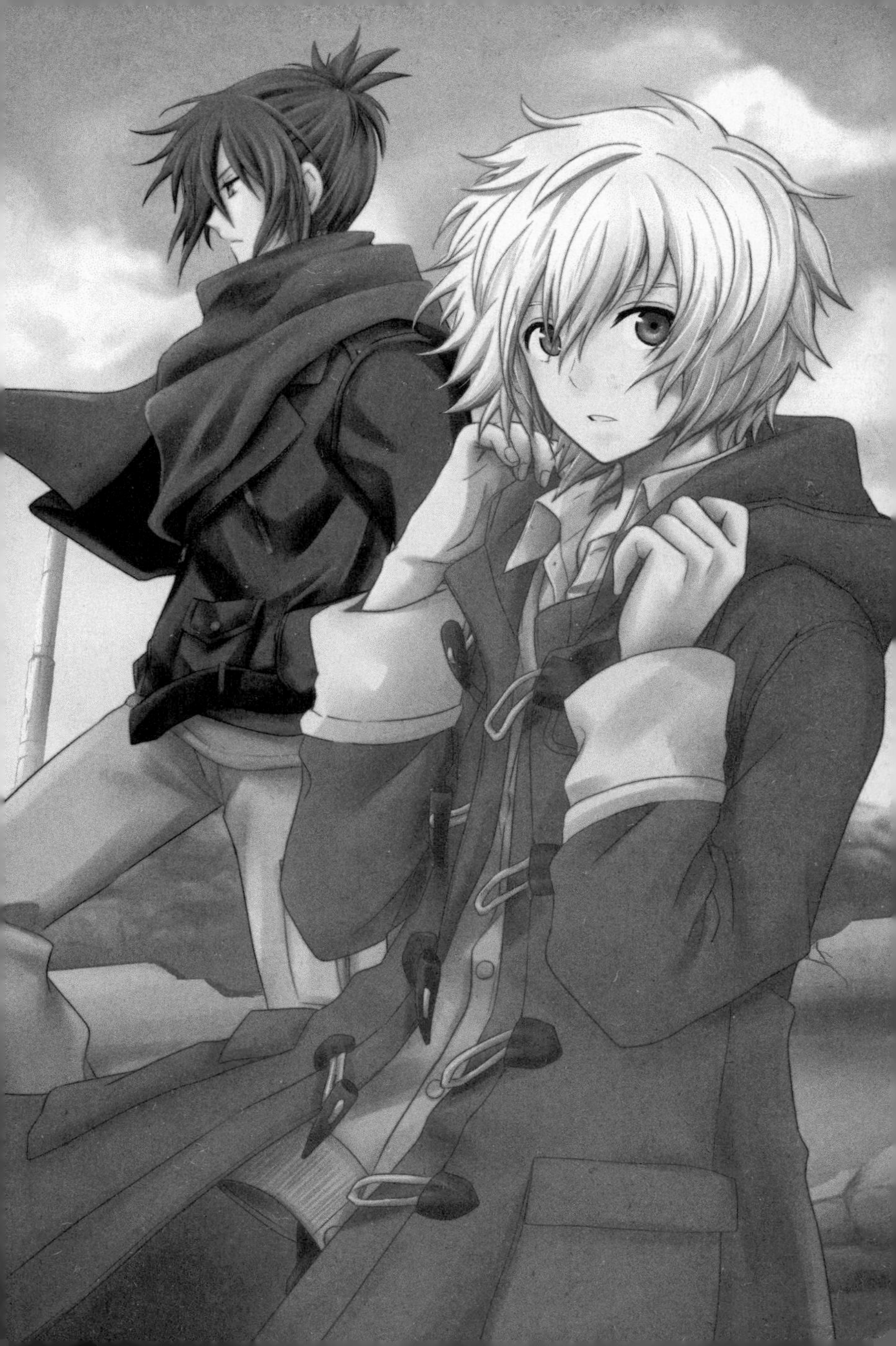

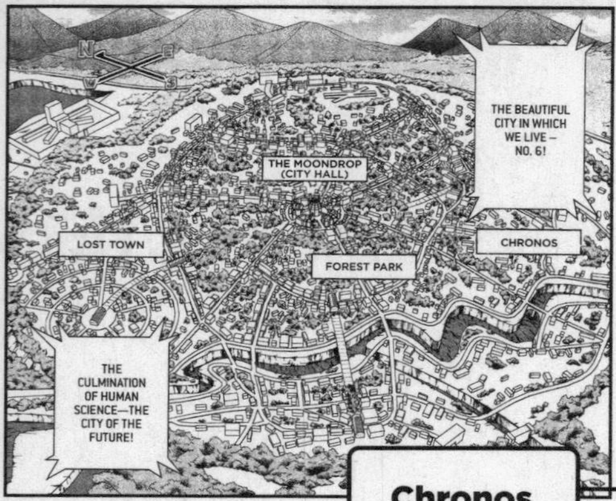
THE BEAUTIFUL CITY IN WHICH WE LIVE — NO. 6!
THE MOONDROP (CITY HALL)
LOST TOWN
CHRONOS
FOREST PARK
THE CULMINATION OF HUMAN SCIENCE—THE CITY OF THE FUTURE!

Inside No. 6

Upper Class

The center of the town, with the Moondrop (City Hall) as its apex.

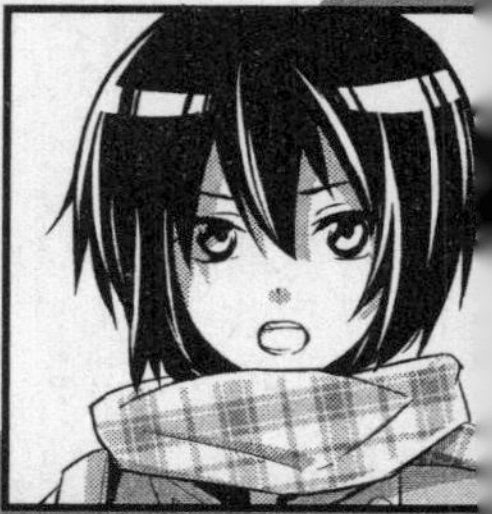

Chronos

The top-class residential area, open only to special elite citizens.

Lost Town

The lower-class residential area for the city's disenfranchised.

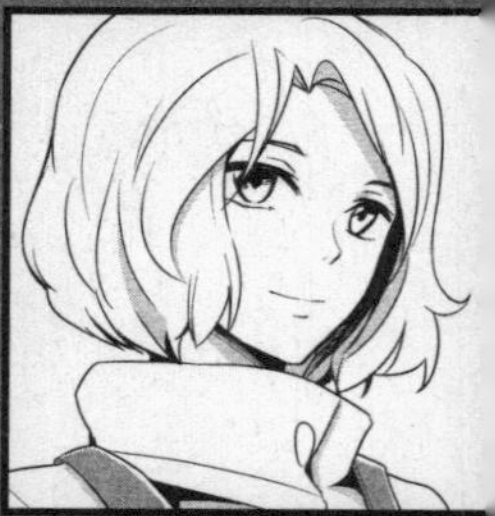

KARAN

Shion's mother. Operates a bakery in Lost Town.

The Outskirts

West Block

The dangerous special zone outside the walls of the city. A criminal correctional facility is located there.

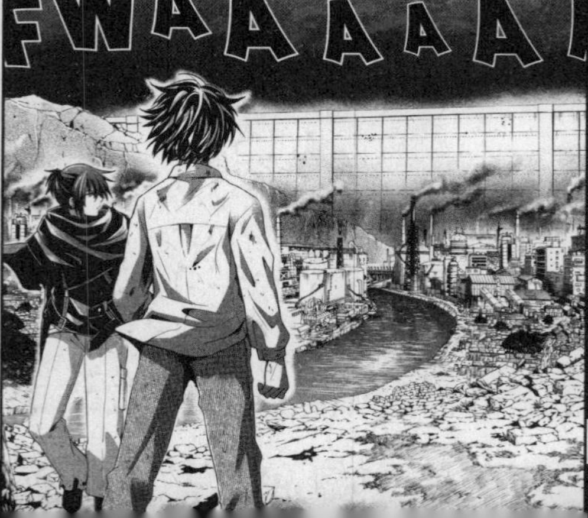
FWAAAAA

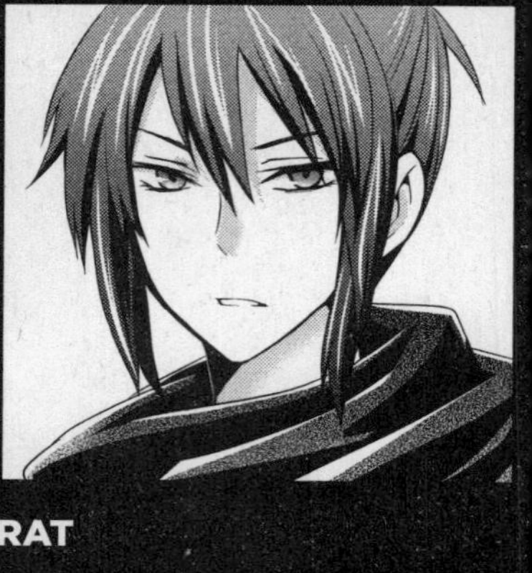

RAT

Four years ago, Shion saved his life in Chronos. Is he a criminal escaped from the correctional facility?

NO.6 STORY and CHARACTERS

SAFU

A childhood riend who's in ove with Shion. An elite researcher who specializes in neuroscience.

The sacred city of No. 6: a collection of the best human science has to offer. The city recognized Shion for his high intelligence, and granted him a life of limitless freedom as a member of the super-elite. But on his twelfth birthday, Shion sheltered a fugitive boy known only as Rat, and was stripped of all his special privileges. Four years later, a mysterious corpse was discovered at the Forest Park Administration Center where Shion worked. The next day, his coworker rapidly aged and died. A single black bee chewed its way out of the corpse.

Under suspicion for his coworker's murder, Shion was being transported to the Public Security Bureau when Rat appeared to rescue him, and together they escaped the city! They arrived safely in West Block, but Shion began to show symptoms of infection by the black bee...

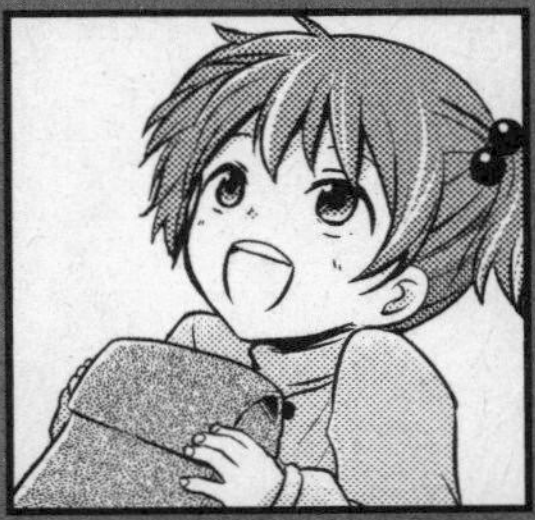

LILY

A little girl and regular customer at Karan's bakery.

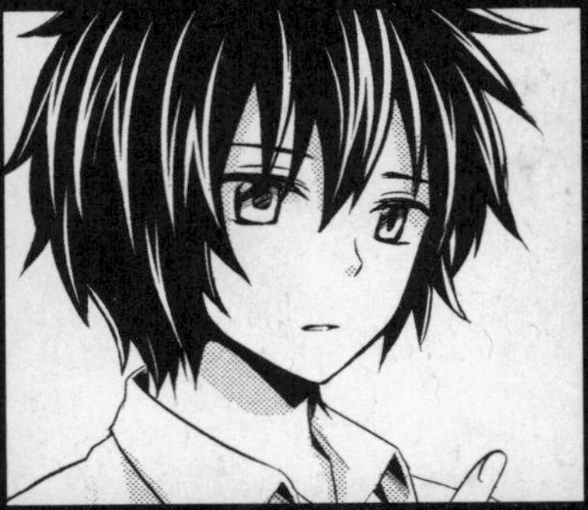

SHION

A fallen elite who became a working student. Suspected of murder, he is on the lam in West Block.

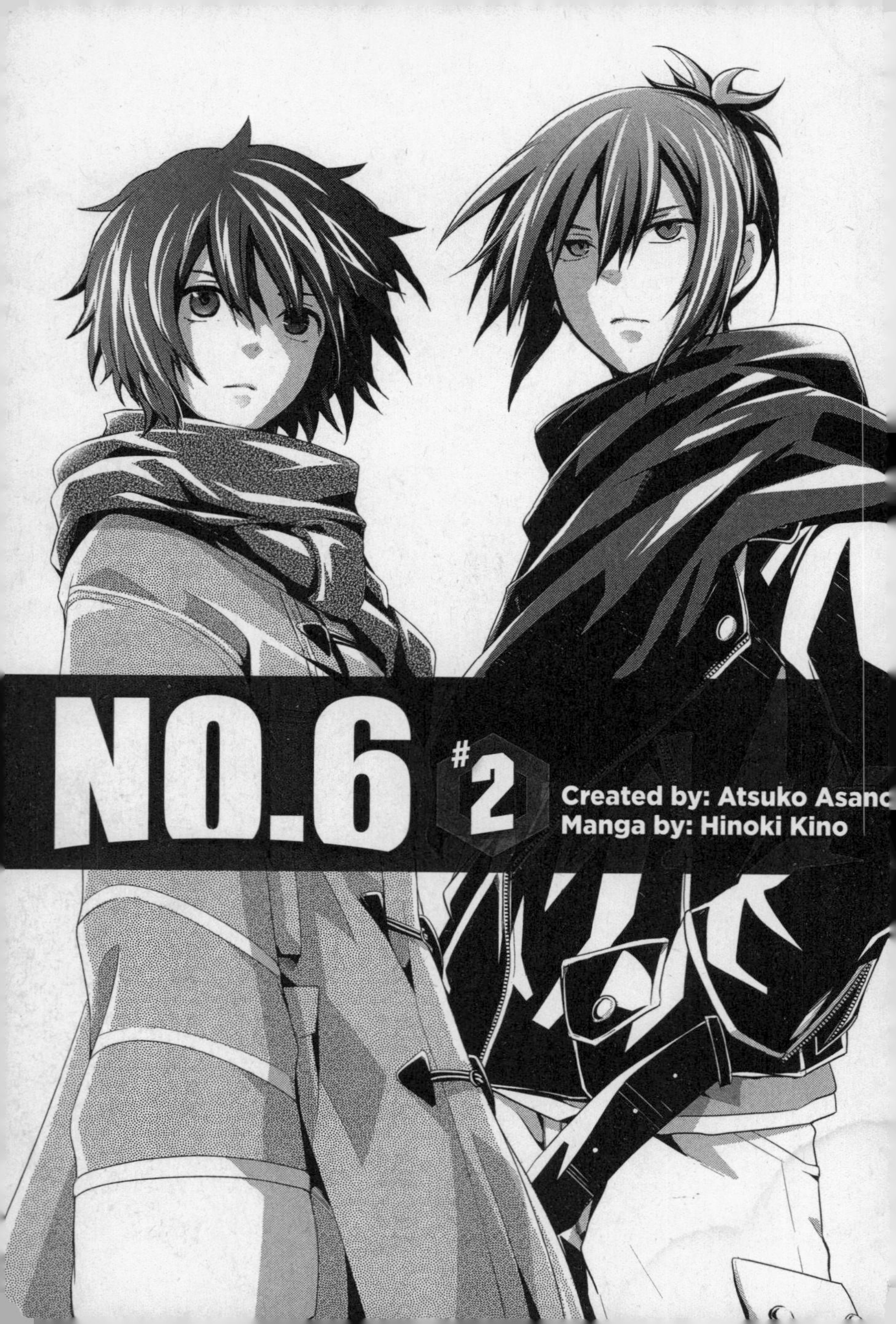
NO.6
#2
Created by: Atsuko Asano
Manga by: Hinoki Kino

Simon Gray was born in 1936. His plays include *Butley,
Otherwise Engaged, Quartermaine's Terms* and *Japes.* He is the
author of the bestselling *The Smoking Diaries* and has also
written many plays for television and radio, several novels and
four books about his experiences in the theatre, including *Fat
Chance* (published by Granta Books), *An Unnatural Pursuit
and Other Pieces* and *How's That for Telling 'Em, Fat Lady?.* He
lives in Holland Park, London.

Also by Simon Gray

Non-fiction

AN UNNATURAL PURSUIT AND OTHER PIECES
HOW'S THAT FOR TELLING 'EM, FAT LADY?
FAT CHANCE
THE SMOKING DIARIES

Fiction

COLMAIN
SIMPLE PEOPLE
LITTLE PORTIA
A COMEBACK FOR STARK
BREAKING HEARTS

Stage plays
published by Faber and Faber

WISE CHILD, DUTCH UNCLE, THE IDIOT, SPOILED, BUTLEY, OTHERWISE ENGAGED, DOG DAYS, MOLLY, THE REAR COLUMN, CLOSE OF PLAY, STAGESTRUCK, QUARTERMAINE'S TERMS, THE COMMON PURSUIT, MELON, HIDDEN LAUGHTER, THE HOLY TERROR, CELL MATES, SIMPLY DISCONNECTED

published by Nick Hern Books

JUST THE THREE OF US, THE LATE MIDDLE CLASSES, JAPES

Television plays

THE CARAMEL CRISIS, DEATH OF A TEDDY BEAR, A WAY WITH THE LADIES, SLEEPING DOG, SPOILED, PIG IN A POKE, THE DIRT ON LUCY LANE, THE PRINCESS, MAN IN A SIDE-CAR, PLAINTIFFS AND DEFENDANTS, TWO SUNDAYS

Radio plays

THE HOLY TERROR, THE RECTOR'S DAUGHTER, SUFFER THE LITTLE CHILDREN, WITH A NOD AND A BOW

Television films

AFTER PILKINGTON, QUARTERMAINE'S TERMS, OLD FLAMES, THEY NEVER SLEPT, THE COMMON PURSUIT, RUNNING LATE, UNNATURAL PURSUITS, FEMME FATALE

Films

BUTLEY, A MONTH IN THE COUNTRY

ENTER A FOX

Simon Gray

Granta Books

London

Granta Publications, 2/3 Hanover Yard, Noel Road, London N1 8BE

First published in Great Britain by Faber and Faber Limited 2001
This edition published in Great Britain by Granta Books 2005

A CIP catalogue record for this book
is available from the British Library.

1 3 5 7 9 10 8 6 4 2

Printed and bound in Great Britain by
Bookmarque Limited, Croydon, Surrey

For Victoria

This afternoon. Today is the 10th of November, the first day of my diary. The reason I've decided to keep a diary again is not to chart the usual miseries to do with the production of a new play, although there is, in fact, a new play called *Japes* (working title), but to learn to write fluently on my computer, Workgroup Server 7250/120, generally known as an Apple. Any miseries detailed here, on this Apple, will therefore be incidental to a far greater plan, one which might lead to a radical change in my life – possibly even to a restructuring of my whole personality. If I have a whole personality. At the moment I suspect that I have only a partial, not to say a morsel – and not a choice one at that – of a personality. As for the rest of me – well, I suppose it's inevitable that, as one gets older, key parts of one's physical self turn into a burden, in the case of the stomach – this one's anyway – into a noticeably sagging and shapeless burden that gives no hint, I hope, to the passing observer of the tumult that it contains. Inevitable too that, as one's outer self swells, thickens, coarsens, one's inner self, one's soul, psyche, ego, super-ego and id – and particularly id – all shrink. Shrivel might be the better word. And that, I think, will be the title of this diary. Shrivelling. Or possibly – the possibility suggested by the number of pleasing misprints I conjured up during the course of writing this – but is this writing, what I'm doing on an Apple? – I'll call it – I'll call it, well, something else entirely. But now enough of all this fol-de-rol. To our muttons.

But I didn't get to my muttons. Went to bed instead. Let's face it, what I'm really doing here on Thursday, no Friday, yes, it's now ten to two in the morning, so we've passed into Friday. But

1

here's what I've decided to do – try to do. Swear I'll try to do. Tomorrow – no, fuckwit, later today, this afternoon or evening, Friday, I'm going to devote my diary to telling the story of the fate of my last play, *The Late Middle Classes*, and on into the story of what's happening, failing to happen, with my new play *Japes* (working title). And I'll keep at it, until I get myself up to date, by which time I fully expect to be fluent on my Apple. There will of course be interruptions from my daily life, or recent and bitter memories that I may feel obliged to disclose, for my health's sake – my recent experience at the Gate Cinema for instance. But my main muttons are quite clear, and must be stuck to. So I'll put down an opening sentence or two in a new paragraph, and pluck it up from there tomorrow. Later today, I mean, of course. So.

'Last Sunday Victoria (wife) and I travelled up the Thames by boat to Greenwich, the Greenwich Theatre, in fact. It would have been an enchanted journey –' There. That's an opening sentence and a half.

Had a hard time getting to sleep, and then a very muddled dream in which I led an acquaintance of mine (not really a friend, an elderly literary critic I bump into now and then at parties), a solitary and a bachelor, gay or gayish, I suppose, gentle-mannered and full of mild enthusiasms for forgotten writers of the Edwardian period – you know the type. Let's call him Edmund, as that's his name. In this dream I passed Edmund on the pavement, half saluting him, then realised who he was, called after him. He turned, recognised me in a slightly muffled sort of way; when I got closer I saw that he was blind, his eyes like small hardboiled eggs, swimming in milk. We embraced. I asked him where he was going, he gave me an address, I said, 'But you can't get there by yourself,' and took charge of him, holding him by the arm, or the hand. We went up and down the ramps of what seemed like underground car parks, until suddenly a milk float skewered in front of us and also around us, surrounding us with metal grilles and iron bars, but the driver, impassive but not malevolent, manoeuvred and manoeuvred us, eventually squeezing us through into a tunnel that led us back

2

towards a pavement, with people on it. Edmund, now wearing a dress, bounded and skipped along the pavement, I caught up with him just before he tumbled into traffic, took him, now thoroughly a her but still completely Edmund (who, as I say, I don't really know) and led her along to her final address, which we didn't get to, because I woke up. It wasn't a nightmare or a bad dream, even – if anything it was a good dream in a bad night, perhaps a dream in which I acted out what I yearn to act out with some of the people in my life, leading them through blindness and imprisonment back to pavements and relationships – the cross-dressing and gender change I'd probably better not try to fathom, although they were sexless complications, and not even complications, as they affected neither Edmund's identity, nor my sense of him. It was the sleep around this dream that was difficult; hard to come by.

I wasn't up until two p.m., a really rotten hour to breakfast at, especially if you find that you're not alone even though your wife is out, that there's a man you've never seen before moving about at the end of the hall, busy with implements. I decided that he wasn't a burglar – a burglar would surely have taken me into account in some way, not just worked around me as I ate my breakfast and scanned the newspapers. Then I saw a little note from Victoria on the table reminding me that the electrician might be around when I woke up. So that was all right then. I came upstairs, here, to my study, calling out for George (dog). No George. Out with Victoria, I assumed. I gave one last call, on the off-chance, and was answered, or thought I was answered, by the electrician. I went to the top of the stairs. He stood at the bottom, a youngish man, tall, dark-haired. A touch public schooly in his posture, not threatening, but distinctly commanding. I was wearing my woolly dressing gown, making it difficult to be commanding back, even though I thought he was answering to my call for a dog. 'No, no,' I said. 'All right. It was just George. Our um – dog – must be out. My wife's out.'

'I need to look at your cheese board.' That's what I heard him say. 'Cheese board? Want the cheese board?' It didn't strike me as odd that an electrician should want to look at our cheese board,

I've always accepted that any trade but my own has mysteries, but I felt oddly about it, if I can make this distinction – perhaps it was being in the woolly dressing gown at the head of the stairs – Barbara Stanwyck in *Double Identity*, *Indemnity*, fool, *Indemnity*, Barbara Stanwyck making her entrance in a tight skirt, coming down the stairs in a tight skirt, was there a chain around her ankle, light gold chain? Well, it's a ridiculous, not to say impertinent comparison with me at the top of the stairs in a woolly dressing gown, even if the electrician could have passed himself off as Fred McMurray, which he couldn't because of his overalls. He said what it was he wanted again, but this time the 'cheese' part of it was slurred. 'What board?' I said. 'What board?' coming half way down the stairs. It was the fuse board. So I went on down the stairs, then down further stairs to the basement, to show him, after a prolonged search, where the fuse board wasn't. There were a lot of other boards there all right, burglar alarm boards, telephone boards, boards to do with the television, so it was perfectly reasonable, in my view, to expect to find the fuse board among them. He went back up the basement steps ahead of me, darted into a room off the kitchen, and located the fuse board. As soon as I saw it I knew I'd known it was there all along. I'd been to it once or twice to press switches, which is all you have to do nowadays to change a fuse.

The effect of this little encounter was to make me feel that I'd be better off fully dressed. So I put on my clothes, and became a proper part of the day, a part of the day that was now actually beginning to fade – nevertheless I decided I should do something more active than sit at my desk and fiddle about on this keyboard, trying yet again to pick up that sentence – 'Last Sunday Victoria (wife) and I travelled up the Thames by boat to Greenwich, the Greenwich Theatre, in fact. It would have been an enchanted journey –' and putting it down again. I can see why I didn't go on with it and still can't – far too much effort – so in short I decided to go out onto the streets, which I did. I roamed purposelessly about the Holland Park neighbourhood, thinking of Christmas presents, and whether I should walk up to Notting Hill to the cashpoint. What was I doing out when

I should be in at work – any work? The fact is I simply don't feel right, in fact feel morally ill, if I'm out and about with no work behind me. At the moment, I don't even have any work in front of me, really, except doing the diary on the computer, which doesn't count. It's not that I'm blocked, but ever since I finished *Japes* (working title) I've been in limbo within myself imaginatively – nothing stirs, nothing, and I'm beginning to reach a stage at which I suspect that this emptiness is final, that the best thing would be to accept it and seek around for alternative employment – but what employment? Who would have me, what could I do that would be useful?

I occasionally have a vision of myself renouncing everything, like the Christian prince in *The Near and the Far*, a novel by L. H. Myers that is set in sixteenth-century India. Having fulfilled all his worldly obligations, this prince leaves his princedom along with his wife, children, grandchildren, some of whom are Buddhists and some Hindus, and goes off to tramp about the world – to what purpose I can't remember – on a quest it must have been, possibly a spiritual quest, or more practically, he wanted to perform good works among the starving multitudes – but having rendered himself penniless, rupeeless, what good works could he perform, apart from the transmission of the Christian faith? – but Myers, himself a Marxist, can't seriously have proposed that his hero should end up as an indigent Christian missionary in sixteenth, or was it seventeenth-century India, especially as his (the hero's) strong suit had always been an enigmatic silence on matters spiritual – well, it's forty years since I read it, I might be misremembering it – I hope I am, as it doesn't make much sense when I try to put it together. I liked it very much, though, at the time. Perhaps because Leavis thought highly of it, or anyway hadn't proscribed it. I seem to recall that Myers himself was very rich, a very rich homosexual Marxist from an old Cambridge family, who lived his life with unassuming sumptuousness – went even short distances in a chauffeur-driven car, etc. – until, still quite young, he killed himself. He left a note to the police, apologising for any mess he made, so I imagine he used a gun.

Well, I was ruminating about the possibilities of abandoning the world myself, not like Myers, of course, with a gun, more along the lines of the prince, even though I didn't exactly have a princedom to give up, but even so how would I get by, minute by minute so to speak, without such conveniences as friends, food, a bed for the night, Victoria, George, films at Whiteleys – did I have in me the makings of a lofty-minded, teetotal tramp, or would I have to go back to drinking to justify my new mode of existence? Thus was I ruminating when I found myself outside Cullens, a local grocery store. On the pavement, at my feet, was a tramp, dwarfish with matted, ginger hair, a matted ginger beard and toothless. This disgusting creature sitting cross-legged and reeking, both his arms clawing eagerly up at me, as if he were pleading to be lifted and clasped to my bosom, had three distinct effects on me. It obliterated the fantasy I'd been entertaining of adopting his sort of life-style; it prevented me from entering Cullens and making a purchase; and finally it made not giving him money a duty, instead of merely a pleasure – this is posturing. I frequently give money to tramps, beggars, etc., sometimes because I feel sorry for them – is one allowed to feel sorry for people any more, even tramps, beggars, etc? Or is it compassion one has to feel, in which case I can't, outside my range – so I scooted away from his upstretched arms, did a furtive U-turn further up the pavement, scooted back towards him, dropped a coin somewhere in his vicinity (not one of the new two-pounders, I hope), and then back home to put down this summary of my life as it has been lived so far today – thus failing once again to get to my muttons.

Muttons. Last Sunday Victoria (now established wife) and I travelled up the Thames by boat to Greenwich, the Greenwich Theatre, in fact. It would have been an enchanted journey if I hadn't been feeling bilious. I feel permanently mildly bilious, the consequence of a loss of about a yard or so of intestine to the surgeon's knife, itself the consequence of twenty-five years of excessive, or aggressive might be the better word, yes, aggressive drinking, in fact excessive aggressive drinking. When I look back on it now I sometimes see it in terms of a heavyweight

6

boxing match. Me versus champagne and Scotch, ending in my defeat somewhere in the middle of the twelfth round by a knockout, a technical knockout, that is, because here I am still conscious, or so I believe, but unable to come out at the bell, unable even to get off my stool, when it comes to taking on a glass of alcohol. So a technical knockout, given that an actual knockout is death. And now back to going up the Thames on Sunday mid-afternoon, feeling intensely bilious. Nerves, you see. More of this later.

Friday 12th November, lunch-time, although for me it's just after breakfast and a walk with Victoria and George. George is in fact a bitch, though not in her sexual behaviour – she constantly attempts to rape our large, fluffy black tom, neutered, whose name is Errol. Errol likes being raped by George, rolling about under her paws and even submitting occasionally to a brief sort of humping. They seem to love each other, sitting or lying side by side, eating out of each other's bowls, even walking into rooms together. The other two cats, Tom and Harry, both female, hate them – but then they're not that keen on each other, either . . .

None of which brings me back to the boat to Greenwich. Nevertheless here we are again, on the boat to Greenwich, Sunday afternoon, in the company of about fifty other people, who were either in the theatrical profession or employees of Barclays Bank, the sponsors of this event. I supposed the banking people were the ones I didn't know, the ones who were dressed for an eveningish rather than an afternoonish outing, long dresses, tailored suits. And there was a little knot of Irish who were hanging about somewhere near us, chain-smoking like me, but unlike me, relaxed and chatty, with unchurning stomachs and steady bowels – well, I say that, but how can I know what was going on inside? They too might have been stuffed with Immodium, but from the look and sound of them, as they drank their drinks, they were in every respect OK with themselves, inside and out, raffishly at ease, glad to be on a jaunt up the Thames, every one a likely playwright, and at least one of them, probably the youngest, the one with the quiet laugh, an award-winner. After so many years in the business, one has a nose for these things. These people. Young Irish playwrights with quiet laughs win the awards these days. Even drunken young Irish playwrights with abusive manners win awards, or at least one of them does – I've seen him at it.

So what was I doing there, what was the point of cruising up the river with a rotten stomach, unable to drink (which is, or used to be, three-quarters of the point of this kind of occasion) in order not to collect the Irish-bound award? I keep saying Irish, very sloppy of me, Northern Irish I should be saying, as these Barclays awards cover only Britain, and therefore only Northern Ireland, on top of which their accents – though this doesn't invalidate anything I've said above, apart from moving the drunk one, who I suppose is Irish in some way or another, off the boat and out of the frame. What I mean is this: there I was in a boat on the Thames without a drink in my hand, surrounded by bankers and theatricals with drinks in both their hands in some cases, and there was also this little gaggle of low-key but triumphant Northern Irish – I couldn't make out why I'd agreed to come – well, I'd been asked a month or so in advance, so far in advance that I'd have agreed to go to virtually anything on the understanding that that much time would never pass. And then I suppose I felt I needed to make the effort – I'm so out of the habit of going anywhere, having become almost agoraphobic since my hospital experiences. In hospital I went to too many places I didn't want to be at without having to move from my bed. So when the invitation to Greenwich and the Barclays awards came up I thought I must make a start, must try and get to somewhere apart from the local cinema and the restaurant across the road, give Victoria an outing with a bit of purpose and uncertainty to it – the uncertainty coming from not knowing until one's name was either read out or not read out whether one had or hadn't won the award – I don't know if I've made that bit clear, absolutely clear, anyway. That was why we were there.

And there was also the Thames, swollen and mysterious in the darkness; well, it wasn't dark yet, really, more yellowish, so let's say there was also the Thames, swollen and mysterious in the yellowishness – no, let's not, let's just say that I thought of T. S. Eliot, not because of the poems, really, though some lines kept popping in and out of my head, but because when I was about eleven and we were living in Chelsea, I used to push my baby brother Piers along the embankment in his pram, and quite regularly I'd see T. S. Eliot pushing John Hayward about in his wheelchair, sometimes we'd pass each other on the pavement – I don't know how I knew it was T. S. Eliot, not from my parents, they wouldn't have known, but I suppose somebody told me who he was and what he did, or I found out subsequently and put two and two together. Anyway, I often connect T. S. Eliot and the Thames, while he of course connected Shakespeare and Spenser with the Thames, but then his was a better-connected mind.

So there was the Thames to make it worthwhile. And a funny conversation with one of the actors about football. And a long exchange with two other actors (married to each other) about the BBC's current diktat against middle-class English accents in their dramas, even when the parts called for middle-class English accents – apparently, too, actors going up for parts in these series are advised by their agents to omit any reference to their stage careers, however distinguished, no, *especially* if they're distinguished. So actors who've been trained to speak clearly and precisely then have to re-train themselves to speak in slovenly elisions, often totally against character. And I've noticed, I said, that the only young actresses who speak clear and precise English, even in period pieces, even in Jane Austen, turn out to be American – Gwyneth Paltrow, for instance, who gets regularly cast in such parts, presumably on the grounds that as she's American she doesn't realise that a proper accent is improper, and therefore her getting it right is just an accident born out of her ignorance, not the fault of the BBC's Drama Department, or whatever they call it these days, who merely and innocently wanted a big-name American beauty, how were they to know she spoke old English too? So that was a pleasant conversation, pleasantly unpleasant I suppose is what it was. Looking at the river in its last stretch when it was finally dark,

I stopped thinking T. S. Eliot. *Our Mutual Friend* is what came to mind, Rogue Riderhood fishing out the corpses of suicides for money.

At Greenwich the whole pack of us formed a crocodile, the Irish winner and pals somewhere towards the front, I think, Victoria and self finding our natural places towards the rear, and thus we trailed past the *Cutty Sark*, so beautiful in its lines that its days must be numbered, given the days we live in – and on to the theatre – getting slightly lost on the way as the head of the crocodile mysteriously vanished, and its tail foolishly chose to follow Victoria and myself, who were turning up and down streets on guesswork. Fortunately a middle-aged couple from the very tip of the tail advanced past us and conducted us to the doors of the theatre, and suddenly we were in our seats on an aisle on the left-hand side the auditorium. I was suddenly terrified that I was going to win. If I won I'd have to get up onto the stage and shake hands with somebody – with Ned Sherrin, for one, as he was the master of ceremonies, but there'd be somebody else too, to take the award from Ned Sherrin and pass it on to me with a shake of the hands, and then I'd have to speak, out loud, in front of, if not actually to or at all the people in a theatre that seemed pretty well packed. At least I wouldn't have to make a speech, one of those speeches in which one is obliged to thank everybody connected with the production, which would mean trying to remember all their names when I'd probably have been unable to remember the name of my own play, even though it had just been announced – well, I wouldn't have to make one of those speeches if I won, because Barclays and Ned Sherrin had devised between them a revolutionary format in which no speeches were made, Ned Sherrin merely asking the award winner a question or two, of a non-probing nature presumably – but nevertheless they'd be questions to which just a shake or nod of the head would be an inadequate response, speech would certainly be involved, and that was it, for me, the nightmare, having to make public utterance. I've never been very good at it, never liked doing it – odd, really, as I was a university lecturer for about twenty years, and during the first fifteen or so of those I lectured several times a week – on Shakespeare, Chaucer, Blake, Wordsworth, and most frequently on Dickens – feeling a trifle nervous and shaky before each lecture, but perfectly fluent, in command, once I'd begun, even now and then enjoying the sensation of being two people simultaneously, the lecturing person and the rather cool accomplice who stood both beside and within him. So I'd motored along smoothly enough for most of those fifteen or so years, sometimes using notes, sometimes not, always with a text in hand to refer to, passages marked for reading out, nervous and shaky beforehand, OK once I'd got going, until one time, one lecture, the nerves and the shakiness went right through the lecture and on to the end, past that into a blankness until I found myself back in my office, trembling in my chair at my desk. It was like that from then on, I couldn't understand it, although really it was just common or garden stage fright, I suppose, but because of it I had to give up lecturing. Probably what happened is that the cool accomplice at my shoulder took himself one day into the audience and became a sardonic and dismissive, possibly a jeering, observer. And certainly the person I'd least like to see when facing an audience would be a person like myself.

The ceremonies began with two little musical numbers, each followed by an award-giving, during which I studied the Ned Sherrin question-and-answer routine quite closely. He limited himself to two questions, and they were indeed innocuous – deftly designed to convey his familiarity with the winner's CV, while demanding only a short paragraph in reply. I noticed with relief that he was disposed to cut off the paragraph if it showed any tendency to expand itself. In almost no time, we were at the best play category. One of the three contenders was, as I'd assumed, the Northern Irish chap with the low laugh. I wished him well. The other I didn't take in properly, but I wished him or her well, too. The third was me. Sheila Hancock somehow manifested herself at Ned Sherrin's side. She had a large white envelope in her hand, which she opened with nary a fumble, and there she was, reading out my name on a sheet of paper before she'd even extracted it from the envelope, and there

I was, making my way from my aisle seat, down the aisle, towards the stage – it was very brightly lit, the two figures, Ned Sherrin and Sheila Hancock badly out of focus but stark, waiting for me. One of the difficulties of this post-alcohol stage of my life is that I appear to be drunk far more often than I used to do when I was drunk. In those days my legs would carry me about quite normally, until suddenly they'd give out completely. These days, however, my legs never give out completely, they simply waver purposelessly, as if the rest of me were an unanticipated burden. This happens most frequently in difficult light, in the gloaming, for instance, or when there are abrupt contrasts of light and shade – as there were now, between the stage and the auditorium. It was humiliating to be reached down to, and assisted up the steps to the stage by Sheila Hancock – what was Ned Sherrin doing, he was much nearer to me, after all? She actually had to cross in front of him before reaching down to me, but he stood, hands folded across his stomach, smiling with disengaged pleasure at this spectacle of a large, probably inebriated man being virtually lifted onto the stage by a delicate woman. Then either Ned or Sheila Hancock handed me a black box, and Ned pestered me with a question – about, I think, whether there were any plans for a new production of *The Late Middle Classes*, a production that would actually get into the West End, and possibly stay there a while, for a little run. His point being that the first, and so far only, production of *The Late Middle Classes* had made it to the very brink of the West End before toppling backwards, so to speak, and out of sight at Richmond. I can't remember how I answered him, although I did manage coherent speech of a jammed-up and graceless kind. He gave me my other question, to which I responded curtly, then somehow I made it back to Victoria and my seat and safety, my box in my hands.

I wish, of course, I'd been able to answer his first question at length. In fact, I'd have loved to have told him, and the rest of the audience, the whole story of *The Late Middle Classes*, from the day I'd finished writing it to my sitting there on an aisle seat in the stalls of the Greenwich Theatre, my trophy in one hand, my

wife's hand in the other. Most of the people there, being of the
theatre, would almost certainly have found it, if not enthralling,
then at least reminiscent of experiences of their own, but I
believe the story reaches out beyond the theatre, into the world
immediately around it, and beyond that into further worlds – in
fact, when I've finished transcribing it on this Apple I might try
to smuggle a copy into a space capsule so that a distant
generation, cut off from its past by some cataclysm (the present
educational system, for instance) will fish it out of the ether in
one of their sky-nets, and having deciphered it, will understand
and even feel compassion for this strangely heroic little figure,
the 'English playwright', and the murky and predatory world in
which he struggled to survive. I'm thinking of starting my own
web site. I must find out what a web site is exactly, I have a
general sense that it's a source of information about oneself for
the benefit of others, and that it works through the Internet,
which I'll also find out about . . . Now I've launched myself into
this computer I can surely do all those things that everybody
else has been doing for decades, I might learn to drive at last,
even get my licence, it would surely be a comfort to Victoria to
find an extra pair of hands on the steering wheel when she
comes to sharp curves, sudden inclines, slippery surfaces. I'll
find out about e-mail too. Victoria gets e-mail. She's shown me
some of it. But muttons, muttons, we're straying a long way
from our muttons again, the immediate muttons being the writing of *The Late Middle Classes*. The black box on my lap in the
aisle seat, by the way, contained a silver goblet on which was
inscribed the one word, 'Barclays'.

Muttons. The writing of *The Late Middle Classes*. I didn't write
it, actually. I dictated it. There it is, staring back at me from the
screen of this computer, the admission or confession I suppose it
is – yes, more a confession, as I feel a peculiar shame about this,
that I dictated *The Late Middle Classes*, every word of it. After all,
writing, writing is what one does or claims to do, therefore one
feels morally obliged to perform the physical act of writing –
and for complete authenticity one must do it, as I've done it for
the last forty years, on an Olympia portable typewriter. They're

not truly portable, by the way, Olympia portables. Too heavy. But when it comes to it, shame or not, the only way I could have written *The Late Middle Classes* was to say it all aloud to my assistant, Sarah Moorehead, who is the only person I can say a piece of writing aloud to in the whole world – I can't even say writing aloud to myself, I've tried it on a recording machine, and couldn't get past the first sentence. But Sarah's been around for fifteen years now, has been taking dictation of letters and such stuff for most of those years, and knows how to be there without seeming to be present; so one morning I said, 'Hey, let's try this,' and began to speak a few lines of dialogue, and we were off. It was quite exhausting, less exhausting physically than writing, of course, as I simply sat slumped and chain-smoking – chain-smoking is in itself pretty exhausting, but then I do that anyway, whatever my other activity – but exhausting in its tension, the tension coming from my complete dependence on Sarah.

I had to teach myself to keep myself away from the play whenever she was absent, and during her absence I wouldn't let myself write down anything, not even little notes or snatches of dialogue, as if dictating were itself a form with strict rules, so I had to pick up at 2.30 p.m. every afternoon (except Saturdays and Sundays) where I'd left off at 6.00 the previous evening. That's how *The Late Middle Classes* came to be written, by speaking it aloud to Sarah three and a half hours an afternoon every afternoon except weekends until it was finished, about two months after we'd started. Then she put it on the machine – this Apple, as a matter of fact – and I spoke out corrections and it was done. The quickest play I'd ever written.

Most of my plays go through fifteen or so complete drafts, and take at least a year, sometimes two or even three years. But then the story of the play came directly out of my own life, as did all the characters. The location was Hayling Island, Hampshire, where I was born. The period was 1952, still very much post-war, when everything from chocolate and eggs to information about sex was in short supply, especially if you were, as I was, a twelve-year-old boy (I'm not saying there was more of anything for twelve-year-old girls either). Naturally, a play being a play

14

and memory being what it is, the actual facts and the fictional facts are now muddled together, and I'm sometimes no longer sure whether I'm remembering facts from the play or facts from my life – for example there is the known fact of me as a twelve-year-old in Putney enduring the unendurable attentions of the pederastic maths teacher, Mr Burn; while on the other hand, in *The Late Middle Classes*, and now pretty well fixed in my memory as an equally known fact, there is an eleven-year-old me, called Holly Smithers, who lives on Hayling Island, and at least partially welcomes the devotions of the possibly pederastic music teacher, Mr Brownlow. Sometimes I remember his first name as John, as it was in life, sometimes as Thomas, as in the play, but really to both Holly and myself he was always Sir, even when we were calling him by his Christian name, which he'd ordered us to do – any failures of intimacy being intimately punished.

I think I'll stop now. No, I'll go on a bit longer as I may not be able to pick it up tomorrow, which is going to be an arduous day of ugly practicalities, chief among them the drawing up of a new will. When I do stop I'll leave half a sentence that will be waiting for me here, to be completed when I come back. I find the thought consoling, that between beginning a sentence and ending it, you can make a new will, lose some of your health, most of your money, some friends, and your temper, without anyone being able to tell unless they're alert to the shifting rhythms in your prose. So Mr Burn then, as I believe I know him to have been, before I confused him into Mr Brownlow.

Mr Burn was round and short and he always smelled of sweet powders, different combinations of powders, I suppose, as the powdery smell, and the intensity of the tickle in my nostrils, varied from day to day. His face was always pale, but dully pale from the powder, and his lips were red, nearly crimson. It was like a toned-down clown's, Mr Burn's face, with the large, pale sweet-smelling cheeks, the full red lips, and the coal-black eyes that flickered over you, if you were me, taking in every desirable aspect of your body, and flickering into you to take in all that part of you that you prayed was concealed from all the eyes in the world, including God's eyes, because it was the shameful part of you, the part that was most shamefully you. He had splayed feet and asthma, and would paddle with a soft, rolling gait between the aisles, wheezing as his eyes flickered from this boy to that until they developed the habit of flickering only at me – of course they took in every other boy in the room too, took in their awareness of him. I was the target though. I knew it from my hot flushes, the prickling of my scalp. He excited me from the beginning, Mr Burn, I wonder if that's how he –

That's the sentence I wrote and left suspended, the one above, 'He excited me from the beginning, Mr Burn, I wonder if that's how he –' and I sat down to it the moment I got back from the day's unpleasant business but I wasn't in a state to make sense of what I'd written, let alone complete the sentence – in fact while I was staring down at it I got the shakes, had to take a pill or two and put myself to bed. By the time Victoria got home, I was feeling OK, certainly OK enough to go out for dinner (Orsino's) and once we were settled at a table, with the meal under way, I began to feel OK, was perfectly relaxed really until I began to talk about my will. Changing it had turned out to be quite an easy matter, I said – not surprisingly, as I have nothing at all to leave except my copyrights, which are virtually worthless, and my curses, which won't work. So far so good. But then, having hoped I wouldn't but had somehow known all along I would, I got on to my brother Piers – how I'd had to cut him out of the will, so it was this, yet another official marking him out of life by marking him out of my will that had caused the shakes earlier, and now brought them back again in the form of a monologue – on and on I went, the circumstances of his death, the needlessness of it, alcohol, fucking alcohol, on and on. And then, fair's fair after all, turn and turn about after all, we talked of Victoria's brother Amschel, younger than Piers, who had died on the day of Piers' funeral. Over coffee we managed to get on to other things – films we wanted to see, what about George, giving her some puppies, giving ourselves some of George's puppies, and there we were, walking home, the bad part of the day gone. As soon as we were in I jogged eagerly up the stairs to the study and sat down to Apple, and there was the sentence waiting for me to complete it at last – 'So he excited me from the beginning, Mr. Burn, I wonder if that's how he –' and I completed it and I was off, finding what seemed a marvellously fluent way of weaving snatches of autobiography and family history through a longish synopsis of *The Late Middle Classes*, touching on my parent's matter-of-fact, middle-class anti-semitism, along with my father's loathing of homosexuals – 'pansies' was his favoured word, Oscar Wilde was 'evil', etc. – and his adulteries, how I'd found out about them (my mother told me) and then how my two brothers, Piers and my older brother Nigel, had found out about them (I told them). I worked right through until three or four this morning, took a pill, listened to some music, went to bed feeling that the day was coming to a pretty good end, after all.

When I sat down to my Apple again this afternoon, there it still was on the screen, 'So he excited me from the beginning, Mr. Burn. I wonder if that's how he –' and nothing followed, there it was, still suspended, still waiting to be completed. So gone, lost, wasted, all those hours of tapping out old family secrets in my finest, easiest, wryest style. And further gone, lost, wasted, are the hours I've spent today trying to get Apple to retrieve all those lost hours of work. I'm going to give up now, take an early bath (it's 3.37 a.m.) and hope that by tomorrow I will have come to accept the disappearance of a thousand words or so as a crucial part of the exercise, a necessary because instructive part of the exercise of teaching myself how to be on comfortable terms with Apple. At the moment I feel like a wife suddenly undeceived – how many other times has Apple done it? How can I trust him not to do it again? How can we go on together without trust?

It's 4.30 in the afternoon of the next day, no, same day, Thursday, and I'm just back from walking George in the small churchyard up the road. I've only been up a few hours – I must try and alter my sleeping–waking pattern because at this time of year there's so little light, and it diminishes, diminishes, beginning to darken as my day begins. Such a lovely day today, too, when I first looked out after breakfast – with that brightness to it that

17

makes you know, before you go out into it, that it's very cold. By the time I got back the brightness had gone, the gloom that was gathering was all the colder, shroud-like is what London winter afternoons are, they remind me far more than long sunny afternoons of my boyhood – of walking along the pavement, towards Putney tube station, my hand in Mr Burn's, or some years later, walking home to Chelsea from my school in Westminster along the embankment, and now this afternoon, walking with George in the grounds of the church up the road where – I might as well report it while it's still fresh, not to say raw – an unseemly incident took place. Now the grounds of this church are exclusive to residents, there are railings, and a gate which you have to open with a key, which sometimes doesn't work and you have to reach through the railings and manoeuvre it into the lock from the side you're not on – a perilous process if you're trying to get out, as you might drop your keys through the railing onto the pavement, from which they might be snaffled up by a passer-by – there are quite a few young men, no, be fair and accurate, young women too, who would be quite pleased to snaffle your keys up from the pavement and dash off with them – no, not bother to dash, just move on with your keys in their pocket, leaving you and George locked in the churchyard, or would they? Is this late-life paranoia? They'd probably toss the keys back, even hand them to you through the railings, in the manner of young men and women from time immemorial – but whichever they'd do, why am I going on about them, as I made my entrance with the key perfectly easily this afternoon – oh, yes, I was leading up to the woman, the young woman with the child, too bundled up to be sexually determinable, the child, that is, not the woman – they were the only other people in the churchyard, and the woman was frankly and openly displeased to see us, George and myself. I'm quite used to giving various degrees of displeasure as I go through life, in my prime I was capable of dishing it out deliberately, nowadays it's accidental, but perhaps I give off an atmosphere of long-accumulated, infantile resentments, thus having the same appeal, say, as a cheese at once over-ripe and immature. Anyway, it's my contention (I'll offer further evidence shortly) that people are likely to respond unfavourably to me before they even know me (after they know me is not necessarily a different story, by the way), in fact virtually on sight, as was the case with this young woman and her sexually muffled child.

Sexually muffled – why did I write that? Ah yes, because of the effect produced, or that we are constantly being reminded is produced, by middle-aged-to-elderly men hovering in places where there are children about. That's why it's a good idea, if you're a middle-aged-to-elderly man, to arm yourself with a dog when you go to a park – a man with a dog, carrying a ball for the dog and a book for himself and aiming at a bench, especially if he keeps his eyes lowered and has a slightly unsteady gait, is a less alarming proposition than the same man without any of those props. Actually they're not props. I throw the ball. George chases it, I sit on the bench. I read my book – if a newspaper I prefer to take the *Guardian*, as it's the most ostentatiously watchful on most moral matters, particularly those to do with children, and is only a problem in being virtually unreadable – by me, anyway. But this afternoon I wasn't carrying a book or a newspaper, and had forgotten the ball, so all I had was George herself to offer against the baleful looks of the mother – I took her to be the mother, rather than an au pair or an abductress, she had the look of a mother, bored, angry, vigilante. I let George off the lead noisily and theatrically, to draw her attention to the obvious reason for sharing the churchyard with her and her infant, and then hurried towards the furthest bench, eyes averted, but had to stop when I realised that George was crouching for what seemed to be a sumptuous crap. When she'd finished, and done her little, and highly sympathetic, dance of joy and relief, I went over to the tree where there's a shovel and a hole in the ground, the hole covered by a lid, picked up the shovel, scooped up George's crap, lifted up the lid, dropped the crap into the hole, put the shovel back in position and then – in fact before there could be any 'and then', at least on my part – I heard her voice. It had a throb in it. 'It's done another one over there.' She was pointing to somewhere George and I hadn't been, indeed hadn't yet had a chance to be. 'Can't be hers,' I said. 'She's just done one here.' I pointed to the spot, still slightly soiled. 'Yes, well it did that other one too.' I shook my head. 'Not her,' I said. 'We've only just got here.'

Out of politeness, though, I did go and look. And there was a mountain of crap, far beyond George's limited capacity, and furthermore, to an expert eye, which I had, not at all fresh. I began to lay down all this evidence, clearly exculpating George entirely, when she raised the stakes with a boldly uttered, unblinkingly delivered lie. 'I saw it do it.' Well, I couldn't, could I? We would have ended up in the courts, and then me in jail, no doubt – so I plodded back and scooped the poop – I'd like it to be known that I'd have done as much anyway, believing that dog-owners have a responsibility for the reputation of dogs in general. (What was the child doing during all this, I wonder, messing up its knickers, I sincerely hope.) She watched me until I'd finished, then she left, presumably taking the child with her. I hadn't once seen her face properly – having heard the voice, I couldn't face the face, I knew it would be self-righteous and long-suffering, and for sure she was a *Guardian* reader, possibly even a *Guardian* columnist – in fact, I suddenly remembered one of the moments when I realised how much I loathed the *Guardian*, it was when I came across a piece on why all dogs should be put down, the woman who wrote it seeming to be rabid and in need of putting down herself – could this woman and that woman be one and the same woman? Not just a *Guardian* reader, but a *Guardian* writer? The *ur Guardian* writer herself? – enough, enough, enough of this, two good friends of mine actually write for the *Guardian*, possibly even read it. So enough of this and on to – on to the Gate, yes, as the other recent example of my ability to arouse dislike in people the instant – almost the instant before, it seems – they clap eyes on me.

I mean, why – why at the Gate of all cinemas, my local cinema, the cinema I've been popping into every week for about fifteen years? But to take it in sequence, with the expostulations and rhetorical questions and expletives coming in their proper place, at the end, it went like this: a few days before I'd set myself to learn how to write on Apple, which would make it about ten days ago, I fell into a mid-afternoon gloom, fading down with the light, I suppose, but worse than usual, and decided that a film might help, might even animate me. I looked in the *Standard*, checked up on the Gate, and saw that a film called *Run, Lola, Run* was running there – I'd picked up bits and pieces about this film, had some idea that it had received generally favourable reviews, suspected that one of these might have come from the *Standard* itself, but in spite of that decided to give it a whirl. So, still loaded down internally (psychically, not gastrically) but with some small prospect of lightening up in sight, I trudged to the bus stop on Holland Park Avenue and waited for a bus to Notting Hill. It was then about 5.15, the programme began at 5.20, the film itself therefore, I guessed, at half past five. The bus trip would take five minutes, at the very most, so I was OK for time. Or would have been if a bus had turned up within the next fifteen minutes, which it didn't. So at about the time the film was to begin, I began the trek up to Notting Hill, my first steps coinciding with a small smattering of rain. (Fortunately I'd remembered to bring my hat, a furry, leathery thing I'd bought in a shop that sells motorcycle equipment. I have to wear it, or something like it, in London rain, which otherwise poisons my scalp, bringing it up in lumps and filling my hair with large flakes of dandruffy white – murdered skin, it must be, and one of the many consequences of the operation on my intestines. I go into all this about the hat – that it wasn't some luxury feature or fashion accessory I was wearing on my head, it was a medical necessity – because I suspect it played a part in what follows.)

All in all, and with a growing sense that I wasn't going to make the beginning of the film, it was a miserable little journey, and no doubt I cut a pretty miserable spectacle when I finally presented myself at the ticket counter, behind which was a young man, black, handsome, smilingly alert, who'd obviously been exchanging jokes with an entourage of friends or colleagues who were lolling around in the foyer. I asked him how much of *Run, Lola, Run* I'd missed. He said about fifteen minutes. Now, unlike the *Guardian* in the churchyard, he had a nice voice, if a touch actory, not to say camp – a dab of camp to it, yes, but friendly in effect if not, as it turned out, in intention. 'Fifteen minutes. Oh. Well, I don't mind.' 'I do,' he said. I took this for what it wasn't – a sympathetic sharing of the disappointment. 'Well, anyway, I'll buy a ticket,' I said, fumbling pocket-wards. 'No, you won't,' his smile going all around the lobby, to friends, colleagues. 'What?' I said, really and truly not understanding this perfectly simple sentence. 'Too late,' he said. 'If you'd come a few minutes earlier, I might have considered it. But I'm not going to disturb my audience now, when they're just getting into the film.' His manner, I must report in all fairness, was in no respect rude – in fact, it was full of – of, well, *joie de vivre* was what it was full of, and much appreciated by friends and colleagues. Now there was a lot I could have said to this, beginning with – 'Audience? What audience at 5.20 in the afternoon, at the Gate!' to 'And what would you have done if I'd booked and prepaid with my credit card on the phone?' with lots of stuff in between about International Law and Human Rights. I might also have pointed to the customer who had just purchased a plastic mug of coffee and was returning to her seat while he'd been busy returning me to the pavement and the rain. But I didn't say anything until I was going out through the doors – some mumbled words over my shoulder, the only distinct one being, probably, 'fascist'.

Pathetic. Where were the fires of yesteryear? I knew where the snows were, and the ice – in my soul, my soul. So what was it about me, what had he seen, that young man, so smiley and shiny and confident, that had tempted him into making me a butt for his little comedy? And that's where I believe my hat comes into it, could it have been my hat, which made me resemble some debris left over from the day the Wall fell? Or was he simply sexist and ageist, seeing before him elderly, white and (but not ostentatiously, I do believe) heterosexual? What he should have seen, of course, was a sad case of triple handicap, calling if not for the sale of a ticket, then at least for the compassion that, though I lack it myself, there is currently, or so

22

we're told, an abundance of in this country – but perhaps it's a fastidious and discriminatory compassion, not to be slopped over the likes of me – these my thoughts as I trudged home from the Gate, in the rain and the gloom.

There are times when one has to take action. The next day I tracked down the ownership of the Gate to a company called Oasis – can it be connected to the musical group? – and discovered the name of the manager, a woman called Lynn, I forget what, but certainly Lynn something. I then composed a long, poignant letter detailing the events related above, and received the next day, or the day after, an urgently apologetic fax that left me feeling, after several readings, both triumphant and humiliated. Humiliated because – well, perhaps because I'd wasted several hours of my shortening span on a matter that a nobler man would have brushed from his memory a moment after hitting the pavement in the rain. There were other people on the pavement in the rain, after all, one or two of them no doubt feeling as rejected as I did, homeless possibly. But the power of rancour, the spasms of energy induced by a grudge – shaming, really. That's my point. I realise that I've motored a long way away from *The Late Middle Classes*, partly because I've been so distracted by the diurnal anguishes of life – I really must try to rise above them, get back to what I was mainly trying to do, which was to give a synopsis of the play. Well, here I am, risen above the diurnal anguishes etc., and so here without further to-do is the synopsis.

The time: the summer of 1955. The place: Hayling Island, Hampshire. The characters: Holly, a boy of twelve; his mother, Celia, an ex-sports teacher, in her mid-thirties; his father, Charles, an adulterous pathologist, nearing forty; Mr Brownlow, a Jewish piano teacher; Ellie, Mr Brownlow's widowed mother, very Austrian, a recluse. The action: Mr Brownlow falls in love with Holly; Ellie lets the cat out of the bag to Charles; Celia finds out that Charles is unfaithful; family falls apart in unsavoury bursts of English middle-class anti-semitism, etc. The main action is in fact a long interruption of a scene between the adult Holly and the aged Mr Brownlow in which feelings from thirty years

23

before are left undeclared, and nothing much is resolved. That's it. That's the play, synoptically.

The day after I'd finished dictating it, Sarah furnished me with half a dozen printed copies, run off, as a matter of no interest, from the printer attached to this very Apple. Big box of a thing, hums, a laser. I fingered one of these copies with nausea then gave it back to her. While she took them off to be bound somewhere in Notting Hill, I sat listlessly at my desk, not so much worn out by the task completed as drained in advance by the task ahead – i.e., the attempt to get the play produced, which meant sending it out, waiting for responses, not getting angry when no responses were immediately forthcoming, not getting angry when tepid, unencouraging or ambiguous responses finally arrived – this, for me, is the truly ghastly part of play-writing, and the prospect of it somehow taints the work itself. I can't even bear to hold it in my hand, however handsome the binding, elegant the printing, professional the whole sleek appearance of it, let alone open it and begin to read it – the truth is I can't even bear to see it – I put it around the corner of a shelf, as if it were something shameful that I need to keep close at hand but out of sight. Years ago I could scarcely keep a copy of something newly made out of my grasp, picking it up almost as soon as I'd put it down, flicking through the pages to pause for long dips of reading – I can't account for this change, nor specify when it took place – but there it is, no sooner have I done it than I'm ashamed of it – and yet I'm always in such a frenzy to get it done, driving myself on to the moment when I can stuff it out of sight. Nevertheless, certain rituals have to be performed. I asked Sarah, who has a much more robust attitude to the finished product – and she'd had to listen to this one and write it down as it was being spoken to her, then write down different versions again and again, then transcribe the whole – anyway, I asked her to send two copies off, one to Judy Daish (my agent) the other to Harold Pinter (a playwright). Harold is always the first recipient of anything I write and in his package I enclosed a note which was in fact a coded invitation to direct the play – coded because I didn't want him to have to turn me down directly, which would be embarrassing for him, painful for me. A third copy, or perhaps really the top copy, I put outside Victoria's study door. And that was as far as I could go at the moment. I don't know how I got through the hiatus – a prolonged one, because I changed my mind about sending off Harold's package, deciding instead to wait until I'd had a discussion with Judy. In the meanwhile Victoria read the play, gave it the nod, which meant I could hold my head up domestically, at least.

Judy was very clear that the play should be sent to Trevor Nunn at the National Theatre. I said that before dispatching it to Trevor Nunn I'd like to have Harold's opinion, and hinted at my hope that he'd want to direct it. We left it that I'd get it around to Harold the following day. I put in a new covering note, which was word for word the same as the old one, apart from the date, of course, and sent it around. The next day I wasn't having lunch in my then usual place Chez Moi across the road – scrambled eggs, bacon, elderflower wine, coffee and a newspaper or a book – having elected instead to go up to the Halcyon, where once upon a time I used to have my usual lunch – the reason for this small interruption to the current routine (most of my routines remain absolute and inflexible until they are changed on a whim or out of boredom, for another absolute and inflexible routine) was that I was having dinner that night at Chez Moi and had had dinner there the night before and was probably going to have dinner there the following night, so – so by God so – so what? So only that I'm explaining a) why Harold, who knows my routines, turned up at Chez Moi expecting to find me at my scrambled eggs, elderflower wine. etc., when I was actually up the road at the Halcyon having a chicken and mayonnaise sandwich, and a sea-breeze (cranberry and grapefruit juices, minus, in my glass, the vodka). I found out about his visit that evening when Victoria and I went to Chez Moi for dinner and Philippe, the maître d', asked in his impeccably French English if Harold had managed to find me, he'd been looking in for me at lunch – and when we got home there indeed was a message from Harold on my answering machine, a few words about the play, clearly favourable, could we meet the next day at Chez Moi for lunch?

I left a message on his machine saying yes, Chez Moi for lunch, and spent a comparatively peaceful night that lasted inevitably until nearly dawn, listening to lots of Schubert, I think it was Schubert.

The next day, over lunch, Harold told me that he liked the play very much indeed. He assumed, though, that I wouldn't want him to direct, as he wasn't available until the following spring, nearly fourteen months away. I thought about this, the pros and cons, although there was only one con – fourteen months is a long time to wait in the life of a hitherto unperformed play. On the other hand, during those fourteen months, I might find the courage to pick the play up, turn over its pages, glance into it, possibly even read it all the way through, and anyway all the pros were overwhelming, the main one being that I thought Harold and the play went together, were somehow already together in spirit – it's astonishing how inward he becomes with a work – after only one proper reading, he is able to quote scenes and even lines, raise questions about what are, at such an early stage, details really. He was a little worried about the play's title, suspecting that *The Late Middle Classes* might be making a sociologically and historically diagnostic claim beyond the play's intentions, but we shelved that for the moment and moved on to the major question – where should we have it done?

There are many differences between Harold's professional life and mine. One of the major ones is that when he finishes a play he can pretty well choose and quite rightly, it seems to me, which theatre he would like to have produce it. With me, it's a question of flogging the play from house to house, steeling myself for rebuffs and attendant humiliations – in fact I feel that in many houses I'm *persona non grata*, sight unseen, play unread. It would be too flattering to myself to say that the artistic directors of these theatres see me as a maverick – rather they see me as someone whose work they are not obliged to do, but whose work they are obliged to read before not doing – they reject me by prevarication usually, always with courtesy, generally with compliments.

26

But to cut back to the nub, Harold shared Judy's view that it should go to the National. 'But they probably won't want to do it,' I said. Harold brushed this aside with muscular assertions of his faith in Trevor Nunn, his confidence in his judgement, taste, etc., and the rest of lunch we spent celebrating what would be, we counted them up, our eighth production together. For the first six of these productions I'd attended almost every day of rehearsal, standing beside him cheek by cheek, jowl by jowl, but for the last production, *Life Support*, I'd been in hospital – on life support, as a matter of fact – and missed every rehearsal, run-through and most of the tour. Finally seeing the production in Bath, just before its move into London, I discovered that Harold was perfectly capable of directing my plays without bacon-saving interventions from me.

A moment ago I was sitting at my desk with Vincent Cronin's biography of Napoleon, had in fact just finished reading Napoleon's address to the troops of the Sixty-Ninth Battalion, who had just failed to take Acre in what was to be their last attempt: 'I'll rig you out in skirts! Pull down their breeches! You've got cunts between your legs, not cocks! Pull the breeches off those sissies!' is how Napoleon's speech goes in Cronin's translation, and I was about to settle down and ponder all the occasions when I'd have liked to have adopted the same tone, the same manner, above all the same vocabulary – well, that was what I was doing at my desk when my eye happened to stray to this. By which I mean the screen of my Apple which is across the room, on my other desk. No, that's nonsense – it's on this desk, of course, the one I'm now sitting at and tapping at, the other desk being the one I was reading Napoleon's noble speech at. So on this desk the screen, which had been cluttered with words the last time I'd noticed it, had gone blank – 'put itself to sleep' in the language of those that have achieved that sort of relationship with their Apples – and I suddenly realised as I jabbed him awake and he filled his screen with what I hoped was the same clutter that I'd left him with – suddenly realised that it's been a couple of days, several, I don't know how many since I recorded a date.

So here is the present one. It is, as I type this, almost exactly three a.m., Monday morning. Monday, 22nd November. It's no good my back-tracking, and trying to put in all the missing dates. I couldn't possibly remember where I started, finished, started again. And besides I've taken the sleeping pill and there's a Beethoven piano concerto on the CD – I love music so much, obvious music anyway, Haydn, Bach, Chopin, Mozart, Elgar, Beethoven, that I often wish I weren't so unmusical, anyway such an unconcentrated listener, thoughts drifting all over the place, failing to identify passages that stir all kinds of memories, passages I've heard time after time. I sometimes believe that if I'd been able to play an instrument, or sing in tune, my life would have been different and better. The same holds true if I'd won Wimbledon. No it doesn't. Ridiculous analogy. You can only win Wimbledon once – well, five or six times if you're Borg or Sampras – but you can play a musical instrument right up to your last breath, well, it would depend on the instrument and what you're dying from, you probably couldn't manage it if you were a singer or a flautist, for instance, but you might at the piano, and ideally of course, at the harp – look, all I mean is I wish I had a gift for music, a practitioner's gift, however trifling, even for the drums or the cymbals – the pill is beginning to work. So back to my other desk and the end of the concerto, a waily bit with violins now, reproachful. Back later today, to finish off my lunch with Harold, or if it's already finished, to try to piece together what happened next.

Tomorrow as promised. Correction. Same day as usual, still 22nd November, but now a quarter to one in the afternoon, a flat, cold, grey afternoon that offers nothing one wants to share with it, only duty – but duty to what? – forces one out of bed at all, on such days. Oh, of course, duty to George, who needs her walk, and George's need will almost certainly become my pleasure – the grimness of the day never seems to get to her, she'll bound after her ball, lose it, pause for a crap and a merry dance, then forget that she's lost her ball, forget even that she's been playing with it, around and around we'll go, both of us sort of sniffing at the grass and the fallen leaves, and I'll keep

28

shouting 'Ball, George, where's your bloody ball?' and she'll go sniff sniff, nose burrowing under the little piles of leaves, all bustle and purpose, but I'll know that really her ball is the last thing on her mind, she's forgotten it in all the other smells, and in the end if I don't find it myself it won't be found at all – well, it'll be too cold to read a book and especially the *Guardian*, so why not look for her ball when she loses it in the hope of turning up the one we lost two or three days ago – with luck we'll have the place to ourselves, and when we come back we'll be quite pleased with the way the day is going – well, she's always pleased with the way the day is going, I think, after romping in the churchyard she likes to rape Errol for a little, then fall asleep on one of her many beds, on her back, feet sticking straight up, afraid of nothing.

So with that in prospect, back in the interim to the lunch with Harold at Chez Moi a year and a half ago. No, no point, nothing to add. On then, to the next stage in the progress of *The Late Middle Classes*. There was, of course, a gap while we waited for the National, in the person of Trevor Nunn, to read the play. Then another gap after Judy had written to Trevor Nunn, reminding him that he'd been sent the play to read. Then another gap, and another, each marked by phone calls from Judy to Trevor Nunn, and then at long last – well over two months after he'd received the play – a letter from Trevor Nunn to Judy, which she passed on to me, in which he explained his reasons for turning the play down, in spite of his having enjoyed reading it. No, not in spite of – that was actually his reason for turning it down, that he'd enjoyed reading it – indeed so enjoyed reading it that he was convinced it didn't need 'the protective environment' of the National (unlike, presumably, *Oklahoma*, settled in for months on months at the Olivier, in an environmentally protected run-up to its West End transfer – an unworthy thought, I now think, Rogers and Hammerstein's money-spinners having passed into the classical repertoire and so helping to fund the protected environment that a new play like mine doesn't need, especially, as Trevor Nunn also pointed out, with a commercial asset like Harold at its helm. We were West End bound, so why bother with the National anyway? was his other way of putting it).

There was also in this letter a rather natty exhibition of practical criticism, in the old Cambridge style. His reading of the text, *close* reading was what he signalled, had revealed to him that this was really an old play of mine, possibly very old indeed, perhaps almost a piece of juvenilia, now lightly refurbished and being passed around as freshly minted goods. He found the main evidence for this attribution, not in the play's style or structure, but in certain arithmetical miscalculations – the ages of the characters frequently failing to correspond to the dates given, for instance. This was true. Harold had also noticed it, but had put it down (correctly) to my sloppiness – we'd have to sit down at some point, he'd said, and work it all out, the numbers, with pen, paper and possibly an abacus – no, he didn't mention an abacus – before we went into rehearsals. But then in all fairness Harold was quite used to my getting dates, etc., wrong, whereas Trevor Nunn hadn't, to my knowledge, had the pleasure of reading one of my scripts before. Though, as a matter of fact, he's since had the pleasure of reading, or rather of not yet getting around to reading, another script of mine – *Japes* (working title) – which Judy sent to him about nine weeks ago. But I'll get to that when I get to that.

I told Harold the news, who received it with darkly couched surprise, and in due course we passed on to other possibilities. Harold was keen on the Almeida, which had housed quite a few of his own plays recently. I had much the same feeling about the Almeida as I'd had about the National, that it would be to me a closed shop, and that further rejection was therefore in store. I didn't put it quite so openly to Harold, having a degree of dignity, an appearance of stoicism, to preserve, but I hinted reservations along those lines. 'We'll see,' he said, 'but I can't imagine, I really can't, after all they're not – well, they'll surely see.' What they saw, with commendable speed – they being the two artistic directors, Jonathan Kent and Ian McDiarmid – was that they didn't care for it. They'd been 'genuinely excited', whichever of them did the reporting reported to Judy, by the dark poetry of the first act, but correspondingly disappointed, presumably also 'genuinely', by the lack of said 'dark poetry' in the second act. They really didn't want to produce this play, Judy said. Whichever of the two Judy had spoken to had been most emphatic on this point. No, they wouldn't be involved in any way in the production of this play on their stage, the stage of the Almeida Theatre. I was all the things I'd expected to be: hurt, humiliated, wounded, mortified; on top of which I was at a loss, I couldn't identify any 'dark poetry' in the first act. I hadn't set out to write any dark poetry in any scene of either act, where had their sense of dark poetry come from, a sense so strong that they actually missed it when it was no longer there? 'Where, in my text, Harold, where in the first act is there the merest hint . . .?' etc., etc., etc. He said, well, the play seemed to him in some ways poetic, in some ways dark, but those certainly weren't the terms in which he would want to discuss it, it had little to do with what was clearly there to be read, really couldn't understand, was really very surprised that these two, or which-ever of them was responsible, he supposed it must be both of them, as they were known to operate together in matters of this sort, virtually joined, he seemed to imply, at the psychic hip – so my consolation had to be that the Almeida hadn't rejected me twice, only once, at double strength.

So where to now?

Where to now, in this here and now, is to the churchyard with George.

Back. She lost her ball. I don't know how she did it, all I know is that she was nuzzling it through the leaves while I was scooping up her crap, and when I returned from the bin, she was scampering about in the distance, a long way from where I'd left her, no ball in sight. We spent about half an hour looking for it, at least I did – she seemed totally uninterested, frolicking along at my side or scuttling off after a squirrel . . . She's now sitting at the top of the stairs outside my study, looking alert. I've never known a dog with such a casual attitude to her possessions. The only items she keeps close tabs on are pieces of food – a slice of cold ham, a biscuit, half a carrot, items she's been given to eat on the spot, in your company, while you're eating something yourself – these items she frequently carries off, through the flap, out into the garden, where she buries them, and is liable to bear back through the flap months later, in a different season altogether, and drop on the floor with a flourish. When I was in hospital Victoria used to wake to an old scrap of something or other disgusting – ham, biscuit, carrot or bone – on my pillow. She chose to interpret this as a message of support. There are more sinister interpretations possible – among them that George was beginning to take over the vacant side of the bed, making it into her own turf, to keep her treasures in.

I intended to go on here, after the walk with George, to the play's next port of call, the Hampstead Theatre Club, but have decided to call it a day. Suddenly find all this raking over depressing. Also self-inflammatory. Particularly the Hampstead Theatre Club.

Tuesday, 23rd November, 3.45 p.m. Part of the problem is the darkness, that now gathers mid-afternoon – as I write this, in fact. Even in lighted rooms it's there, around you, leaking into you. On top of which everything electronic in my life seems to falter at my touch – this Apple, for instance, which has taken to changing its typography at whim, or perhaps in an ill-judged response to my mood, shrivelling into small italics, then swelling into block capitals, double spacing itself – well, the whole business is still very strange to me so I try to take care but inevitably I lapse into a dangerous jauntiness, my fingers behaving as if they now know where to go instinctively, and when I glance up at the screen I discover that not even the last words are what I know I've written, and I then further discover that these last words are floating inside a previously completed paragraph – I suppose that while the cursor drifts away, I plough on, head bowed, in the wrong context. But at least what goes wrong comes out of my still-forming relationship with my Apple, and there is an explanation for it, however irritating. But how do you, can I, explain the abrupt closing down of my cable system on television the day before yesterday? It just stopped working, or rather refused to come on when I pressed the button on the remote, so depriving me of all the channels where the best sport and most of the worst films are to be found. No sooner had I got that fixed – yesterday – than my video machine, on which I record the best sport and most of the worst films so that I can watch them at an hour of my choice, did exactly the same thing – failed to come on, offering me only a blank screen with two large zeros on it. I called in a Greek, who took the video away but promised me faithfully that he'd have a replacement within an hour that's already passed. In both these cases I did nothing different, nothing personal, merely turned them on.

I was about to begin my account of our dealings with Jenny Topper and the Hampstead Theatre Club when Peter Hall, just back from the *Evening Standard* awards, phoned to inform me that the editor had said in his closing speech that *The Late Middle Classes* might well have won the 'Best Play in London' award if only it had managed to get to London. As it was, not one of the plays on offer either in the West End or in the capital's sub- sidised theatres was, in the judging panel's view, good enough to be considered for the award, which, for the first time ever, was therefore going to go unawarded. I don't quite know how I feel about this – after all, if *The Late Middle Classes* had won the *Evening Standard* award as the Best Play in London, it wouldn't have won the Barclays award for the Best Play out of London, and I'd never have got all the way down the river to Greenwich, merely just up the road to the Savoy. On the other hand, if it had won the *Evening Standard* award it might now be settling in for a long London run, with weekly cheques, so forth – so I sat for a while, ruminating on the strange and still continuing after-life of *The Late Middle Classes*. 'You'll appreciate me when I'm gone,' as my mother used to say – on which, to Jenny Topper, Artistic Director of the Hampstead Theatre Club.

I've never met Jenny Topper, though I've always liked her name, so pregnant with associations – school prefect, Fred Astaire, hanging, laughter, light brown hair – no, that's Jeannie, but same sort of thing – a topper as a beverage that you add to a beverage, a chocolate bar, woolly hats, and for some reason turtles. None of these associations, except possibly the hanging one, lurked in her letter to Judy – a letter the like of which, I have to say, the like of which I've never, ever, so forth, so on, such a sentence completes itself, when spoken, not with words but with gestures and plosives . . . but what it could be boiled down to, her letter, was this: that Ms Topper was prepared to entertain the possibility of a production in her theatre on the required dates (she had available exactly the right dates) if Harold and I were prepared 'to sit down' with her to work out the play's real but unrealised themes. The most real of these unrealised themes, so unrealised on my part that I hadn't even realised it was there, not even as an under-theme, was the theme of artistic genius cruelly thwarted by middle-class conventions. After the three of us had realised the unrealised themes, the three of us would then address ourselves to the themes that were actually there, realisably there, but without any claim or need to be there, were in fact merely cluttering up the story. She admired the writing, by the way, which she said was 'beautiful'. Of all the compliments I've come to fear, 'beautifully written' is the one I've come to fear most. A play shouldn't be beautifully written unless, for dramatic purposes, there is a character in it who speaks beautiful writing, so to speak. If it's to be any good a play can only be truthfully written, which means the characters speak as the characters would have spoken in this or that situation – from time to time they may find resources within themselves that enable them to speak as if from beyond themselves (the prerogative of fiction) and therefore beautifully, but the resources must be recognisably, even if astonishingly, the characters', not the writer's. With luck and at his best the writer will pass unrecognised through a play, only identifiable at the end in the effect of a whole experience – if he's lucky, and been at his best.

Well, I'm only talking here, in a bloated sort of way, about the sort of plays I try to write, long to write successfully. There are completely other sorts of plays for instance, which are plays of so completely another sort that I could call them 'beautifully' as well as 'wittily', 'dazzlingly', 'fizzishly' etc. written and intend it as a compliment. But with *The Late Middle Classes*, some of whose 'themes' Ms Topper found to be in need of resuscitation, others of suppression, her 'beautifully written' was the compliment that follows the insult to the injury – hey I've just watched Chelsea overwhelm Feyenoord, a Dutch side. Chelsea were, well – witty, dazzling, fizzing, all that and yes, beautiful too, really they played beautifully written football, failing only to put the ball into the net with the regularity their beautiful writing deserved. They won three–one, when it should have been six or seven–nil. Odd how English sides, even when composed almost entirely of foreigners, find scoring so difficult. They must have made about fifteen chances, of which they took three, two of them scrappily. The Dutch made one chance, and took it cleanly. Supposing the Dutch had made only three more chances, they'd have won four–three, at least according to my calculations. Well, tomorrow – no, today (it's one a.m.) England meet – meet? – South Africa in the first test, at Johannesburg, to be shown live here on television, beginning in six hours' time. I shall therefore be in bed for the whole of the first session, so I'll have to record it. And then what? When do I watch it, I mean, as I'll be up in time for the second and third sessions, which I can therefore watch as they're taking place – would there be any point in watching the first session after I've seen the second and third sessions? – of course I can always stagger it, watching the first session on the video up here while recording the second session on the video downstairs, then watching the second session on the video downstairs while recording the third session on the video up here, which I can then watch up here – and before I know it really, tomorrow's first session will be on me, being recorded, while I'm still in bed. And then I could begin the whole process again. Every day for five days. Assuming, that is, that England last five days. Perhaps I'd better settle for the highlights on Channel Four – only forty-five minutes. Forty-five minutes, to cover six hours! Like doing *Lear* in the intervals. Still, better than becoming addicted. I could never become addicted to *Lear*, though I suppose I could pretend to be, so that whenever I'm invited to see it I could refuse, explaining that I'm in recovery – 'one day at a time, you know, of not seeing *Lear*, I've just about made it to the third step –'

Well, Harold was pretty steely about it, her letter – the idea that he should bunker down with Ms Topper and sort through the 'themes' of a play he was going to direct. It didn't sit well with him, it really didn't. And here I have to admit I let myself down rather. Quite a bit, actually. I was already pretty demoralised by the responses from the National and the Almeida, and I'd begun to panic – imagining, perfectly plausibly the way things were going, that we'd end up homeless – or, just as bad, really, that the dates on which Harold was available would slip by, I'd not only have nowhere to go, but I'd have no one to go there with. So I made what was really an obscene proposition: 'Well, look, Harold, what we could do is this, this is the sort of thing we could do. I mean.' Or words to that effect. 'What?' Harold rather growled at me down the telephone, I remember the growl and assume the telephone, as I don't believe I could have got even this far face to face. 'What do you mean, exactly? What exactly are you talking about?' I mentally amended all the ruling pronouns in the following, from the plural to the singular. 'Well, I could sit down with Topper and listen to everything she's got to say, and pretend to take it very seriously, make notes and nod and that sort of thing, and then bustle off to think about it all – it'll be just like dealing with those BBC script conferences, which only had to take place because they started employing script editors and so one had to learn to listen away to their nonsense, but in the end one didn't change anything at all, but kept thanking them for all their marvellous insights and suggestions – I'm sure I could do the same sort of thing with Topper, give her a sense, you know, of her own – her own value, that she has a contribution to make, that's probably all she really wants. Needs.' He thought about it, not at all fulminatingly. For one thing, he could see where my worries were. 'Look,' he said, 'it's your play. You have to do what you think is right for it and whatever you think is right for it, I'll be happy to direct it.' This was, it seems to me, the most generous and imaginative thing Harold could possibly have said. It left me free to . . .

Thursday, 25th November, a few minutes past 11.00 a.m., therefore a few minutes past lunch in Johannesburg. I turned on the television to find the start of the second session was delayed – is being delayed – by rain. A stroke of luck, I thought, as I could whip through my recording of the first session and catch up, then dove-tail into resumed play, live. Perfect. I wound back, spent ten minutes watching England's first four wickets go down for two runs – yes, that is the right way around. Not two runs for four wickets, normal England performance, but four wickets for two runs, double the normal England performance. No, double the normal England performance would have to be four wickets for no runs, let's look at it that way. No, let's not look at it at all. So I didn't look at it at all. Atherton's shattered stumps, Donald's joyous leap, who needs it? – especially as it's only a game.

. . . Leaving me free to do what, precisely, Harold's generous and imaginative response? When it came down to it, free to demean myself by going up to Hampstead to sit and sup with Ms Topper. And to sup with Ms Topper, I'd need a long spoon – well, more likely an earnest and grateful aspect, the very sort of aspect that comes least naturally to me, my natural aspect being, I believe, furtive and Welsh, eager to take offence. Anyway the more I entertained the thought, the thought of sitting and supping themes with Ms Topper, the less pleasant I seemed to myself. And therefore the angrier I became with Ms Topper – what made her think, by what right, and so on into plosives and gestures, not forgetting plosive gestures and gesturing plosives until I finally phoned Judy and no way, under no circumstances, who did she (Ms Topper, not Judy), by what right, etc., plosively. Judy said she quite understood, and that, triumphantly, was that: no theatre, but vanity unviolated.

Now all of the above, from having the play flatteringly rejected at the National, then having it emphatically rejected at the Almeida, and then having to reject Hampstead's equivocal and insulting semi-acceptance took up months. I suppose there were considerable pauses for reflection between each step, but I can't remember them. All I do remember is that at this stage – the post-Hampstead stage – I told Judy that I'd like to be kept uninformed of the next bout of rejections, she could send it where she thought there was hope, and let me know only when there was something worth knowing – i.e., that someone somewhere thought it was worth doing, and could do it at Harold's dates. So I've no idea where it went next, or after that, or after that, or whether Harold knew – we never discussed it, not even when the play had been doing its rounds for eight or nine months, and Judy's skilful reticence helped me into the sort of calm that's not far removed from stupor, when suddenly I thought of Watford.

Oh Christ, there's a pile of crap on my lavatory floor. I just popped in for a pee, and there it was, not a pile really, but little sausages laid neatly, side by side, so a row really. A row of crap. Theoretically, in a house of six, there are six suspects, but three of them, the two humans and the dog, can be eliminated without further thought. This leaves the three cats, Errol, the neutered stray, whose psychological profile doesn't fit, has no protests to make, no further territories to secure, is perfectly adjusted and gastrically sound. So, by process of elimination, we come to Harry (the large, female grey) and Tom (the sleek black female with elegant white patches on chin, throat and forepaws). Of the two, Harry has numerous previous convictions, having been seen arriving at or hurriedly departing from one of the areas (there are about four, not counting her current favourite, my bathroom) subsequently found to be despoiled, and has now and then been actually observed in the act of despoiling them – not that she hurries off, not until she gets to a corner at the top of the stairs, and even then she merely picks up a bit of speed as she trots down the stairs. Tom, more elusive, has fewer clear-cut convictions, but has been caught just often enough to confuse the issue. Generally, I plump for Harry – well, give a dog a bad name – but in the immediate case my intuition goes for Tom. Partly because she's just appeared outside at the window, bowing her head slightly, as she always does when she wants to be let in. Something too pat about it, as if presenting me with an alibi – 'Look, here I am outside, so how could I have been inside a mere few minutes ago, crapping in your bathroom?' – quite easily, is the answer to that. In through the kitchen cat flap, along the hall, up the stairs, into the bathroom, a quick, well-organised crap, then back down the stairs, along the hallway, through the kitchen into the garden, up the wall, on to the terrace, then there you are in front of my window, with bowed head. Well, whether it's Harry or Tom, something has to be done, apart from cleaning up, I mean, and squirting toxic chemicals over the patch, and something more than was done a few days ago, when Victoria introduced into the house an enormous cat-tray, placed it on one of the spots Harry (almost certainly Harry) has been favouring recently, and filled it with litter. The litter, golden yellow in colour, is thus far unsullied, indeed unruffled, unsurprisingly as it's given a wide berth, not just by Tom, Errol and George, but self-evidently by Harry too.

It's got to 4.00 a.m. And I am very tired. I'll stop now, please. But where has the day gone? What have I done, apart from putting in time with my Apple, sporadically? Went for a walk with Victoria and George. Read a treatment of a film about Duveen and Berenson which I may or may not be asked to write, had a long dinner with a director and a producer who are the ones who may or may not ask me to write it. Did a lot of lying down, not feeling very well. That was my day, now all gone, so stop now. Go.

It's Friday, 26th November, quarter to midnight. Don't want to talk about the day so far, even to myself. Anyway, only fifteen minutes of it left, then it'll be over, and I can claim, yet again, the start of a new day – eventually, if I stay up long enough, it'll be dawn. On which thought, back to my thinking of Watford, the real question now seeming to be, why hadn't I thought of it a long time before, when the play was shuttling to and from points unknown to me – if I had I might have saved Judy a vast quantity of letters, phone calls, faxes, embarrassment. And then it suddenly struck me, after I'd suddenly thought of Watford, that Judy had already thought of Watford, had in fact offered the play to Watford, had had it rejected by Watford, she'd by now sent it even further north, it was possibly being rejected well beyond Leeds, by now – but I had a feeling about Watford, a good feeling – in fact, I've had a good feeling about Watford ever since the early seventies, when they did the first, sometimes the only, revivals of my plays, and in two cases, the first productions of plays that eventually moved into the West End. Stephen Hollis, the then artistic director, had become a close friend, and when he moved to the States, was instrumental in bringing me over to co-direct a play of mine, *Molly*, at the Charleston Festival, the Charleston that's in North Carolina (there's another in another state, I believe, but I really see no need to look it up on the map), and another play of mine, *Dog Days*, when he was artistic director in Dallas, which any fool knows is in Texas, no, Kansas, no, where the fuck is Dallas? – yes, Texas, I should know as I once wrote a whole section of a book about being there, Kennedy was shot there, so Texas of course is where Dallas was. And is.

So. From Watford to North Carolina and then to Texas with Stephen Hollis, and a lot of laughter in all three spots. 'I've been thinking – what do you think about Watford?' I said to Harold. 'Watford. Yes. Yes, very happy memories of Watford.' Sometime in the late sixties, early seventies, he'd played Lennie in *The Homecoming* at Watford – directed by Stephen Hollis, as a matter of fact – and liked the thought of going back. So to Judy next – no, she hadn't quite got to Watford yet, she'd give it a try, do some checking. She phoned back almost immediately, to report that Watford had the right dates available. Already Watford was coming up trumps – all it had to do now, to be perfectly satisfactory on all counts, was to want the play. Giles Croft, the artistic director, read the play over a weekend, and declared a great enthusiasm for it. And there it was, dates were agreed, the matter was settled, Watford would present *The Late Middle Classes* in February, 1998. In a matter of days Eileen Diss, who has designed so many of my plays, was signed up to do the set, Mick Hughes, who has lit so many of my plays, was signed up to do the lighting; and so in no time every aspect of the production was complete – well, apart from the casting, of course.

But even the casting, generally such an agony in the first production of a new play, was a doddle after the prolonged agony of finding a theatre. Harriet Walter was everybody's first choice for Celia – and in fact every member of the cast, bar one, was on the agreed short list. The one was, inevitably, for the part of twelve-year-old Holly. There are no doubt crowds of twelve-year-old millionaires in Hollywood whose faces and names are well known to the world as they shuttle beween the studios and the clinics – but surely none in these islands – although I might be quite wrong about this, I never watch the indigenous soaps in which even six-year-olds, for all I know, may be making fortunes for parents they will subsequently sue for either child abuse or misappropriation of funds, or both – all I'm trying to get around to saying in this spasm of misanthropy or is it child-hatred? No, no, it's *successful*-child-hatred, I must ask one of my classically trained friends the ancient Greek for 'successful child', I know the word for hatred – all I'm trying to get around to saying is that we had to audition lots of fourteen-year-old boys before casting a fifteen-year-old girl, and her thirteen-year-old sister, in the part. These two girls, half-Indian on their father's side, were referred to by the company as the Bedi boys, Bedi being their last name, I hasten to add. Their secret was scrupulously guarded – after all, we didn't want audiences admiring them for their brilliance in passing themselves off as boys, but for their brilliance in the part of Holly. They appeared in the programme as Sam (for Sarah) and Alex for (Ann) Bedi, which I suppose could be taken as a professional extension of the customs of our household where the two female cats and the female dog go about under male names. Glancing up at this paragraph I see that from the way I've written it I give the impression that the Bedi boys appeared on stage simultaneously in the part of Holly. In fact they alternated after Sarah, the older, had broken the part in.

The casting of the Bedis ended my participation in the production. Harold phoned up most evenings to keep me abreast of rehearsals, we had a couple of lunches, and several dinners, but these were social, not professional. I scarcely remember him so completely happy while in rehearsals, a matter that wasn't, I hope, wholly to be explained by my absence from them. I went to see a couple of late run-throughs, and of the few notes I had, only one was controversial – that Nicholas Woodeson was playing Brownlow with a German accent, whereas I'd written him in an English one. I raised the subject with Harold on the train back from Watford: he was mildly aghast, feeling that it was too late – the first public performance was only four or so days away. This seemed to me a doubtful argument – in my experience, once actors have found their characters they can change accents without much difficulty. During the course of our discussion – argument, I suppose it was, really – I became tongue-tied. Harold was beginning to get his frown going, his voice was developing the husky rasp, so in the end I chickened out, decided to wait until I got home and could fight from my bunker with telephone and fax. I sent two faxes and left a couple of telephone messages at a time when I knew he was out, thus giving him the chance to take in how strongly I felt, and digest all my arguments before responding. He didn't respond at all – at least not directly. When he phoned back my bulletins went unmentioned, he had urgent thises and thats to discuss, a request for a few small cuts, and a few extra lines of dialogue. I couldn't bring myself to raise the subject again, thinking that if he'd missed the messages, so be it, God's will, etc., and if he'd seen and heard them, then he'd made up his mind, better trust to his director's instinct, etc. – shades of Munich here? – and eventually my agitation about the accent dwindled to acquiescence as the first night approached, and then to full acceptance on the first night, when – I had to admit to Victoria – I could no longer imagine Brownlow without a German accent.

Which brings me to the first night itself with all its usual and unusual agonies – but hey, no it doesn't, I've forgotten one element in my account of the negotiations with Watford – a crucial element, actually, as on it the later unfolding of our tale depends. A friend of Giles Croft, the artistic director, her name was Sonia Wasserman – no, that's not quite her name. Check it out[1] – who was associated in some way with a new production

---

1. Her name is Sonia Friedman, in fact.

company called (check this out too. Call it for now – West End Bound) WEB, had come across the script in his flat or office (better say office) and asked if she could read it, had read it, liked it so much that she'd shown it to people at WEB, who also liked it, liked it so much, in fact, that they offered to take the production on tour, with a view to bringing it into London. And there it was. From nowhere at all to Watford, and now from Watford to Bath, Brighton, Richmond, towns west, east, north and south, and finally London – all this arranged in a matter of days, hours almost. It is thus that the fickle finger, the massy wheel, time's whirligigs, etc., manage to retain our interest. On which note, and with the first night coming up tomorrow, pills now, music, bed.

Right up to the afternoon of the first night, I kept myself deep in my new play, *Japes* (working title) – an excellent tactic, really, as it stopped me from getting the shakes until a few hours before curtain up. I remember absolutely nothing about the journey to the theatre – whether Victoria and I went alone, or with Harold and Antonia or what – and my proper memory of the evening begins with the performance itself. The cast played as if they'd been at it for months and were still enjoying it, Eileen's set, Mick's lighting both worked so perfectly that they were unnoticeable, while the director – this is the bit that's difficult to decribe, as I've never had an experience quite like it, not in any of Harold's previous productions of my plays, though I'd admired them all – but for me it was like this, that while it was a completely realised production, beautifully flowing and out there in the world, living a life of its own, Harold himself was somehow present in every detail, in every detail I could feel his feeling for the play. As I've said, nothing like this had happened before, and I also sensed in it something valedictory, of a collaboration completing itself, perhaps. As for the play itself – I found myself bewildered by it, mostly seeing it out there, and independent, living the life Harold had given it, nothing to do with me at all, really, and then I'd be abruptly jolted into a spasm of ghastly clarity, like a little fit, really, when all I could see was that same old me, the same old abominable me, predictable, calculating, contrived, and yet look at me! strutting shamelessly about before the people of Watford like a drunken nude – the embarrassment, the shame of it, how did I dare, what made me suppose that I could ever? etc., and then back to seeing the play with almost psychotic detachment, admiring the production, the actors, the lighting, the costumes, etc., and the audience for sitting through it without audible protest, no sighs, groans, coughs from the graveyard, etc. Actually, as truth is truth and one is obliged to tell it they seemed to have enjoyed their evening quite a lot. I'm not going here just on the negative evidence listed above – there was positive evidence too, most importantly in the closeness of concentration, absorption. For instance, I'd noticed that when a line spoken in the first scene was echoed in the last scene, there was a ripple of appreciation, and not only for themselves for remembering it. At the interval the bar had been a-buzzing and a-hopping, or so Giles Croft informed those of us who were standing about in one of the theatre's offices, striking the familiar nonchalant and dignified poses, and afterwards at a public party (rather too public for my taste) lots and lots of people came up and said lots and lots of the sort of thing that, let's face it, lots and lots of people tend to say on these occasions – but at the least, at the very least, there was a distinct lack of commiseration in their looks and tones, one has surely learnt to interpret all the (half-)disguised signals – the shifting eyes, the slight droop in the voice, the brevity of the exchange – or has one? The eyes could shift from shyness, the voice droop from reverence, the exchange be brief from an inadequate vocabulary, a surfeit of emotion – but possibly the best clue as to how the evening had gone came from the SWEB representative – yes, I think it was SWEB, not WEB[2] – but what can the 'S' stand for? who introduced himself in droves all over the place, exclaiming again and again on how much he was looking forward to guiding the production out of Watford into its tour, then out of its tour and into the West End. He shook my hand several times, or was it that several SWEB representatives shook it once? – Giles

---

2. Neither, as it turns out. It is ATC, Associated Theatre Companies.

Croft was exuberant, as was his friend Sonia Wasserman, who was also, now I come to think of it, a SWEB representative – the key representative, in fact. Anyway, Harold, his wife Antonia, our agent Judy, my wife Victoria, all confirmed to each other in front of me that the evening had gone well, 'remarkably well', Harold put it; and if it hadn't, at least it had gone.

I had only the one perfectly routine worry – what to do about the critics. Not that there's anything to be done about the critics that would be acceptable in what we think of as a civilised society – and when it comes right down to it, I don't really believe anything ought to be done about them anyway. They are there as a natural part of the playwright's unnatural world, condensing all those propositions about life itself, its 'ups and downs', 'swings and roundabouts', 'hills and valleys', 'slings and arrows' – no, that's all one way, isn't it, 'slings and arrows', though in fact there are three particular critics who are always 'slings and arrows', at least for me – for other playwrights they may be swings and roundabouts, hills and valleys, etc., but I'll get to them when they turn up, in more general terms the history of my reviews is similar to the history of my relationship with the subsidised theatres. If you were to look through them, the hundreds upon hundreds of them, you would find that I don't actually seem to have a history – or to put it in publishing terms, a backlist. With each new play, it seems to be a case of 'here he is again, whoever he is', as if I were straight out of the egg, really, though not a particularly fresh one. On the other hand at least I've been reviewed. There are lots of writers, some of them far better writers than me, perhaps – how would one know? that's my point – who've never been reviewed at all, or perhaps only once, killed off early by lethally inept producers, directors, actors, husbands, wives – and who knows, possibly even dogs – and here was I with *The Late Middle Classes* flourishing away at Watford, worrying only about how to keep the critics at bay at least until we got to London. But still – I mean, why soil our experience in Watford before we'd properly begun even? And would we even make it out of Watford to those towns east, west, north and south if the national newspapers warned them in advance that a turkey was heading in their direction? This simple, if cowardly, strategy of dealing with the critics by putting them off until the last moment turned out to be a non-starter. As Watford was giving the world première of *The Late Middle Classes*, Watford was entitled to all the attention that was going, even if some of it proved to be unwanted. So I tried to look at the matter more positively – that getting our bad reviews in Watford would save us all the bother of going to London and closing there almost immediately. But why was I expressing such a lack of confidence in my play, I was asked. A question to which I couldn't give a sensible answer, especially to people who were investing a great deal of time and money in it.

All the national dailies, and one Sunday, came in to review it on the Tuesday or Wednesday of the following week, which meant – protocol and honour somehow demanded it – that Harold and I had to be in, too. I remember peering at them during the interval, through the crack in the door of our office – a section of the bar had been made over to them, there was a table with plates of food, bottles of wine spread out. I tried to distinguish one from another as they swarmed around it – I could see there was a woman, a rather attractive youngish woman – could that be a critic? And there was a large, bearded man who was dispensing lavish hospitality to himself standing next to a man strangely limbed and featured, grubby, with something on top of his head, a wool hat, and there were one or two alert-looking, middle-aged men who greeted each other cheerily, as if they were hooking up at their usual pub, at their usual hour. I reported my findings to the room at large, and was told by one of the theatre personnel that the cluster at the table were more likely to be the Friends of Watford Theatre, or was it the Patrons and Guests of the Watford Theatre? – some such body was expected in that night, and were almost certainly clustered around the table I was observing, while the critics, almost equally certainly, were clustered around a table at the other end of the bar, not to be seen through the crack in our door. Or so he thought. Or so he claimed he thought. I thought they were the critics. And were they all there, at whichever table, all of the critics? Yes, well, all except the Sundays, the 'heavy' Sundays. One 'light' Sunday was in but the 'heavies' were being held back until London. So that, then, was to be our strategy: to be swept into the West End by the dailies and one light Sunday, then enthroned there by the heavy Sundays; an astute way, one might think, of honouring the Watford première while keeping an eye on metropolitan interests. On the other hand, it meant that we'd have to go through the same process twice, nerves (and reputation, possibly) shredded twice, and the stomach – the old stomach . . .

The reviews over the next few days were OK, some more than OK, several very good indeed. The *Mail* and the *Standard* were very bad. These past few years I have come to expect very bad reviews, these are my 'slings and arrows', from the man from the *Mail*, the man from the *Standard* and the man from the *Sunday Times*. Actually the man from the *Sunday Times* (who was being held back for London) is the odd one out of the three, the other two began by hating my plays, and haven't yet stopped, why should they, as my plays go on being by me, and they go on being themselves, presumably? but the man from the *Sunday Times* started by loving my plays, and with a strange, almost unnerving passion (once even comparing me favourably with God), and then without any transitional phase whatever, no lukewarm reviews, followed by disappointed reviews, followed by exasperated reviews, not one of the above, turned on me one Sunday morning and savaged me rather like – well, like an Alsatian, now I come to think of it, like the Alsatian that gets from your feet to your throat while the smile is still on your lips – though actually the one Alsatian I know well (his name is Jack) – is a gambolling, playful creature, only alarming when he goes quite still, and fixes his eyes with simmering intensity on Victoria's face – oh, I suddenly remember that he's twice had to appear in court, for biting a boy, and the postman [3] – but all in all Jack is the model of a Good Alsatian. I'm talking here of the *Sunday Times* man in terms of the Bad Alsatian – I really feel a sudden need to get back to George at this point, although I have nothing to say

---

3. Me too, since writing this.

about her that isn't complimentary, nothing new to say at all, but still, her restfulness – of all the dogs I've owned, or shared ownership with, George is the most restful – and by that I don't mean that she lies about in a torpor, as some dogs do. Dogs in shops, for instance. They have to sit or lie there in self-induced or owner-trained unawareness, while every so often the door opens and people enter, along with gusts of smells, noise and life, and yet there they have to sit as if senseless. Or, at the very best, if they're allowed, go to greet customers with a few punctilious wags of their tail, then back to their posts, recumbent – some of them make the most of it by assuming an air of authority, part of the management, alert even when asleep.

Which brings me to Wittgenstein. I've had many problems with Wittgenstein in my time, mainly because I don't understand his writing – even when I understand the sense I miss out on the meaning, it can't possibly mean what I understand it to mean, 'Our understanding of the world depending on the way we interpret the silence around us', for example. Well, for one thing, what silence? In the nearest I ever get to silence, I hear only the din of my self, lamentable and clamorous, nothing that needs interpretation, nothing worthy of interpretation. Otherwise it seems a tautology – how can there be a difference between understanding and interpretation in that particular sentence, if you alter the position of the two words so that you get: 'Our interpretation of the world depends on the way we understand the silence around us' it strikes me as being exactly the same proposition, really, and just as useless. But then again, I may be misremembering this famous quotation, he might have written something entirely different. Besides, I'm only bringing Wittgenstein up here because of dogs, what he said about dogs, or is reported to have said in the couple of memoirs of him I've come across – for one thing, he claims that dogs can't be said to wait for people. They have no sense of time, therefore how can they experience waiting or indeed any form of anticipation. No doubt he said this with the air of intense concentration that apparently characterised all of Wittgenstein's utterances – but that doesn't exonerate the sentence on the page, does it? At least if I'm remembering it correctly. A man who doesn't believe dogs wait and anticipate! For dogs life is in part a nightmare of waiting and anticipating – a man who doesn't know that is quite simply a man who has never spent time with a dog. Perhaps the problem for Wittgenstein as he appears in the memoirs is that he didn't expect his more slap-happy observations to be memorialised, though he's always made to deliver them as if he did – I suspect his celebrated dictum about lions and speech – 'If a lion could speak, we would be unable to understand it,' is roughly how it goes – was actually the product of sustained thought, I'm sorry to say . . . Well, I mean, we would only know a lion was speaking because we could understand it – at least to the extent of understanding that it was making, or attempting to make, speech, which is already to understand something important about the lion – which of course doesn't make, or attempt to make speech, being a lion. And being a lion, he doesn't know, or care, that he's a lion. Certainly not enough to want to talk about it. Even with Wittgenstein.

All the above is fol-de-rol, evasion. What I don't want to talk about any more, not even with myself, is the man from the *Sunday Times*, the part he played in my immediate past, with *The Late Middle Classes*, the part he might play in my immediate future, with *Japes* (working title). It's coming up to midnight, Monday, 29th November, and in a few minutes time it will be the start of a day during which I have to go all the way to Lewes, to see someone I really don't want to see – look, I might as well go back to the man from the *Sunday Times*. As a topic he gets the nod over my expectations of the day that's already on us.

The thing about the man from the *Sunday Times* who wasn't coming to Watford is that he came to Watford. Not on the day all the other critics came, but by himself, on a Monday. 'But I thought it was understood he wasn't coming. He was being held back with the other Sundays. For London.' Well no, he was the Sunday who wasn't being held back. He was the Sunday who was being brought forward. 'Why?' 'Well, they must have thought it was a good idea, obviously.' 'Who? Who thought it was a good idea?' 'Well, SWEB.' This was pretty well how the conversation went, as I remember it from my end of the line. I suppose it was Judy on the other end, as all my information about this sort of thing came through her. 'So SWEB actually invited him to Watford? On his own? On a Monday? On the worst performance night they actually invited him, and on his own? Yes?' Yes. SWEB wanted him to come, he wanted to come, there was nothing to be done about it. 'Well,' I said, suddenly feeling that my panic was both unbecoming and unnecessary, the more unbecoming for being unnecessary, 'Well, it doesn't really matter anyway. He can't hurt us now, can he? We've already got enough decent reviews from the dailies – and the light Sunday, that was good too.' There was probably one of those pauses that makes one hate the telephone. 'Ah well, you see, Sonia Wasserman says that Howard Panter is a *Sunday Times* man. A bit of a *Sunday Times* man.' What could it mean that Howard Panter, the man from SWEB, was suddenly declaring himself to be 'a bit of a *Sunday Times* man'? Well, it probably meant that Howard Panter, the man from SWEB, held to the belief that audiences came to the theatre when the man from the *Sunday Times* summoned them, went elsewhere or stayed at home when the man from the *Sunday Times* so advised them. If that was indeed Howard Panter's belief, then he wasn't going to wait until we got to London to find out which it was going to be in our case. I suddenly realise that I have so far failed to mention Howard Panter – mainly because he's been irrelevant. But now here he is, on the verge of being overwhelmingly relevant.

When I'd first learnt that he was at the top of SWEB, or behind it, or in some way significantly around in it, I'd been pleased, really, as I'd had quite a lot to do with Howard Panter fifteen years ago. He'd produced a play of mine, *The Common Pursuit*, which I directed myself with a group of young comic actors – Rik Mayall, Stephen Fry, John Sessions and John Gordon Sinclair – all of them then in their mid-to-late twenties. We had a pretty merry time, in fact I've never enjoyed myself so much in a rehearsal room. Howard Panter had been an impeccable producer – that is to say, completely invisible unless required, which he mainly wasn't. Now that he had bobbed up again in this new context, I tried to recall him properly from back then. What I came up with was a strained-looking man with a strained but jolly voice, rather like a ship's purser, really, who has come to rely on a bluff manner to conceal a justified terror of the sea. At no point in our association during *The Common Pursuit* had he ever mentioned theatre critics, as I remembered it, not even the man from the *Sunday Times*, but those were undoubtedly different days, when being brave was cheaper. And easier, if you had a large handful of young and famous comics, and therefore a guaranteed audience. Well, with *The Late Middle Classes* we had no guaranteed audience; what we did have was a group of exceptionally fine actors, an exceptionally fine production (even the critics who didn't care much for the play admired the production) in a play that could be fairly described as having been well received by the audiences at Watford – and well received, too, by Howard Panter himself. He'd written to me after the second or third performance, congratulating me on a truly wonderful evening, he was much looking forward to bringing it to London, etc. – although not exactly a promissory note, it held more than a whiff of promise in it. Best of all, he'd signed it himself, with a legible signature.

But, but, but – so far and no further I began to suspect, without a blessing from the man from the *Sunday Times*, who wasn't going to give us one. 'He's not going to give us one,' I actually did say to Judy, and also did actually tell her to pass this on, not as a prediction, but as a fact, to Sonia Wasserman, for her to pass on to Howard Panter and all other hands at SWEB. Judy who – strangely, given her profession of literary agent – takes a more sanguine view of human nature than I do, refused to believe a) in the inevitability of a bad review from the man from the *Sunday Times*, or b) that the play's long-term future depended on it. Harold who – strangely, given his professions of playwright, director, actor, all-round observer of the world's cruelties – also takes a more sanguine view of human nature than I do, also refused to believe in a) or b). With respect to a) he said I ought to give the man a chance, after all, he wasn't a complete idiot, surely? Let's not jump the gun. In respect to b) he said, it wasn't possible, just not possible that if the gun we weren't going to jump nevertheless went off, it was still out of the question that Howard Panter and SWEB would fail to fulfil their obligations, they weren't complete cowards, surely?

The man from the *Sunday Times* gave us a bad review. Very small and very bad. That evening Victoria and I had dinner with Harold and Antonia in a neighbourhood restaurant. There wasn't much to say about the review, really, though we all said quite a lot. I again raised the question of the Panter–SWEB reaction – began to voice fears that had become more than fears, then backed away – after all, what was the source of my conviction, when it came down to it, what was it based on but Sonia Wasserman's letting drop to Judy that Howard Panter was 'a bit of a *Sunday Times* man'? Either you saw the darkling plain or you didn't. So we cut away to other matters, and ended the evening, as is the way with such evenings, with bursts of merriment, at whose expense I can't remember.

It's half past one on the morning of Wednesday, 30th November. No, 1st December. Can that be right? Yes, it's right all right, I've just checked a newspaper, Monday's *Standard*, the *Standard* of Monday the 29th, so Tuesday the 30th, thirty days hath September, April, June, and November, and as today is definitely Wednesday, and as Wednesday is definitely the first of December, we're into the Christmas month. So it was on the last day of November, yesterday in fact, although it still feels like today, that I went to see Margot in Lewes.

Now I've got that clear let me try and get the rest of it clear – I mean about Margot, yesterday afternoon. I've talked about it briefly with Victoria, but she was too tired after the dinner party to listen to what would really amount to yet another version of my autobiography – she's never met Margot except in my anecdotes, for instance as the legendary figure from the morning after the first night of *Dutch Uncle*, and so as the embodiment of a certain kind of cruelty – that's how Victoria knows her, as a fictional joke-monster, so at first she didn't know who I meant when I told her I might have to go to Lewes to see Margot – 'Oh, her! But I thought she lived in Germany.' Actually she lives in

The Hague, has lived there and in other parts of Holland and Germany for the last thirty years or so which is why it's a bit of a puzzle her turning up suddenly in a hospital in Lewes, all she's written in her note is that she's in St Margaret's Hospital, Glasgow Street, Lewes, she expects to be there for about ten days, if I want to see her, don't bother to phone as they're stupid with messages, just turn up any afternoon after two. If I was too busy, she wrote in a PS, it didn't matter. Of course, I said to Victoria, now I knew she was there, I'd have to go, wouldn't I? If our roles had been reversed and Victoria had put this question to me, it would have been rhetorical – but from me to her it was really a whine for help – 'Please answer that with, "No, of course you don't have to go, in fact with your health, etc." ' – but Victoria has her weaknesses, and thinking that I'm a good person is one of them, so she assumed I was going, and so I assumed I was going. I'll go next week,

I said, 'I'll send her a note saying I'll go next Wednesday,' which I did, thus allowing seven or eight days for the possibility of a card or a phone call from Margot saying wonderful news, she was cured earlier than expected of whatever it was that had brought her to a hospital in Lewes, she was off back to The Hague on the morrow, sorry we'd missed each other, thanks for thinking of me, etc., but there was no note or phone call and yesterday, no, it was the day before yesterday, I phoned the hospital and was told she was still there. The man I spoke to had the usual hospital accent – i.e. foreign, he seemed unable even to pronounce the word 'hospital' properly, making it sound like 'hosbitch', so Spanish, probably – I don't know why I'm going into all this, the preliminaries to going to see Margot in Lewes – oh yes, I do, it's because concentrating on what doesn't matter very much while practising away on Apple might help me slide into what I really want to do, need to do as a matter of fact, which is to describe what happened this afternoon between Margot and me, which was itself quite naturally – I'm beginning to see – the consequence of all that's happened and never happened between Margot and me since we were students at Dalhousie University, back in Halifax, Nova Scotia. Now I've already said that I've turned her cruelty (the *Dutch Uncle* affair, for instance) into the stuff of anecdotes, so that's a help, a start, her cruelty – the truth is that she's not cruel, she's not even unkind really, in my view, at least not deliberately unkind, it's rather that she's exceptionally, well, frank, I suppose would be the word – I would say fearlessly frank, except that courage never seems to come into it – it simply doesn't occur to her not to blurt out what she thinks and feels, but then why should it as she never notices (at least I hope she doesn't) the dire effect this often has on people – it's almost as if she's a sort of autistic, in that she can't (or won't?) read unmistakable signals of distress – warning scowls when she's half way through a sentence, trembling lips when she's got to the end of it. On she tramples, straight into the next sensitive area, trample, trample, trample. Nobody in my experience has ever told her to be careful, let alone to shut up – perhaps because such injunctions would involve explanations, 'You see, Margot, why I'm so hurt by what you've just said' – which in turn would involve peeling back scabs, opening up old wounds, making bad worse.

I remember once, though, thinking that one could always silence her without having to explain anything, simply by killing her – which brings me to *Dutch Uncle*, the morning after its first night, the first night of my second play, thirty-one years ago, when Margot and I were both thirty-three, half our lifetimes ago almost, but why am I going into that, time and the fever sort of stuff – oh, well, obviously – but. Here it is, pretty well as I've told it to Victoria more than once, probably to quite a few other people too, more than once. Imagine me stumbling out of bed, still half drunk and full of despair, trying to ready myself to face up to the reviews by binning them without looking at them – I knew what they would say, were duty-bound to say, for once no hard feelings – or there wouldn't be as long as I didn't read them. There were no newspapers on the mat in the hall, obviously too early, hadn't come yet, but what was that strange noise, guttural and honking, coming from the kitchen? Could it be a voice? Whose voice, wife and kiddies still in bed, I'd just seen them there, but definitely a human voice – oh, of course,

Margot's voice! Whose else? given the gutturalness, the honk-ingness, and of course she was staying the night (at her own invitation) – all the way from Munich or wherever just to see *Dutch Uncle*, what a friend! so I shambled into the kitchen, and there she was on the telephone, turning her back on me as if demanding privacy but also actually raising her voice – 'No, I mean it, appalling, appalling! People kept leaving – no, no, *before* the interval! and at the end the response! – well, it was like being at a bad funeral. That's it. I've got it exactly. A bad funeral.' I remember thinking, yes she had, she'd got it exactly, as I sat down and looked over the reviews which she'd left carefully spread out on the counter, including some from newspapers we didn't have delivered, which she must have gone out and bought, therefore. She'd given pride of place to the *Daily Mail*, quite rightly as it had a two-page spread, headlined 'WHY NOT BRING BOOING BACK TO THE THEATRE?' and there was a photo-graph, embedded in the text like a little round tombstone, of my face, cheeks bloated, eyes piggy and forlorn, beneath two differently styled eye-brows, one tufty, one almost bald, and I re-member half wondering at what stage in the evening – the interval perhaps? – it had been taken, while half listening to Margot now honking and gutteraling compassionately on about the poor actors, what must they be feeling at the thought of having to do it again tonight, after reading those reviews! But not for many nights afterwards she didn't think – punctuating herself with her barking laugh or her smoker's cough, and it came to me quite clearly – all I had to do was to reach into a drawer, then two quick steps, a thrust, a last honk, bark, cough –! And then – then we 'd talk funerals, a good funeral this time, hah, hah . . .

I could go on like this about Margot, there's more, lots more, but given the events of this afternoon, no, yesterday afternoon, I might as well get to the heart of the matter, the lack of heart, that is. Margot and I never had an affair, never even slept together. The closest we got to sex was back then in the (nineteen-)fifties, in Halifax, Nova Scotia – 'necking' it was called, though actually in our case the neck didn't really come into it, and nor did anything below it. I don't believe I even put a hand on the wodges of clothing beneath which her breasts could be thought to lie. She was a heavy dresser, the young Margot, swathed even in the hot Nova Scotian summers – the sun played havoc with her skin, the cold with her chest – and it wasn't until we were in our mid-thirties, and I was married with two children, that I at last saw her body. It was encased in a hideous green and pink one-piece bathing costume – actually that's what it looked like, a costume – for a musical comedy, perhaps, as performed in the village hall, and therefore perfectly right for the beach at Lyme Regis (she had come from Munich, I think it was, to stay with us for a week), and I saw in spite of the greens and pinks and the baggy bit around her bottom, that she had quite a shapely body, sturdy but definitely shapely, with fine breasts, rounded buttocks. Also I suddenly realised how pretty she was, had always been, with her neat Teutonic face and her intelligent grey eyes – and her mouth has – had in Halifax, Nova Scotia, and still had that summer in Lyme Regis – a charming over-bite, I think it's called, the tips of her front top teeth just showing above her under-lip when she laughed. At Lyme Regis her very blonde fine hair was cropped short, which didn't suit her, made her look slightly brutal, but in Halifax, Nova Scotia, she'd worn it long, down to the small of her back. Apart from the hair, though, she was rather stunning, really, and I could certainly see that if I knocked fifteen years off her age, and got her out of the bathing costume, she was everything that a sex-crazed lad of nineteen should have wanted, especially in Halifax, Nova Scotia – although this particular sex-crazed lad hadn't wanted it, even in Halifax, Nova Scotia, and what's more wouldn't have wanted it even if he'd known about the shapely breasts, rounded buttocks etc., at least not if they were on offer from Margot – which they were, as a matter of fact, she'd more than hinted it several times, and once virtually said it outright, quite angrily. I didn't fancy her, that was the thing. I was going through the most sexually undiscriminating period of my life (it went on for a very long time, this period, I was a rancorous virgin right into my early twenties), but however hard I tried I simply could not bring

56

myself to fancy Margot. And I did try very hard indeed – hours before we'd arranged to meet up I'd put myself to bed and mull over my favourite fantasies, invent some new ones and work away on those, while at the same time of course practising complete self-abstention, sometimes with complete success – anyway I often left the house in a highly excitable state, in fact choosing to slip out by the back door rather than face my mother's kiss – but it was no good, never any good, conviction collapsed, excitement dribbled away the moment she was in front of me – it was perhaps her voice that put me off, already a chain-smoker's at five a day (I'd started her off); it was perhaps her smell, of pepperminty lotions and something else faintly acrid; perhaps it was the thought of her widowed mother, obese, carping and Lutheran; and it was perhaps the sort of remark she was just beginning to go in for, recognisably hurtful, even by Nova Scotian standards – but there was one thing far worse than all these things put together, and that was that she loved me. She would have died for me, I think. Well, if not for me, with me.

For my part I certainly didn't love Margot, no, and I did on many occasions hide from her, yes, most frequently after I'd discovered that her mother had put it about that we were 'going steady' (she'd seen Margot sitting on my knee on her porch), and in those days in Halifax, Nova Scotia, a couple 'going steady' was a couple going steadily towards the altar of one of Halifax's seventy-eight churches, so, yes, there were many occasions when I darted up the steps of the Dalhousie library or nipped behind a pillar when I saw her thickly swaddled figure galloping briskly in my direction, but – this is the point – there were also many occasions when I went looking for her, hunting for her, prowling around the campus like a wolf on heat (that can't possibly be right but wow!) so urgent was my need for her, because there was this in Margot that I did actually, well, love: she made me feel like a writer. She read everything I wrote, poems, plays, short stories, fragments of novels, meditative essays, everything, with total attention, with devoted and critical, sometimes savage but always total attention. She could even quote me to myself. That's what I loved in her.

Before this afternoon, yesterday afternoon, I hadn't seen her for eleven years – eleven years and three months, we calculated it at, yesterday afternoon. We've spoken regularly on the telephone, Christmas, birthdays, etc., and we've written, she much more often than me, long letters, almost essays, about the detestability of her colleagues, particularly the ones doing gender and racial studies, and the self-righteous dimness of her students. I never read them very carefully. I don't know any of the people, after all, and her handwriting is difficult, thin and small, in light blue ink. I sometimes sit down determined to write her a proper letter, but mostly I find it an effort to stretch myself to a second page. I always send her copies of my plays, of course. She reads them promptly, responds to them thoughtfully, sometimes sharply – and that's been our relationship for the last eleven years and three months, up until yesterday afternoon. And that's the way I'd have liked it to go on, with perhaps fewer and shorter letters from her, no letters at all from me, a short phone call every other Christmas. Still in each other's lives, in a neglectful sort of way, would have been fine by me. As I've already said, I think, I absolutely dreaded seeing her again, and as I've certainly already said, since coming out of hospital I pretty well dread the thought of having to go anywhere at all, and most especially to a hospital, even when someone else is the patient. So what with the dread of having to take a train to see her, along with the dread of seeing her in a hospital, along with the dread of actually seeing her at all –

So I thought it through in stages – up in time for breakfast (midday), order a taxi for the station (Victoria) half an hour before needed, on arrival at Victoria purchase return ticket immediately, then pick up newspapers, Diet Cokes, a sandwich, find the platform, go to it, wait patiently, smoke heavily on the assumption that it'll be a no-smoking train, make sure to get off at the right station (Lewes), make sure to give the right name (St Margaret's) and the right address (Glasgow Road) to the taxi driver in Lewes, and make sure to book him to return in an hour. It was all a bit of a triumph, really, in that I got through all the stages just as I'd organised them mentally, though of course each stage as lived had its own quite different organisation, the taxi arrived too early, the train was late, the sandwich was inedible, the Diet Coke warm, I had to walk to town for a taxi, and then when I got to St Margaret's, Glasgow Road, at pretty well the time I'd expected, the low, light, cheerful little building, rather like an infant school from the outside, with a sort of playground entrance, turned out not to be a hospital but a hospice, and Margot is dying. She has a cancer that was endlessly misdiagnosed in Holland and Germany, and has come to Lewes because some relatives on her father's side live there – an uncle and two cousins. Also some colleagues, ex-students, the family who live in the flat above hers in The Hague, will probably want to come to the funeral, and she couldn't really expect them to fly out to Nova Scotia, could she, which she'd anyway long ago ceased to think of as home.

She's very far gone, I think, her cheeks sunk and her teeth exposed and protruding, and she was wearing a turban, so I suppose she must be bald – but her voice is quite strong, no, not strong, vigorous if whispery. She sat on the bed hunched and chain-smoking, sipping from a mug of vodka and lime – they know how to treat you in Lewes, she said, when you're dying, she almost certainly wouldn't have been allowed vodka and fags in Holland, certainly not in Germany, how long was I staying, not for long, please, she didn't want me to stay for long, or to come again, she had too much to say to me, I too little to say to her, a goodbye was necessary, a short one would do. I handed her *Japes* (working title), which I'd brought her instead of flowers and chocolates. I couldn't think what else to do with it, as I was holding it, and it was obviously intended for her. She thanked me for it, said she'd try to read it. I said she was always my best reader, the one at my shoulder, and she said no, she didn't think she'd get to read it after all, why waste a copy, and handed it back to me. I tried not to see her hand or arm, as I took it. 'That's it,' she said, 'That's enough. I'll let you know when the funeral is.' A small version of the familiar bark. 'I mean somebody will. You don't have to come.' I said, 'Of course I will, of course I'll come.'

I got up, hovered. She nodded at me. I bent, kissed her on the side of the forehead, and went to the door. She said something I didn't quite hear. 'What?' I said. 'What, Margot?' 'Doesn't matter,' she said, and jabbed me out with her cigarette. As I went into the sort of playground a short young man with blond hair passed me, carrying some books – they looked like German books – and a carrier bag from an off-licence. I wondered if he was one of the cousins, or a colleague or ex-student, or whether in fact he was visiting Margot in particular at all, he might have been a doctor or a priest. The taxi was faithful to its hour, which meant I had a long wait at the gates of the playground. I sat on a bit of wall, out of breath, and smoked, and thought about what I thought I'd heard Margot say, which was, 'I haven't hated you for years.' And then a little something else, which might have been, 'Isn't that a pity?' I don't know – I could have got both bits wrong. For instance it might have been 'I haven't rated you for years. Your work's got shitty.' I hoped so. Much more Margot. And it would explain why she gave me *Japes* (working title) back, rather than just leaving it to be disposed of, in due course.

When I got home, after an OK journey, the life stages approximating to the mental stages (I ordered myself a taxi on my mobile, the first time I've used it – successfully, at least) I couldn't think what to do, feeling ropy and still agitated, my stomach all over the place. Victoria came in, late apparently, and we had to rush straight out to the small dinner party. The people were agreeable, the food decent, but what was I doing there, at the end of such a day? I felt oddly like a criminal, on parole from somewhere ghastly, Margot's little cubicle of a room, I suppose, where I wasn't wanted. When we got back from the dinner I sat on the edge of the bed and talked to Victoria about Margot for a short while, I think I've already mentioned this, until she fell asleep, then I came in here, put down all of the above. It's dawn, there are the birds, definitely time for a sleeping pill, possibly two, and then tomorrow, or whenever it is I next sit down to this Apple here, I will with luck be back to where I was before I went to Lewes.

Well, here I am. But where am I in fact?

Oh, yes, on the tour. So we're forgetting Lewes, gone from Watford, moved to Brighton. But back to Watford for the moment.

Yes, last week at Watford. Man from SWEB tells us that six, yes, six West End theatres (six!) are desperate to bring us in so SWEB was active on many (many!) fronts – 'You can imagine!' said the man from SWEB. We also learnt that we were on our way to breaking some of Watford's box-office records. Subsequently, the world was informed – the world hanging on to its hat for this one – that we'd actually broken all of Watford's box-office records, including some that had never previously been recorded. So here it was, or seemed to be: a play that had been rejected by London management after London management was heading triumphantly towards London, by way of a tour which was also turning out to be something of a triumph – and now I can finally move us on to Brighton, where two couples (and not in their dotage) introduced themselves in the foyer of the Theatre Royal in order to tell me that they'd enjoyed the show even more than at Watford, where they'd seen it twice. I allowed myself the luxury of believing them. After all, why should they lie about this, when they surely had so many more important things to lie about? I think I'll stop here – not in the mood. I've just written a long letter to Margot talking about our past, how much it's always meant to me, how much I'll miss her – here it is on the screen, so immaculate, so impersonal, so fraudulent and so permanent – and yet all I need to make it vanish is a few taps of my fingers, a whisking about of my sensor – or is it my cursor I whisk about? – whichever it is, I've just done it. Now let's get to Richmond on Thursday – no, let's not. Let's get to my sleeping pill, some music, and then to bed with Victoria and George, George and Victoria.

Tuesday the what? Well, around the second week of the Christmas month, 2.00 a.m., having just returned from dinner with an old friend, let's call him Rupert. I used to be very fond of him, I suppose I still am, really, but recently, let's face it, we've had some pretty dodgy outings together – since I gave up drinking, as a matter of fact. One of the penalties of having to remain sober is you don't get much of a move on when it comes to moods over dinner tables, while your companion (i.e. Rupert), if drinking too much, is likely to be travelling all over the place. I feel guilty about this sometimes, treacherous, really, as up to two or so years ago I used to swing about, usually harmoniously, or at least in equal disharmony – but these days here I am, stuck in the state in which I started the evening, my mind not really much fixed on the conversation once it begins to take antic and slovenly leaps – I keep smiling, nodding, grunting, as I try to fix my mind on the prospect of pudding, puddings having entered my life in a big way now that alcohol has left it. Anyway, it was like that this evening with Rupert, only more so, as he arrived at the restaurant in the state in which he usually leaves it, his side of the conversation – most of the time it was the only side – was a chaos of befuddled anecdotes, bewildering non-sequiturs, slurry and sometimes belligerent laughter, every now and then he seemed to be accusing me of something, I couldn't make out what, but probably of being sober, when it came down to it – by the time we hit the pavement I was holding him up, virtually – I had a terrible time getting him a taxi, they kept drawing up and then veering away at speed when they realised what was on offer, and the one I finally got I had to bribe with a twenty-pound note – I'd also paid his share of the bill, by the way, which was much more than twice mine, I should think, because of all the booze. Well, the next time we meet it should be for lunch, but then he sometimes drinks pretty heavily at lunch too. Well, breakfast then – except that I'm never up for breakfast – but still, something or other – 'Keep your friendships in constant repair,' said Dr Johnson. 'Cling to those who cling to you.' Not that Rupert and I have ever actually clung to each other, but we go back nearly forty years or so, and we've had some times – I'd better stop now, don't feel up to going from my evening with Rupert to that Thursday in Richmond. I'll do it tomorrow . . .

Well, it is tomorrow, though only a few hours after I wrote the above, being now 1.45 a.m. on Monday, the 9th or so of

December, anyway the day which brings me to Thursday in Richmond – but the reason I've started again so soon after I'd hoped I'd finished is that it wasn't in Richmond that that Thursday took place, I've just realised it can't have been, because by Richmond the future of *The Late Middle Classes* was over and done with, so not at Richmond, not at Woking, I'm sure of that, therefore the Thursday night when it all didn't happen, or rather when it became clear to me that nothing was going to happen must have happened in Brighton. Yes. I've just checked with Victoria. She says, of course it was Brighton. So that's where I go from later today. That Thursday night (but why am I so sure it was a Thursday, when it comes down to it? But I am. It was.) in Brighton.

It is now 11.15 a.m., same day, with that Thursday in what's turned out to be Brighton waiting to be unfolded. But before I get to that I suppose I ought to report briefly on a telephone call I've just had from Sheila (let's call her), Rupert's first wife and still a friend of mine. She wanted to know why I'd sent him around to her last night. I said that I hadn't, I'd sent him home. She said that Rupert said I'd put him in a taxi and sent him to her. Oh Christ, I said, I must have given the taxi driver his old address, from habit, sorry, is everything all right? Well, no, it wasn't all right, as soon as she'd let him in he'd vomited over the floor and the sofa, she'd had to sponge him down, etc., heave him into a mini-cab. She spoke as if I'd primed, loaded and aimed him at her quite deliberately – so of course lots of apologies from me, then the usual 'How's Victoria? How's Pepe?' – her current other half, an Argentinian – 'We must see each other some time,' etc., but I could tell from her tone that she still holds me responsible in some way – odd, as his drinking was one of the reasons she threw him out, but now, without any thoughts at all on the damaging effect alcohol continues to have on my social life, my bank balance and my health, even though I've given it up – to that Thursday in Brighton. By that point in the tour, just over half way, Howard Panter and his team from SWEB had run through five of the six theatres that had been in hot pursuit when we were in Watford – a couple had dropped out because the shows they thought were dying were suddenly in robust health. One or possibly two had pegged out earlier than anticipated, had had to be replaced before our tour was up. In short, the only theatre now available to us was the Gielgud. I couldn't help feeling that the dwindle from six theatres to one in a few short weeks was ominous – especially as at least three of them seemed to me, in terms of intimacy, more suitable than the Gielgud – previously known as the Globe – which I always feel cowed by, even under its new name – perhaps because an early play, one that had taken me eight years to write, had closed there (albeit when it was the Globe) a week or so after opening. It had unhappy associations, therefore, of imminent death, the theatre once known as the Globe, now as the Gielgud. On the other hand it was a theatre – the only theatre left – that wanted us, and whenever we get down to the only theatre that wants us, that theatre is good enough for me, even if it's completely unsuitable.

So the important thing, as far as everyone connected with the company was concerned, was that negotiations were proceeding smoothly with the Stoll Moss group (the proprietors of the Gielgud), and if there was a slight problem – this had come to me from Judy a few days earlier – one more investor with thirty pounds, hey hey, thirty *thousand* pounds at his or her disposal, and inclined for a gamble in the theatre, would solve it. Problem already solved, I told Judy, as I myself was able to furnish precisely some such investor, in the form of an old friend of mine who had read the play soon after it was finished, and even back then, when there were no signs of a production to invest in, had wanted to invest in it. I passed her name on to Judy, who proceeded to put Howard Panter and SWEB in touch with her in New York. So there she was, waiting, ready to sign contracts, post cheques, whatever was needed – and there were SWEB and Panter delighted to have her name, telephone and fax numbers, claiming they would make contact the moment they knew for sure that they actually needed one last investor with thirty thousand to invest. An odd sum, Victoria pointed out, an odd sum to be short, when you consider that Howard Panter and SWEB are presumably professional enough to have made all their calculations in advance, and that these calculations would have involved quite a few hundred thousand pounds, odd then, that in those large terms such a smallish sum should threaten to be a sticking point, what would have happened, what would happen indeed, if the author hadn't happened to have a friend who happened to have thirty thousand pounds to hand, and a personal interest in this particular play's future – yes, strange that they should need it at all – unless, of course, somebody had pulled out just as they were coming to the wire.

But by and large there was a great deal of euphoria abroad that night at Brighton. In the office – I might have got the town wrong, and the theatre wrong, but I remember the office and my place in it, I was at the desk like the chairman of the board, ginger ale and cigarettes to hand; Harold, Antonia, Victoria, were seated or standing with their champagne, Sonia Wasserman – have I described her? Pretty, youngish woman, frizzy brown hair, an air of capable femininity – capable femininity, what on earth does that mean? Well, I know what it means really, it means that her capability and her femininity seemed inextricable, you enjoyed the softness of her face and voice, while admiring the succinctness with which she answered questions, issued news bulletins, and was able to tell us now, in the Richmond office that the talks between Panter–SWEB and the Stoll Moss gang were proceeding apace – the only slight worry, not to be worried about, was a show hovering in the provinces that was also making a bid for the Gielgud, but apart from this completely unworriable worry, Sonia informed us, nobody could see any reason that *The Late Middle Classes* shouldn't go straight into the Gielgud at the end of its tour. The Gielgud was currently empty, it was waiting, we were needed. Words to that effect.

'What is this show in the provinces?' somebody asked.

It was a musical.

'What sort of musical?'

She didn't know.

'Well, what's it called?'

She didn't know.

'Well, where is it? Where does it come from, where's it performing?'

The North, she said. Somewhere in the North. But she didn't know which part of the North. Didn't know anything about it at all really, apart from its being in the North and wanting to come south, all the way south, into the Gielgud. I said it must be a bit difficult for Panter–SWEB to find itself bidding against a show they couldn't give a name to, whose provenance and current whereabouts were also unknown – a bit like *The Maltese Falcon*, really.

'Ah, *The Maltese Falcon*,' said Harold. 'Now there was a film!'

And so we were off for a while on *The Maltese Falcon*, Sidney Greenstreet, Peter Lorre, Elijah Cook Junior, Humphry Bogart, until we came back on track, no, onto a nearby track, with an account from the Brighton house manager of the wonderful audiences they'd been having, even the matinees, etc., throughout which my concentration was feeble, as little bells were ringing. I suffer from tinnitus, by the way, but I don't get bells, I get a high electrical whining – it tends to come on at times of stress, so there in the office of the Theatre Royal, Brighton, warning bells were ringing, stress-induced electricity was whining, because the fact is that I didn't believe, not for a minute, that Panter–SWEB didn't know which musical currently playing in the North was in direct competition with them for the sole remaining West End berth. Or if they didn't know, it was only because they couldn't be bothered to find out. Perhaps it was beneath SWEB's and Howard Panter's dignity, their own will was so clear, their honour so unimpeachable – alternatively, they didn't care who was going into the Gielgud, as long as it wasn't them. Us, rather. *The Late Middle Classes*.

I muttered all this to Victoria before the curtain went up, and began to mutter it again at the interval, as we made our way back to the office – in which, I noticed, Sonia Wasserman was already sitting, in the middle of a conversation on the telephone – so either she had beaten me out of the auditorium by some minutes, a clear impossibility as nobody ever beats me out of the auditorium at the intervals of my own plays – or, which seemed to me the only physically plausible explanation, she had only pretended to be going into the first act when she'd left the office with the rest of us, had in fact doubled back to the office as soon as she'd seen us safely dispatched to our different seats. Well, why shouldn't she? There was a life to be lived outside my play, especially by an attractive young woman, there were lots of good reasons for foregoing the first act in favour of the telephone – to say hello to lovers, friends, family, to make business deals, restaurant bookings, murder threats to musicals playing up north – whatever, so I don't know why I minded so much, but I did – not minded angrily, but minded suspiciously. Suspiciously minded. Which Victoria says I am, about some things; but, imbecilically, not about others – the things that matter, perhaps. Because really there was no point my being suspicious of Sonia Wasserman for being on the phone when we came into the office; and no point in being therefore even more suspicious at the way she got off the phone, by hanging up abruptly, and smiling around at us with furtive radiance. She then left the room, seeming to say, 'Oh, I must go and find a phone,' which is perhaps what she did say, really meaning a phone on which she could have a decent, or even an indecent conversation without being looked at suspiciously by the likes of me. Then Harold and Antonia came in, perhaps other people too came in, I don't remember, all I remember is that eventually everybody else, including Victoria, went back to watch the second act and I alone sat lingering there, I don't know why, not because I couldn't face the second act, which I couldn't, really – but nor was I attempting to lay some sort of trap for Sonia Wasserman – I was just as surprised at her coming back into the office as she was to find me in it. Less embarrassed, though, as I was the author and she was purportedly only at the theatre to be among the audience. She said she was looking for a phone. I gestured to the one she'd used some twenty-five minutes earlier. She looked at it, nodded. I said I'd be slipping back into the theatre in a minute, just polishing off my ginger ale. Well, she said, it wasn't urgent.

Odd, it suddenly strikes me, that she didn't have a mobile. Everybody – certainly everybody who goes about life in theatre management and such occupations – seems to have a mobile these days – seemed to, too, in those days, which were under a year ago. Perhaps hers was broken. Or she didn't like them, the sense of being reachable, available – well, she probably wished she had one now, and was using it somewhere else – instead of stuck in the office having to make conversation with me. Difficult conversation, because I suddenly enquired after Howard Panter's health. Fine, she said. He was fine. I said I was glad to hear it, he'd had a tendency to apoplexy, heart-attacks, when we'd last had anything to do with each other. Oh, he's over all that, she said. Very robust. I mentioned the letter he'd sent me during Watford, in which he'd said he was looking forward to working with me again, moving *The Late Middle Classes* into the West End. 'Ah well,' she said, 'ah well now, Howard won't actually be doing that. He's not going to be doing *The Late Middle Classes*. He's leaving that side of things entirely alone, from now on. From now on, he'll be doing the big musicals. That side of things.' I made a little joke about his possible interest in a mystery-cloaked musical hovering about the northern provinces, but I don't think it was heard, or if heard, understood, because Sonia Wasserman, with a serious little frown and lots of serious little nods, was being eloquent on the subject of SWEB, the complex juggling and rejigging that had seen Howard Panter move himself sideways, or around, or upwards – anyway, to an arena of concerns from which he need no longer address as much as a glance in our direction. 'I'll be dealing with the plays part of things,' she said. 'That'll be my job.' And *The Late Middle Classes*? Yes, yes. That would be her job too. She did something that's probably translatable, if you're a student of body language, that I can't translate but remember clearly – a sweeping-something-out-of-her-hair kind of gesture. So she would be taking over the putting in, so to speak, of me and mine? She would, yes, and now she must, really she must get back, didn't want to miss the rest of the second act – I sat on for a bit, not really pondering this, just letting it settle – the realisation that there was to be no London future (well, apart from a week in Richmond) for *The Late Middle Classes*. But then I'd already assumed as much, really, from the moment I'd been told that Howard Panter was 'a bit of a *Sunday Times* man'.

The two hours after the show were, though only for me, I hope, utterly disgusting. There was a party in an Italian restaurant close by. Harold, or whoever had arranged it, had taken a large section of the upstairs room. There were two long tables, at one of which Harold, Antonia, Victoria and I sat with members of the cast plus, towards the bottom end with head lowered but animated, Sonia Wasserman. She seemed to be deeply mixed into the party without somehow being a part of it – however much she shrugged, gesticulated, laughed, stretched even, she remained sunk – morally sunk, I suppose, from my view of her – in her chair. She made absolutely sure her eyes never strayed up the table towards director (and wife), author (and wife) – well, who can blame her, after all what would she see but me, my face, no doubt expressing all kinds of things from which guiltless people would also avert their eyes. What was horrible though, was the cheery trustingness of everybody else's behaviour. Awful phrases – 'When we get to the West End' from Harriet, or 'I wonder what the Gielgud dressing rooms are like, anybody familiar with the dressing rooms at the Gielgud?' – I remember this about dressing rooms particularly distinctly, though I don't remember who said it. Harold was all laughter, anecdotes, beams, with a speech portending. He likes making speeches, he's very good at them, forceful, witty, genial – but those words don't get it, really, the full flavour of a Harold speech, which is something to do with the imposition of a very strong personality, a darkish personality imposing itself in sunny hues – I know lots of people who speak well, urbanely, fluently, with idiosyncratic charm – but nobody I've ever come across simply takes possession of a party or dinner party, that sort of occasion, as Harold does, and leaves it as a prime memory of the event.

So in due course, with three or four vigorous raps of a piece of cutlery on the table, he rose and spoke. It was mostly a speech of thanks to the cast, for the imagination and devotion they had brought to their work – though I think he used the word 'tasks' – he was charmingly funny about the Bedi boys, who were girlishly delighted and properly proud of what he said both about them and across the table directly to them – a few very moving (for me) words about the play. Then, with an unsuccessful look around for Sonia Wasserman, who had made herself invisible to all but the most implacably focused eye, he talked of the months to come in London, where a different sort of challenge would be offered by audiences, said a few words about the tensions we'd all of us had to endure while waiting for the right theatre – but that was what it was like these days, we no doubt all of us had stories to tell, but now, raising his glass, a toast to the Gielgud future of *The Late Middle Classes*. All glasses were raised not only in response to the toast but also in a salute to Harold, among them the Wasserman glass, though tentatively, at half-mast. For me, in spite of knowing what I knew, the occasion had at least had its moments, the moments of simple and proper honouring, really, is what they amounted to. For her, knowing what she knew, virtually every moment must have been quite ghastly – the more so for her having insisted on making herself (or rather, I suppose, Howard Panter and SWEB) the hostess of a party she hadn't even known was going to take place until she was invited to it. There is surely an analogy for how she must have felt – something to do with undertakers having to celebrate with tomorrow's customers, or executioners throwing a party on the lip of a mass grave – no, they're not right, don't work, let's just say that Sonia Wasserman took an early leave from the party, thus managing to escape the gratitude of her guests.

In the car, on the way back to London, I told Victoria what was what. She refused to believe me – I was always paranoid about the intentions of producers, she said – (but when had I been wrong, I asked her) and I didn't have any information to go on, not even soft information (which is what?) let alone hard information, not a single fact, it was all a matter of what I made of Sonia Wasserman's expressions, her behaviour over the telephone, her shyness at the dinner table – how could I blame her for not answering a straight question when I hadn't, according to my own account, even actually asked her one? The conversation went on like this in the way that such conversations do, round and round – and in the end I realised it was no good my saying again and again, 'If only you'd been there, you'd have seen what I mean,' because if she had been there, she almost certainly wouldn't have seen what I meant – how could she, as she wouldn't have been me, and therefore wouldn't have been looking for it. Perhaps that is what's meant by a paranoiac, still best defined, in my view, as someone who knows all the facts. So we left it there for the night. Got home, I assume, to George, Errol, Harry, Tom, and the night in Brighton, which for so long during my writing of this I've confused (though only in date and venue) with the night in Richmond, was over. Therefore, I suppose, maintaining the chronological spirit, on to the night in Richmond.

I have, by the way, got a mild viral infection. It's a Thursday, 7.45 p.m. I have just got out of bed, having spent most of the day there. I'm on my own as Victoria's in Leeds – on her way back by now – where she went to help her god-daughter move her possessions out of her university lodgings and back to London over the Christmas holidays. I don't know if I'm up to Apple this evening, much better if I'd stayed away from him until my chest and head cleared, but actually, I feel – on top of feeling ill – I feel irritable, very irritable. The sort of state in which I hate almost every aspect of the world I find myself in. Perhaps because I'm sixty-three and suspect that I'm a kind of Rip Van Winkle, but in my case I didn't sleep for forty years, I blinked one day – I don't even know on which day, in which year, but I certainly blinked sometime some years ago, and there I was, struggling to get along in a world in which all the points of reference were quite different. Still are. About a quarter of the news is devoted to people who are famous in London, or in England, or in the UK, or world-famous even, and I've never heard of them before. How can this happen? Logically, experientially, it would appear to be impossible. They can't have exploded into being household names, they must have got there in stages – and the way they're written about certainly presupposes a long acquaintance (frequently even a long, hostile acquaintance) with the subject, in fact it's part of the point that we're keeping them company on their journey from comparative obscurity through accelerating fame and riches to who knows what, public obloquy perhaps. But I've gradually worked out something about the professions of these to me, completely anonymous people – anonymous in that not only do I not know their names when I hear them, I've already forgotten them the moment after I've heard them. What I've worked out is that they are in branches of show business that didn't exist until I blinked – or weren't considered of public consequence until I blinked. They are people who read out the news, for instance, at peak hours on television. They are people who compère quiz shows, or chair discussion panels. They are people who have been playing the same part in soap operas for twenty or thirty years. They are singers in groups, or possibly even single singers, or one of a pair of singers. Or comics. Or gardeners. Or cooks. Or women.

These are the professions of the celebrities I can never identify, stories about whom mystify, irritate and sometimes terrify me – the possibility exists, after all, that in failing to identify them I'm also failing to understand not just simple facts, but key laws about the world I find myself in at the age of sixty-three – and it may turn out that they're not merely social laws but evolutionary and therefore natural laws, and that all my habitual points of reference are becoming truly meaningless except to my friends, most of whom seem also to have blinked. But what is it that one dreads about this state of affairs? After all, death will come as death always does to all the famous people I've never heard of, and when it does – if I'm still around, that is – I'll hear even more about them for a short while, and then less about them, and then nothing at all, and it won't matter in the slightest that I still won't know who they were or the real meaning of what they did. Can I really find this a consoling thought? Really, it's not even a thought, more a jeer, really, yah-booh, death too, for you and you and you – whoever you are, you and you, death, oblivion – the jeer of a sixty-three-year-old with a touch of bronchitis. A blinker.

But here's something else that might explain my present (but passing, I trust) confusion and indecency of spirit. When I finally got out of bed, having been licked into full wakefulness by George – she does this, laps her tongue heavily over half my face as soon as it shows signs of consciousness; I have contradictory feelings about it – the sensation itself is unpleasant, after all hers is a rough tongue, and as I've said she applies it heavily; but the instinct behind it, which I take to be protective, fills me with gratitude, especially when Victoria is off molly-coddling god-daughters or whatever – well, when I finally got out of bed, dressed myself, washed George's saliva off my face, I went into my study, wondering whether I had it in me to sit down and pick up, as I'd said I was going to, on that night in Richmond. Then I saw there were several messages on my answering machine. I played back, and got clicks and the most eerie vacancy, that's what it sounded like, a noisy vacancy with stabbing clicks at short intervals, and then the usual definitive ping, meaning the messages were over. All three of them. I did that thing – dialled 1974, no, 1471, and there was the usual voice, informing me that I'd had a phone call at 16.22 on 10th November. Which is the day I started this diary, a day under a month ago. So what had happened to all the phone calls since, had they been wiped, had they never in fact taken place, were the three phone calls I hadn't had just now harbingers of future calls, the ones I'm never going to get, as well as ghostly cries from all the dead calls since 10th November, when I first sat down and started to teach myself how to write on this computer? Anyway, it was very upsetting, suddenly bringing back the hallucinatory episodes I went through in hospital – although for those there had at least been an explanation of a clear, scientific kind. I had merely been poisoned by the anaesthetic – not deliberately poisoned of course, or even accidentally poisoned in the sense that I'd been given the wrong one or too much of it – I have an allergy to opium is all it turned out to be, and as the anaesthetics generally used in major operations are opium-based, just as the sedatives and pain-killers used after major operations are also opium-based, you can see how everything follows in a perfectly logical and understandable sequence. First the opium-based anaesthetic administered during a major operation on my stomach, then lashings of opium-based painkillers and sedatives, then, with the recognition that I was being killed by a multiplicity of poisonous palliatives, the withdrawal of virtually everything that is normally recognised as life-sustaining – food, water, all medicines – living (once the word has been deprived of its vital content) off a drip for three weeks.

Both these periods, the poisoning period and the withdrawal from poisoning period, therefore caused me to hallucinate – usually in the form of conspiracies against my person, my career and my reputation. At the centre of the conspiracy was usually to be found a doctor, who had suborned and seduced all the other doctors, as well as the nurses and my loved ones. These conspiracies were acted out in scenes so vivid that they only differed from reality by being more real, more unavoidable. In one of the earliest ones, I watched and listened helplessly as all the young doctors and nurses took turns on the ward telephone to make contact with their agents, to negotiate deals for a film script based on the short stories of Daphne du Maurier – I kept attempting to shout out that these were my short stories, I'd been given them to adapt for films (this bit was true. I'd finished two of them just before becoming ill), I owned and loved them. Nothing audible came from me because an oxygen mask was clamped over my nose and there were tubes in my mouth. Nevertheless the young doctors, all of them extremely beautiful, by the way, radiant, could understand me perfectly, which is why they kept smiling at me, winking and nodding. And then there was the black woman in the bed opposite mine. She moaned and moaned and then she was dead. Her family came and clustered about the bed in fine clothes; and then a very slight black woman, middle-aged and frail, possessed of a great but mild authority, came into the ward and called – it was really a calling forth – one of the nurses, an Irish girl who had been very nice to me, called her forth, and said, 'Oh Mary, how could you? We trusted you.' And the nurse began to cry and said, 'Oh, I'm sorry, so sorry, I didn't mean to, oh, I'm sorry.' And the black woman slapped her across the face, not a vicious slap but worse than that, a slap of dismissal for ever, and went away. The Irish girl crouched on the floor sobbing and blaming herself. I was very indignant, mumbling words of comfort. Then other nurses appeared, gently but quite pitiless, and led the girl off, telling me to mind my own business, it was her fault, she deserved everything. Now as I say this happened as an event in my life, not witnessed or observed merely but felt by me as a participant. It was only when I saw Victoria's expression as I told her about it on her visit that I guessed that it had only happened to me, and not to the nurses – I could see all around me the nurses, including the Irish girl, behaving as they always did, good and proper nurses. But still there was some truth at the centre of the hallucination. The black woman who had been in the bed opposite me had gone. She had died during the night – and indeed some black women, dressed in their best clothes, came in while Victoria was there with me, carrying flowers and fruit, expecting to find their friend where they'd left her the day before. That seemed to me as I watched it, and saw Victoria's face, less vivid than what hadn't happened, except to me, during the night. And for some time I suspected Victoria, the nurses, were covering up the truth, that either the Irish girl had murdered the black woman, or she had been assaulted and victimised by a religious sect composed of her fellow nurses and the families of patients. In other words, the hallucination wasn't abruptly expelled by an acknowledgement that that was what it must have been, an hallucination, it perpetrated itself as an experience lived through, actually lived through, surfacing as such in memory and susceptible to various conspiratorial interpretations – I'm still not sure at what point I began to refer to it with any confident casualness as 'one of my hallucinations', but it wasn't until some time after I'd left the hospital, and begun to recover physical strength.

A few years before that illness and the operation, I'd gone through a different sort of hallucinatory passage – it lasted about six weeks, I suppose, and it happened while I was in otherwise the best of health, i.e., smoking and drinking to the normal excess without noticing any particular ill effects, sound in mind, wind and limb, working hard, with gusto. Nothing wrong with me at all, in fact, except that green shrubs sprouted out of my head, from time to time, and less frequently from other parts of my body. My arms would turn into branches, my face become a bush, my fingers long beans. They would last, these experiences, episodes is probably the correct term, as in episodic fits, for instance, they would last for a minute or two, on bad days they would recur every twenty minutes, the anticipation of them being the more horrible for knowing that it – the anticipation – was somehow also the cause. Forcing myself to pretend that it wasn't going to happen, that a part of my body wasn't going to turn into a green growth, or grow a green protuberance, seemed to force it to happen more painfully, willed resistance creating the tension from which this bustly life erupted. I grew positively to fear the colour green, only moderately in clothes or in and on inanimate things, but vegetables, green vegetables on a plate were terrifying, frozen peas the vilest and most threatening. It was like being assaulted at any moment of the day, and when fully conscious, by a nightmare.

And this was virtually my doctor's diagnosis. He listened thoughtfully to my account in his consulting room, requested time to take advice from possible specialists in the field (what field, I wondered – horticultural psychology perhaps) summoned me back a couple of days later, and informed me gravely that there was little doubt that I was suffering from what was known as 'waking nightmares' – which would certainly have seemed a perfectly reasonable description if it had been offered by a layman over a glass in a pub, for instance, but pretty skimpy coming from a pro at thirty-odd quid a crack (not including cab fare), especially as it turned out to be not only his diagnosis but pretty well his proposed remedy as well. He did, it's true, suggest that I cut down on my drinking somewhat – there was some news on my blood tests that indicated I would shortly be in trouble with my liver – there might be a connection here between liver and waking nightmares. I considered this phase of the consultation to be an impertinent intrusion into my personal habits, and noted sardonically that the good doctor had recently had a few crates of wine delivered, they were there waiting for him in the hall. How evidence that the good doctor enjoyed his wine invalidated any observations he had to make about my own alcohol consumption I can no longer understand, but I was more innocent in those days, and when it came to drinking, completely fearless. It took vastly more impertinent intrusions – the death of a brother, and my own near death – to teach me a salutary cowardice. Nevertheless, nevertheless, the fact remains that I went on drinking as I'd always drunk, and nevertheless, nevertheless, my mind stopped producing verdant outcroppings on my body, not stopped all at once and suddenly, rather they petered away, to green thoughts in a green shade, then to wisps of green thinking, then memories of wisps – but there still lurks in me the fear that one day, on a sudden moment, I will suddenly find myself gaping in horror at a cluster of frozen peas on a plate, and shoots will spring from my cheeks again.

The truth is, that nothing that happened that Thursday in Richmond was as bad as any day of my life when I was, or rather felt, perfectly well and successful, while enduring the 'waking nightmares'. For one thing, nothing in particular happened that Thursday night in Richmond, I now realise, because by then everything that was going to happen had already happened, it had in fact been announced to the world at large that the life of *The Late Middle Classes* would end with the last night of the run in Richmond, so have I all along been confusing not just my Brightons and my Richmonds, but also my Thursdays and my Saturdays? And have I possibly been making all sorts of other confusions as well, Pinters with Panters, Harolds with Howards, who knows what a mess and a muddle my memory has been making of this perfectly simple history of deceit, double-dealing, treachery, murder and so forth. I will now try and sort it out. No, I won't. For the last two days I've buried Margot – or rather, the fact of Margot, that she's dead. Refused to think about it is all I mean of course. A man with a German accent phoned, left a short message on my machine saying she'd died 'serenely' during the night, and then gave the funeral details. He had a cheerful, upbeat voice – I wondered if it was the short, blond man I'd seen going into the hospice, carrying books and something from the off-licence. Perhaps I should stop for the night – now Sunday morning, half past midnight, and anyway last night I'd resolved not to come near the Apple for twenty-four hours, give it and myself a break, concentrate on the major issues in life – currently the second test match in South Africa, for instance, where once again England has its back to the wall. A magnificent South African batsman, whose face is squeezed by the vice-like helmet around it into a sort of boiled potato with knobs and slits for features, is hammering our bowling all over the place – sometimes he looked like something from a computer game, no, a relative to robo-cop, that's it, a virtual reality creation with nothing human visible even in close-up, while our boys, whether in close-up – sweating, grimacing, scowling or in long shot – scrambling, tumbling, sprawling – looked whatever is the opposite of virtual in their reality, pathetic, frail, mortal – losers, losers. But actually if you subtracted this unfairly advantaged hero's innings from the South African total, we batted much better than they did. That's one way of looking at it, as at many other things. Foolishly.

Actually, it's pretty foolish even to glance in the direction of Richmond on that Saturday night.

At Richmond on Saturday night there was a party of the kind that is now probably known as a 'closure' party. It was a dismal affair, confined to the cast and company and a few friends – outsiders, who must have wished in that atmosphere of grim relaxation that they'd remained outside. The management had been excluded, as a punishment – some punishment! – for the sheer shoddiness of their manners – they'd announced the news that negotiations with the Gielgud had broken down and they were terminating the production at Richmond in a fax (signed SWEB) to the company manager, who was ordered to read it out to the cast – yes, that's how the director and author got the news from Howard Panter, Sylvia Wasserman, SWEB *et al.*, about the fate of *The Late Middle Classes* – they got it from the cast, who got it from the company manager, who got it from a fax from who knows which of the above. But of course it wasn't really news at all, at least not to me – I'd known it for an absolute fact ever since that Thursday night at Brighton when Sylvia Wasserman came into the office in search of a telephone, and found, to her poorly concealed horror, me. So I'd endured none of the ups and downs, hopes and despairs, that Harold, Judy, Victoria, the cast had had to endure. Now all I had to endure was the painful struggle of not allowing myself to say 'I told you so', before I found relief by saying it, quite often, to quite a few people. Actually none of them believed me – could not, would not believe that we'd failed to make it to the West End because Howard Panter was 'a bit of a *Sunday Times* man'. It was not until a few months ago that I at last found a little honour in my own country. Judy bumped into someone from SWEB on an unrelated (to *The Late Middle Classes*) occasion, who admitted to her that yes, it was the man from the *Sunday Times* that did for the play, the management had lost its nerve and faith, both of which it had had in abundance, of course, until the man from the *Sunday Times* . . . Oh, by the way and while I remember, my friend in the States, who had been waiting to invest her thirty thousand pounds in the transfer to the West End eventually received a fax from SWEB regretting that her money wouldn't be needed for *The Late Middle Classes*, but they would be grateful if she would keep it to hand for forthcoming SWEB productions, they would be in touch.

Now that's almost that, about all of that. Shortly I shall come to this – by which I mean the current progress towards the production of my new play *Japes* (working title) but there's one thing I shouldn't omit from my account of the spectral after-life of *The Late Middle Classes*. When we got the official bad news at Woking – no, not now, sleeping pill now, and then some music. It's 1.30 a.m., on Friday, 17th December. They're replaying three hours of cricket on Sky at 2.00 a.m. – the last day of the test match. I've missed most of it, but know the result – a draw, very hard fought, apparently – particularly hard fought against one of the umpires, who gave three of our chaps out when they clearly (clearly, when seen on television replays, that is), perfectly clearly, were still in. Morally still in, that is. Because physically they were perfectly clearly out, wherever they were. Anyway, it'll be delightful to watch – I'll be able to boil away with rage at the evident, visible injustices – injustice in action again and again – while secure in the knowledge that we overcame and ultimately triumphed. A draw being, in English cricket terms, a triumph. Still, let me remind the world that South Africa had previously won their last eleven home test matches. We've put a stop to that. And now perhaps we can start ruining other things for them – we've got a pretty good record, historically, of messing up South Africa, right back to the Boer War, for which I believe somebody or other (the Queen? the Archbishop of Canterbury? the Prime Minister?) is currently apologising. Let's hope that after this tour is over we'll have lots more to apologise for. Anyway, I've got a decent pre-bed time before me. That's the thing. But Margot's funeral tomorrow – no, today, this afternoon. That's the other thing.

Friday 17th December, half past midnight. The journey back was quite appalling. We'd just got past Haywards Heath when there was an announcement to the effect that there was a points failure further up the line, we were therefore returning to Haywards Heath. At Haywards Heath we were told that we were transferring to the fast track, which would get us into London, Victoria Station, not much later than if we'd stayed on the slow track. We then jolted about in the station for a while, official but distraught voices coming through the window, taking me back through four decades and train journeys across Spain at the dead of night – the same incompetence filling the air, the same certainty of interminable delays, the same listlessness gathering in the soul. There was no destination, there never had been a destination, there was always only going to be this stuffy compartment, the voices outside, stops that started suddenly, stopped immediately, this was it, for ever and ever – a Connex official, so obese he had to run down the corridor sideways, paused briefly to shout out an instruction, a warning, a greeting, who knows – then there was an announcement to the effect that our trip down the fast line would be a slow one, there had been a fatality on the track, just outside East Croydon, 'I'm sorry about that,' the impersonal, rather grating voice concluded. I couldn't understand what puzzled me about this announcement until I realised that I couldn't recall ever hearing a first person pronoun in a railway announcement before – perhaps they've borrowed this intimate approach from the airlines where the pilots always claim personal responsibility for every aspect of the flight, from the weather to the failure of the sound system on the film they're therefore not going to show – anyway it was disturbing having it on the train, off-key, this sourceless voice connecting itself with a corpse somewhere outside East Croydon. 'I'm sorry about that.'

Off and on during all this I'd been trying to get my mobile to work. It's a new one, and I'm unfamiliar with it – so neat and compact that my fingers kept hitting the wrong buttons, the screen flashing up meaningless logos and slogans, and when I made occasional contact with Radio Taxis I'd get a few rings, followed by whimperings and silence. Eventually I thought I heard a voice, jabbered out a message, heard a little wisp of an answer, then a humming noise that I recognised as my tinnitus, and gave up. We got into Victoria nearly an hour late. I trudged through the station, trudged through the station hotel, trudged out on to the street where there wouldn't be any taxis. There was one, stationary, right in front of the doors. I hurried to it, knocked on the window. The driver shrugged negatives at me, to indicate that he was booked, waiting, waiting for someone. Waiting for me? Me? Gray, yes, waiting for Gray. So that's how I came home from Margot's funeral. In style.

The funeral itself didn't have much style, really. In fact, you could even say that as funerals go it was right down there with the first night of *Dutch Uncle*. It was held in a Baptist chapel near the prison, which is a rather grand little building, by the way, the prison, like a low castle, historical but with a homely aspect. Everything in Lewes seems to be pleasing in that sort of way – its hospices, its prisons – though not quite its Baptist chapel, red-brick and squat. There were seven of us – eight, including me – a middle-aged couple, who I took to be the cousins, sitting on wooden chairs at the front; and a little cluster of what could only be academics, two men and three women. There was no small, blond man. I sat at the back, as close to the door as I could get. The service, such as it was, was in German, conducted by a tall man, half bald, in a dark suit, more like Philip Larkin or an undertaker than a pastor, with a rather sharp, cutting voice – anyway, it had an edge to it, almost hostile. There were readings from the five academics, some Goethe and Heine poems and a long patch of prose from Nietzsche – that's the name I seemed to catch, Nietzsche, one of the women did him, rather cheerful, with a nice, light voice – the other two women were big, and elderly, and one of them sniffed a lot, not emotional sniffs, more like a tic, the sort that would drive you mad in five minutes – she read for ten, but it seemed like hours, the whole business seemed like hours and hours, though it was only about thirty-five minutes, forty at the most. There was no music, no climax, no tears, not even a coffin, so there was no purpose, really, that I could feel. I wondered about Margot's body – why wasn't it here, and where was it? Still in the hospice? Or in a funeral parlour in Lewes? Or being shipped to Nova Scotia or back to The Hague? And of course I looked down at my hands a lot, embarrassed, afraid that I was suddenly going to let out a yap of laughter. I didn't really notice how it ended, but suddenly the Larkinish undertaker figure was speaking again and suddenly he wasn't speaking, and the two cousins, if they were the cousins, were moving shyly towards the academics. I hovered about for a few seconds, saw that the pretty woman and the sniffing woman were looking in my direction, so I made a kind of ambiguous gesture with my hand (*ave atque vale, requiescat in pace*, etc.) and left.

I picked up a taxi as it was coming out of the prison drive, went straight to the station, and began the appalling journey home which at least – now I come to think of it – provided a corpse. Anyway, I was home at last, that was the main thing. Victoria was out for the evening, and I was having dinner with an old friend, Tony Gould, at eight, which gave me an hour alone in the house with George and Errol, both in rather low spirits, I thought. No, not low, but uncharacteristically sedate –

George didn't greet me at the door, but lay at the top of the stairs, staring woodenly at me. Errol was lying in the hall, inert, his eyes open but unresponding. I had to step over him, which I thought was a bit much. I filled their plates in the kitchen, called them in. Neither stirred. I decided Victoria had already fed them – overfed them – and I'd come in on them while they were becalmed by digestion. Or they'd had too much simulated sex. After a heavy meal. Or perhaps there was nothing about me that aroused their interest. Probably just that – lack of interest in me, personally, because when Tony rang the bell George raced downstairs and sniffed greedily around the bottom of the door and bounded about him when I let him in, while Errol rolled to his feet, sauntered forward and offered himself archingly, for some stroking. I commented on this somewhat bitterly to Tony as we crossed the road to Chez Moi. He said the kind of thing people say when they've been singled out for favoured attention by other people's pets, something modest and yet inward with the ways of animals – 'I expect it's because I'm slightly damp. They like the smell of damp I've noticed – well, on my clothes anyway.' Something like that Tony said, as we crossed to the restaurant, though it probably wasn't exactly that, as there was no reason for him to be damp, that I knew of – it wasn't raining, and it hadn't been all day.

Well here it is, Monday morning, 2.15 a.m., and scrolling back I see that everything I wrote yesterday was about Friday (Margot's funeral) so Saturday's missing, the whole day of the day before yesterday, I can't remember any part of it, what we did in it, Victoria and I – and it's not good enough just to say that it therefore can't have been anything memorable – this might be the beginning of the end, Alzheimer's, senile dementia, or the start of the good times, no memory means nothing to worry about, not even about having no memory, but while I've still got a bit of one, I'd better use it to wrap up the story of *The Late Middle Classes* at last. Here goes. Once it became a publicly acknowledged fact that we weren't going to the Gielgud, or indeed anywhere in the West End I decided – no, not true, Victoria decided – that we should try to get as many of the people who hadn't yet seen it – the people, that is, that one hoped would actually like it, or at least enjoy some aspects of it – the acting for instance, or the warm-blooded fluency of Harold's production – to look in on it during its week at Richmond – or even the week before at Woking, if they could face the hassle of getting to Woking, which I doubted. Among those I wrote to were some of the Sunday reviewers who had missed it at Watford, these being among the reviewers who I believed liked (among many sorts of plays) the sort of plays I tried to write, even if they didn't always like the plays I actually wrote – honourable reviewers, I reckon them to be, who, unlike the Doge of Venice, say, find many things more interesting about a play than the thought of themselves being at it. I made it clear that I wasn't expecting reviews – favourable reviews would be too late to help the show, and unfavourable ones . . . Quite a few of the people we asked went to Richmond, and some, including the man from the *Sunday Telegraph*, even went to Woking, so the last two weeks of *The Late Middle Classes* were bustly and well attended, were almost festive in fact, except at the final party, a sorry little affair which I think I've already described. On top of which two reviews appeared on the Sunday after we closed, one in the Sunday Telegraph, the other in the *Independent on Sunday*, both of them favourable – and therefore wanted after all. So there it was: there had been three excellent Sunday reviews for *The Late Middle Classes*, and only one dud: but the dud had come early and it had come from the man on the *Sunday Times*, and so forth and so forth and so forth, whine, whine, whine . . .

Although when you look at it coolly, there's not much to whine about. Everywhere the play was allowed to go, it was a success, played to full houses, got lots of standing ovations (the actors did, I mean) and even sanctification in the press as the play that, denied its rightful place in London, exposed the West End for the corrupt shambles it had become – all that sort of thing. I enjoyed a period of quiet, scrupulous martyrdom, laying just the right amount of blame in exactly the right places in a perfectly judged tone – it must have been pretty well judged, anyway, because I heard from here and there that I was taking it 'very well' and, less flatteringly, 'surprisingly well', and then there was the award for being the Best-Play-out-of-London, followed by the phantom award for being the Best-play-in-London-if-only-it-had-got-there. Mentions are still popping righteously up in the press – one today in the *Spectator*, as a matter of fact, lamenting the injustice done to *The Late Middle Classes*, what a scandal, etc. – all of which seems to me vastly better than a dismal little run in the Gielgud, né Globe, the predictable fate of the musical, *Bandboy*, I think it was called, or *Boyband*, which usurped it – I mean, what chance did it have, infamous as a usurper before it had even opened? So let's admit it, I might even have reason to be grateful to the man from the *Sunday Times* for writing the review that kept my play out of London, even though that was never his intention – he could scarcely have expected or wanted the producer to take it as an instruction to foreclose, after all. But then many good results, as Porphyrus Quintus once famously pointed out, 'come forth from undesign'.

But there is another history of the play, its publishing history, that ran alongside its theatrical history, well, let's rush through it, it's nothing that should be lingered over. It's this – that some weeks after I'd finished *The Late Middle Classes*, I did as I always did and asked Judy to send a copy to my publishers, Faber, so that they'd have the published play ready before the first performance, copies could then go into the theatres (when found) for sale at the counter that deals in chocolates, ice-cream, T-shirts, baseball caps, balloons, etc., or perhaps at the other counter that just deals in programmes – anyway, to have it available to audiences who, having just seen the play, might persuade themselves that they want to read it, as well. And who knows, they might actually read it – check out a scene at leisure, over dinner afterwards perhaps, to settle a bet on how it ended, was that awful line always there or was it stuck in at the last minute to cover a set change, that sort of thing – but of course for me, as for all other playwrights, the larger point is to have the book in circulation once the production has ended – giving it an after-life, as something to be read when it can no longer be seen, and also the chance of a further production life – quite often a play gets revived because a director has come across it in a bookshop, in the library, on the shelf of a colleague – in other words, for the playwright, there is a world of hope in the thought of the play just being around, waiting to be picked up, opened, rediscovered, produced, acclaimed – such hopes help to keep playwrights ticking along in their daily gloom, and in their dotage.

With *The Late Middle Classes*, and for the first time ever, Judy showed a marked reluctance to send the script to Faber. 'But why not?' She just didn't think it a good idea to send it just yet – given their new policy. What new policy? I hadn't heard of a new policy, what was it about, this new policy of Faber's? It was about their not publishing a new play until it had been guaranteed a West End production. That was their new policy, the whole of it, and it had been endorsed, by the Chairman of Faber, Matthew Evans himself. Harold has a phrase that would cover my reaction to this, rather a dead phrase, actually, that nevertheless comes to such life in his mouth – 'It took my breath away!' I found myself saying, Harold style: 'You've taken my breath away!'

Nevertheless, a fact is a fact, whatever one's reaction to it. This is something one usually learns by the time one gets to one's sixties, although the disinclination to believe unpleasant ones remains as strong as it did in one's earlier years – which is why, no doubt, I went on expostulating with Judy, taking her through my relationship with Faber, which went back to my first novel, sent to them when I was twenty-four, unsolicited – that long ago, nearly forty years ago, when publishers received, read and occasionally published unsolicited novels – and I'd chosen Faber (Faber and Faber as they then were) because they were the only publishers I knew about, the publishers of Pound, Eliot, Auden, with Eliot still on the board – the only publishers still in existence who were a part of our literary history – I think I remembered down the phone to Judy what it had been like, the moment I'd opened the letter from Frank Pike, of Faber and Faber, inviting me to London to discuss the publication – discuss the publication! – it was the best single moment of my writing life, about the finest letter I'd ever received, the invitation to go up to London, to meet Frank Pike in the offices of Faber and Faber at 24 Russell Square to discuss –

And of course being a Faber and Faber author – the mere thought of it, let alone actually being able to say it aloud, 'Actually, Faber and Faber actually' when asked, followed by lots of proud little complaints about how little they gave one as an advance, how slow they were in getting from manuscript to print, how inactive when it came to 'pushing' one's novels – getting the buggers into the shops and actually selling them – 'gentlemanly', one finally always boiled these complaints down to, 'a bit too gentlemanly, but still one wouldn't dream of leaving them. After all, who would one even think of going to, if one ever even dreamt of leaving Faber and Faber?' And who, by the way, would have one? was the secret thought . . . And so I went on proudly and complainingly as Faber and Faber published my first four novels and then my first two plays – now I'm writing here of forty years ago, and, good God yes, even as I put the words down I suddenly recall that what happened a year or so ago with the Faber Chairman Matthew Evans and *The Late Middle Classes* also happened those forty years ago with the then Faber and Faber Chairman (now dead, I expect) and a play I'd just written, called *Soiled*. No, *Spoiled* I mean, of course. *Spoiled* . . . Almost exactly the same thing happened with *Spoiled*, but at least with this excuse – that forty years ago publishing plays was almost as new to Faber and Faber as writing them was to me, so inevitably they approached it with gentlemanly and bowed-down caution, fearing that it might turn out to be a different game entirely from publishing novels, cook-books, gardening books, poetry, and great poetry – it still came as something of a shock, though, in fact it took my breath away, when Frank Pike, my editor, told me that Faber and Faber were going to withhold publication of *Spoiled* until it had been produced on the stage, and the reviews were in. Good reviews – publication by Faber and Faber. Bad reviews – no publication by Faber and Faber. What about mixed reviews? I asked. 'Well, exactly. The trouble is, they still aren't sure that they should be doing plays at all, they need endorsements from other sources.'

What! From theatre reviewers! Could this be right? It didn't sound even honourable, at least to me, that they should be entrusting decisions about what they published to theatre critics. Would they start applying the same principles to novels and poetry? Why not hand the choice of publication over to reviewers completely, sending them the piles of manuscripts and asking them to send back the ones they approved of, no, not send back, why bother, send straight to the printers – put the others out with the rubbish – and so on, I went, and on, to poor old (then poor young) Frank Pike who agreed with every word I said, but as is so often the way with people who agree with every word you say, they're not the people who caused you to say it, nor the people who can do anything about it.

Anyway, apart from harassing young Frank Pike into old Frank Pike, it never occurred to me that there was anything I could actually do but wait for *Spoiled* to be produced, and hope for good reviews, lots and lots of good reviews – but how many did I need, how good did they have to be? Questions to which Frank Pike could give no answer, they hadn't worked it out yet, they were still new at plays, he kept reminding me – and I never found out because when *Spoiled* was finally produced (at the Haymarket in 1971) the script was already in the bookshops, having been published some months earlier by Methuen. (In fact, the reviews were pretty decent, especially from the man – who was several men or more before the present man – from the *Sunday Times*.)

This, for me, dramatic move – the change of play publishers from Faber and Faber to Methuen – came about by accident. Geoffrey Strachan, the plays editor at Methuen, had dropped in on his friend and my then agent, Clive Goodwin, came across the script while waiting for Clive to come off the telephone (which he sometimes did), started to read it, took it home, read it, asked if it was available for publication, and there I was, with no effort on my part, suddenly rolling along with two prestigious publishers, one putting out my novels, the other putting out my plays. This satisfying and vanity-tickling situation lasted until Methuen was taken over by a vast American company called Octopus some eight years ago, and the usual panic ensued – nobody knew quite what would happen, but it was supposed that the Americans would be looking for an immediate profit by selling off this, cutting down that – on the plays side Geoffrey Strachan, the Methuen publisher, felt unable to guarantee the continuation of the list, the chief plays editor Nick Hern went off to establish Nick Hern Books, some of the playwrights stuck with Methuen, others went to different publishers, I went back, as seemed only natural, to Faber and Faber, who after all were the publishers of my two theatrical diaries, *An Unnatural Pursuit* and *How's That for Telling 'Em, Fat Lady?* – the subject of both of which which was a play, *The Common Pursuit*, published by Methuen. Actually, for all my gratitude to Methuen, to Geoffrey Strachan and Nick Hern, [4] I felt that in going back to Faber I was going home.

Going home turned out to be a big deal, more like a divorce, really, involving meetings with lawyers, along with meetings with other people whose function I never quite grasped (social workers, perhaps?) – not that I minded, in fact I was thrilled to discover this adult publishing world so late in my writing career, flattered that people in those suits and with those low, sage voices should assemble just to meet me, and above all my heart was warmed by how much I was wanted, how lavish the terms offered – a complete edition of my plays, in as many volumes as it took, said volumes to be added to as I wrote further plays, which would always be published separately first, to coincide with their theatrical productions, and of course the business over *Spoiled* would never be repeated – this was a constant refrain, that I was a complete Faber author now, publication guaranteed – of almost anything I wrote, I got the impression, novels, diaries, plays, love-letters, bills of lading, rejected letters to the *Guardian*, an endless flow of myself in print I could envisage, if I wanted to, under the Faber imprimatur – along with a fairly substantial cheque (by my standards, which are very low) in payment for the rights to my backlist, which Faber undertook to keep in print –

---

4. Nick Hern Books are the publishers of *The Late Middle Classes* and *Japes*.

I simply couldn't have asked for more. For one thing I lacked the imagination – I also lacked the sense to get it all down in writing, but then the assurances given at the meetings, along with the tone of these meetings, solemn and rather mysterious – and particularly the way Harold's name would be invoked, never quite in context but as a sort of sacred non-sequitur, a sort of by-the-way, by the way would I pass on Chairman Evans' compliments, assurances of his and the rest of Faber's admiration both for his work and for his passionate political commitments – no doubt I passed all the messages on to Harold as requested – or perhaps I didn't, knowing Harold well enough to know that any decision he made about a publisher he would make without help from me.

As I've said, there was no contract to give final authority to these verbal agreements but then there seemed no need of one – matters proceeded exactly as promised, with the appearance of my novel, *Breaking Hearts* – a novella really, as it ran to scarcely a hundred pages of largish print, though some of those pages, to do with bondage, were described as 'quite heavenly', by a reviewer in a women's magazine – and there was *Fat Chance*, a chronicle of my unsettling relationship with Stephen Fry, again rather brief, which was described as being 'completely without compassion', by a theatre critic, and then there were four plays, *Hidden Laughter*, *Cell Mates*, *Simply Disconnected* and *Life Support*, all published to coincide – well, almost – with the stage productions, and finally, best of all, my collected plays in four plump volumes, which I edited comprehensively and, to tell the truth, rather foolishly, as I rewrote scenes and restructured acts that had worked perfectly well where it really counted – on the stage. I think the problem was that I'd decided, for reasons that I can't remember, but probably of vanity, to call the volumes, not *The Collected Plays of Simon Gray*, presumably on the grounds that this would be too simple and sensible and thus an opportunity wasted, but *The Definitive Simon Gray*, so laying upon myself the obligation to define – and therefore muck up – what was in a sense already self-defined.

So all was well between Faber and myself, all promises honoured on both sides, i.e., I wrote, Faber published, until –

I realise that the rancour is still raw, the blood not yet off the boil, bubble, bubble my blood still boils when I think of Chairman Evans and his policy of no-publication-without-West-End-production, and much more freshly and double double bubble bubble it boiled a year and four months ago to the very day (a lie, of course, let's just say about a year and a half ago) when I first got the news from Judy down the telephone. And so to my letters to Matthew Evans. By the time I got to the thirteenth or so, the one I finally sent, I'd managed to boil myself out of steam, even managed to write out a calm and melancholy message of farewell, as the conclusion to a dignified statement of the facts as I understood them – I avoided any easy emotional references, not reminding him, for instance, that I'd actually been in the offices of Faber and Faber (then at 24 Russell Square, T. S. Eliot's at the top, sometimes when I was visiting he was said actually to be in it!) on the very day that he, Matthew Evans (now of course Lord Evans), had joined the firm – and how young he'd looked! So undisturbed by life that when Frank Pike introduced him I mistook him for a sort of office boy, a sure sign, as we know from the novels of Jeffrey Archer, that he was destined to rule the roost – but as I say I didn't touch on this haunting encounter in my letter, no, I concentrated simply on my long and complicated history with the house of Faber, and with the house (or houses?) of Faber and Faber, a double history of severance, reconciliation, betrayal and now severance again – in other words I addressed Matthew Evans in his representative self as Chairman, the embodiment of the great tradition, the keeper of the flame, the guardian of values, that sort of thing, and it was in that spirit that I pointed out the implications of his new policy – that in deciding to appoint London's theatrical producers, Howard Panter, *Desert Island Discs*, OBE, *et al.* to the posts of commissioning editors at Faber, just as a long-gone predecessor had once decided to appoint theatre reviewers, the men from the *Mail*, the *Standard* and the *Sunday Times, et al.* to the posts of commissioning editors – but did I really go into all the *Spoiled* stuff, however apt? No, I've just forced myself to check the letter, I didn't go into all the *Spoiled* stuff – fortunately, really, as from Chairman

Matthew Evans' point of view it wouldn't have been in the slightest apt, he wasn't even there in the *Spoiled* days, or if he was, he was merely on the rise.

My last words, just before my melancholy and dignified leave-taking, were a plea that he reconsider his new policy – not on my behalf, as I'd already made the decision to leave Faber – if it's possible, that is, for a playwright to leave a publisher who isn't going to publish his plays – but on behalf of Faber itself, all it stood for, its traditions, values, the flame, etc. When I had to look at my copy just now, I could see that it was a rather pathetic business, my letter, beaten out on my old Olympia portable, mistakes corrected in pen, with suspicious splodges here and there – coffee, I hope, and I hope not to be found on the original. It received no response, this thirteenth or so draft, the one I sent, not even an acknowledgement that it had been received and read. In fact my next communication from Faber came several months later in the form of a bill – I'd ordered some copies of my own work (just because Faber couldn't sell them doesn't mean I can't give them away) which Faber had sent c/o Clive Goodwin, my ex-agent, now twenty years dead. The note I enclosed with my cheque – which I sent direct to Chairman Evans – was short and playful, asking him whether I hadn't received his reply to my letter because he'd posted that too to my dead agent, or possibly to someone else long in the grave, my parents, for instance – I added that I was glad that at least some of the Faber traditions (i.e., incompetence) were flourishing – that sort of playful. To this Chairman Evans did respond, saying that he'd passed my cheque on to the appropriate office, and explaining that he hadn't replied to my previous letter because he hadn't wanted to engage in 'a slanging match about the past' – which, inevitably, prompted me to engage him in a slanging match about the past. Letters passed back and forth, a case of the rapier against the blunderbuss is how I liked to see it, skill and thrust of thought on my side, clumsiness and ill-judged blastings on his, what fun! Especially as all the harm he could do he'd already done, he hadn't left himself a target to aim at – or so I believed, until one afternoon Judy reported that Chairman Evans had just phoned her to ask whether I knew that I'd only been invited back to Faber because of Harold.

She asked him what he meant by this, he refused to say what he meant by this, but what he meant by this was obvious, that I'd been his bait for larger prey, the worm for the fish, the cheese for the mouse, the mouse for the cat, whatever – so the blunderbuss had found a target after all, and my rapier pride was pasted all over the walls of my little study to prove it. Still, what was pride when there were serious issues of principle to be dealt with? I decided to ignore his call – which hadn't anyway been made to me – and wrote him a cool by-the-way sort of letter asking him, by the way, if he'd warned the other playwrights on the Faber list of his new policy – if he hadn't I felt obliged to do it for him. His reply consisted of a statement of my recent royalties, and a note daring me to send copies to the other playwrights – which I duly did, along with copies of his covering letter, along with copies of both sides of our correspondence to date. The fellow playwrights expressed shock, outrage, etc., at the Chairman's behaviour, while possibly savouring the vertiginous contrast between their royalties and mine. On occasions like this I always try to keep somewhere in mind the memory of Giuseppe de Lampedusa, who failed during his lifetime to sell a single copy of *The Leopard*. But which would you have preferred to write, I ask myself, *The Leopard*, or a novel by one – any one – of the celebrated novelists of the last twenty-five years? Make that fifty years. Actually, this is a pretty stupid question – if you broke it into two parts, a) whose novel would you prefer to have written, and b) whose royalties would you prefer to have collected, you're likely to get two sensible answers.

But the brute fact is – back to Chairman Evans – the brute fact is that Chairman Evans was right. I can't pretend, least of all to myself, that I'm a heady commercial prospect – I sometimes think that if only I could stir up some academic interest, get myself onto syllabuses, then regularly onto the examination papers – but as far as I know there's only been one full-length book about me – it arrived through the post about five years ago, unannounced and unexplained, with a cover so drab that I'd probably have tossed it into the waste-paper basket if I hadn't glimpsed my name in the title. It was part of a series, casebook I think it was, yes, a casebook, and from a quick and painful dip I got the impression that it was mainly aimed at psychiatrists with a special interest in sexual abnormalities (homophobia as camouflage for paedophilia, sort of thing – well not 'sort of thing', the thought lay at the centre of at least three of the essays) – while the straight literary-critical stuff was actually rather wounding, no need to recall any of it really.

And that, thank God, is the end of that – of the history of my dealings with all publishers up to this stage of my life, of the history of *The Late Middle Classes* on all immediate fronts. Rolling it, no, scrolling it to its beginning, it slides smoothly up the screen, up the screen and down again, an effortless flow, but of course it was all effort, picking away at the depressing little tale hour after hour for several days now, taking no note of anything else going on in my life, swearing as my fingers jam or hit the wrong logo and find myself caught in an Apple trap, and frames containing boxes of instructions fill the screen, but with no little boxes to tap your cursor on and release you back to the sentence you were struggling with, and may no longer even be there, or not as you remembered it – I think I'll go and check on George, I haven't seen her for a while and that's unusual when Victoria's out – not that there's any need really, she's bound to be perfectly safe – and indeed she is, as there she was (and still is, I hope) stretched out on the sitting-room sofa, where she's not allowed to be, but too asleep to be interfered with.

As I stroked her, I noticed a small group of Muslims going past the window, presumably heading towards the mosque which is almost next to the synagogue around the corner from the church in the grounds of which George and I walk together – all three religions within a stone's throw of each other, so to speak – sometimes I have a longing to join one of the groups, trudge along with them, particularly the Muslims, the women in their shapeless layers of black cloth, trailing behind the men in their black, baggily respectable suits, the children, heavily shod and bespectacled, herded between them – no shouting or laughter, in fact no communication at all, just the slow devoted trudging. I wonder how I would look to myself if I saw myself passing the window – mute and joyless, I expect, like any other man heading for a mosque, a synagogue, even a church, the only outward difference I would note is that my passing self is also carrying a lead, at the end of which is George, pulling, pausing, chivvying, unaware of God present or God absent. But it's a big difference, when you think about it and also, when you think about it, no man has the right to be mute or joyless when in the company of a dog like George. I have heard Catholics claim that dogs are inferior to humans because they lack souls. But how can they lack what they don't need?

Stopping here. It's nearly four in the morning of Christmas Eve. I'm going to stay away from Apple until Boxing Day, perhaps the day after. Don't know why, really, but it seems the right thing to do, the seasonal thing.

Christmas morning, 1.00 a.m. Just back from midnight mass. For the first time I found myself loathing the communion service. Sanctimonious paganism is what it seemed to be, something furtive and nasty running through it. And before that the business of clasping hands with other members of the congregation, people one has no reason for touching, no desire to touch, and yet one can't refuse an extended hand, especially if it's an ethnic one, which I supposed that this one was, from the nice firm grasp, full of goodwill and the eyes brimming with gladness and sharing – I wonder what my grasp felt like to him, soft, nasty grasp, full of ill-will, I expect, and as for my eyes . . . There was an emotional wreck of a woman standing by the door where she'd been handing out the order of service sheets and candles that we had to light and hold (why? Don't want to know, actually). She was about fifty, in loose baggy trousers, a short anorak, and spangled slippers. Her face was swollen and heavily made up, her hair straggly. During the service she led in the hymns and the responses, always getting in a beat earlier than everyone else, arms folded, head up to show she didn't need to consult the sheet in her hand. When we got to the flesh-pressing bit, she stuffed herself into the arms of various women, tears running down her cheeks, then when the vicar, an enormous young man with a moonyish face and large spectacles, got to the blessing she chattered away, nearly drowning him out – I thought at first it was to herself, but there was an awkwardly attentive younger woman standing near, so I suppose it must have been to her.

At the end of the service the vicar advanced with heavy, apprehensive tread to the door, to wish Happy Christmas to the departing congregation, visibly bracing himself as she heaved herself at him, wrapped her arms around him like a wrestler. He let her tuck in for a bit, extricated himself with an experienced kiss and caress, got to the door, through it to the pavement, leaving the field inside to her – she lunged about, embracing here, embracing there, I suppose her victims were known to her, but we did a large loop around her just in case, made it safely out onto the pavement and a comparatively sane handshake with the vicar, who I suppose can't be held responsible for the psychological make-up of his parishioners, though he can for the imbecility of his sermon, shot through with a weird gynaecological imagery asking us to allow the baby Jesus to be born inside us.

I've always liked Christmas services before, for the usual reasons, I expect – I think of my parents, my mother gaunt with cancer and dying during her last Christmas, insisting on going to church on Christmas morning – rightly so, the pain would have been the pain wherever she was, so why not be where she'd always been on Christmas morning, her husband and two of her sons beside her and her memories of other Christmases with her parents, so the generations keeping in touch, the living and the dying with the dead – but none of that happened for me tonight, just that woman, so desolate and greedy; the communion, with its symbolic cannibalism, the great white disc of pseudo-bread, the cheap and shiny chalice and goblets – never again. I shall never enter a church again except to look at the architecture and read the memorial plaques. But never for a service, except in a coffin, of course. Next year, if I'm still with us, it'll be at home with Bach, though of course I'll be pleased if

Victoria chooses to fling herself into my arms, no moment inopportune for that.

Now I really will close myself down on this until Boxing Day at the earliest. But I'll have to avoid television, at least unscouted forays – last night, was it last night, or the night before? – anyway, one night recently I flicked on, sped through Sky, paused at an incomprehensible image, a great bulge of white flesh it seemed to be, and in fact was, a side of breast in fact, a side of breast drooping out of a harness worn by a truly tawdry woman, with another harness around her hips, a strap going between her dappled legs. She was carrying a whip. A voice over, male and nasal, proclaimed that we were now about to endure the tormenting pleasures of the bondage chamber, and the camera adjusted sideways to take in a man roughly the same age as the woman, with a face, particularly the nose, almost suably similar to that of the fine American actor, still alive but old now, Malden, Karl Malden, that's it, the priest in *On the Waterfront* – so this Karl Maldenish man was also wearing a harness, his hands bound in leather cuffs in front of him, a collar around his neck with a lead hanging from it. 'Kneel down!' said the woman, with a ghastly flap of breasts. 'Kneel down, scumbag.' She was English, North London accent. The man knelt. I don't know how it panned out, as I switched off.

Christmas night, 11.30. Just checking in, really, to report that I haven't forgotten my vow of abstinence – also to report, while it's still going on but coming to an end, that it's been a nice day, but difficult to get through all the same. I've been half-waiting for the telephone – for me, Christmas has often been the time for really bad phone calls, the ones from hospitals announcing illness and the imminence of death. I prefer the telephone not to ring at all at Christmas, even at the best of times, and in some crucial respects these last years have been the worst of times, though there is no 'worst' when it comes to times, when it comes to times we live by comparatives only. Judy Daish and I had a tradition of meeting for a New Year drink, our toast always being along the same lines – that, well, the year coming couldn't be as bad as the one finishing – last year we remembered just how many years in succession we'd raised our glasses to this foolish proposition, and at last refrained from doing so. This year we aren't even meeting for the drink, hoping, I suppose, that by eliminating the ritual, we'll eliminate what had come to seem like the consequences. On the other hand, I've just popped downstairs to do a check-up: there they are – Victoria; my daughter Lucy; her husband James. Upstairs my two grand-daughters, Madeleine and Georgina, are asleep. That's quite enough for now, thank you, I'll settle for that, celebrate it, in fact – and even celebrate my son-in-law James, just putting his head around the door to ask if I could let him have a packet of cigarettes, he couldn't find his own, he suspected that George had eaten them.

Boxing Day. Actually Boxing Day is over, the day after Boxing Day just begun. There's nothing I want to write down at the moment, really, except as an *aide-memoire*, and why should I need one, in what circumstances will I ever need to know what I did on Boxing Day, 1999, why should I ever need to care? But just in case – got up at midday. Took the grandchildren to the Holland Park playgrounds as promised. Not particularly surprised to discover that they were padlocked against children, would remain so, a notice told us, until 4th January, meanwhile the playground staff wished us a Happy Christmas, New Year. Came home for lunch. Seen through a window we might have looked like one of those seventeenth-century Dutch interiors, there was cheese on the table, cold ham, fruit, bottles of wine, we were clearly in some way family, and the light would have been about right too, thin and dying outside, glowing warmly around us.

I stumbled up to bed in the early evening, fell into an irritable half-sleep, the Christmas coma. I started out of it once or twice, thinking I'd heard the phone ring – some call I'd been expecting – oddly, Margot came into it somehow, and also Piers, and vaguely my parents – phone calls from the dead. Victoria finally stirred me into full consciousness telling me I'd better get a move on, we were already late for dinner with Harold and Antonia. The phone rang. It was Emma, Victoria's sister, to announce that she'd just landed at Heathrow back from Calcutta a day late, there'd been a hijacking in Delhi, flights had been cancelled, postponed, etc. – I realised, from Victoria's expression when she listened to her sister's voice, that she too had spent much of the day half-listening for a call, but in her case a necessary call, one from the living, which had finally come and brought relief.

It is five in the morning of the first day of the New Year, the first day of the next thousand years. Also of the first day of the rest of my life – I think that's what they say in rehab clinics, after detox, 'Welcome to the rest of your life,' which always sounds to me rather threatening, as if it were a consequence of the life so far lived, or of some dismal task you've failed to perform, like eating the rest of your greens: welcome to the rest of your greens, and you'll stay there until you finish them; welcome to the rest of your life, and you're staying here until you finish it.

A couple of days seemed to have hopped by without my noticing whether I sat down to Apple or not. I spent one of those days – and one of those nights – in bed with what I take to be the medical version of the dreaded millennium bug, a wheezy chest, an unlocatable headache (I wasn't even sure it was in the head), a combination of listlessness and irritability – many things seem to be working to grind me down, from the pervasive circumstances of my life to the inhaling of cigarette after cigarette – also I keep having odd glimpses of myself as a man who belonged to the last century, if not the last millennium – I feel that if only I'd managed to get myself on television more often I could have straddled the breach – odd phrase, can it be right? Where did it come from? I can't mean what the image conjures up – myself with one foot in 1999 and the other in 2000, being pulled apart and gradually splitting up the middle as the two centuries grow away from each other, thus transforming myself into a kind of giant, almost mythological – no, all I meant was that if I'd somehow contrived to appear on television, however briefly, in the dying moments of the last century, say around 11.58 on Friday night, and then for the same amount of time on Saturday morning before dawn, I would have been seen to belong to neither one century nor the other, but just to be hanging around in a general sort of way in the present. But I wasn't on television. I wasn't even on the radio. Nor was I in the newspapers, come to that, naming my favourite ten books of the last year/century/millennium/of all time – my face was unseen, my voice unheard, my tastes unprinted – a goner, really. And a long-gone goner, at that – last invited to be visible back in the seventies, when visibility was still incidental to the main business, which was the writing, if you were a writer, the cooking, if you were a chef, the drinking, if you were an alcoholic – now the real business seems to be about being on television, you do your time as a heavy drinker, for instance, in order to do your cleaning up in front of the camera – but I have memories of occasions of my own back then, when alcohol dissolved all fear and I strutted my stuff on talk shows and so forth.

I cut quite a figure, according to some American friends (one of them an investor) – 'You looked drunk, you sounded drunk, everybody hated you, including Billy Rose, he wanted you to die, dead in front of him would have been better than another minute of you live.' 'Live, I thought it was recorded, they could cut me.' 'Billy Rose is live. That's the point of him.' Billy Rose, or it might have been David Rose, or Johnny Rose, but it was definitely Rose, happened in New York, during early previews of one of my self-directed plays, *The Holy Terror*, I think it must have been. I'd spent most of the day in rehearsal, with bottles of champagne to hand, then the evening in the theatre for a preview, glasses of whisky at the interval, a few more whiskies after the curtain, and then been driven straight to the studio for the chat with Rose. I don't remember anything about it, in fact I didn't remember it as it was taking place, all I have to go on are the subsequent recriminations – I'd spoken with great precision, apparently, and very slowly, in the manner of a drunk drunkenly imitating sobriety, and everything I'd said had sounded spiteful and conceited, especially on the subject of American directors and theatre critics. Actors, my own actors, I'd patronised, presenting them as warm-hearted, ignorant, loveable, completely devoted to me as a human being, in awe of my achievements as director and writer – my tone not far removed from that of an ante-bellum plantation owner talking of his slaves – in a matter of minutes I'd done the work of ten bad reviews, but there was still something to be done that I'd left undone. Rose, Billy or David, desperate to get me off screen, bade me farewell with one of those fatal questions – 'Any last thing you want to share before –' The last thing I wanted to share before – included the word 'fucking', encased in a thought about the 'surprisingly high' intelligence level of New York theatre audiences, they seemed to understand quite a bit of me, including some of my jokes, and I hoped this would continue to be the case during the whole length of our run (which turned out to be too short, ten days or so, to present a serious test). After Rose in New York I turned down every request to appear on television until I stopped receiving requests, and though I sometimes long to receive them again, I'd be too frightened to accept them, I expect.

That's where I stopped yesterday, on the afternoon of 4th January. I meant to go on for a while, thinking I was aiming towards some momentary conclusion, some point I'd been tending to, but there it was, I suddenly felt very ropey, went to bed for an hour or so with George – Victoria was out doing the sort of thing people used to do in the sort of novels people used to write, taking tea, yes, taking tea with her sister Emma. I lay in bed with George, feeling cold and miserable, wishing I'd remembered to put on the bed-socks I'd been given for Christmas, unable to get to sleep, unable to read, not perfectly conscious, grateful for George's spine pressing through the covers against mine, but in a dreary, drifting state, really, the state in which you're on the verge of doing some terrible accounting, but to no purpose, as it's too late to make additions, and the subtractions go on without you, it almost seems, even while you're lying cold and curled in bed, not doing harm, not even checking the figures in the columns however close you are to the verge . . . well, it was pretty horrible, the uselessness of it, I mean, is this what I gave up drink for, apart from not being dead, that is, and I began to tell myself how it was three years ago, when by this stage in the day I would have been, well, at a different stage of a different sort of day with at least a bottle and a half of champagne in me, the bleakness and the self-pity arriving much later, at the hour traditional to the dark night, etc. – in those days, when I went to bed in the afternoons I was usually in a kind of daze, to which I added a further layer of daze with a temazepam – the combination of alcohol and temazepam giving me two or three hours of deep, drugged sleep, from which I would awake, semi-drugged, shuffle unsteadily towards consciousness with a few glasses of champagne, and then life would stir again, not too much of it, just enough to be comfortable in until after midnight, then spasms of ferocious work accompanied by glass after glass of champagne until exhaustion trailed into depression which was countered by more champagne, a temazepam, bed and ten to twelve hours of sleep.

So altogether I must have slept thirteen to fifteen hours a day, the waking hours given over almost entirely to work, with no attempt at all at a social life, apart from tottering little trips to Whiteleys to the cinemas there, though I mainly slept through the films or drifted out of them to sip glasses of white wine at one of the nearby bars. Was it any consolation to Victoria, I wonder, that at least she always knew exactly where her husband was, and also where he was heading in short order – to the hospital or the morgue, taking exactly the same route taken by my younger brother (ten years younger) the year before – my taxi running along the same streets as his ambulance, my body half-carried along the same corridors to the same emergency room, then into the same ward for life-support, but whereas he continued in a straight line from life-support to the hospital morgue, I took a turning off into wards he'd been too far gone to get into, received procedures he'd had no hope of surviving. So from that to this – in bed in the mid-afternoon, spine to spine with George, sleepless, self-pitying, sober, waiting for the distant click of the front door, which George of course always picks up on before me, launches herself away from my spine with an exuberant kick, thuds to the floor, scampers out of the room – and then I hear the door, its click, the sound of it shutting, then the clamour in the hall, footsteps on the stairs, and then they're both in the room, George back on the bed, Victoria sitting on its edge.

Tuesday. This is something else I have to put up with now that I'm sober – not just going through trivial, rancour-inducing experiences, I went through those, probably more of them, when I was drunk, but I didn't keep remembering them, no, worse, didn't keep consciously reminding myself of them, nursing them along, encouraging them to flourish, like a sort of addict, really, desperate for his mouthful of bile – so let me get around to the latest 'incident' – there was this woman at the box office – no, start again, what happened was this – we decided to see the revival of Noël Coward's *Song at Twilight*, starring a brace of Redgraves, no, the third actor in the three-hander was also a Redgrave by marriage, which therefore gave us a complete cast of Redgraves, Vanessa, Corin and Corin's wife, Kika Markham, which sounded inviting enough, and furthermore, it's playing at the Gielgud (né Globe), the very theatre that might have been housing *The Late Middle Classes* if only – so on top of everything else, here was a chance to show the world (i.e., Victoria and myself) that I'm not a mean-spirited dog-left-out-of-the-manger, that I greet the large pricks and the little victories with equal relish, all forms of experience a joy sort of stuff – and it was in this spirit that I phoned the Gielgud box office, only to find myself grappling with the kind of woman I thought had been turfed out of West End box offices a decade or so ago. In fact, as she announced before our conversation began, she wasn't a Gielgud Theatre employee, she was an employee of Stoll Moss, the company that owned a number of theatres, the Gielgud amongst them. No, that's not right, she made no such announcement, why on earth should she, what would be the point of her announcing down the telephone, 'I am not an employee of the Gielgud Theatre, I am an employee of the Stoll Moss Company that owns the Gielgud Theatre among others.' No, what she probably said was, 'Stoll Moss box office, which theatre do you want to book for?' And I presumably said, 'Gielgud, please,' and the negotiation proceeded apace, although to tell the truth I found her voice irritating, young but with the kind of middle-class accent my mother had – OK in its time but ghastly now, and wilful – and I was also irritated by her insertion of herself into every possible sentence, as in: 'Where would you like me to put you? I can put you anywhere you like, I have seats at all prices, yes, I have aisle seats everywhere,' this last in response to my question about the availability of aisle seats – I have to sit on an aisle seat, preferably near an exit, because I sometimes suffer from theatregoer's claustrophobia, need to make a sudden dash for it – 'I can put you in any seat you want,' which was, of course, good to hear in one way, to know we could sit where I wanted, but bad to hear in another – no one connected with the performing side of the theatre enjoys a box-office voice informing the public that every seat in the house is available, because they know the public will be picking up implicit information – i.e., this show is a bummer, nobody else in the whole world wants a seat at this show, it's a complete bummer, and of course they also imagine hearing the same voice saying the same thing of one of their shows, even if they haven't got a show on at the moment – and indeed I actually did hear it once years ago when I had a play running at this very theatre when it was called the Globe, same bloody theatre – but I've been into all that, the Globe–Gielgud business. The play in question was called *The Rear Column*, by the way, and one afternoon I phoned to check the box office to find out how it was going – actually I knew how it was going, so I got what I deserved, I suppose – and there was this male voice, I can still hear it, informing me with a whinny, that I could have any seat, absolutely any seat in the house if I really wanted one – 'No need to book, just come along at eight and you can have a seat anywhere you want.'

Well, I let it pass then, at the Globe, because I was so mortified, and I let it pass now at the Gielgud because I wasn't in the mood for trouble. I booked the tickets, paid for them with my credit card, listened while she told me in that voice, with that accent, that my tickets couldn't be exchanged, weren't refundable, I was to pick them up at the box office at 7.30. 'But it begins at eight o'clock,' I said. 'That's right. Eight o'clock.' 'So why should I pick up the tickets at half past seven, they're already paid for, why should I get there half an hour early?' 'Because that's when they've got be picked up.' And that's when I found out I was in the mood, after all. I said that I planned to arrive at the theatre at about five minutes to eight, possibly even one minute to eight, and would expect to find my tickets ready for me. She said that if I arrived at one minute to eight it was unlikely that I'd have the tickets by eight o'clock, in which case I'd be refused admission until the interval, no refunds – in other words it was a heavy skirmish, but quite brief, and concluded with my cancelling the tickets. 'Fine,' she said. 'By all means, cancel the tickets' – but the voice was faltering, and I tried to imagine that the accent was on the verge of slipping forward to the year 2000. 'Which means,' I said, 'which means that the theatre has just lost sixty pounds, and Stoll Moss, isn't it, has just lost the booking fee as well. The management will be delighted to hear all this.' Then I said goodbye – it is my firm belief that people should never just hang up on people, certain formalities should be observed that allow a way back into further negotiation. After a pause she hung up. I considered it a complete victory, even though cancelling the tickets also meant that I'd cancelled the evening's projected entertainment and I hadn't plotted an alternative.

So it was either turning up at the Gielgud ticketless, on spec, or it was nothing. Spec seemed preferable since it carried with it the possibility of taking the battle into the lobby of the Gielgud. I made sure we arrived at the box office at the very last minute, where I was frustrated by a pleasant and helpful man, middle-aged and balding, who sold us two tickets for seats on an aisle by an exit, and we enjoyed a cast of Redgraves in a well-directed late play by Noël Coward that neither of us had seen before. As for the audience, some young, some old, some medium, but all ages responsive and concentrating, enjoying their own concentration in fact – just the sort of people you'd like to have at a play of your own, only lots more of them, of course, and perhaps *The Late Middle Classes* might after all, if only, if only – but no point thinking along those lines at this hour, it's three a.m., much better to think about how to put the skids under the girl in the box office – I saw from the programme that I know the producer, I could give him a ring in the morning – but no, really! Let someone else do the dirty work for once – time for the sleeping pill, for some music and for Troyat's life of Tolstoy, which to my bewilderment I'm re-reading, I hadn't meant to, merely picked it up as I was passing the bookshelf, opened it casually, my eye caught a sentence about Leo resolving at the age of seventeen to become 'moderately perfect' at playing the violin, so of course I read on, and now I'm stuck with a book I never intended to read again, though it gave me a lot of pleasure the first time round. But there are so many books I haven't read at all, or good books that get even better every time I read them, including a lot by Tolstoy, come to think of it. I haven't read *The Death of Ivan Illyich* for ages, and it's probably a story one should make oneself live through once a year, well, perhaps less than that as one gets older, when it's somehow in the system whether one reads it or not, in fact I can't see any reason at all for reading it again, just by naming it I've brought it to the surface, and at a moment when I don't particularly want to think about it, or actually particularly don't want to think about it. So I'll take my pill and drift towards bed. Goodnight.

Actually, it wasn't goodnight, and here I still am, about to apple away on my Apple again. Why? Do I really think that putting into words how I passed the last three hours or so will confer meaning, value, even dignity on them? You can't really find meaning, value and dignity in having watched an old tape of *Law and Order*, followed by a younger tape of Manchester United losing a football match in Brazil. It's almost dawn, I can hear the bloody birds, full of their usual shit – the noise is probably great when you're getting up, but not when you're trying to put yourself to bed after hours of watching videos, with your stomach full of Diet Coke and smoke in your lungs. The problem is, have I taken the sleeping pill? I've just scrolled back to where I say I'm going to, but did I? Tomorrow I'll go and visit Piers' grave.

Wednesday afternoon. It was a beautiful midday, beautiful up there at Kensal Green Cemetery. Piers is in Rowan Garden, a new section, pastoral and domestic in feeling, with its own little gate. I've become very fond of it, it settles me down and makes me quite peaceful, although actually his tombstone is undeniably ugly. When I chose it in the shop it was lying in the corner softened by shadow, and I was in a bad state, hurrying through this part of the business, out of focus and a bit drunk, not able to imagine it upright in daylight. Upright in daylight it is squat and brutally assertive, reminiscent of Mussolini architecture, and would have embarrassed Piers – or he might have found it funny, I hope, as I did the second or third time I saw it – the first time I was appalled and ashamed – but what made it worse the first few times was that it was on its own at the beginning of a row, all the space beside it one way not yet taken, and a big gap before the graves began the other way – really it had the effect of a military outpost, a lumpish and suppressive thing. Now, though, new tombstones have filled in on either side, and it looks more and more as if it belongs in the company, is even beginning to weather a bit. In another four years it'll be all right. I took flowers with me, daffodils still surviving from Christmas which I plucked from the vase in the hall as I stepped out to the taxi, and I enjoyed the ride – it's only about twenty minutes, looking out into the sunny streets, glancing down at a newspaper that someone had left in the back – and then I was there, suddenly in front of his gravestone, arranging the flowers at the foot of the stone, cleaning its black top with the flat of my hand. I sat on the bench I'd had placed directly in front of his grave, his bench I suppose, as his name is on it, and just melted around for a while, remembering and regretting without getting angry, which I sometimes do.

There were a couple of middle-aged Serbs (probably – there are a lot of Serbian graves in Kensal Green), one of them weeping into a handkerchief, the other fussing around with a candle and flowers, and a group of four, a middle-aged man and three women of descending ages, possibly a mother, a wife, a daughter, but the man didn't look like a husband to any of the three women, more like a son to the older one, and a brother to the other two. He was very pale, black hair pasted back, and clothes that looked old but freshly pressed, as if he hadn't worn them for a long time – a recently released convict, possibly.

I didn't take in the women properly, but like the man they were ill at ease, walking very close together in a little batch and glancing about as if they might have come to the wrong cemetery – and when they got to the far side of the section, they began to hunt about among the gravestones, picking over them as if they were at a market and needed to find bargains – but one of the women was carrying flowers, I seem to remember. They were very sad, touching. I don't think they found the grave because they passed me again quite soon, still close together, not talking, the woman still carrying flowers, and crossed the road to another part of the cemetery.

I walked up and down the path a while, smoking and making a few remarks to Piers about this and that, trying to keep it light and easy, unreproachful and unapologetic, and then paused in front of one of the graves I always pause at, eight down from Piers, on the right, as you face him. The headstone is rather jaunty, yellowy-grey in colour, with a photograph of a young man embedded in a little glass dome at the top. He is bareheaded, dark hair cut short, round, handsome face with slightly childlike features, unformed anyway, as if he hasn't grown into them yet. He is dressed in shiny black leather, mounted on a powerful motorbike, a helmet under one arm, the other resting on the handlebars. Underneath this is inscribed 'In Loving Memory Of Andrew Crabb' and underneath that 'A Dear Son, Brother And Friend' and underneath that 'Born 12th February 1963. Died 10th April 1996' and underneath that is written in curling, flourishy letters the following poem:

> He rode through life
> Fast and free
> His candle burning bright
> And through the smoke that we still pass
> He left us with his light

For the first time I worked out from his dates that he was just two days short of thirty-three years and two months old when he smashed himself up on his motorbike, some five months younger than my son, Ben, is now. I suddenly became interested in this question of ages, how long the dead in Piers' vicinity had spent in the world. I suppose I must have checked on about fifteen gravestones, and found two, both men, on which the arithmetic worked out at forty-nine – the age Piers was when he died. Altogether three out of sixteen, if one included Piers – but that must be unusual, surely, a freak clustering – 'clustering', isn't that the right word, the word they use when compiling statistics of this sort?

I picked up some bits of rubbish lying around in Piers' area, dead flowers, a cigarette packet and a sandwich wrapper that was under his bench, that sort of stuff (though there wasn't much, really, not for these days, in fact it's a very well tended cemetery, especially the Rowan Garden section), put them in the carrier bag I'd used for his flowers, dumped the carrier bag into a bin, then walked over to the little gate, but instead of leaving I found myself going back to Andrew Crabb's grave. I copied the inscription into my newspaper, then sat down again on Piers' bench, smoked a couple of cigarettes, just pleased to be where I was, and in the sunshine. As soon as I got home I sat down to write this, and now, just as I'm putting down these words, the light is beginning to go. But I had quite a lot of it, for once. It seems a long time since I've had such a light-hearted day, or so much of a day.

It's 11.00 a.m., on Monday, 10th January. I've been up since half past nine, my earliest since we were in Greece, in the late summer. It's as sunny as yesterday, and being up that much earlier, I'll have more if it. Then if I can hang on until early evening, not going back to bed until dark, I'll have had virtually a full day. And tomorrow why not the same, more and more as we come out of winter into spring, life beginning to stir again. I wish that life would stir in me again, that I could get down to some work again at last. But I think I've become paralysed by *Japes* (working title) and what it's come to mean to me. Because the thing about *Japes* (working title) is, well, I have a feeling about it that I've never had about any of my other plays, though I know one always tends to say that about one's last piece of work, but the feeling this time, which I've certainly never had before, is that this is it, this is the last, there isn't another one in me, never will be. To go on from here I'd have to begin a new life, or discover an unexpected self, which probably amounts to the same thing, and it's too late for that. 'I am what I am' – no, one generally says that as an apology, meaning, 'Sorry, didn't mean to, can't help it, nothing I can do about it, I am what I am – see.' Or as an epitaph, with a bit of a boast underneath – 'I am what I am – and they don't come any better, at least of my sort – right?' So let's try, 'I have become what I am' – which at least contains the suggestion of a natural process completed – it also contains a sinister ambiguity, now I look at it: it also strikes me as completely meaningless, now I look at it again. The question therefore is, what did I think it meant, 'I have become what I am?' And the next question is, 'Where is the ambiguity?' Yes, unambiguously meaningless is how the phrase 'I have become what I am' now seems to me, so let's get off its case and try and think out what I really want to say about my attitude to *Japes* (working title).

Well, if I believe it's my last play, and I do, then simply and obviously I want to get it on the stage in the fashion that will do it most honour, and preferably in my lifetime. In other words this is not a play I can afford to be shy about or ashamed of simply because it's written by me. It's true that I still haven't picked up the script, which is therefore still lying almost out of sight, and whenever my eye flickers towards it, my whole head immediately swivels away from it, but still, in my heart, in my soul, in my blood and in my bone, and in my water too-ooo-ooo – isn't that how the song goes? in my water too-ooo-ooo – because that's where the play lives, in all those elements and spheres and organs of my being, which means I don't actually have to read it again, or even pick it up to know that it's OK, or if not OK in the terms that finally matter – Tolstoy, say, or Chekhov – it's OK in terms of my little life, the only life I've ever had, at least as far as I know – though I met a soothsayer once in Greece, a small bearded man with dull but canny eyes, who felt my fingertips, caressed the palms of my hands, and informed me that I'd so far had fifty-seven lives, most of them lived as a great warrior, a few of them as a poet and comforter – he actually used that word, 'comforter' – and in one or two of the lives I'd been very quiet, sort of lying low, I suppose. This sooth-sayer, who came from Essex or Kent, and was called Higgens, something along those lines, was completely convincing. He was also rather expensive, at thirty pounds per half-hour. Barry Humphries, who happened to be staying on the same island, had many consultations with this man Higgens, but then of course Barry Humphries has three or four lives going on at virtually the same time and in the present, so presumably he had two or three hundred past lives to discuss – but what has Barry Humphries got to do with all this, why am I writing about Barry Humphries? Whatever the reason, I'm stopping here to go for a walk.

A slow stroll up to Notting Hill, limbs working awkwardly, as if I were newly out of hospital. Stopped at the chemist, to explore their anti-smoking shelves, came away with a cigarette holder and some tubes full of a nicotiney substance to help simulate smoking, smokeless smoking – I can see immediate possibilities, for instance, in No Smoking zones, if I put holder in my mouth, raise lighter to nicotiney tube, pretend to light up, would it be an offence? Well, they'd make it into one, somehow, a smoker impersonating a smoker in a non-smoking zone – these thoughts revolving, puffing an actual cigarette, I made it up to the big bookshop in Notting Hill, Waterstone's, slightly puzzled at being nodded at by four or even five passers-by, not one of whom I recognised, not one of whom seemed to be my sort of person – there was a short man in an expensive overcoat and tall, fur hat who gave a wink and smile with his nod, almost as if he were trying to pick me up, but on the other hand he did look like someone I might have met – in rehearsals, perhaps, when I was directing, but no, not much of the actor about him, an actor would have been more overt in reminding me who he was. Or in trying to pick me up. I was extremely depressed by the num-ber of books in the shop and left immediately. I would have walked all the way home if a taxi hadn't happened by. When I got in Victoria looked at me in surprise, asked me if I'd walked.

Yes, I said, I had. Which was true enough, but then I ruined it by saying, 'There and back.' Why? A completely pointless lie, which I shall have to correct at some point. Why? Because these days lying makes me feel ill – not a moral matter, a physiological one. Post-operative, I suppose, the guts for lying were snipped out, along with certain digestive valves, so I can't swallow my own deceits without feeling I'm going to throw them straight up, or have them out in a bout of diarrhoea. Now I know this sounds unlikely, pretentious probably, but it's a fact, a medical fact, that lying makes me ill, from slightly to extremely, depending on the size of the lie, or more accurately, its nature, what it's about – mild queasiness if I lie for social reasons – i.e., to get out of something I don't want to do – but immense upheavals if I lie about something important, my feelings about a friend's work, for example, to hear myself saying that I've admired something I haven't admired, or to hear myself laughing at jokes I haven't found funny, that sort of thing does a Pinocchio-like number on my stomach. I wonder why it is, then, that whenever a character in an American film or play vomits from emotional or moral distress, I feel contempt for the writer, actor, director, whichever I choose to hold responsible. Perhaps if they built it into the film's plot that the character is suffering from a malfunction of whatever connects the gastric system to the nervous system, I might go along with it – but as it is, authenticating one's integrity by vomiting every time it's affronted! – though come to think of it, I remember being told by one of my doctors that the stomach has an entirely independent nervous system, can I have got that right? And independent from what? And does it follow that the gastric system also has an independent moral system – if so, it might explain my medical history. I've just popped into Victoria's study, to tell her that in fact I didn't walk back from Waterstone's, I'd taken a taxi in fact. She looked rather puzzled, as if wondering why I thought she had a need for this information.

Tuesday, 11th January, 11.15 a.m. Up an hour ago, not as early as yesterday, but then it's a rotten day, the sort of day you couldn't guess the time of by glancing out of the window –

wet, cold and grey, with a corresponding effect on morale. Nevertheless, here I am, in front of Apple because things have begun to move positively at last with *Japes* (working title). Let's begin with where we were until yesterday – though it's pretty well the same old *The Late Middle Classes* story, same old circuit, with a few stops left out. Begin this time with the end of the writing (not dictated, written on my Olympia portable), which was late August.

Once again Judy phoned Trevor Nunn's office, left a message asking whether he'd be interested in reading a new play by me, got a message back saying that he would, indeed he would be interested, by coincidence he had a break from directing coming up, he was going to devote it to reading, please send the play around as soon as possible. After four, possibly five weeks of silence from Trevor Nunn and desperate for some professional reaction, I sent the play to one of the West End's most distinguished producers (*Desert Island Discs*, OBE, that sort of thing). He phoned within two days to say he'd been deeply affected, wanted to read it again. Two days later he phoned, and said tersely, somewhat emotionally, that 'It must be done, it must be done,' and indicated that he would like to be involved in the doing of it, what did I think? I said I wasn't sure it was a play for the West End, especially the West End as it now is, perhaps it ought to start somewhere more modest. Well, what did I think of Hampstead, he asked? I thought about Hampstead, while trying not to think about my previous experiences at Hampstead. I said it was clearly the right sort of place to start, if one was thinking of starting at a place like that, as one was. He said he knew Jenny Topper well, was seeing her that evening, in fact, should he pass the play on to her? Fine, I said. A few days later I heard from Judy that she'd heard from *Desert Island Discs*, OBE, that Jenny Topper liked the play very much, made no mention of 'themes' important or unimportant, present or absent, would certainly like to do it at Hampstead, but couldn't fit it in until the summer of the coming year. I said that was fine by me – as long as a date could be fixed I was willing to wait, when precisely in the summer? There followed a protracted silence from Hampstead –

and indeed from *Desert Island Discs*, OBE, who hasn't phoned me since the 'It must be done' declaration – followed by a message from Judy that Jenny Topper couldn't guarantee a date in the summer after all, it might have to be later, perhaps into the following New Year, the problem apparently being that she'd commissioned a large number of plays, which seemed suddenly to be arriving by the truck load, and of course her first duty was to these commissioned plays – each one, when it arrived, taking up a place towards the front of the queue, *Japes* (working title) being shuffled further and further to the back of it, she'd let us know when she could be more specific.

Since then, a further word from Jenny Topper hinting that the New Year of next year was no longer on the cards, seeming to leave us with a possibility of a date on calendars not yet in existence. I suppose it was before I gave up on Jenny Topper completely – although not officially, by actually withdrawing the play – that I wrote to Trevor Nunn pointing out that the play had now been with him for over two months, and that Judy had come to the view that he had no intention of reading the play in the near future, if at all. I got back a letter from Trevor Nunn denouncing Judy for spreading vile rumours, he was brimming with the intention of reading the play, would be getting around to it as soon as he'd got *The Merchant of Venice* out of the Olivier and into the Cottesloe, where it belonged – no, sorry, wrong way around, out of the Cottesloe into the Oliver, so a matter of expansion not contraction – anyway, when he'd done that, which was taking him twenty-eight hours a day in a nine-day week, he would settle down to some serious reading – actually, I'm not sure I want him to go that far, ordinary reading would do perfectly well – and as soon as he'd done that he'd be in touch immediately. That letter came to me some, what, two months, yes, it must be two months ago, nothing since. So all in all *Japes* (working title) has been with, in some sense of the word or other, Trevor Nunn for four months. Now by my calculations if he hangs on to it one and a half times longer than he's already hung on to it, he'll have spent longer not reading the play than I spent in writing it.

So technically, for the last few months, the play has been on offer to three different managements – Trevor Nunn, *Desert Island Discs*, OBE, the Hampstead Theatre Club – but in fact we were in the doldrums, the same sort of doldrums we'd been in with *The Late Middle Classes*, when suddenly, a mere two days ago, a fresh wind sprang up – a new ship hove into view – a voice called across the water, and – well, what happened was this. A playwright friend of mine, Hugh Whitemore, who's read and likes *Japes* (working title) phoned to say that a producer friend of his, Michael Redington had mentioned that he was looking for a play to produce, did he by any chance have at his disposal, or know of any playwright who might have at his or her disposal – therefore, Hugh asked, could he pass the play on to Michael Redington? With my blessings, I said, my full blessings, and lo! yesterday Michael Redington, a pleasant and excitable-sounding man, and clearly of the highest intelligence, phoned to say that he very much liked *Japes* (working title), so did his co-producer, Barbara Matthews, they very much wanted to produce it, how did I feel? I told him how I felt and on Friday, at 5.00 p.m. we're to have a meeting with the director, Peter Hall – but have I mentioned Peter Hall yet?

About a month ago I sent him *Japes* (working title) in his role of colleague, professional reader, friend, although I admit that lurking somewhere in the front of my mind was the hope that he'd want to direct it, his had been the first name I'd put to Judy when we'd discussed directors. He phoned a few days later to say he liked it, in fact liked it 'very much indeed'. We talked about it for a bit, skirting around the directing issue, moved on to a discussion of the calamitous state of the theatre, particularly the West End, etc., agreed to talk again very soon. A week or so later I wrote him a letter formally inviting him, he phoned back to say that he was pleased to accept, there were two patches of time available to him in his calendar, October and November of this year, February and March of next year, were they agreeable? They were agreeable, I phoned Michael Redington and told him about Peter Hall, was he agreeable? He was very agreeable, in fact couldn't imagine a better director, he knew Barbara

Matthews would feel the same, so – so – well, so suddenly, out of nothing from nowhere, here I amazingly am, with a director and a producer, wanting only a theatre and a cast. Now that's that up to date, that's enough, I'll finish here, take it up again after the meeting with Michael Redington, Barbara Matthews and Peter Hall on Friday. No, I'd better write to Trevor Nunn while I'm in the mood, which I'm not, but best to get it over and done with.

Done with. A virtuous little note, saying that the play has now been with him for four months, time to go elsewhere – actually it took about seven drafts to get it down to these few lines, and that was after I'd written several lengthy drafts in which I tried to combine irony with outrage – the sort of struggle that can take more hours out of a life than a life, a little life anyway, has to spare. A thought that leads on to the thought that it's time for a walk with George, for whom this little life always has time to spare, and for whom Victoria yesterday bought a rubber bone with big knobs on the ends – it doesn't have much bounce, which will make it harder to lose than a ball, but also make it less fun for George, but really, whose fault is that?

Just back from the meeting, which I almost forgot – not that there was a meeting at 5.00 p.m. but that it was today – I'd pushed it vaguely into the future, sometime later in the week, then realised after lunch that today, being Friday, is later in the week. Once I'd remembered it, I was off and running – an hour earlier than was strictly necessary in fact, to make sure that I was on time.

I spent my spare hour at the Garrick Club, which is only a few minutes walk from Michael Redington's office. I've been a member of the Garrick for seven years or so, but scarcely go there, my interest having been drained by the seven or so previous years I'd spent on its waiting list. In fact I don't really feel I belong, a feeling reinforced by a friend, a long-time member who seems to have smuggled his son in at the age of thirteen or so, and himself sits on all sorts of committees to do with wine and possibly even with women, how to get in more of the former and keep out most of the latter, that sort of thing – all in all, he's a very serious member, so serious that he refuses to take my own membership seriously, actually denying it to my face on two separate occasions – 'But you're not a member, I assure you you're not, you can't be, if you were I'd have known about it!'

There seemed to be nobody at the Garrick apart from the doorman, who, since he greeted me with a nod of recognition, must have mistaken me for somebody else. I couldn't think what to do, not being familiar with the lay-out, and having no one around whose movements I could track. I was very conscious of myself alone as I went up the large staircase, walked along the landing, looked at portraits of Garrick, and then checked out the rooms, one of them a small reading room with all the day's newspapers on a table, the other a large room, I don't know what you'd call it, a tea-room, a reception room, a drawing room, well, really it was exactly the kind of room you'd expect to find in a club, lots of small tables with, I was glad to see, ash-trays on them, enormous windows looking out over Garrick Street. There were portraits on the wall, too many too close together, it was difficult to find one in particular to look at, but what suddenly caught my eye at the end of the room, was a white sculpting, I suppose in marble, that suggested an image clearly impossible in such surroundings. But I went up to it and there it was, unmistakable under its bell jar, a fine and sturdy woman holding down over her out-thrust knee an equally fine but slender woman whose skirt was hitched up over her waist, so that her buttocks, round and firm, were exposed. The woman who was holding her down with one hand, held in her other hand, upraised, either a fan or a paddle, it was hard to make out which. The whole effect, cool and poised, insouciant would really be the word, I suppose, was very pleasing. I stood bent over it a while with my spectacles on, trying to see the ex-pressions on the two faces – above all I wanted to know whether they were both enjoying themselves, or was there serious busi-ness afoot? They were very neatly carved, but the whiteness made it difficult to distinguish the features, though I could make out that both of them had lovely, tumbling hair. I was suddenly anxious that someone would come in and find me bending there, slightly too engrossed perhaps, so I put my spectacles away and sauntered about, wondering how I could get some coffee. There was a sort of bronze button in the wall beside the door. I pressed it without much hope, really, sat down at one of the tables, lit a cigarette.

A girl of about twenty, very pretty and wearing a little apron, suddenly appeared. She was French. So there I was, alone in the Garrick with a French maid. In fact she was so French that she didn't understand anything I said – not even my request for coffee. Finally I did it in French, she giggled and did little curtsies at me, and went off. When she came back she was carrying a tray of coffee and a muffiny thing. I asked what it was, the muffiny thing, and she said it was 'tease cake'. I drank the coffee, ate half the tease cake, had a cigarette, finished off tease cake and coffee, checked on my watch that it was about time to leave, discovered actually that I was on my way to being late, then realised I hadn't paid. I pressed the button again. As I waited I realised I didn't know how one paid. Did one offer cash? – I could see that offering my credit card would be out of order and could one seriously write out a cheque for a pot of coffee and a tease cake? Was there some way of putting it on account? Did I have an account? This wasn't a problem I could solve with the French maid, as I couldn't make her understand what the problem was – I stopped short of '*l'addition, s'il vous plaît*'. I noticed though that she had a little order book in her hand, and a pen. Gently, almost timidly, I took both from her, wrote my name down, pressed pad and pen back into her hands, which I refrained from patting. She did her giggle and curtsy, and went off. I waited a few seconds, so as not to seem to be following her, went off myself, down the stairs, and with a familiar nod at the doorman was out of the Garrick, thinking that perhaps it is my sort of club after all, at least during the hours when there's nobody in it.

The Michael Redington office, or rather the office of his co-producer, Barbara Matthews, is down an alley off Long Acre – a sinister little alley, especially at that hour in the dark, but I imagine it's always dark down that alley, always sinister. The office itself was at the top of steep stone stairs that kept turning off at quite sharp angles – going up them was exactly like going backstage – something exciting about it, conspiratorial, adultery and murder in the air, or perhaps just the memory of all those times I'd climbed all those similar stairs to tell lies to actors before giving them notes – the confidence in my eyes concealing panic, the answering panic in their eyes concealing more panic.

Barbara Matthews's room is extremely small, without being cosy. Strictly a working room for a limited number of people. There were only the four of us, and we used up all the seating, especially as Peter Hall is of majestic proportions, but even so we didn't seem cramped, or crammed together – possibly because everyone was quite at ease, apparently enjoying each other's company, as we first of all confirmed Peter Hall's availability, then went on to discuss casting. In between the one and the other Peter Hall made a speech to the effect that he wanted very much to do the play but if we got the right actors with the wrong (from his point of view) dates, we must go with the actors, he would step aside. This seemed to me not only honourable but pertinent. *Japes* (working title) is a three-character play with three enormous parts – actually, it's a four-character play, with three enormous parts, one of the actors playing two parts – and we can't get by without the best possible actors. There's no point in naming the three actors we're starting with, I suspect they'll all be doing films, but we'll give them a whirl, and when they've each said, no thanks, we'll go on to the best possible three and then three more of the best possible, not going down the line but across it, if you follow, until – I hope – we come up with three of the best some time in the future, anyway before we begin rehearsals. But for me the real point about the meeting is that it took place. I sat through it thinking, in a dull or dazed sort of way, but with the old tingle tingling, 'Well, here we are again then, here we go again.'[5]

5 To Colchester this time. *Japes* opens there mid-November. After Colchester, to London – or not, as the case may be.

Monday, 17th January. A letter from Trevor Nunn. It must have crossed mine in the post. Is that a coincidence or has he got extraordinary antennae? Anyway, he offers me terrifically warm New Year salutations, goes on to congratulate me on the writing, characterisation and dialogue, of *Japes* (working title) but feels he is unable to offer a slot to the play on the grounds that a) it's too depressing, b) it would do very well in the West End, especially with Harold at the helm, and c) – this comes between his a) and his b) – it contains a speech by one of the characters which could be construed as an attack on Patrick Marber's *Closer* and audiences might therefore think that the National was attacking itself for having put *Closer* on in the first place. He concludes the letter by suggesting that he, Harold and I should have lunch one day soon to discuss a project for the National. I've already written my response, without too much effort, really, merely pointing out that I have the greatest respect for *Closer*, that I'm surprised he should confuse me with one of the characters in my play, and then further confuse the character in my play with the National itself. I make no reference to the proposed lunch and conclude with a return of his New Year salutations. I suppose I'll post it tomorrow or the day after, for the moment I like having it on my desk, where it looks both impressive (the envelope is long and white, rather handsome) and personal – I've written the address in my own hand, not knowing yet how to print out envelopes from Apple here. Actually, now I've learnt to write on Apple – I can 'copy', 'find', and even 'cut' and 'paste' – I shall soon cease to use it, I think. It'll be back to the Olympia portable, but to do what is the problem?

Oh, George has just come into the room. No, that's not right. She didn't simply come into the room, sniff about at my feet, go out again, as she usually does, she bustled into the room, straight past me at the desk here and out onto the porch – I'd just opened the French windows to let the smoke out – she went onto the porch, peered intently through the railings. Then I heard what I knew I was going to hear, the deep chortling from the garden, the chortle of the fox that now visits regularly – perhaps every night. And George – who usually barks vibrantly, proud of the noise she is making at any dog she hears, even in the far distance – is all silent, fascinated bustle when the fox is stalking about, doing his chortling. I know it's a male fox, there's a sexual sub-tone to the noise he makes. And stalking is actually the right word for the way this fox moves, I know because we've both seen him at it, Victoria and I, picking his way along the high wall in the moonlight, full of purpose, stalking – what else could he be doing? Of course we fear for George – what attitude do foxes take to dogs, especially small light-coloured half-Westies, who've not yet encountered violence in their three years of life? And what is going on in George, who has left the porch, gone down-stairs and there goes the dog flap so she's out in the garden, the fox is giving a chortle. Now there is silence. I've just looked down from the porch. It's too dark to see anything. I called 'George, George,' a few times, but low, because of the neigh-bours. I shall have to go down myself. There's the chortle again. I'm going down.

Here I am, back. I opened the door, and George came straight in, business-like, went past me up the stairs into the bedroom. She's already settled down beside Victoria, moulded herself into the curve of Victoria's stomach, seems to be asleep. Victoria's fast asleep. I switched off her bedside light, left mine on as I always do, came back to Apple to write it all down, and to puzzle over what can be going on, between George and this fox. I can't say I like it much.